DEVIANCE ACROSS CULTURES

DEVIANCE ACROSS CULTURES

Robert Heiner

Plymouth State University

New York   Oxford
OXFORD UNIVERSITY PRESS
2008

Oxford University Press, Inc., publishes works that further Oxford University's
objective of excellence in research, scholarship, and education.

Oxford New York
Auckland Cape Town Dar es Salaam Hong Kong Karachi
Kuala Lumpur Madrid Melbourne Mexico City Nairobi
New Delhi Shanghai Taipei Toronto

With offices in
Argentina Austria Brazil Chile Czech Republic France Greece
Guatemala Hungary Italy Japan Poland Portugal Singapore
South Korea Switzerland Thailand Turkey Ukraine Vietnam

Published by Oxford University Press, Inc.
198 Madison Avenue, New York, New York 10016
http://www.oup.com

Library of Congress Cataloging-in-Publication Data
Heiner, Robert
    Deviance across cultures / Robert Heiner.
        p.   cm.
    Includes bibliographical references.
    ISBN 978-0-19-517710-7 (cloth)—ISBN 978-0-19-517709-1 (pbk. : alk. paper)   1.
Deviant behavior—Cross-cultural studies.   I. Title.
    GN493.5.H45 2007
    302.5′42—dc22   2007001616

9 8 7 6 5 4 3 2 1

Printed in the United States of America
on acid-free paper

this book is dedicated to Gresham Sykes
for inspiring a half century of inquiry

CONTENTS

Preface xi
Acknowledgments xiii

PART 1 EXPLAINING DEVIANCE 1

The Normal and the Pathological 3
EMILE DURKHEIM

On the Sociology of Deviance 7
KAI T. ERIKSON

Social Structure and Anomie 15
ROBERT K. MERTON

Techniques of Neutralization: *A Theory of Delinquency* 26
GRESHAM M. SYKES AND DAVID MATZA

A Control Theory of Delinquency 32
TRAVIS HIRSCHI

Conceptions of Deviant Behavior: *The Old and the New* 41
JACK P. GIBBS

The Search for Scapegoat Deviants 45
JEFFERY S. VICTOR

PART 2 MORAL PANICS 51

Moral Panics in History 53
ERICH GOODE AND NACHMAN BEN-YEHUDA

The Classic Moral Panic: *Mods and Rockers* 60
KENNETH THOMPSON

The Devil Goes to Day Care: *McMartin and the Making of a Moral Panic* 68
MARY DEYOUNG

Penis Panics   79
ROBERT E. BARTHOLOMEW

PART 3   SEX AND SEXUALITY   87

The Cochón and the Hombre-Hombre in Nicaragua   89
ROGER N. LANCASTER

Women in Lesotho and the (Western) Construction of Homophobia   94
K. LIMAKATSO KENDALL

Paraphilias Across Cultures   106
DINESH BHUGRA

PART 4   PROSTITUTION   117

Prostitution and the Status of Women in South Korea   119
ROBERT HEINER

Big Sister Is Watching You! *Gender Interaction and the Unwritten Rules of the Amsterdam Red-Light District*   126
MANUEL B. AALBERS

PART 5   DRUGS   139

Rx Drugs
60 MINUTES (TRANSCRIPT)   141

Healthy Nightclubs and Recreational Substance Use: *From a Harm Minimization to a Healthy Settings Approach*   147
MARK A. BELLIS, KAREN HUGHES, AND HELEN LOWEY

Why Ritalin Rules   158
MARY EBERSTADT

Pumped-Up Panic   166
DAYN PERRY

PART 6   CORPORATE DEVIANCE   177

Regulation, White-Collar Crime and the Bank of Credit and Commerce International   179
BASIA SPALEK

Corruption Scandals in America and Europe: *Enron and EU Fraud in Comparative Perspective*   191
CRIS SHORE

PART 7 DEVIANCE AND RELIGION 199

Nones on the Run: *Evangelical Heathens in the Deep South* 201
ROBERT HEINER

Caught Up in the Cult Wars: *Confessions of a Canadian Researcher* 216
SUSAN J. PALMER

Suicide Bombers: *The "Just War" Debate, Islamic Style* 227
JOHN KELSAY

PART 8 MENTAL ILLNESS 233

On Being Sane in Insane Places 235
DAVID L. ROSENHAN

Schizophrenia in the Third World 243
RICHARD WARNER

PART 9 EPILOGUE: *A Freedom-Deviance Trade-Off?* 255

Lessons in Order 257
DAVID H. BAYLEY

PREFACE

One of the more resounding principles in the sociology of deviance is that the defining quality of deviance resides in the audience and not in the person or the behavior. That is, there is nothing inherent in the behavior or the person that makes it or him or her deviant. Rather, a behavior or person is deviant because an audience defines it or him or her as such. This proposition is the essence of labeling theory and of social constructionism, and it suggests that a sociological understanding of deviance requires us to study the audience. Further, an understanding of the audience requires us to examine its cultural milieu because, quite simply, audiences react differently depending upon the cultural and historical context in which they reside. Thus, for example, behaviors which led to the label of "witch" in medieval Europe would be seen as normal, rebellious, idiosyncratic, or the product of mental illness in other times and cultures. Thus, deviance is culturally relative and the study of deviance is most appropriate for a cross-cultural analysis such as this book is designed to facilitate.

We tend to judge other cultures and their standards by the standards of our own. This tendency is called "ethnocentrism" and it is, to an extent, natural and unavoidable; but it stands in the way of objective understanding and is one of the great bugaboos of social scientific inquiry. One very common manifestation of ethnocentrism is the tendency to view customs in other cultures as being strange, exotic, or bizarre, and a book such as this runs the risk of catering to this tendency. I was ever-conscious of this dilemma when selecting articles for this volume and did my best not to make this a look-how-weird-they-are book. It is my hope that the combination of articles contained herein and the introductions that precede each article will make it clear to the reader that the United States is just as "weird" as "they" are and that the same processes that generate and influence deviance in other cultures do so in our own. Further, I expect that our ethnocentric tendencies will be counterbalanced by the fact that deviance in other cultures will be seen as more distant and therefore less threatening than deviance in our own culture, thus improving our ability to understand the phenomenon of deviance more objectively.

This book was made possible by a host of friends and professionals who assisted and inspired me. I want to thank the people who anonymously reviewed the proposal and provided me with encouragement and very useful criticism. I am also grateful to Joyce Bruce, Khuan Chong, Joann Guilmett, John Krueckeberg, Kathryn Melanson, Bryon Middlekauff, Nikki Nunes, and Alice Staples for their positive attitude and able technical assistance. Finally, I wish to thank those at Oxford University Press, in particular, Peter Labella, Sherith Pankratz, Chelsea Gilmore, and Andrew Fargnoli. Their professional expertise guided me every step along the way to completing this project, and it was a pleasure working with them.

ACKNOWLEDGMENTS

Aalbers, Manuel B., Republished with permission of the *Journal of Sex Research*, from "Big sister is watching you! Gender interaction and the unwritten rules of the Amsterdam red-light district." Manuael B. Aalbers, vol. 42, no. 1, Feb 2005, pp. 54–62 (edited); permission conveyed through Copyright Clearance Center, Inc.

Bartholomew, Robert E., "Penis Panics: The psychology of penis-shrinking mass hysterias." *Skeptic*, vol. 7, no. 4, 1999, pp. 45–49 (edited). Reprinted with permission.

Bayley, David H., Republished with permission of the University of California Press from *Forces of order: Policing modern Japan* (revised edition). Berkeley: University of California Press, 1991, pp. 168–182 (edited); permission conveyed through Copyright Clearance Center, Inc.

Bellis, Mark A., Karen Hughes, and Helen Lowey, Reprinted from *Addictive Behaviors*, vol. 27, Mark A. Bellis, Karen Hughes, and Helen Lowey, "Healthy nightclubs and recreational substance use: From a harm minimisation to a healthy settings approach," pp. 1025–1035, Copyright 2002, with permission from Elsevier.

Bhugra, Dinesh, "Disturbances in objects of desire: Cross-cultural issues." *Sexual and Relationship Therapy*, vol. 15, no. 1, 2000, pp. 67–78 (edited). Reprinted with permission from Taylor and Francis, Ltd. (http://www.tandf.co.uk/journals).

DeYoung, Mary, "The devil goes to day care: McMartin and the making of a moral panic." *Journal of American Culture*, vol. 20, no. 1, Spring 1997, pp. 19–25 (edited). Reprinted with permission from Blackwell Publishing.

Durkheim, Emile, *The rules of sociological method*. Translated by Sarah A. Soloway and John H. Mueller, edited by George E. G. Catlin, University of Chicago, 1938, pp. 64–73. Public domain.

Eberstadt, Mary, "Why Ritalin rules." *Policy Review*, issue 94, April/May 1999, pp. 24–40 (edited). Reprinted with permission.

Erikson, Kai T., *Wayward puritans: A study in the sociology of deviance*. Published by Allyn and Bacon, Boston, MA, 2005. Copyright © by Pearson Education. By permission of the publisher.

Gibbs, Jack P., "Conceptions of deviant behavior: The old and the new." *Pacific Sociological Review*, vol. 9, Spring 1966, pp. 9–11. Reprinted with permission from the University of California Press.

Goode, Erich, and Nachman Ben-Yehuda, *Moral panics: The social construction of deviance.* Cambridge, MA: Blackwell, 1994, pp. 4–11. Reprinted with permission.

Heiner, Robert, "Prostitution and the status of women in South Korea." *International Journal of Contemporary Sociology*, vol. 29, no. 1, April 1992, pp. 115–123 (edited). Reprinted with permission.

Heiner, Robert, "Evangelical heathens: The deviant status of freethinkers in Southland." *Deviant Behavior*, vol. 13, no. 1, 1992, pp. 1–20 (edited). Reprinted with permission from Taylor and Francis, Ltd. (http://www.tandf.co.uk/journals).

Hirschi, Travis, *Causes of delinquency.* Piscataway, NJ: Transaction, 2002, pp. 16–30. Reprinted with permission.

Kelsay, John, "Suicide bombers: The 'just war' debate, Islamic style." Copyright 2002 *Christian Century*. Reprinted by permission from the August 14–27, 2002, issue of the *Christian Century*. Subscriptions: 49/yr. from P.O. Box 378, Mt. Morris, IL 51054. 1–800–208–4097.

Kendall, K. Limakatso, "Women in Lesotho and the (Western) construction of homophobia," from *Female desires: Same-sex relations and transgender practices*, edited by Evelyn Blackwood and Saskia Wieringa, New York: Columbia University Press, 1999, pp. 157–178 (edited). Reprinted with permission from the author.

Lancaster, Roger N., Republished with permission of the University of California Press from *Life is hard: Machismo, danger, and the intimacy of power in Nicaragua.* Berkeley: University of California, 1992, pp. 237–245 (edited); permission conveyed through Copyright Clearance Center, Inc.

Merton, Robert K., "Social structure and anomie." *American Sociological Review*, vol. 3, 1938, pp. 672–682. Public domain.

Palmer, Susan J., "Caught up in the cult wars: Confessions of a Canadian researcher," from *Misunderstanding Cults: Searching for objectivity in a controversial field*, edited by Benjamin Zablocki and Thomas Robbins, University or Toronto Press, 2001, pp. 99–121 (edited). Reprinted with permission from the publisher.

Perry, Dayn, "Pumped-up hysteria." *Reason*, vol. 34, no. 8, pp. 32–39. Reprinted with permission.

Rosenhan, David. L., "On being sane in insane places." *Science*, vol. 179, 1973. Excerpted. Copyright © 1973 AAAS. Reprinted with permission.

Shore, Cris, "Corruption scandals in America and Europe: Enron and EU fraud in comparative perspective." *Social Analysis*, vol. 47, no. 3, Fall 2003, pp. 147–152. © 2003 by Berghan Books. Reprinted with permission by the publisher.

60 Minutes, "Rx Drugs," © CBS Worldwide Inc., All Rights Reserved, Originally broadcast on 60 MINUTES on December 27, 1992, over the CBS Television Network.

Spalek, Basia, "Regulation, white-collar crime and the Bank of Credit and Commerce International." *The Howard Journal*, vol. 40, no. 2, May 2001, pp. 166–179 (edited). Reprinted by permission from Blackwell Publishers.

Sykes, Gresham M. and David Matza, "Techniques of Neutralization: A theory of delinquency." *American Sociological Review*, vol. 22, 1957, pp. 664–670. Public domain.

Thompson, Kenneth. From *Moral Panics*, Kenneth Thompson, Copyright © Routledge 1998. Reproduced by permission of Taylor and Francis Books UK.

Victor, Jeffery S., *Satanic panic: The creation of a contemporary legend*. pp. 195–200. Reprinted by permission of Open Court Publishing Company, a division of Carus Publishing Company, Peru, IL from *Satanic panic: The creation of a contemporary legend* by Jeffery S. Victor, Copyright © 1993 by Open Court.

Warner, Richard, From *Recovery from Schizophrenia*, 3rd edition, Copyright © Brunner-Routledge 1998. Reproduced by permission of Taylor and Francis Books UK.

PART 1

Explaining Deviance

THE NORMAL AND THE PATHOLOGICAL

EMILE DURKHEIM

In one of the most classic statements about crime and deviance in the history of sociology, Durkheim asserts that since crime occurs in all societies throughout history, then it must be seen as normal and not as a sign of an unhealthy society. Because societies allow and encourage a certain diversity of thought, we are all different and that differentness accounts for both deviance and innovation. If it were not for that differentness, there would be no crime and there would be no social change; societies would remain absolutely stagnant—a condition that is not only undesirable but also impossible.

To rephrase Durkheim, crime is the price that we pay for a free society. This is not to say that the more crime the better. Indeed Durkheim does acknowledge that rising crime rates are cause for concern.

Crime is present not only in the majority of societies of one particular species but in all societies of all types. There is no society that is not confronted with the problem of criminality. Its form changes; the acts thus characterized are not the same everywhere; but, everywhere and always, there have been men who have behaved in such a way as to draw upon themselves penal repression. If, in proportion as societies pass from the lower to the higher types, the rate of criminality, i.e., the relation between the yearly number of crimes and the population, tended to decline, it might be believed that crime, while still normal, is tending to lose this character of normality. But we have no reason to believe that such a regression is substantiated.

Many facts would seem rather to indicate a movement in the opposite direction. From the beginning of the [nineteenth] century, statistics enable us to follow the course of criminality. It has everywhere increased. In France the increase is nearly 300 per cent. There is, then, no phenomenon that presents more indisputably all the symptoms of normality, since it appears closely connected with the conditions of all collective life. To make of crime a form of social morbidity would be to admit that morbidity is not something accidental, but, on the contrary, that in certain cases it grows out of the fundamental constitution of the living organism; it would result in wiping out all distinction between the physiological and the pathological. No doubt it is possible that crime itself will have abnormal forms, as, for example, when its rate is unusually high. This excess is indeed, undoubtedly morbid in nature. What is normal, simply, is the existence of criminality, provided that it attains and does not exceed, for each social type, a certain level, which it is perhaps not impossible to fix in conformity with the preceding rules.[1]

Here we are, then, in the presence of a conclusion in appearance quite paradoxical. Let us make no mistake. To classify crime among the phenomena of normal sociology is not to say merely that it is an inevitable, although regrettable phenomenon, due to the incorrigible wickedness of men; it is to affirm that it is a factor in public health, an integral part of all healthy societies. This result is, at first glance, surprising enough to have puzzled even ourselves for a long time. Once this first surprise has been overcome, however, it is not difficult to find reasons explaining this normality and at the same time confirming it.

In the first place crime is normal because a society exempt from it is utterly impossible. Crime, we have shown elsewhere, consists of an act that offends certain very strong collective sentiments. In a society in which criminal acts are no longer committed, the sentiments they offend would have to be found without exception in all individual consciousnesses, and they must be found to exist with the same degree as sentiments contrary to them. Assuming that this condition could actually be realized, crime would not thereby disappear; it would only change its form, for the very cause which would thus dry up the sources of criminality would immediately open up new ones.

Indeed, for the collective sentiments which are protected by the penal law of a people at a specified moment of its history to take possession of the public conscience or for them to acquire a stronger hold where they have an insufficient grip, they must acquire an intensity greater than that which they had hitherto had. The community as a whole must experience them more vividly, for it can acquire from no other source the greater force necessary to control these individuals who formerly were the most refractory. For murderers to disappear, the horror of bloodshed must become greater in those social strata from which murderers are recruited; but, first it must become greater throughout the entire society. Moreover, the very absence of crime would directly contribute to produce this horror; because any sentiment seems much more respectable when it is always and uniformly respected.

One easily overlooks the consideration that these strong states of the common consciousness cannot be thus reinforced without reinforcing at the same time the more feeble states, whose violation previously gave birth to mere infraction of convention—since the weaker ones are only the prolongation, the attenuated form, of the stronger. Thus robbery and simple bad taste injure the same single altruistic sentiment, the respect for that which is another's. However, this same sentiment is less grievously offended by bad taste than by robbery; and since, in addition, the average consciousness has not sufficient intensity to react keenly to the bad taste, it is treated with greater tolerance. That is why the person guilty of bad taste is merely blamed, whereas the thief is punished. But, if this sentiment grows stronger, to the point of silencing in all consciousnesses the inclination which disposes man to steal, he will become more sensitive to the offenses which, until then, touched him but lightly. He will react against them, then, with more energy; they will be the object of greater opprobrium, which will transform certain of them from the simple moral faults that they were and give them the quality of crimes. For example, improper contracts, or contracts improperly executed, which only incur public blame or civil damages, will become offenses in law.

Imagine a society of saints, a perfect cloister of exemplary individuals. Crimes, properly so called, will there be unknown; but faults which appear venial to the layman will create there the same scandal that the ordinary offense does in ordinary consciousnesses. If, then, this society has the power to judge and punish, it will define these acts as criminal and will treat them as such. For the same reason, the perfect and upright man judges his smallest failings with a severity that the majority reserve for acts more truly in the nature of an offense. Formerly, acts of violence against persons were more frequent than they are today, because respect for individual dignity was less strong. As this has increased, these crimes have become more rare; and also, many acts violating this sentiment have been introduced into the penal law which were not included there in primitive times.[2]

In order to exhaust all the hypotheses logically possible, it will perhaps be asked why this unanimity does not extend to all collective sentiments without exception. Why should not even the most feeble sentiment gather enough energy to prevent all dissent? The moral consciousness of the society would be present in its entirety in all the individuals, with a vitality sufficient to prevent all acts offending it—the purely conventional faults as well as the crimes. But a uniformity so universal and absolute is utterly impossible; for the immediate physical milieu in which each one of us is placed, the hereditary antecedents, and the social influences vary from one individual to the next, and consequently diversify consciousnesses. It is impossible for all to be alike, if only because each one has his own organism and that these organisms occupy different areas in space. That is why, even among the lower peoples, where individual originality is very little developed, it nevertheless does exist.

Thus, since there cannot be a society in which the individuals do not differ more or less from the collective type, it is also inevitable that, among these divergences, there are some with a criminal character. What confers this character upon them is not the intrinsic quality of a given act but that definition which the collective conscience lends them. If the collective conscience is stronger, if it has enough authority practically to suppress these divergences, it will also be more sensitive, more exacting; and, reacting against the slightest deviations with the energy it otherwise displays only against more considerable infractions, it will attribute to them the same gravity as formerly to crimes. In other words, it will designate them as criminal.

Crime is, then, necessary; it is bound up with fundamental conditions of all social life, and by that very fact it is useful, because these conditions of which it is part are themselves indispensable to the normal evolution of morality and law.

Indeed, it is no longer possible today to dispute the fact that law and morality vary from one social type to the next, nor that they change within the same type if the conditions of life are modified. But, in order that these transformations may be possible, the collective sentiments at the basis of morality must not be hostile to change, and consequently must have but moderate energy. If they were too strong, they would no longer be plastic. Every pattern is an obstacle to new patterns, to the extent that the first pattern is inflexible. The better a structure is articulated, the more it offers a healthy resistance to all modification; and this is equally true of functional, as of anatomical, organization. If there were no crimes, this condition could not have been fulfilled; for such a hypothesis presupposes that collective sentiments have arrived at a degree of intensity unexampled in history. Nothing is good indefinitely and to an unlimited extent. The authority which the moral conscience enjoys must not be excessive; otherwise no one would dare criticize it, and it would too easily congeal into an immutable form. To make progress, individual originality must be able to express itself. In order that the originality of the idealist whose dreams transcend his century may find expression, it is necessary that the originality of the criminal, who is below the level of his time, shall also be possible. One does not occur without the other.

Nor is this all. Aside from this indirect utility, it happens that crime itself plays a useful role in this evolution. Crime implies not only that the way remains open to necessary changes but that in certain cases it directly prepares these changes. Where crime exists, collective sentiments are sufficiently flexible to take on a new form, and crime sometimes helps to determine the form they will take. How many times, indeed, it is only an anticipation of future morality—a step toward what will be! According to Athenian law, Socrates was a criminal, and his condemnation was no more than just. However, his crime, namely, the independence of his thought, rendered a service not only to humanity but to his country. It served to prepare a new morality and faith which the Athenians needed, since the traditions by which they had lived until then were no longer in harmony with the current conditions of life. Nor is the case of Socrates unique; it is reproduced periodically in history. It would never have been possible to establish the freedom of thought we now enjoy if the regulations prohibiting it had not been violated before being solemnly abrogated. At that time, however, the violation was a crime, since it was an offense against sentiments still very keen in the average conscience. And yet this crime was useful as a prelude to reforms which daily became more necessary. Liberal philosophy had as its precursors the heretics of all kinds who were justly punished by secular authorities during the entire course of the Middle Ages and until the eve of modern times.

From this point of view the fundamental facts of criminality present themselves to us in an entirely new light. Contrary to current ideas, the criminal no longer seems a totally unsociable being, a sort of parasitic element, a strange and unassimilable body, introduced into the midst of society.[3] On the contrary, he plays a definite role in social life. Crime, for its part, must no longer be conceived as an evil that cannot be too much suppressed. There is no occasion for self-congratulation when the crime rate drops noticeably below the average level, for we may be certain that this apparent progress is associated with some social disorder. Thus, the number of assault cases never falls so low as in times of want.[4] With the drop in the crime rate, and as a reaction to it, comes a revision, or the need of a revision in the theory of punishment. If, indeed, crime is a disease, its punishment is its remedy and cannot be otherwise conceived; thus, all the discussions it arouses bear on the point of determining what the punishment must be in order to fulfil this role of remedy. If crime is not pathological at all, the object of punishment cannot be to cure it, and its true function must be sought elsewhere.

NOTES

1. From the fact that crime is a phenomenon of normal sociology, it does not follow that the criminal is an individual normally constituted from the biological and psychological points of view. The two questions are independent of each other. This independence will be better understood when we have shown, later on, the difference between psychological and sociological facts.

2. Calumny, insults, slander, fraud, etc.

3. We have ourselves committed the error of speaking thus of the criminal, because of a failure to apply our rule (*Division du travail social*, pp. 395–96).

4. Although crime is a fact of normal sociology, it does not follow that we must not abhor it. Pain itself has nothing desirable about it; the individual dislikes it as society does crime, and yet it is a function of normal physiology. Not only is it necessarily derived from the very constitution of every living organism, but it plays a useful role in life, for which reason it cannot be replaced. It would, then, be a singular distortion of our thought to present it as an apology for crime. We would not even think of protesting against such an interpretation, did we not know to what strange accusations and misunderstandings one exposes oneself when one undertakes to study moral facts objectively and to speak of them in a different language from that of the layman.

ON THE SOCIOLOGY OF DEVIANCE
KAI T. ERIKSON

Flowing from Durkheim's assertion that deviance is universal and functional, below Erikson speculates about the necessary role performed by deviants in the community. According to Erikson, the deviant helps the community establish its moral boundaries and, therefore, its identity as a community. An understanding of this process helps us to understand why the coverage of crime and deviance constitutes such a large proportion of the daily news in ours and other societies. It also helps us to understand one of the great paradoxes in the sociology of social control; that is, do we really believe that we can take society's deviants, force them into extremely deviant environments (e.g., a prison or a mental hospital), and expect them to come out less deviant?

Human actors are sorted into various kinds of collectivity, ranging from relatively small units such as the nuclear family to relatively large ones such as a nation or culture. One of the most stubborn difficulties in the study of deviation is that the problem is defined differently at each one of these levels: behavior that is considered unseemly within the context of a single family may be entirely acceptable to the community in general, while behavior that attracts severe censure from the members of the community may go altogether unnoticed elsewhere in the culture. People in society, then, must learn to deal separately with deviance at each one of these levels and to distinguish among them in his own daily activity. A man may disinherit his son for conduct that violates old family traditions or ostracize a neighbor for conduct that violates some local custom, but he is not expected to employ either of these standards when he serves as a juror in a court of law. In each of the three situations he is required to use a different set of criteria to decide whether or not the behavior in question exceeds tolerable limits.

In the next few pages we shall be talking about deviant behavior in social units called "communities," but the use of this term does not mean that the argument applies only at that level of organization. In theory, at least, the argument being made here should fit all kinds of human collectivity—families as well as whole cultures, small groups as well as nations—and the term "community" is only being used in this context because it seems particularly convenient.[1]

The people of a community spend most of their lives in close contact with one another, sharing a common sphere of experience which makes them feel that they belong to a special "kind" and live in a special "place." In the formal language of sociology, this means that communities are boundary maintaining: each has a specific territory in the world as a whole, not only in the sense that it occupies a defined region of geographical space but also in the sense that it takes over a particular niche in what might be called cultural space and develops its own "ethos" or "way" within that compass. Both of these dimensions of group space, the geographical and the cultural, set the community apart as a special place and provide an important point of reference for its members.

When one describes any system as boundary maintaining, one is saying that it controls the fluctuation of its consistent parts so that the whole retains a limited range of activity, a given pattern of constancy and stability, within the larger environment. A human community can be said to maintain boundaries, then, in the sense that its members tend to confine themselves to a particular radius of activity and to regard any conduct which drifts outside that radius as somehow inappropriate or immoral. Thus the group retains a kind of cultural integrity, a voluntary restriction on its own potential for expansion, beyond that which is strictly required for accommodation to the environment. Human behavior can vary over an enormous range, but each community draws a symbolic set of parentheses around a certain segment of that range and limits its own activities within that narrower zone. These parentheses, so to speak, are the community's boundaries.

People who live together in communities cannot relate to one another in any coherent way or even acquire a sense of their own stature as group members unless they learn something about the boundaries of the territory they occupy in social space, if only because they need to sense what lies beyond the margins of the group before they can appreciate the special quality of the experience which takes place within it. Yet how do people learn about the boundaries of their community? And how do they convey this information to the generations which replace them?

To begin with, the only material found in a society for marking boundaries is the behavior of its members—or rather, the networks of interaction which link these members together in regular social relations. And the interactions which do the most effective job of locating and publicizing the group's outer edges would seem to be those which take place between deviant persons on the one side and official agents of the community on the other. The deviant is a person whose activities have moved outside the margins of the group, and when the community calls him to account for that vagrancy it is making a statement about the nature and placement of its boundaries. It is declaring how much variability and diversity can be tolerated within the group before it begins to lose its distinctive shape, its unique identity. Now there may be other moments in the life of the group which perform a similar service: wars, for instance, can publicize a group's boundaries by drawing attention to the line separating the group from an adversary, and certain kinds of religious ritual, dance ceremony, and other traditional pageantry can dramatize the difference between "we" and "they" by portraying a symbolic encounter between the two. But on the whole, members of a community inform one another about the placement of their boundaries by participating in the confrontations which occur when persons who venture out to the edges of the group are met by policing agents whose special business it is to guard the cultural integrity of the community. Whether these confrontations take the form of criminal trials, excommunication hearings, courts-martial, or even psychiatric case conferences, they act as boundary-maintaining devices in the sense that they demonstrate to whatever audience is concerned where the line is drawn between behavior that belongs in the special universe of the group and behavior that does not. In general, this kind of information is not easily relayed by the straightforward use of language. Most readers of this paragraph, for instance, have a fairly clear idea of the line separating theft from more legitimate forms of commerce, but few of them have ever seen a published statute describing these differences. More likely than not, our information on the subject has been drawn from publicized instances in which the relevant laws were applied—and for that matter, the law itself is largely a collection of past cases and decisions, a synthesis of the various confrontations which have occurred in the life of the legal order.

It may be important to note in this connection that confrontations between deviant offenders and the agents of control have always attracted a good deal of public attention. In our own past, the trial and punishment of offenders were staged in the market place and afforded the crowd a chance to participate in a direct, active way. Today, of course, we no longer parade deviants in the town square or expose them to the carnival atmosphere of Tyburn, but it is interesting that the "reform" which brought about this change in penal practice coincided almost exactly with the development of newspapers as a medium of mass information. Perhaps this is no more than an accident of history, but it is nonetheless true that newspapers (and now radio and television) offer much the same kind of entertainment as public hangings or a Sunday visit to the local gaol. A considerable portion of what we call "news" is devoted to reports about deviant behavior and its consequences, and it is no simple matter to explain why these items should be considered newsworthy or why they should command the extraordinary attention they do. Perhaps they appeal to a number of psychological perversities among the mass audience, as commentators have suggested, but at the same time they constitute one of our main sources of information about the normative outlines of society. In a figurative sense, at least, morality and immorality meet at the public scaffold, and it is during this meeting that the line between them is drawn.

Boundaries are never a fixed property of any community. They are always shifting as the people of the group find new ways to define the outer limits of their universe, new ways to position themselves on the larger cultural map. Sometimes changes occur within the structure of the group which require its members to make a new survey of their territory—a change of leadership, a shift of mood. Sometimes changes occur in the surrounding environment, altering the background against which the people of the group have measured their own uniqueness. And always, new generations are moving in to take their turn guarding old institutions and need to be informed about the contours of the world they are inheriting. Thus single encounters between the deviant and his community are only fragments of an ongoing social process. Like an article of common law, boundaries remain a meaningful point of reference only so long as they are repeatedly tested by persons on the fringes of the group and repeatedly defended by persons chosen to represent the group's inner morality. Each time the community moves to censure some act of deviation, then, and convenes a formal ceremony to deal with the responsible offender, it sharpens the authority of the violated norm and restates where the boundaries of the group are located.

For these reasons, deviant behavior is not a simple kind of leakage which occurs when the machinery of society is in poor working order, but may be, in controlled quantities, an important condition for preserving the stability of social life. Deviant forms of behavior, by marking the outer edges of group life, give the inner structure its special character and thus supply the framework within which the people of the group develop an orderly sense of their own cultural identity. Perhaps this is what Aldous Huxley had in mind when he wrote:

> Now tidiness is undeniably good—but a good of which it is easily possible to have too much and at too high a price.... The good life can only be lived in a society in which tidiness is preached and practiced, but not too fanatically, and where efficiency is always haloed, as it were, by a tolerated margin of mess.[2]

This raises a delicate theoretical issue. If we grant that human groups often derive benefit from deviant behavior, can we then assume that they are organized in such a way as to promote this resource? Can we assume, in other words, that forces operate in the social structure to recruit offenders and to commit them to long periods of service in the deviant ranks? This is not a question which can be answered with our present store of empirical data, but one observation can be made which gives the question an interesting perspective—namely, that deviant forms of conduct often seem to derive nourishment from the very agencies devised to inhibit them. Indeed, the agencies built by society for preventing deviance are often so poorly equipped for the task that we might well ask why this is regarded as their "real" function in the first place.

It is by now a thoroughly familiar argument that many of the institutions designed to discourage deviant behavior actually operate in such a way as to perpetuate it. For one thing, prisons, hospitals, and other similar agencies provide aid and shelter to large numbers of deviant persons, sometimes giving them a certain advantage in the competition for social resources. But beyond this, such institutions gather marginal people into tightly segregated groups, give them an opportunity to teach one another the skills and attitudes of a deviant career, and even provoke them into using these skills by reinforcing their sense of alienation from the rest of society.[3] Nor is this observation a modern one:

> The misery suffered in gaols is not half their evil; they are filled with every sort of corruption that poverty and wickedness can generate; with all the shameless and profligate enormities that can be produced by the impudence of ignominy, the range of want, and the malignity of despair. In a prison the check of the public eye is removed; and the power of the law is spent. There are few fears, there are no blushes. The lewd inflame the more modest; the audacious harden the timid. Everyone fortifies himself as he can against his own remaining sensibility; endeavoring to practice on others the arts that are practiced on himself; and to gain the applause of his worst associates by imitating their manners.[4]

These lines, written almost two centuries ago, are a harsh indictment of prisons, but many of the conditions they describe continue to be reported in even the most modern studies of prison life. Looking at the matter from a long-range historical perspective, it is fair to conclude that prisons have done a conspicuously poor job of reforming the convicts placed in their custody; but the very consistency of this failure may have a peculiar logic of its own. Perhaps we find it difficult to change the worst of our penal practices because we *expect* the prison to harden the inmate's commitment to deviant forms of behavior and draw him more deeply into the deviant ranks. On the whole, we are a people who do not really expect deviants to change very much as they are processed through the control agencies we provide for them, and we are often reluctant to devote much of the community's resources to the job of rehabilitation. In this sense, the prison which graduates long rows of accomplished criminals (or, for that matter, the state asylum which stores its most severe cases away in some back ward) may do serious violence to the aims of its founders; but it does very little violence to the expectations of the population it serves.

These expectations, moreover, are found in every corner of society and constitute an important part of the climate in which we deal with deviant forms of behavior.

To begin with, the community's decision to bring deviant sanctions against one of its members is not a simple act of censure. It is an intricate rite of transition, at once moving the individual out of his ordinary place in society and transferring him into a special deviant position.[5] The ceremonies which mark this change of status, generally, have a number of related phases. They supply a formal stage on which the deviant and his community can confront one another (as in the criminal trial); they make an announcement about the nature of his deviancy (a verdict or diagnosis, for example); and they place him in a particular role which is thought to neutralize the harmful effects of his misconduct (like the role of prisoner or patient). These commitment ceremonies tend to be occasions of wide public interest and ordinarily take place in a highly dramatic setting.[6] Perhaps the most obvious example of a commitment ceremony is the criminal trial, with its elaborate formality and exaggerated ritual, but more modest equivalents can be found wherever procedures are set up to judge whether or not someone is legitimately deviant.

An important feature of these ceremonies in our own culture is that they are almost irreversible. Most provisional roles conferred by society, those of the student or conscripted soldier, for example, include some kind of terminal ceremony to mark the individual's movement back out of the role once its temporary advantages have been exhausted. But the roles allotted the deviant seldom make allowance for this type of passage. He is ushered into the deviant position by a decisive and often dramatic ceremony, yet is retired from it with scarcely a word of public notice. And as a result, the deviant often returns home with no proper license to resume a normal life in the community. Nothing has happened to cancel out the stigmas imposed upon him by earlier commitment ceremonies; nothing has happened to revoke the verdict or diagnosis pronounced upon him at that time. It should not be surprising, then, that the people of the community are apt to greet the returning deviant with a considerable degree of apprehension and distrust, for in a very real sense they are not at all sure who he is.

A circularity is thus set into motion which has all the earmarks of a "self-fulfilling prophesy," to use Merton's fine phrase. On the one hand, it seems quite obvious that the community's apprehensions help reduce whatever chances the deviant might otherwise have had for a successful return home. Yet at the same time, everyday experience seems to show that these suspicions are wholly reasonable, for it is a well-known and highly publicized fact that many if not most ex-convicts return to crime after leaving prison and that large numbers of mental patients require further treatment after an initial hospitalization. The common feeling that deviant persons never really change, then, may derive from a faulty premise; but the feeling is expressed so frequently and with such conviction that it eventually creates the facts which later "prove" it to be correct. If the returning deviant encounters this circularity often enough, it is quite understandable that he, too, may begin to wonder whether he has fully graduated from the deviant role, and he may respond to the uncertainty by resuming some kind of deviant activity. In many respects, this may be the only way for the individual and his community to agree what kind of person he is.

Moreover this prophesy is found in the official policies of even the most responsible agencies of control. Police departments could not operate with any real effectiveness if they did not regard ex-convicts as a ready pool of suspects to be tapped in the event of trouble, and psychiatric clinics could not do a successful job in the community if they were not always alert to the possibility of former patients suffering relapses. Thus the prophesy gains currency at many levels within the social order, not only in the poorly informed attitudes of the community at large, but in the best informed theories of most control agencies as well.

In one form or another this problem has been recognized in the West for many hundreds of years, and this simple fact has a curious implication. For if our culture has supported a steady flow of deviation throughout long periods of historical change, the rules which apply to any kind of evolutionary thinking would suggest that strong forces must be at work to keep the flow intact—and this because it contributes in some important way to the survival of the culture as a whole. This does not furnish us with sufficient warrant to declare that deviance is "functional" (in any of the many senses of that term), but it should certainly make us wary of the assumption so often made in sociological circles that any well-structured society is somehow designed to prevent deviant behavior from occurring.[7]

It might be then argued that we need new metaphors to carry our thinking about deviance onto a different plane. On the whole, American sociologists have devoted most of their attention to those forces in society which seem to assert a centralizing influence on human behavior, gathering people together into tight clusters called "groups" and bringing them under the jurisdiction of governing principles called "norms" or "standards." The questions which sociologists have traditionally asked of their data, then, are addressed to the uniformities rather than the divergencies of social life: how is it that people learn to think in similar ways, to accept the same group moralities, to move by the same rhythms of behavior, to see life with the same eyes? How is it, in short, that cultures accomplish the incredible alchemy of making unity out of diversity, harmony out of conflict, order out of confusion? Somehow we often act as if the differences between people can be taken for granted, being too natural to require comment, but that the symmetry which human groups manage to achieve must be explained by referring to the molding influence of the social structure.

But variety, too, is a product of the social structure. It is certainly remarkable that members of a culture come to look so much alike; but it is also remarkable that out of all this sameness a people can develop a complex division of labor, move off into diverging career lines, scatter across the surface of the territory they share in common, and create so many differences of temper, ideology, fashion, and mood. Perhaps we can conclude, then, that two separate yet often competing currents are found in any society: those forces which promote a high degree of conformity among the people of the community so that they know what to expect from one another, and those forces which encourage a certain degree of diversity so that people can be deployed across the range of group space to survey its potential, measure its capacity, and, in the case of those we call deviants, patrol its boundaries. In such a scheme, the deviant would appear as a natural product of group differentiation. He is not a bit of debris spun out by faulty social machinery, but a relevant figure in the community's overall division of labor.

NOTES

1. In fact, the first statement of the general notion presented here was concerned with the study of small groups. See Robert A. Dentler and Kai T. Erikson, "The Functions of Deviance in Groups," *Social Problems*, VII (Fall 1959), pp. 98–107.

2. Aldous Huxley, *Prisons: The "Carceri" Etchings by Piranesi* (London: The Trianon Press, 1949), p. 13.

3. For a good description of this process in the modern prison, see Gresham Sykes, *The Society of Captives* (Princeton, N.J.: Princeton University Press, 1958). For discussions of similar problems in two different kinds of mental hospital, see Erving Goffman, *Asylums* (New York: Bobbs-Merrill, 1962) and Kai T. Erikson, "Patient Role and Social Uncertainty: A Dilemma of the Mentally Ill," *Psychiatry*, XX (August 1957), pp. 263–274.

4. Written by "a celebrated" but not otherwise identified author (perhaps Henry Fielding) and quoted in John Howard, *The State of the Prisons*, London, 1777 (London: J. M. Dent and Sons, 1929), p. 10.

5. The classic description of this process as it applies to the medical patient is found in Talcott Parsons, *The Social System* (Glencoe, Ill.: The Free Press, 1951).

6. See Harold Garfinkel, "Successful Degradation Ceremonies," *American Journal of Sociology*, LXI (January 1956), pp. 420–424.

7. Albert K. Cohen, for example, speaking for a dominant strain in sociological thinking, takes the question quite for granted: "It would seem that the control of deviant behavior is, by definition, a culture goal." See "The Study of Social Disorganization and Deviant Behavior" in Merton et al., *Sociology Today* (New York: Basic Books, 1959), p. 465.

SOCIAL STRUCTURE AND ANOMIE

ROBERT K. MERTON

In one of the most often-cited works in the American sociology of deviance, Merton asserts that much of the crime and deviance in our society stems from the extraordinarily strong emphasis our culture places on the goal of financial success. The strong belief that Americans hold in the existence of "equal opportunity for all" implies that the goal of success is equally available and those who do not achieve it have only themselves to blame. Yet the problem is that there is not equal opportunity and that millions of Americans are set up to fail. The result can be frustration, hostility, anomie, and crime.

While other countries may have higher rates of poverty, the correlation between crime and poverty is not as strong in those societies because the emphasis on financial success and the belief in equal opportunity are not as strong; therefore, the frustration engendered by poverty is not as keen in those countries as it is in the United States.

There persists a notable tendency in sociological theory to attribute the malfunctioning of social structure primarily to those of man's imperious biological drives which are not adequately restrained by social control. In this view, the social order is solely a device for "impulse management" and the "social processing" of tensions. These impulses which break through social control, be it noted, are held to be biologically derived. Nonconformity is assumed to be rooted in original nature.[1] Conformity is by implication the result of a utilitarian calculus or unreasoned conditioning. This point of view, whatever its other deficiencies, clearly begs one question. It provides no basis for determining the nonbiological conditions which induce deviations from prescribed patterns of conduct. In this paper, it will be suggested that certain phases of social structure generate the circumstances in which infringement of social codes constitutes a "normal" response.[2]

The conceptual scheme to be outlined is designed to provide a coherent, systematic approach to the study of socio-cultural sources of deviate behavior. Our primary aim lies in discovering how some social structures *exert a definite pressure* upon certain persons in the society to engage in non-conformist rather than conformist conduct. The many ramifications of the scheme cannot all be discussed; the problems mentioned outnumber those explicitly treated.

Among the elements of social and cultural structure, two are important for our purposes. These are analytically separable although they merge impercept-ibly in concrete situations. The first consists of culturally defined goals, pur-poses, and interests. It comprises a frame of aspirational reference. These goals are more or less integrated and involve varying degrees of prestige and senti-ment. They constitute a basic, but not the exclusive, component of what Linton aptly has called "designs for group living." Some of these cultural aspirations are related to the original drives of man, but they are not determined by them. The second phase of the social structure defines, regulates, and controls the acceptable modes of achieving these goals. Every social group invariably couples its scale of desired ends with moral or institutional regulation of permissible and required procedures for attaining these ends. These regulatory norms and moral imperatives do not necessarily coincide with technical or efficiency norms. Many procedures which from the standpoint of *particular individuals* would be most efficient in securing desired values, e.g., illicit oil-stock schemes, theft, fraud, are ruled out of the institutional area of permitted conduct. The choice of expedients is limited by the institutional norms.

To say that these two elements, culture goals and institutional norms, operate jointly is not to say that the ranges of alternative behaviors and aims bear some constant relation to one another. The emphasis upon certain goals may vary independently of the degree of emphasis upon institutional means. There may develop a disproportionate, at times, a virtually exclusive, stress upon the value of specific goals, involving relatively slight concern with the institutionally appropriate modes of attaining these goals. The limiting case in this direction is reached when the range of alternative procedures is limited only by technical rather than institutional considerations. Any and all devices which promise attainment of the all important goal would be per-mitted in this hypothetical polar case.[3] This constitutes one type of cultural malintegration. A second polar type is found in groups where activities ori-ginally conceived as instrumental are transmuted into ends in themselves. The original purposes are forgotten, and ritualistic adherence to institutionally prescribed conduct becomes virtually obsessive.[4] Stability is largely ensured while change is flouted. The range of alternative behaviors is severely lim-ited. There develops a tradition-bound, sacred society characterized by neo-phobia. The occupational psychosis of the bureaucrat may be cited as a case in point. Finally, there are the intermediate types of groups where a balance between culture goals and institutional means is maintained. These are the significantly integrated and relatively stable, though changing, groups.

An effective equilibrium between the two phases of the social structure is maintained as long as satisfactions accrue to individuals who conform to both constraints, *viz.*, satisfactions from the achievement of the goals and satisfactions emerging directly from the institutionally canalized modes of striving to attain these ends. Success, in such equilibrated cases, is twofold. Success is reckoned in terms of the product and in terms of the process, in terms of the outcome and in terms of activities. Continuing satisfactions must derive from sheer *participation* in a competitive order as well as from eclipsing one's competitors if the order itself is to be sustained. The occasional sacrifices involved in institutionalized conduct must be compensated by socialized rewards. The distribution of statuses and roles through competition must be so organized that positive incentives for conformity to roles and adherence to status obligations are provided *for every position* within the distributive order. Aberrant conduct, therefore, may be viewed as a symptom of dissociation between culturally defined aspirations and socially structured means.

Of the types of groups which result from the independent variation of the two phases of the social structure, we shall be primarily concerned with the first, namely, that involving a disproportionate accent on goals. This statement must be recast in a proper perspective. In no group is there an absence of regulatory codes governing conduct, yet groups do vary in the degree to which these folkways, mores, and institutional controls are effectively integrated with the more diffuse goals which are part of the culture matrix. Emotional convictions may cluster about the complex of socially acclaimed ends, meanwhile shifting their support from the culturally defined implementation of these ends. As we shall see, certain aspects of the social structure may generate countermores and antisocial behavior precisely because of differential emphases on goals and regulations. In the extreme case, the latter may be so vitiated by the goal-emphasis that the range of behavior is limited only by considerations of technical expediency. The sole significant question then becomes, which available means is most efficient in netting the socially approved value.[5] The technically most feasible procedure, whether legitimate or not, is preferred to the institutionally prescribed conduct. As this process continues, the integration of the society becomes tenuous and anomie ensues.

Thus, in competitive athletics, when the aim of victory is shorn of its institutional trappings and success in contests becomes construed as "winning the game" rather than "winning through circumscribed modes of activity," a premium is implicitly set upon the use of illegitimate but technically efficient means. The star of the opposing football team is surreptitiously slugged; the wrestler furtively incapacitates his opponent through ingenious but illicit techniques; university alumni covertly subsidize "students" whose talents are largely confined to the athletic field. The emphasis on the goal has so attenuated the satisfactions deriving from sheer participation in the competitive activity that these satisfactions are virtually confined to a successful outcome. Through the same process, tension generated by the desire to win in a poker game is relieved by successfully dealing oneself four aces, or, when the cult of success has become completely dominant, by sagaciously shuffling the cards in a game of solitaire. The faint twinge of uneasiness in the last instance and the surreptitious nature of public delicts indicate clearly that the institutional rules of the game are *known* to those who evade them, but that the emotional supports of these rules are largely vitiated by cultural exaggeration of the success-goal.[6] They are microcosmic images of the social macrocosm.

Of course, this process is not restricted to the realm of sport. The process whereby exaltation of the end generates a *literal demoralization*, i.e., a deinstitutionalization, of the means is one which characterizes many[7] groups in which the two phases of the social structure are not highly integrated. The extreme emphasis upon the accumulation of wealth as a symbol of success[8] in our own society militates against the completely effective control of institutionally regulated modes of acquiring of fortune.[9] Fraud, corruption, vice, crime, in short, the entire catalogue of proscribed behavior, becomes increasingly common when the emphasis on the *culturally induced* success-goal becomes divorced from a coordinated institutional emphasis. This observation is of crucial theoretical importance in examining the doctrine that antisocial behavior most frequently derives from biological drives breaking through the restraints imposed by society. The difference is one between a strictly utilitarian interpretation which conceives man's ends as random and an analysis which finds these ends deriving from the basic values of the culture.[10]

Our analysis can scarcely stop at this juncture. We must turn to other aspects of the social structure if we are to deal with the social genesis of the varying rates and types of deviate behavior characteristic of different societies. Thus far, we have sketched three ideal types of social orders constituted by distinctive patterns of relations between culture ends and means. Turning from these types of *culture patterning*, we find five logically possible, alternative modes of adjustment or adaptation by *individuals* within the culture-bearing society or group.[11] These are schematically presented in the following table, where (+) signifies "acceptance," (−) signifies "elimination," and (±) signifies "rejection and substitution of new goals and standards."

Our discussion of the relation between these alternative responses and other phases of the social structure must be prefaced by the observation that

MODES OF ADAPTATION	CULTURE GOALS	INSTITUTIONAL MEANS
I. Conformity	+	+
II. Innovation	+	−
III. Ritualism	−	+
IV. Retreatism	−	−
V. Rebellion[12]	±	±

persons may shift from one alternative to another as they engage in different social activities. These categories refer to role adjustments in specific situations, not to personality *in toto*. To treat the development of this process in various spheres of conduct would introduce a complexity unmanageable within the confines of this paper. For this reason, we shall be concerned primarily with economic activity in the broad sense, "the production, exchange, distribution, and consumption of goods and services" in our competitive society, wherein wealth has taken on a highly symbolic cast. Our task is to search out some of the factors which exert pressure upon individuals to engage in certain of these logically possible alternative responses. This choice, as we shall see, is far from random.

In every society, Adaptation I (conformity to both culture goals and means) is the most common and widely diffused. Were this not so, the stability and continuity of the society could not be maintained. The mesh of expectancies which constitutes every social order is sustained by the modal behavior of its members falling within the first category. Conventional role behavior oriented toward the basic values of the group is the rule rather than the exception. It is this fact alone which permits us to speak of a human aggregate as comprising a group or society.

Conversely, Adaptation IV (rejection of goals and means) is the least common. Persons who "adjust" (or maladjust) in this fashion are, strictly speaking, *in* the society but not *of* it. Sociologically, these constitute the true "aliens." Not sharing the common frame of orientation, they can be included within the societal population merely in a fictional sense. In this category are *some* of the activities of psychotics, psychoneurotics, chronic autists, pariahs, outcasts, vagrants, vagabonds, tramps, chronic drunkards, and drug addicts.[13] These have relinquished, in certain spheres of activity, the culturally defined goals, involving complete aim-inhibition in the polar case, and their adjustments are not in accord with institutional norms. This is not to say that in some cases the source of their behavioral adjustments is not in part the very social structure which they have in effect repudiated nor that their very existence within a social area does not constitute a problem for the socialized population.

This mode of adjustment occurs, as far as structural sources are concerned, when both the culture goals and institutionalized procedures have been assimilated thoroughly by the individual and imbued with affect and high positive value, but where those institutionalized procedures which promise a measure of successful attainment of the goals are not available to the individual. In such instances, there results a two-fold mental conflict insofar as the moral obligation for adopting institutional means conflicts with the pressure to resort to illegitimate means (which may attain the goal) and inasmuch as the individual is shut off from means which are both legitimate *and* effective. The competitive order is maintained, but the frustrated and handicapped individual who cannot cope with this order drops out. Defeatism, quietism, and resignation are manifested in escape mechanisms which ultimately lead the individual to "escape" from the requirements of the society. It is an expedient which arises from continued failure to attain the goal by legitimate measures and from an inability to adopt the illegitimate route because of internalized prohibitions and institutionalized compulsives, *during which process the supreme value of the success-goal has as yet not been renounced*. The conflict is resolved by eliminating *both* precipitating elements, the goals and means. The escape is complete, the conflict is eliminated, and the individual is associated.

Be it noted that where frustration derives from the inaccessibility of effective institutional means for attaining economic or any other type of highly valued "success," that Adaptations II, III, and V (innovation, ritualism, and rebellion) are also possible. The result will be determined by the particular personality, and thus, the particular cultural background, involved. Inadequate socialization will result in the innovation response whereby the conflict and frustration are eliminated by relinquishing the institutional means and retaining the success-aspiration; an extreme assimilation of institutional demands will lead to ritualism wherein the goal is dropped as beyond one's reach but conformity to the mores persists; and rebellion occurs when emancipation from the reigning standards, due to frustration or to marginalist perspectives, leads to the attempt to introduce a "new social order."

Our major concern is with the illegitimacy adjustment. This involves the use of conventionally proscribed but frequently effective means of attaining at least the simulacrum of culturally defined success-wealth, power, and the like. As we have seen, this adjustment occurs when the individual has assimilated the cultural emphasis on success without equally internalizing the morally prescribed norms governing means for its attainment. The question arises, Which phases of our social structure predispose toward this mode of adjustment? We may examine a concrete instance, effectively analyzed by Lohman,[14] which provides a clue to the answer. Lohman has shown that specialized areas of vice in the near north side of Chicago constitute a "normal" response to a situation where the cultural emphasis upon pecuniary success has been absorbed, but where there is little access to conventional and legitimate means for attaining such success. The conventional occupational opportunities of persons in this area are almost completely limited to manual labor. Given our cultural stigmatization of manual labor, and its correlate, the prestige of white collar work, it is clear that the result is a strain toward innovational practices. The limitation of opportunity to unskilled labor and the resultant low income cannot compete in terms of *conventional standards of achievement* with the high income from organized vice.

For our purposes, this situation involves two important features. First, such antisocial behavior is in a sense "called forth" by certain conventional values of the culture *and* by the class structure involving differential access to the approved opportunities for legitimate, prestige-bearing pursuit of the culture goals. The lack of high integration between the means-and-end elements of the cultural pattern and the particular class structure combine to favor a heightened frequency of antisocial conduct in such groups. The second consideration is of equal significance. Recourse to the first of the alternative responses, legitimate effort, is limited by the fact that actual advance toward desired success-symbols through conventional channels is, despite our persisting open-class ideology,[15] relatively rare and difficult for those handicapped by little formal education and few economic resources. The dominant pressure of group standards of success is, therefore, on the gradual attenuation of legitimate, but by and large ineffective, strivings and the increasing use of illegitimate, but more or less effective, expedients of vice and crime. The cultural demands made on persons in this situation are incompatible. On the one hand, they are asked to orient their conduct toward the prospect of accumulating wealth and on the other, they are largely denied effective opportunities to do so institutionally. The consequences of such structural inconsistency are psychopathological personality, and/or antisocial conduct, and/or revolutionary activities. The equilibrium between culturally designated means and ends becomes highly unstable with the progressive emphasis on attaining the prestige-laden ends by any means whatsoever. Within this context, Capone represents the triumph of amoral intelligence over morally prescribed "failure," when the channels of vertical mobility are closed or narrowed[16] *in a society which places a high premium on economic affluence and social ascent for all its members.*[17]

This last qualification is of primary importance. It suggests that other phases of the social structure besides the extreme emphasis on pecuniary success must be considered if we are to understand the social sources of antisocial behavior. A high frequency of deviate behavior is not generated simply by "lack of opportunity" or by this exaggerated pecuniary emphasis. A comparatively rigidified class structure, a feudalistic or caste order, may limit such opportunities far beyond the point which obtains in our society today. It is only when a system of cultural values extols, virtually above all else, certain *common* symbols of success *for the population at large* while its social structure rigorously restricts or completely eliminates access to approved modes of acquiring these symbols *for a considerable part of the same population* that antisocial behavior ensues on a considerable scale. In other words, our egalitarian ideology denies by implication the existence of noncompeting groups and individuals in the pursuit of pecuniary success. The same body of success-symbols is held to be desirable for all. These goals are held to *transcend class lines*, not to be bounded by them, yet the actual social organization is such that there exist class differentials in the accessibility of these *common* success-symbols. Frustration and thwarted aspiration lead to the search for avenues of escape from a culturally induced intolerable situation; or unrelieved ambition may eventuate in illicit attempts to acquire the dominant values.[18] The American stress on pecuniary success and ambitiousness for all thus invites exaggerated anxieties, hostilities, neuroses, and antisocial behavior.

This theoretical analysis may go far toward explaining the varying correlations between crime and poverty.[19] Poverty is not an isolated variable. It is one in a complex of interdependent social and cultural variables. When viewed in such a context, it represents quite different states of affairs. Poverty as such, and consequent limitation of opportunity, are not sufficient to induce a conspicuously high rate of criminal behavior. Even the often mentioned "poverty in the midst of plenty" will not necessarily lead to this result. Only insofar as poverty and associated disadvantages in competition for the culture values approved for *all* members of the society are linked with the assimilation of a cultural emphasis on monetary accumulation as a symbol of success is antisocial conduct a "normal" outcome. Thus, poverty is less highly correlated with crime in southeastern Europe than in the United States. The possibilities of vertical mobility in these European areas would seem to be fewer than in this country, so that neither poverty per se nor its association with limited opportunity is sufficient to account for the varying correlations. It is only when the full configuration is considered, poverty, limited opportunity, and a commonly shared system of success-symbols, that we can explain the higher association between poverty and crime in our society than in others where rigidified class structure is coupled with *differential class symbols of achievement*.

In societies such as our own, then, the pressure of prestige-bearing success tends to eliminate the effective social constraint over means employed to this end. "The-end-justifies-the-means" doctrine becomes a guiding tenet for action when the cultural structure unduly exalts the end and the social organization unduly limits possible recourse to approved means. Otherwise put, this notion and associated behavior reflect a lack of cultural coordination. In international relations, the effects of this lack of integration are notoriously apparent. An emphasis upon national power is not readily coordinated with an inept organization of legitimate, i.e., internationally defined and accepted, means for attaining this goal. The result is a tendency toward the abrogation of international law, treaties become scraps of paper, "undeclared warfare" serves as a technical evasion, the bombing of civilian populations is rationalized,[20] just as the same societal situation induces the same sway of illegitimacy among individuals.

The social order we have described necessarily produces this "strain toward dissolution." The pressure of such an order is upon outdoing one's competitors. The choice of means within the ambit of institutional control will persist as long as the sentiments supporting a competitive system, i.e., deriving from the possibility of outranking competitors and hence enjoying the favorable response of others, are distributed throughout the entire system of activities and are not confined merely to the final result. A stable social structure demands a balanced distribution of affect among its various segments. When there occurs a shift of emphasis from the satisfactions deriving from competition itself to almost exclusive concern with successful competition, the resultant stress leads to the breakdown of the regulatory structure.[21] With the resulting attenuation of the institutional imperatives, there occurs an approximation of the situation erroneously held by utilitarians to be typical of society generally wherein calculations of advantage and fear of punishment are the sole regulating agencies. In such situations, as Hobbes observed, force and fraud come to constitute the sole virtues in view of their relative efficiency in attaining goals—which were for him, of course, not culturally derived.

It should be apparent that the foregoing discussion is not pitched on a moralistic plane. Whatever the sentiments of the writer or reader concerning the ethical desirability of coordinating the means-and-goals phases of the social structure, one must agree that lack of such coordination leads to anomie. Insofar as one of the most general functions of social organization is to provide a basis for calculability and regularity of behavior, it is increasingly limited in effectiveness as these elements of the structure become dissociated. At the extreme, predictability virtually disappears and what may be properly termed cultural chaos or anomie intervenes. This statement, being brief, is also incomplete. It has not included an exhaustive treatment of the various structural elements which predispose toward one rather than another of the alternative responses open to individuals; it has neglected, but not denied the relevance of, the factors determining the specific incidence of these responses; it has not enumerated the various concrete responses which are constituted by combinations of specific values of the analytical variables; it has omitted, or included only by implication, any consideration of the social functions performed by illicit responses; it has not tested the full explanatory power of the analytical scheme by examining a large number of group variations in the frequency of deviate and conformist behavior; it has not adequately dealt with rebellious conduct which seeks to refashion the social framework radically; it has not examined the relevance of cultural conflict for an analysis of culture-goal and institutional-means malintegration. It is suggested that these and related problems may be profitably analyzed by this scheme.

NOTES

1. E.g., Ernest Jones, *Social Aspects of Psychoanalysis*, 28, London, 1924. If the Freudian notion is a variety of the "original sin" dogma, then the interpretation advanced in this paper may be called the doctrine of "socially derived sin."

2. "Normal" in the sense of a culturally oriented, if not approved, response. This statement does not deny the relevance of biological and personality differences which may be significantly involved in the incidence of deviate conduct. Our focus of interest is the social and cultural matrix; hence we abstract from other factors. It is in this sense, I take it, that James S. Plant speaks of the "normal reaction of normal people to abnormal conditions." See his *Personality and the Cultural Pattern*, 248, New York, 1937.

3. Contemporary American culture has been said to tend in this direction. See Andre Siegfried, *America Comes of Age*, 26–37, New York, 1927. The alleged extreme(?) emphasis on the goals of monetary success and material prosperity leads to dominant concern with technological and social instruments designed to produce the desired result, inasmuch as institutional

controls become of secondary importance. In such a situation, innovation flourishes as the *range of means* employed is broadened. In a sense, then, there occurs the paradoxical emergence of "materialists" from an "idealistic" orientation. Cf. Durkheim's analysis of the cultural conditions which predispose toward crime and innovation, both of which are aimed toward efficiency, not moral norms. Durkheim was one of the first to see that "contrairement aux idees courantes le criminel n'apparait plus comme un être radicalement insociable, comme une sorte d'element parasitaire, de corps étranger et inassimilable, introduit au sein de la société; c'est un agent regulier de la vie sociale." See *Les Règles de la Méthode Sociologique*, 86–89, Paris, 1927.

4. Such ritualism may be associated with a mythology which rationalizes these actions so that they appear to retain their status as means, but the dominant pressure is in the direction of strict ritualistic conformity, irrespective of such rationalizations. In this sense, ritual has proceeded farthest when such rationalizations are not even called forth.

5. In this connection, one may see the relevance of Elton Mayo's paraphrase of the title of Tawney's well-known book. "Actually the problem is not that of the sickness of an society; it is that of the acquisitiveness of a sick society." *Human Problems of an Industrial Civilization*, 153, New York, 1933. Mayo deals with the process through which wealth comes to be a symbol of social achievement. He sees this as arising from a state of anomie. We are considering the unintegrated monetary-success goal as an element in producing anomie. A complete analysis would involve both phases of this system of interdependent variables.

6. It is unlikely that interiorized norms are completely eliminated. Whatever residuum persists will induce personality tensions and conflict. The process involves a certain degree of ambivalence. A manifest rejection of the institutional norms is coupled with some latent retention of their emotional correlates. "Guilt feelings," "sense of sin," "pangs of conscience" are obvious manifestations of this unrelieved tension; symbolic adherence to the nominally repudiated values or rationalizations constitute a more subtle variety of tensional release.

7. "Many," and not all, unintegrated groups, for the reason already mentioned. In groups where the primary emphasis shifts to institutional means, i.e., when the range of alternatives is very limited, the outcome is a type of ritualism rather than anomie.

8. Money has several peculiarities which render it particularly apt to become a symbol of prestige divorced from institutional controls. As Simmel emphasized, money is highly abstract and impersonal. However acquired, through fraud or institutionally, it can be used to purchase the same goods and services. The anonymity of metropolitan culture, in conjunction with this peculiarity of money, permits wealth, the sources of which may be unknown to the community in which the plutocrat lives, to serve as a symbol of status.

9. The emphasis upon wealth as a success-symbol is possibly reflected in the use of the term "fortune" to refer to a stock of accumulated wealth. This meaning becomes common in the late sixteenth century (Spenser and Shakespeare). A similar usage of the Latin fortuna comes into prominence during the first century B.C. Both these periods were marked by the rise to prestige and power of the "bourgeoisie."

10. See Kingsley Davis, "Mental Hygiene and the Class Structure," Psychiatry, 1928, 1: esp. 62–63; Talcott Parsons, *The Structure of Social Action*, 59–60, New York, 1937.

11. This is a level intermediate between the two planes distinguished by Edward Sapir; namely, culture patterns and personal habit systems. See his "Contribution of Psychiatry to an Understanding of Behavior in Society," *Amer. J. Sociol.*, 1937, 42:862–870.

12. This fifth alternative is on a plane clearly different from that of the others. It represents a *transitional* response which seeks to *institutionalize* new procedures oriented toward revamped cultural goals shared by the members of the society. It thus involves efforts to change the existing structure rather than to perform accommodative actions within this structure, and introduces additional problems with which we are not at the moment concerned.

13. Obviously, this is an elliptical statement. These individuals may maintain some orientation to the values of their particular differentiated groupings within the larger society or, in

part, of the conventional society itself. Insofar as they do so, their conduct cannot be classified in the "passive rejection" category (IV). Nels Anderson's description of the behavior and attitudes of the bum, for example, can readily be recast in terms of our analytical scheme. See *The Hobo*, 93–98, *et passim*, Chicago, 1923.

14. Joseph D. Lohman, "The Participant Observer in Community Studies," *Amer. Sociol. Rev.*, 1937, 2:890–898.

15. The shifting historical role of this ideology is a profitable subject for exploration. The "office-boy-to-president" stereotype was once in approximate accord with the facts. Such vertical mobility was probably more common then than now, when the class structure is more rigid. (See the following note.) The ideology largely persists, however, possibly because it still performs a useful function for maintaining the status quo. For insofar as it is accepted by the "masses," it constitutes a useful sop for those who might rebel against the entire structure, were this consoling hope removed. This ideology now serves to lessen the probability of Adaptation V. In short, the role of this notion has changed from that of an approximately valid empirical theorem to that of an ideology, in Mannheim's sense.

16. There is a growing body of evidence, though none of it is clearly conclusive, to the effect that our class structure is becoming rigidified and that vertical mobility is declining. Taussig and Joslyn found that American business leaders are being *increasingly* recruited from the upper ranks of our society. The Lynds have also found a "diminished chance to get ahead" for the working classes in Middletown. Manifestly, these objective changes are not alone significant; the individual's subjective evaluation of the situation is a major determinant of the response. The extent to which this change in opportunity for social mobility has been recognized by the least advantaged classes is still conjectural, although the Lynds present some suggestive materials. The writer suggests that a case in point is the increasing frequency of cartoons which observe in a tragi-comic vein that "my old man says everybody can't be President. He sasy if ya can get three days a week steady on W.P.A. work ya ain't doin' so bad either." See F. W. Taussig and C. S. Joslyn, *American Business Leaders*, New York, 1932; R. S. and H. M. Lynd, *Middletown in Transition*, 67 ff., chap. 12, New York, 1937.

17. The role of the Negro in this respect is of considerable theoretical interest. Certain elements of the Negro population have assimilated the dominant caste's values of pecuniary success and social advancement, but they also recognize that social ascent is at present restricted to their own caste almost exclusively. The pressures upon the Negro which would otherwise derive from the structural inconsistencies we have noticed are hence not identical with those upon lower class whites. See Kingsley Davis, op. cit., 63; John Dollard, *Caste and Class in a Southern Town*, 66 ff., New Haven, 1936; Donald Young, American Minority Peoples, 581, New York, 1932.

18. The psychical coordinates of these processes have been partly established by the experimental evidence concerning *Anspruchsniveaus* and levels of performance. See Kurt Lewin, *Vorsatz, Willie and Bedurfnis*, Berlin, 1926; N. F. Hoppe, "Erfolg und Misserfolg," *Psychol. Forschung*, 1930, 14:1–63; Jerome D. Frank, "Individual Differences in Certain Aspects of the Level of Aspiration," *Amer. J. Psychol.*, 1935, 47:119–128.

19. Standard criminology texts summarize the data in this field. Our scheme of analysis may serve to resolve some of the theoretical contradictions which P. A. Sorokin indicates. For example, "not everywhere nor always do the poor show a greater proportion of crime . . . many poorer countries have had less crime than the richer countries. . . . The [economic] improvement in the second half of the nineteenth century, and the beginning of the twentieth, has not been followed by a decrease of crime." See his *Contemporary Sociological Theories*, 560–561, New York, 1928. The crucial point is, however, that poverty has varying social significance in different social structures, as we shall see. Hence, one would not expect a linear correlation between crime and poverty.

20. See M. W. Royse, *Aerial Bombardment and the International Regulation of War*, New York, 1928.

21. Since our primary concern is with the socio-cultural aspects of this problem, the psychological correlates have been only implicitly considered. See Karen Horney, *The Neurotic Personality of Our Time*, New York, 1937, for a psychological discussion of this process.

TECHNIQUES OF NEUTRALIZATION

A Theory of Delinquency

GRESHAM M. SYKES AND DAVID MATZA

Why do people violate the rules in which they believe? Put another way, we all need to feel good about ourselves and good people do good things while bad people do bad things. So why do juvenile delinquents do bad things when such behavior can jeopardize their capacity to feel good about themselves? The answer, according to Sykes and Matza, is because juveniles are able to neutralize the wrongfulness of their acts using the techniques outlined below.

Key to understanding the role these techniques of neutralization play in deviant behavior is appreciating that these are not mere "rationalizations" that are used to explain the behavior after it has taken place; these techniques are employed before the behavior takes place and pave the way for deviance.

As Morris Cohen once said, one of the most fascinating problems about human behavior is why men violate the laws in which they believe. This is the problem that confronts us when we attempt to explain why delinquency occurs despite a greater or lesser commitment to the usages of conformity. A basic clue is offered by the fact that social rules or norms calling for valued behavior seldom if ever take the form of categorical imperatives. Rather, values or norms appear as qualified guides for action, limited in their applicability in terms of time, place, persons, and social circumstances. The moral injunction against killing, for example, does not apply to the enemy during combat in time of war, although a captured enemy comes once again under the prohibition. Similarly, the taking and distributing of scarce goods in a time of acute social need is felt by many to be right, although under other circumstances private property is held inviolable. The normative system of a society, then, is marked by what Williams has termed flexibility; it does not consist of a body of rules held to be binding under all conditions.[1]

This flexibility is, in fact, an integral part of the criminal law in that measures for "defenses to crimes" are provided in pleas such as non-age, necessity, insanity, drunkenness, compulsion, self-defense, and so on. The individual can avoid moral culpability for his criminal action—and thus avoid the negative sanctions of society—if he can prove that criminal intent was lacking. It is our argument that much delinquency is based on what is essentially an unrecognized extension of defenses to crimes, in the form of justifications for deviance that are seen as valid by the delinquent but not by the legal system or society at large.

These justifications are commonly described as rationalizations. They are viewed as following deviant behavior and as protecting the individual from self-blame and the blame of others after the act. But there is also reason to believe that they precede deviant behavior and make deviant behavior possible. It is this possibility that Sutherland mentioned only in passing and that other writers have failed to exploit from the viewpoint of sociological theory. Disapproval flowing from internalized norms and conforming others in the social environment is neutralized, turned back, or deflected in advance. Social controls that serve to check or inhibit deviant motivational patterns are rendered inoperative, and the individual is freed to engage in delinquency without serious damage to his self-image. In this sense, the delinquent both has his cake and eats it too, for he remains committed to the dominant normative system and yet so qualifies its imperatives that violations are "acceptable" if not "right." Thus the delinquent represents not a radical opposition to law-abiding society but something more like an apologetic failure, often more sinned against than sinning in his own eyes. We call these justifications of deviant behavior techniques of neutralization; and we believe these techniques make up a crucial component of Sutherland's "definitions favorable to the violation of law." It is by learning these techniques that the juvenile becomes delinquent, rather than by learning moral imperatives, values, or attitudes standing in direct contradiction to those of the dominant society. In analyzing these techniques, we have found it convenient to divide them into five major types.

THE DENIAL OF RESPONSIBILITY

Insofar as the delinquent can define himself as lacking responsibility for his deviant actions, the disapproval of self or others is sharply reduced in effectiveness as a restraining influence. As Justice Holmes has said, even a dog distinguishes between being stumbled over and being kicked, and modern society is no less careful to draw a line between injuries that are unintentional, i.e., where responsibility is lacking, and those that are intentional. As a technique of neutralization, however, the denial of responsibility extends much further than the claim that deviant acts are an "accident" or some similar negation of personal accountability. It may also be asserted that delinquent acts are due to forces outside of the individual and beyond his control such as unloving parents, bad companions, or a slum neighborhood. In effect, the delinquent approaches a "billiard ball" conception of himself in which he sees himself as helplessly propelled into new situations. From a psychodynamic viewpoint, this orientation toward one's own actions may represent a profound alienation from self, but it is important to stress the fact that interpretations of responsibility are cultural constructs and not merely idiosyncratic beliefs. The similarity between this mode of justifying illegal behavior assumed by the delinquent and the implications of a "sociological" frame of reference or a "humane" jurisprudence is readily apparent.[2] It is not the validity of this orientation that concerns us here, but its function of deflecting blame attached to violations of social norms and its relative independence of a particular personality structure.[3] By learning to view himself as more acted upon than acting, the delinquent prepares the way for deviance from the dominant normative system without the necessity of a frontal assault on the norms themselves.

THE DENIAL OF INJURY

A second major technique of neutralization centers on the injury or harm involved in the delinquent act. The criminal law has long made a distinction between crimes which are *mala in se* and *mala prohibita*—that is, between acts that are wrong in themselves and acts that are illegal but not immoral—and the delinquent can make the same kind of distinction in evaluating the wrongfulness of his behavior. For the delinquent, however, wrongfulness may turn on the question of whether or not anyone has clearly been hurt by his deviance, and this matter is open to a variety of interpretations. Vandalism, for example, may be defined by the delinquent simply as "mischief"—after all, it may be claimed, the persons whose property has been destroyed can well afford it. Similarly, auto theft may be viewed as "borrowing," and gang fighting may be seen as a private quarrel, an agreed upon duel between two willing parties, and thus of no concern to the community at large. We are not suggesting that this technique of neutralization, labeled the denial of injury, involves an explicit dialectic. Rather, we are arguing that the delinquent frequently, and in a hazy fashion, feels that his behavior does not really cause any great harm despite the fact that it runs counter to law. Just as the link between the individual and his acts may be broken by the denial of responsibility, so may the link between acts and their consequences be broken by the denial of injury. Since society sometimes agrees with the delinquent, e.g., in matters such as truancy, "pranks," and so on, it merely reaffirms the idea that the delinquent's neutralization of social controls by means of qualifying the norms is an extension of common practice rather than a gesture of complete opposition.

THE DENIAL OF THE VICTIM

Even if the delinquent accepts the responsibility for his deviant actions and is willing to admit that his deviant actions involve an injury or hurt, the moral indignation of self and others may be neutralized by an insistence that the injury is not wrong in light of the circumstances. The injury, it may be claimed, is not really an injury; rather, it is a form of rightful retaliation or punishment. By a subtle alchemy the delinquent moves himself into the position of an avenger and the victim is transformed into a wrong-doer. Assaults on homosexuals or suspected homosexuals, attacks on members of minority groups who are said to have gotten "out of place," vandalism as revenge on an unfair teacher or school official, thefts from a "crooked" store owner—all may be hurts inflicted on a transgressor, in the eyes of the delinquent. As Orwell has pointed out, the type of criminal admired by the general public has probably changed over the course of years and Raffles no longer serves as a hero;[4] but Robin Hood, and his latter-day derivatives such as the tough detective seeking justice outside the law, still capture the popular imagination, and the delinquent may view his acts as part of a similar role.

To deny the existence of the victim, then, by transforming him into a person deserving injury is an extreme form of a phenomenon we have mentioned before, namely, the delinquent's recognition of appropriate and inappropriate targets for his delinquent acts. In addition, however, the existence of the victim may be denied for the delinquent, in a somewhat different sense, by the circumstances of the delinquent act itself. Insofar as the victim is physically absent, unknown, or a vague abstraction (as is often the case in delinquent acts committed against property), the awareness of the victim's existence is weakened. Internalized norms and anticipations of the reactions of others must somehow be activated if they are to serve as guides for behavior; and it is possible that a diminished awareness of the victim plays an important part of determining whether or not this process is set in motion.

THE CONDEMNATION OF THE CONDEMNERS

A fourth technique of neutralization would appear to involve a condemnation of the condemners or, as McCorkle and Korn have phrased it, a rejection of the rejectors.[5] The delinquent shifts the focus of attention from his own deviant acts to the motives and behavior of those who disapprove of his violations. His condemners, he may claim, are hypocrites, deviants in disguise, or impelled by personal spite. This orientation toward the conforming world may be of particular importance when it hardens into a bitter cynicism directed against those assigned the task of enforcing or expressing the norms of the dominant society. Police, it may be said, are corrupt, stupid, and brutal. Teachers always show favoritism and parents always "take it out" on their children. By a slight extension, the rewards of conformity—such as material success—become a matter of pull or luck, thus decreasing still further the stature of those who stand on the side of the law-abiding. The validity of this jaundiced viewpoint is not so important as its function in turning back or deflecting the negative sanctions attached to violations of the norms. The delinquent, in effect, has changed the subject of the conversation in the dialogue between his own deviant impulses and the reactions of others; and by attacking others, the wrongfulness of his own behavior is more easily repressed or lost to view.

THE APPEAL TO HIGHER LOYALTIES

Fifth, and last, internal and external social controls may be neutralized by sacrificing the demands of the larger society for the demands of the smaller social groups to which the delinquent belongs, such as the sibling pair, the gang, or the friendship clique. It is important to note that the delinquent does not necessarily repudiate the imperatives of the dominant normative system, despite his failure to follow them. Rather, the delinquent may see himself as caught up in a dilemma that must be resolved, unfortunately, at the cost of violating the law. One aspect of this situation has been studied by Stouffer and Toby in their research on the conflict between particularistic and universalistic demands, between the claims of friendship and general social obligations, and their results suggest that "it is possible to classify people according to a predisposition to select one or the other horn of a dilemma in role conflict."[6] For our purposes, however, the most important point is that deviation from certain norms may occur not because the norms are rejected but because others' norms, held to be more pressing or involving a higher loyalty, are accorded precedence. Indeed, it is the fact that both sets of norms are believed in that gives meaning to our concepts of dilemma and role conflict.

The conflict between the claims of friendship and the claims of law, or a similar dilemma, has of course long been recognized by the social scientist (and the novelist) as a common human problem. If the juvenile delinquent frequently resolves his dilemma by insisting that he must "always help a buddy" or "never squeal on a friend," even when it throws him into serious difficulties with the dominant social order, his choice remains familiar to the supposedly law-abiding. The delinquent is unusual, perhaps, in the extent to which he is able to see the fact that he acts in behalf of the smaller social groups to which he belongs as a justification for violations of society's norms, but it is a matter of degree rather than of kind.

"I didn't mean it." "I didn't really hurt anybody." "They had it coming to them." "Everybody's picking on me." "I didn't do it for myself." These slogans or their variants, we hypothesize, prepare the juvenile for delinquent acts. These "definitions of the situation" represent tangential or glancing blows at the dominant normative system rather than the creation of an opposing ideology; and they are extensions of patterns of thought prevalent in society rather than something created de novo.

Techniques of neutralization may not be powerful enough to fully shield the individual from the force of his own internalized values and the reactions of conforming others, for as we have pointed out, juvenile delinquents often appear to suffer from feelings of guilt and shame when called into account for their deviant behavior. And some delinquents may be so isolated from the world of conformity that techniques of neutralization need not be called into play. Nonetheless, we would argue that techniques of neutralization are critical in lessening the effectiveness of social controls and that they lie behind a large share of delinquent behavior. Empirical research in this area is scattered and fragmentary at the present time, but the work of Redl,[7] Cressey,[8] and others has supplied a body of significant data that has done much to clarify the theoretical issues and enlarge the fund of supporting evidence. Two lines of investigation seem to be critical at this stage. First, there is need for more knowledge concerning the differential distribution of techniques of neutralization, as operative patterns of thought, by age, sex, social class, ethnic group, etc. On a priori grounds it might be assumed that these justifications for deviance will be more readily seized by segments of society for whom a discrepancy between common social ideals and social practice is most apparent. It is also possible, however, that the habit of "bending" the dominant normative system—if not "breaking" it—cuts across our cruder social categories and is to be traced primarily to patterns of social interaction within the familial circle. Second, there is need for a greater understanding of the internal structure of techniques of neutralization, as a system of beliefs and attitudes, and its relationship to various types of delinquent behavior. Certain techniques of neutralization would appear to be better adapted to particular deviant acts than to others, as we have suggested, for example, in the case of offenses against property and the denial of the victim. But the issue remains far from clear and stands in need of more information.

In any case, techniques of neutralization appear to offer a promising line of research in enlarging and systematizing the theoretical grasp of juvenile delinquency. As more information is uncovered concerning techniques of neutralization, their origins, and their consequences, both juvenile delinquency in particular and deviation from normative systems in general may be illuminated.

NOTES

1. Cf. Robin Williams, Jr., *American Society*, New York: Knopf, 1951, p. 28.

2. A number of observers have wryly noted that many delinquents seem to show a surprising awareness of sociological and psychological explanations for their behavior and are quick to point out the causal role of their poor environment.

3. It is possible, of course, that certain personality structures can accept some techniques of neutralization more readily than others, but this question remains largely unexplored.

4. George Orwell, *Dickens, Dali, and Others*, New York: Reynal, 1946.

5. Lloyd W. McCorkle and Richard Korn, "Resocialization Within Walls," *The Annals of the American Academy of Political and Social Science*, 293 (May, 1954), pp. 88–98.

6. See Samuel A. Stouffer and Jackson Toby, "Role Conflict and Personality," in *Toward a General Theory of Action*, edited by Talcott Parsons and Edward A. Shils, Cambridge, Mass.: Harvard University Press, 1951, p. 494.

7. See Fritz Redl and David Wineman, *Children Who Hate*, Glencoe, Ill.: The Free Press, 1956.

8. See D. R. Cressey, *Other People's Money*, Glencoe, Ill.: The Free Press, 1953.

A CONTROL THEORY OF DELINQUENCY

TRAVIS HIRSCHI

A great number of theories of deviance look at conditions or traits that are present in the deviant's personality or environment that account for his or her deviance. Control theory is different in that it looks for things that are absent, specifically "controls." In psychoanalytic theory, the superego and the ego act as controls; when they are improperly developed, deviance can be the result. In the sociological version of control theory outlined below by Hirschi, controls take the form of bonds between the individual and society. When these bonds are absent or inadequate, deviance can be the result.

American culture is renowned for the value it places on individualism. The very concept of "individualism" connotes a condition where the bonds between the individual and society are relatively weak. Thus, American culture may be more conducive to deviance than those cultures that place more emphasis on the centrality of the group.

Control theories assume that delinquent acts result when an individual's bond to society is weak or broken. Since these theories embrace two highly complex concepts, the *bond* of the individual to *society*, it is not surprising that they have at one time or another formed the basis of explanations of most forms of aberrant or unusual behavior. It is also not surprising that control theories have described the elements of the bond to society in many ways, and that they have focused on a variety of units as the point of control....

ELEMENTS OF THE BOND

Attachment

In explaining conforming behavior, sociologists justly emphasize sensitivity to the opinion of others.[1] Unfortunately,... they tend to suggest that man is sensitive to the opinion of others and thus exclude sensitivity from their explanations of deviant behavior. In explaining deviant behavior, psychologists, in contrast, emphasize insensitivity to the opinion of others.[2] Unfortunately, they too tend to ignore variation, and, in addition, they tend to tie sensitivity inextricably to other variables, to make it part of a syndrome or "type," and thus seriously to reduce its value as an explanatory concept. The psychopath is characterized only in part by "deficient attachment to or affection for others, a failure to respond to the ordinary motivations founded in respect or regard for one's fellow;"[3] he is also characterized by such things as "excessive aggressiveness," "lack of superego control," and "an infantile level of response."[4] Unfortunately, too, the behavior that psychopathy is used to explain often becomes part of the definition of psychopathy. As a result, in Barbara Wootton's words: "[The psychopath] is...par excellence, and without shame or qualification, the model of the circular process by which mental abnormality is inferred from anti-social behavior while anti-social behavior is explained by mental abnormality."[5]

The problems of diagnosis, tautology, and name-calling are avoided if the dimensions of psychopathy are treated as causally and therefore problematically interrelated, rather than as logically and therefore necessarily bound to each other. In fact, it can be argued that all of the characteristics attributed to the psychopath follow from, are effects of, his lack of attachment to others. To say that to lack attachment to others is to be free from moral restraints is to use lack of attachment to explain the guiltlessness of the psychopath, the fact that he apparently has no conscience or superego. In this view, lack of attachment to others is not merely a symptom of psychopathy, it *is* psychopathy; lack of conscience is just another way of saying the same thing; and the violation of norms is (or may be) a consequence.

For that matter, given that man is an animal, "impulsivity" and "aggressiveness" can also be seen as natural consequences of freedom from moral restraints. However, since the view of man as endowed with natural propensities and capacities like other animals is peculiarly unpalatable to sociologists, we need not fall back on such a view to explain the amoral man's aggressiveness.[6] The process of becoming alienated from others often involves or is based on active interpersonal conflict. Such conflict could easily supply a reservoir of *socially derived* hostility sufficient to account for the aggressiveness of those whose attachments to others have been weakened.

Durkheim said it many years ago: "We are moral beings to the extent that we are social beings."[7] This may be interpreted to mean that we are moral beings to the extent that we have "internalized the norms" of society. But what does it mean to say that a person has internalized the norms of society? The norms of society are by definition shared by the members of society. To violate a norm is, therefore, to act contrary to the wishes and expectations of other people. If a person does not care about the wishes and expectations of other people—that is, if he is insensitive to the opinion of others—then he is to that extent not bound by the norms. He is free to deviate.

The essence of internalization of norms, conscience, or superego thus lies in the attachment of the individual to others.[8] This view has several advantages over the concept of internalization. For one, explanations of deviant behavior based on attachment do not beg the question, since the extent to which a person is attached to others can be measured independently of his deviant behavior. Furthermore, change or variation in behavior is explainable in a way that it is not when notions of internalization or superego are used. For example, the divorced man is more likely after divorce to commit a number of deviant acts, such as suicide or forgery. If we explain these acts by reference to the superego (or internal control), we are forced to say that the man "lost his conscience" when he got a divorce; and, of course, if he remarries, we have to conclude that he gets his conscience back.

This dimension of the bond to conventional society is encountered in most social control-oriented research and theory. F. Ivan Nye's "internal control" and "indirect control" refer to the same element, although we avoid the problem of explaining changes over time by locating the "conscience" in the bond to others rather than making it part of the personality.[9] Attachment to others is just one aspect of Albert J. Reiss's "personal controls"; we avoid his problems of tautological empirical *observations* by making the relationship between attachment and delinquency problematic rather than definitional.[10] Finally, Scott Briar and Irving Piliavin's "commitment" or "stake in conformity" subsumes attachment, as their discussion illustrates, although the terms they use are more closely associated with the next element to be discussed.[11]

Commitment

"Of all passions, that which inclineth men least to break the laws, is fear. Nay, excepting some generous natures, it is the only thing, when there is the appearance of profit or pleasure by breaking the laws, that makes men keep them."[12] Few would deny that men on occasion obey the rules simply from fear of the consequences. This rational component in conformity we label commitment. What does it mean to say that a person is committed to conformity? In Howard S. Becker's formulation it means the following:

> First, the individual is in a position in which his decision with regard to some particular line of action has consequences for other interests and activities not necessarily [directly] related to it. Second, he has placed himself in that position by his own prior actions. A third element is present though so obvious as not to be apparent; the committed person must be aware [of these other interests] and must recognize that his decision in this case will have ramifications beyond it.[13]

The idea, then, is that the person invests time, energy, himself, in a certain line of activity—say, getting an education, building up a business, acquiring a reputation for virtue. When or whenever he considers deviant behavior, he must consider the costs of this deviant behavior, the risk he runs of losing the investment he has made in conventional behavior.

If attachment to others is the sociological counterpart of the superego or conscience, commitment is the counterpart of the ego or common sense. To the person committed to conventional lines of action, risking one to ten years in prison for a ten-dollar holdup is stupidity, because to the committed person the costs and risks obviously exceed ten dollars in value. (To the psychoanalyst, such an act exhibits failure to be governed by the "reality principle.") In the sociological control theory, it can be and is generally assumed that the decision to commit a criminal act may well be rationally determined—that the actor's decision was not irrational given the risks and costs he faces. Of course, as Becker points out, if the actor is capable of in some sense calculating the costs of a line of action, he is also capable of calculational errors: ignorance and error return, in the control theory, as possible explanations of deviant behavior.

The concept of commitment assumes that the organization of society is such that the interest of most persons would be endangered if they were to engage in criminal acts. Most people, simply by the process of living in an organized society, acquire goods, reputations, prospects that they do not want to risk losing. These accumulations are society's insurance that they will abide by the rules. Many hypotheses about the antecedents of delinquent behavior are based on this premise. For example, Arthur L. Stinchcombe's hypothesis that "high school rebellion...occurs when future status is not clearly related to present performance"[14] suggests that one is committed to conformity not only by what one has but also by what one hoped to obtain. Thus "ambition" and/or "aspiration" play an important role in producing conformity. The person becomes committed to a conventional line of action, and he is therefore committed to conformity.

Most lines of action in a society are of course conventional. The clearest examples are educational and occupational careers. Actions thought to jeopardize one's chances in these areas are presumably avoided. Interestingly enough, even nonconventional commitments may operate to produce conventional conformity. We are told, at least, that boys aspiring to careers in the rackets or professional thievery are judged by their "honesty" and "reliability"—traits traditionally in demand among seekers of office boys.[15]

Involvement

Many persons undoubtedly owe a life of virtue to a lack of opportunity to do otherwise. Time and energy are inherently limited: "Not that I would not, if I could, be both handsome and fat and well dressed, and a great athlete, and make a million a year, be a wit, a bon vivant, and a lady killer, as well as a philosopher, a philanthropist, a statesman, warrior, and African explorer, as well as a 'tone-poet' and saint. But the thing is simply impossible."[16] The things that William James here says he would like to be or do are all, I suppose, within the realm of conventionality, but if he were to include illicit actions he would still have to eliminate some of them as simply impossible.

Involvement or engrossment in conventional activities is thus often part of a control theory. The assumption, widely shared, is that a person may be simply too busy doing conventional things to find time to engage in deviant behavior. The person involved in conventional activities is tied to appointments, deadlines, working hours, plans, and the like, so the opportunity to commit deviant acts rarely arises. To the extent that he is engrossed in conventional activities, he cannot even think about deviant acts, let alone act out his inclinations.[17]

This line of reasoning is responsible for the stress placed on recreational facilities in many programs to reduce delinquency, for much of the concern with the high school dropout, and for the idea that boys should be drafted into the army to keep them out of trouble. So obvious and persuasive is the idea that involvement in conventional activities is a major deterrent to delinquency that it was accepted even by Sutherland: "In the general area of juvenile delinquency it is probable that the most significant difference between juveniles who engage in delinquency and those who do not is that the latter are provided abundant opportunities of a conventional type for satisfying their recreational interests, while the former lack those opportunities or facilities."[18]

The view that "idle hands are the devil's workshop" has received more sophisticated treatment in recent sociological writings on delinquency. David Matza and Gresham M. Sykes, for example, suggest that delinquents have the values of a leisure class, the same values ascribed by Veblen to *the* leisure class: a search for kicks, disdain of work, a desire for the big score, and acceptance of aggressive toughness as proof of masculinity.[19] Matza and Sykes explain delinquency by reference to this system of values, but they note that adolescents at all class levels are "to some extent" members of a leisure class, that they "move in a limbo between earlier parental domination and future integration with the social structure through the bonds of work and marriage."[20] In the end, then, the leisure of the adolescent produces a set of values, which, in turn, leads to delinquency.

Belief

Unlike the cultural deviance theory, the control theory assumes the existence of a common value system within the society or group whose norms are being violated. If the deviant is committed to a value system different from that of conventional society, there is, within the context of the theory, nothing to explain. The question is, "Why does a man violate the rules in which he believes?" It is not, "Why do men differ in their beliefs about what constitutes good and desirable conduct?" The person is assumed to have been socialized (perhaps imperfectly) into the group whose rules he is violating; deviance is not a question of one group imposing its rules on the members of another group. In other words, we not only assume the deviant *has* believed the rules, we assume he believes the rules even as he violates them.

How can a person believe it is wrong to steal at the same time he is stealing? In the strain theory, this is not a difficult problem. (In fact . . . the strain theory was devised specifically to deal with this question.) The motivation to deviance adduced by the strain theorist is so strong that we can well understand the deviant act even assuming the deviator believes strongly that it is wrong.[21] However, given the control theory's assumptions about motivation, if both the deviant and the nondeviant believe the deviant act is wrong, how do we account for the fact that one commits it and the other does not?

Control theories have taken two approaches to this problem. In one approach, beliefs are treated as mere words that mean little or nothing if the other forms of control are missing. "Semantic dementia," the dissociation between rational faculties and emotional control which is said to be characteristic of the psychopath, illustrates this way of handling the problem.[22] In short, beliefs, at least insofar as they are expressed in words, drop out of the picture; since they do not differentiate between deviants and nondeviants, they are in the same class as "language" or any other characteristic common to all members of the group. Since they represent no real obstacle to the commission of delinquent acts, nothing need be said about how they are handled by those committing such acts. The control theories that do not mention beliefs (or values), and many do not, may be assumed to take this approach to the problem.

The second approach argues that the deviant rationalizes his behavior so that he can at once violate the rule and maintain his belief in it. Donald R. Cressey had advanced this argument with respect to embezzlement,[23] and Sykes and Matza have advanced it with respect to delinquency.[24] In both Cressey's and Sykes and Matza's treatments, these rationalizations (Cressey calls them "verbalizations," Sykes and Matza term them "techniques of neutralization") occur prior to the commission of the deviant act. If the neutralization is successful, the person is free to commit the act(s) in question. Both in Cressey and in Sykes and Matza, the strain that prompts the effort at neutralization also provides the motive force that results in the subsequent deviant act. Their theories are thus, in this sense, strain theories. Neutralization is difficult to handle within the context of a theory that adheres closely to control theory assumptions, because in the control theory there is no special motivational force to account for the neutralization. This difficulty is especially noticeable in Matza's later treatment of this topic, where the motivational component, the "will to delinquency," appears *after* the moral vacuum has been created by the techniques of neutralization.[25] The question thus becomes: Why neutralize?

In attempting to solve a strain-theory problem with control-theory tools, the control theorist is thus led into a trap. He cannot answer the crucial question. The concept of neutralization assumes the existence of moral obstacles to the commission of deviant acts. In order plausibly to account for a deviant act, it is necessary to generate motivation to deviance that is at least equivalent in force to the resistance provided by these moral obstacles. However, if the moral obstacles are removed, neutralization and special motivation are no longer required. We therefore follow the implicit logic of control theory and remove these moral obstacles by hypothesis. Many persons do not have an attitude of respect toward the rules of society; many persons feel no moral obligation to conform regardless of personal advantage. Insofar as the values and beliefs of these persons are consistent with their feelings, and there should be a tendency toward consistency, neutralization is unnecessary; it has already occurred.

Does this merely push the question back a step and at the same time produce conflict with the assumption of a common value system? I think not. In the first place, we do not assume, as does Cressey, that neutralization occurs in order to make a specific criminal act possible.[26] We do not assume, as do Sykes and Matza, that neutralization occurs to make many delinquent acts possible. We do not assume, in other words, that the person constructs a system of rationalizations in order to justify commission of acts he *wants* to commit. We assume, in contrast, that the beliefs that free a man to commit deviant acts are *unmotivated* in the sense that he does not construct or adopt them in order to facilitate the attainment of illicit ends. In the second place, we do not assume, as does Matza, that "delinquents concur in the conventional assessment of delinquency."[27] We assume, in contrast, that there is *variation* in the extent to which people believe they should obey the rules of society, and, furthermore, that the less a person believes he should obey the rules, the more likely he is to violate them.[28]

In chronological order, then, a person's beliefs in the moral validity of norms are, for no teleological reason, weakened. The probability that he will commit delinquent acts is therefore increased. When and if he commits a delinquent act, we may justifiably use the weakness of his beliefs in explaining it, but no special motivation is required to explain either the weakness of his beliefs or, perhaps, his delinquent act.

The keystone of this argument is of course the assumption that there is variation in belief in the moral validity of social rules. This assumption is amenable to direct empirical test and can thus survive at least until its first confrontation with data. For the present, we must return to the idea of a common value system with which this section was begun.

The idea of a common (or perhaps better, a single) value system is consistent with the fact, or presumption, of variation in the strength of moral beliefs. We have not suggested that delinquency is based on beliefs counter to conventional morality; we have not suggested that delinquents do not believe delinquent acts are wrong. They may well believe these acts are wrong, but the meaning and efficacy of such beliefs are contingent on other beliefs and, indeed, on the strength of other ties to the conventional order.[29]

NOTES

1. Books have been written on the increasing importance of interpersonal sensitivity in modern life. According to this view, controls from within have become less important than controls from without in *producing* conformity. Whether or not this observation is true as a description of historical trends, it is true that interpersonal sensitivity has become more important in *explaining* conformity. Although logically it should also have become more important in explaining nonconformity, the opposite has been the case, once again showing that Cohen's observation that an explanation of conformity should be an explanation of deviance cannot be translated as "as explanation of conformity has to be an explanation of deviance." For the view that interpersonal sensitivity currently plays a greater role than formerly in producing conformity, see William J. Goode, "Norm Commitment and Conformity to Role-Status Obligations," *American Journal of Sociology*, LXVI (1960), 246–258. And, of course, also see David Riesman, Nathan Glazer, and Rouel Denney, *The Lonely Crowd* (Garden City, New York: Doubleday, 1950), especially Part I.

2. The literature on psychopathy is voluminous. See William McCord and Joan McCord, *The Psychopath* (Princeton: D. Van Nostrand, 1964).

3. John M. Martin and Joseph P. Fitzpatrick, *Delinquent Behavior* (New York: Random House, 1964), p. 130.

4. Ibid. For additional properties of the psychopath, see McCord and McCord, *The Psychopath*, pp. 1–2.

5. Barbara Wootton, *Social Science and Social Pathology* (New York: Macmillan, 1959), p. 250.

6. "The logical untenability [of the position that there are forces in man 'resistant to socialization'] was ably demonstrated by Parsons over 30 years ago, and it is widely recognized that the position is empirically unsound because it assumes [!] some universal biological drive system distinctly separate from socialization and social context-a basic and intransigent human nature" (Judith Blake and Kingsley Davis, "Norms, Values, and Sanctions," *Handbook of Modern Sociology*, ed. Robert E. L. Faris [Chicago: Rand McNally, 1964], p. 471).

7. Emile Durkheim, *Moral Education*, trans. Everett K. Wilson and Herman Schnurer (New York: The Free Press, 1961), p. 64.

8. Although attachment alone does not exhaust the meaning of internalization, attachments and beliefs combined would appear to leave only a small residue of "internal control" not susceptible in principle to direct measurement.

9. R. Ivan Nye, *Family Relationships and Delinquent Behavior* (New York: Wiley, 1958), pp. 5–7.

10. Albert J. Reiss, Jr., "Delinquency as the Failure of Personal and Social Controls," *American Sociological Review*, XVI (1951), 196–207. For example, "Our observations show ... that delinquent recidivists are less often persons with mature ego ideals or non-delinquent social roles" (p. 204).

11. Scott Briar and Irving Piliavin, "Delinquency, Situational Inducements, and Commitment to Conformity," *Social Problems*, XIII (1965), 41–42. The concept "stake in conformity" was introduced by Jackson Toby in his "Social Disorganization and Stake in Conformity: Complementary Factors in the Predatory Behavior of Hoodlums," *Journal of Criminal Law, Criminology and Police Science*, XLVIII (1957), 12–17. See also his "Hoodlum or Business Man: An American Dilemma," *The Jews*, ed. Marshall Sklare (New York: The Free Press, 1958), pp. 542–550. Throughout the text, I occasionally use "stake in conformity" in speaking in general of the strength of the bond to conventional society. So used, the concept is somewhat broader than is true for either Toby or Briar and Piliavin, where the concept is roughly equivalent to what is here called "commitment."

12. Thomas Hobbes, *Leviathan* (Oxford: Basil Blackwell, 1957), p. 195.

13. Howard S. Becker, "Notes on the Concept of Commitment," *American Journal of Sociology*, LXVI (1960), 35–36.

14. Arthur L. Stinchcombe, *Rebellion in a High School* (Chicago: Quadrangle, 1964), p. 5.

15. Richard A. Cloward and Lloyd E. Ohlin, *Delinquency and Opportunity* (New York: The Free Press, 1960), p. 147, quoting Edwin H. Sutherland, ed., *The Professional Thief* (Chicago: University of Chicago Press, 1937), pp. 211–213.

16. William James, *Psychology* (Cleveland: World Publishing Co., 1948), p. 186.

17. Few activities appear to be so engrossing that they rule out contemplation of alternative lines of behavior, at least if estimates of the amount of time men spend plotting sexual deviations have any validity.

18. *The Sutherland Papers*, ed. Albert K. Cohen et al. (Bloomington: Indiana University Press, 19561, p. 37.

19. David Matza and Gresham M. Sykes, "Juvenile Delinquency and Subterranean Values," *American Sociological Review*, XXVI (1961), 712–719.

20. Ibid., p. 718.

21. The starving man stealing the loaf of bread is the image evoked by most strain theories. In this image, the starving man's belief in the wrongness of his act is clearly not something that must be explained away. It can be assumed to be present without causing embarrassment to the explanation.

22. McCord and McCord, *The Psychopath*, pp. 12–15.

23. Donald R. Cressey, *Other People's Money* (New York: The Free Press, 1953).

24. Gresham M. Sykes and David Matza, "Techniques of Neutralization: A Theory of Delinquency," *American Sociological Review*, XXII (1957), 664–670.

25. David Matza, *Delinquency and Drift* (New York: Wiley, 1964), pp. 181–191.

26. In asserting that Cressey's assumption is invalid with respect to delinquency, I do not wish to suggest that it is invalid for the question of embezzlement, where the problem faced by the deviator is fairly specific and he can reasonably be assumed to be an upstanding citizen. (Although even here the fact that the embezzler's nonsharable financial problem often results from some sort of hanky-panky suggests that "verbalizations" may be less necessary than might otherwise be assumed.)

27. *Delinquency and Drift*, p. 43.

28. This assumption is not, I think, contradicted by the evidence presented by Matza against the existence of a delinquent subculture. In comparing the attitudes and actions of delinquents with the picture painted by delinquent subculture theorists, Matza emphasizes- and perhaps exaggerates-the extent to which delinquents are tied to the conventional order. In implicitly comparing delinquents with a supermoral man, I emphasize—and perhaps exaggerate—the extent to which they are not tied to the conventional order.

29. The position taken here is therefore somewhere between the "semantic dementia" and the "neutralization" positions. Assuming variation, the delinquent is, at the extremes, freer than the neutralization argument assumes. Although the possibility of wide discrepancy between what the delinquent professes and what he practices still exists, it is presumably much rarer than is suggested by studies of articulate "psychopaths."

CONCEPTIONS OF DEVIANT BEHAVIOR

The Old and the New

JACK P. GIBBS

A cross-cultural examination of deviance quickly reveals that deviance is a culturally relative phenomenon. This insight suggests the futility in identifying deviance as the result of inherent or biological qualities of deviant individuals, as was the case in the early days of criminology. It also suggests that there is nothing inherent in deviant behavior that makes it deviant. Instead, deviance is defined by features external to the deviant and the deviant act, namely, in the audience that identifies the deviance. As we will see in many of the articles in this text, there are political, economic, and cultural factors that help us understand audience reactions.

The ultimate end of substantive theory in any science is the formulation of empirical relations among classes of phenomena, e.g., X varies directly with Y, X is present if and only if Y is present. However, unless such propositions are arrived at by crude induction or sheer intuition, there is a crucial step before the formulation of a relational statement. This step can be described as the way the investigator comes to perceive or "think about" the phenomena under consideration. Another way to put it is the development of a "conception."

... In a field without consensus as to operational definitions and little in the way of systematic substantive theory, conceptions necessarily occupy a central position. This condition prevails in most of the social sciences. There, what purport to be definitions of classes of phenomena are typically general and inconsistent to the point of lacking empirical applicability (certainly in the operational sense of the word). Moreover, what passes for a substantive theory in the social sciences is more often than not actually a loosely formulated conception. These observations are not intended to deride the social sciences for lack of progress. All fields probably go through a "conceptions" stage; it is only more apparent in some than in others.

Of the social sciences, there is perhaps no better clear-cut illustration of the importance of conceptions than in the field identified as criminology and the study of deviant behavior. As we shall see, the history of the field can be described best in terms of changing conceptions of crime, criminals, deviants, and deviation. But the purpose of this paper is not an historical account of major trends in the field. If it is true that conceptions give rise to formal definitions and substantive theory, then a critical appraisal of conceptions is important in its own right. This is all the more true in the case of criminology and the study of deviant behavior, where conceptions are frequently confused with substantive theories, and the latter so clearly reflect the former.

OLDER CONCEPTIONS

In recent years there has been a significant change in the prevailing conception of deviant behavior and deviants. Prior to what is designated here as the
"new perspective," it commonly was assumed that there is something inherent in deviants which distinguishes them from non-deviants.[1] Thus, from
Lombroso to Sheldon, criminals were viewed as biologically distinctive in
one way or another.[2] The inadequacies of this conception are now obvious.
After decades of research, no biological characteristic which distinguishes
criminals has been discovered, and this generalization applies even to
particular types of criminals (e.g., murderers, bigamists, etc.). Consequently,
few theorists now even toy with the notion that all criminals are atavistic,
mentally defective, constitutionally inferior. But the rejection of the biological
conception of crime stems from more than research findings. Even casual
observation and mild logic cast doubt on the idea. Since legislators are not
geneticists, it is difficult to see how they can pass laws in such a way as to
create "born criminals." Equally important, since most if not all "normal"
persons have violated a law at one time or another,[3] the assertion that criminals are so by heredity now appears most questionable.

Although the biological conception generally has been rejected, what is
here designated as the analytic conception of criminal acts largely has
escaped criticism. Rather than view criminal acts as nothing more or less
than behavior contrary to legal norms, the acts are construed as somehow
injurious to society. The shift from the biological to the analytical conception
is thus from the actors to the characteristics of their acts, with the idea being
that some acts are inherently "criminal" or at least that criminal acts share
intrinsic characteristics in common.

The analytical conception is certainly more defensible than the biological
view, but it is by no means free of criticism. Above all, the "injurious" quality of some deviant acts is by no means conspicuous, as witness Durkheim's
observation:

> . . . there are many acts which have been and still are regarded as criminal without
> in themselves being harmful to society. What social danger is there in touching a
> tabooed object, an impure animal or man, in letting the sacred fire die down, in
> eating certain meats, in failure to make the traditional sacrifice over the grave
> of parents, in not exactly pronouncing the ritual formula, in not celebrating
> holidays, etc.[4]

Only a radical functionalism would interpret the acts noted by Durkheim as
literally injuring society in any reasonable sense of the word. The crucial
point is that, far from actually injuring society or sharing some intrinsic feature in common, acts may be criminal or deviant because and only because
they are proscribed legally and/or socially. The proscription may be irrational
in that members of the society cannot explain it, but it is real nonetheless.
Similarly, a law may be "arbitrary" in that it is imposed by a powerful minority

and, as a consequence, lacks popular support and is actively opposed. But if the law is consistently enforced (i.e., sanctions are imposed regularly on violators), it is difficult to see how it is not "real."

The fact that laws may appear to be irrational and arbitrary has prompted attempts to define crime independently of legal criteria, i.e., analytically. The first step in this direction was Garofalo's concept of natural crime—acts which violate prevailing sentiments of pity and probity.[5] Garofalo's endeavor accomplished very little. Just as there is probably no act which is contrary to law universally, it is equally true that no act violates sentiments of pity and probity in all societies. In other words, cultural relativity defeats any attempt to compile a list of acts which are crimes universally. Also, it is hard to see why the violation of a rigorously enforced traffic regulation is not a crime even though unrelated to sentiments of pity and probity. If it is not a crime, what is it?

The search for an analytic identification of crime continued in Sellin's proposal to abandon legal criteria altogether in preference for "conduct norms."[6] The rationale for the proposal is simple. Because laws vary and may be "arbitrary" in any one society, a purely legal definition of crime is not suited for scientific study. But Sellin's observations on the arbitrariness of laws apply in much the same way to conduct norms. Just as the content of criminal law varies from one society to the next and from time to time, so does the content of extra-legal norms. Further, the latter may be just as arbitrary as criminal laws. Even in a highly urbanized society such as the United States, there is evidently no rationale or utilitarian reason for all of the norms pertaining to mode of dress. True, there may be much greater conformity to conduct norms than to some laws, but the degree of conformity is hardly an adequate criterion of the "reality" of norms, legal or extra-legal. If any credence whatever can be placed in the Kinsey report, sexual taboos may be violated frequently and yet remain as taboos. As a case in point, even if adultery is now common in the United States, it is significant that the participants typically attempt to conceal their acts. In brief, just as laws may be violated frequently and are "unreal" in that sense, the same applies to some conduct norms; but in neither case do they cease to be norms. They would cease to be norms if and only if one defines deviation in terms of statistical regularities in behavior, but not even Sellin would subscribe to the notion that normative phenomena can or should be defined in statistical terms.

In summary, however capricious and irrational legal and extra-legal norms may appear to be, the inescapable conclusion is that some acts are criminal or deviant for the very simple reason that they are proscribed.

THE NEW CONCEPTION

Whereas both the pathological and the analytical conceptions of deviation assume that some intrinsic feature characterizes deviants and/or deviant acts, an emerging perspective in sociology flatly rejects any such assumption. Indeed, as witness the following statements by Kitsuse, Becker, and Erikson, exactly the opposite position is taken.

> Kitsuse: Forms of behavior *per se* do not differentiate deviants from nondeviants; it is the responses of the conventional and conforming members of the society who identify and interpret behavior as deviant which sociologically transform persons into deviants.[7]

> Erikson: From a sociological standpoint, deviance can be defined as conduct which is generally thought to require the attention of social control agencies—that is, conduct about which "something should be done." Deviance is not a property inherent in certain forms of behavior; it is a property conferred upon these forms by the audiences which directly or indirectly witness them. Sociologically, then, the critical variable in the study of deviance is the social audience rather than individual person, since it is the audience which eventually decides whether or not any given action or actions will become a visible case of deviation.[8]

> Becker: From this point of view, deviance is not a quality of the act a person commits, but rather a consequence of the application by others of rules and sanctions to an "offender." The deviant is one to whom that label has successfully been applied; deviant behavior is behavior that people so label.[9]

The common assertion in the above statements is that acts can be identified as deviant or criminal only by reference to the character of reaction to them by the public or by the official agents of a politically organized society. Put simply, if the reaction is of a certain kind, then and only then is the act deviant. The crucial point is that the essential feature of a deviant or deviant act is *external* to the actor and the act. Further, even if the act or actors share some feature in common other than social reactions to them, the feature neither defines nor completely explains deviation. To take the extreme case, even if Lombroso had been correct in his assertion that criminals are biologically distinctive, the biological factor neither identifies the criminal nor explains criminality. Purely biological variables may explain why some persons commit certain acts, but they do not explain why the acts are crimes. Consequently, since criminal law is spatially and temporally relative, it is impossible to distinguish criminals from noncriminals (assuming that the latter do exist, which is questionable) in terms of biological characteristics. To illustrate, if act X is a crime in society A but not a crime in society B, it follows that, even assuming Lombroso to have been correct, the anatomical features which distinguish the criminal in society A may characterize the noncriminal in society B. In both societies some persons may be genetically predisposed to commit act X, but the act is a crime in one society and not in the other. Accordingly, the generalization that all persons with certain anatomical features are criminals would be, in this instance, false. True, one may assert that the "born criminal" is predisposed to violate the laws of his own society, but this assumes either that "the genes" know what the law is or that the members of the legislature are geneticists (i.e., they deliberately enact laws in such a way that the "born criminal" will violate them). Either assumption taxes credulity.

The new perspective of deviant behavior contradicts not only the biological but also the analytical conception. Whereas the latter seeks to find something intrinsic in deviant or, more specifically, criminal acts, the new conception denies any such characterization. True, the acts share a common denominator—they are identified by the character of reaction to them—but this does not mean that the acts are "injurious" to society or that they are in any way inherently abnormal. The new conception eschews the notion that some acts are deviant or criminal in all societies. For that matter, the reaction which identifies a deviant act may not be the same from one society or social group to the next. In general, then, the new conception of deviant behavior is relativistic in the extreme.

NOTES

1. Throughout this paper crime is treated as a sub-class of deviant behavior. Particular issues may be discussed with reference to crime, but on the whole the observations apply to deviant behavior generally.

2. Although not essential to the argument, it is perhaps significant that the alleged biological differentiae of criminals have been consistently viewed as "pathological" in one sense or another.

3. See Edwin H. Sutherland and Donald R. Cressey, *Principles of Criminology*, 6th ed., Chicago: J. B. Lippincott, 1960, p. 39.

4. Emile Durkheim, *The Division of Labor in Society*, trans. George Simpson, Glencoe, Illinois: The Free Press, 1949, p. 72.

5. Raffaele Garofalo, *Criminology*, Boston: Little, Brown & Co., 1914, Chapter 1.

6. Thorsten Sellin, *Culture Conflict and Crime*, New York: Social Science Research Council, Bulletin 14, 1938.

7. John I. Kitsuse, "Societal Reaction to Deviant Behavior: Problems of Theory and Method," *Social Problems*, 9 (Winter, 1962), p. 253.

8. Kai T. Erikson, "Notes on the Sociology of Deviance," *Social Problems*, 9 (Spring, 1962), p. 308.

9. Howard S. Becker, *Outsiders*, New York: The Free Press of Glencoe, 1963, p. 9.

THE SEARCH FOR SCAPEGOAT DEVIANTS

JEFFERY S. VICTOR

*There is nothing that
makes us feel so good as
the idea that someone else
is an evildoer.*

Robert Lynd[1]

As Durkheim and Erikson pointed out in earlier readings, the deviant may indeed serve a useful purpose in society by providing others a reason to unite against a common enemy. History shows that society is especially inclined to create deviant categories and hunt for deviants during periods of rapid social change. Change is often unsettling and frequently induces anxiety in people. Scapegoating can provide people with an explanation for their tensions, even if it is false, and sanctioning the deviant can serve to relieve some of these tensions.

THE SOCIAL CONSTRUCTION OF IMAGINARY DEVIANTS

Sometimes societies invent new forms of deviance in order to have scapegoats for deep social tensions.[2] New social deviants are sometimes invented when rapid social change in a society results in widespread dislocation in people's lives, and the resulting frustration, fear, and anger, in turn, causes a great many people to seek scapegoats to blame. These scapegoats are "invented" by moral crusaders who target categories of social deviants to bear the blame for threats to a society's past way of life and its basic moral values.

The labels that a society uses to identify a new category of deviance embody socially constructed stereotypes, which are attributed to a category of people regarded as being deviant.[3] For example, the labels "murderer," "rapist," and "child molester" convey deviant stereotypes. In reality, the actual personality patterns and behavior of people involved in these forms of deviance are quite different from the imaginary stereotypes. In some situations, socially constructed labels for newly defined forms of deviance may precede the actual existence of any behavior or persons which fit the stereotypes embodied in the labels. Such was the case of the label "heretic" in the Middle Ages and "subversive" in the 1950s.

Eventually, moral crusades and witch hunts for social deviants, such as "subversives," "heretics," "witches," or "satanists," set society on a path, whereby individuals are found who seem to confirm the stereotype embodied in the deviant label.[4] In other words, moral crusades may be aimed at deviance which does not exist, and may even create a social type of deviant which did not previously exist, by seeking out, apprehending, and punishing some people. Paradoxically, widespread witch hunts, inquisitions, purges, and persecutions function to confirm the existence of new forms of social deviance.[5]

The labels "Satanism" and "Satanic cult" are socially constructed stereotypes. In actual social usage, the label "Satanism" has vague and elastic meanings. In small town newspaper articles, the label "Satanist" is applied loosely to a wide assortment of social deviants, including: teenage vandals, animal mutilators, and gang murderers, and adult psychopathic murderers, child molesters, and vicious rapists. Similarly, the label "Satanic cult" is used to refer to such widely different groups as juvenile delinquent gangs, unconventional religious groups, and Mafia-style criminal syndicates, all of which are supposedly motivated by worship of the Devil. The point is that claims, rumors, and allegations about criminal Satanism and Satanic cults ultimately arise from people's socially constructed predisposition to find Satanism in many unrelated incidents and activities.

As a form of collective behavior, the Satanic cult scare is a moral crusade similar to the "Red Scare" of the 1950s, albeit on a much lesser scale. It is a witch hunt for moral "subversives" and criminals. There isn't any agreed upon term to describe this pattern of collective behavior. It has been called a moral crusade, a witch hunt, or mass hysteria. However, none of these terms convey the complexity and variation of the social processes involved.

The classic case is that of the European witch-hunting craze, which lasted from the fifteenth through the seventeenth century. The frequent waves of anti-Semitic persecutions, beginning in the twelfth century and continuing through the twentieth century, are another familiar set of examples. In the United States, the anti-Catholic movement of the 1840s through the 1850s and the anti-Communist witch hunts of the 1950s are other examples.

SOCIAL CONFLICT AND THE CREATION OF SCAPEGOAT DEVIANTS

When individuals build up tension from frustration, anger, and fear, they very commonly release their tension in angry attacks upon other people whom they blame for their feelings. For example, when a young husband is suddenly fired from his job, he may come home and verbally attack his wife or kick the family dog. The psychological mechanism is well known. It's called displacement or displaced aggression. We may all use it unintentionally from time to time because it temporarily reduces our feelings of tension. Similarly, when groups of people accumulate a lot of welled-up tension, the collective social process is the same. Groups seek scapegoats to blame, in part, because scapegoating temporarily reduces tension within groups.

However, the creation of scapegoat targets in a society is not only a collective extension of psychological processes. The creation of scapegoat targets tells us a lot about internal social dynamics in a society, because it is also a product of social conflict within a society.

The Search for External Enemies

Societies experiencing a lot of internal conflict and tension often seek common external enemies as a way to unify the conflicting elements within the society. The threat of an external enemy functions to pull together conflicting parties within a society and deflects attention and activity away from their grievances against each other. It pushes them to cooperate with each other and to put less emphasis upon defining their differences. Hostility directed at a common external enemy usually causes conflicting groups to set aside, at least temporarily, their hostilities towards each other.

When a society perceives an external enemy, whether or not there exists any genuine threat to that society's security, it collectively manufactures an evil enemy image.[6] The evil enemy image is a stereotype of the enemy group, which portrays the enemy as having those qualities which are considered most immoral in that society. It is a reverse mirror image of one's own society. Onto it, we project all those qualities we most detest and condemn, the ones that violate our culture's highest values. The evil enemy is seen as having no moral scruples whatsoever.

This contrast stereotype of the evil enemy allows people to exaggerate their own virtues. In contrast to the evil enemy, they grow angel's wings. It also discourages any penetrating criticism of the society by internal dissenters, who would immediately be viewed as traitors. The stereotype of Communist "fanatics" and of the "evil empire" of Communism served this social function in American society starting in the late 1940s.[7] Other evil enemy stereotypes held by Americans have been those embodied in the labels "Japs," "Huns," and Indian "savages."

The Search for Internal Enemies

A search for internal enemies can serve the same function of providing a target for displaced aggression and a unifying force for conflicting elements in a society. This is done by defining some social category of people as being traitors to, or deviants from, the over-arching moral values of a society. When moral values are in dispute in a society, a witch hunt for moral subversives serves the purpose of clarifying and redefining the limits of moral conduct. The internal enemy can be a useful proxy target, a stand-in, for attacks between powerful conflicting elements in a society. Conflicting groups can direct their attacks safely against the proxy target, without having to engage each other directly. Normally, a society dares not choose genuinely powerful internal enemies to function as scapegoat targets.

Research on American racism illustrates this social dynamic. American scapegoating of Black people becomes more common when there is heightened internal conflict between groups of white people in society. One research study, for example, found a high correlation between the frequency of lynchings of Blacks in the South and periods of economic stress and social conflict arising from sharp drops in the price paid to farmers for cotton.[8] Another study found greater racist behavior in areas of the country in which there was greater income inequality between white people than in areas where the income differences between whites was much less.[9] In Europe, Jews have traditionally served this unifying social function of being a proxy scapegoat target for conflicting groups of Christians.

These same conflict-unifying social functions of scapegoating are also found in small groups.[10] Research on family relationships, for example, has found that conflict-ridden marriages sometimes keep a "united front" by scapegoating a child in the family.[11] Marriage partners can displace their hostilities towards each other by blaming a child for their marital discord. The scapegoated child may actually be responsible for some disturbing behavior, but it gets exaggerated and distorted in the eyes of its parents. In some cases, the behavior may even be entirely a product of the parents' invention. Moreover, the two parents fight each other through their attacks upon the child. Thereby, on the surface at least, they may seem to be cooperating effectively. One of the consequences for the child can be emotional harm.

The fact that the internal enemy, or deviant category, need not actually exist in the society (but is instead socially constructed through the scapegoating process) is recognized by the eminent sociological theorist, Lewis Coser.

> The inner enemy who is looked for, like the outer enemy who is evoked, may actually exist: he may be a dissenter who is opposed to certain aspects of group life or group action and who is considered a potential renegade or heretic. But the inner enemy also may be "found," he may simply be invented, in order to bring about through a common hostility toward him the social solidarity which the group so badly needs.... If men define a threat as real, although there may be little or nothing in reality to justify this belief, the threat is real in its consequences—and among these consequences is the increase in group cohesion.[12]

REFERENCES

1. Robert Lynd (cited in Rudolf Flesch) *The Book of Unusual Quotations* (New York: Harper Bros., 1957), p. 80.

2. Nachman Ben-Yehuda, *The Politics and Morality of Deviance* (Albany, NY: State University of New York Press, 1990).

3. Erich Goode, *Deviant Behavior*, 3rd ed. (Englewood Cliffs, NJ: Prentice-Hall, 1990).

4. Nachman Ben-Yehuda, "The European Witch Craze of the 14th to 16th Centuries: A Sociologist's Perspective," *American Journal of Sociology* 86, no. 1 (1981): 1–31; Elliott P. Currie, "Crimes Without Criminals: Witchcraft and Its Control in Renaissance Europe," *Law and Society Review* 3, no. 1 (August 1986): 7–32.

5. Albert J. Bergesen, "Political Witch Hunts: The Sacred and the Subversive in Cross-National Perspective," *American Sociological Review* 42, (April 1977): 220–33; Jerry D. Rose, *Outbreaks: The Sociology of Collective Behavior* (New York: The Free Press, 1982).

6. Brett Silverstein, "Enemy Images," *American Psychologist* 44 (June 1989): 903–13; Jerome D. Frank, "The Face of the Enemy," *Psychology Today*, Nov. 1968, 24–29.

7. Howard F. Stein, "The Indispensable Enemy and American-Soviet Relations," *Ethos* 17 (Dec. 1989): 480–503.

8. Joseph T. Hepworth and Stephen G. West, "Lynchings and the Economy: A Time-Series Reanalysis of Hovland and Sears," *Journal of Personality and Social Psychology* 55, no. 2 (1988): 239–47.

9. Michael Reich, "The Economics of Racism," *Problems in Political Economy: An Urban Perspective*, ed. David M. Gordon (Lexington, MA: D. D. Heath, 1971): pp. 107–13.

10. Lynn S. Kahn, "The Dynamics of Scapegoating: The Expulsion of Evil," *Psychotherapy: Theory, Research and Practice* 17 (Spring 1980): 79–84; Jeffrey Eagle and Peter M. Newton, "Scapegoating in Small Groups: An Organizational Approach," *Human Relations* 34, no. 4 (1981): 283–301; Fred Wright, et al. "Perspectives on Scapegoating in Primary Groups," *Group* 12 (Spring 1988): 33–44; Gary Gemmill, "The Dynamics of Scapegoating in Small Groups," *Small Group Behavior* 20 (Nov. 1989): 406–18.

11. Ezra F. Vogel and Normal W. Bell, "The Emotionally Disturbed Child as the Family Scapegoat," *The Family*, rev. ed. (New York:. Free Press, 1960, 1968), pp. 412–25.

12. Lewis Coser, *The Function of Social Conflict* (New York: Free Press, 1956), p. 107.

PART 2

Moral Panics

MORAL PANICS IN HISTORY

ERICH GOODE AND NACHMAN BEN-YEHUDA

Occasionally, as we will see in this section of readings, societies get whipped up into a frenzy of alarm about some problem of deviance. When this happens, things are rarely what they seem. That is, factors, other than a sudden invasion of deviants, are usually at the root cause of the alarm. Much as Gibbs explains in his discussion of the old and the new conceptions of deviance, it is the qualities of the audience and of the culture and not of the deviants and the deviance that best defines a moral panic.

In [the following] episodes, people have become intensely concerned about a particular issue or perceived threat—which, as measured by concrete indicators, turns out not to be especially damaging—and have assembled, and taken action, to remedy the problem; yet, somehow, at a later point in time, they lost interest in the issue or threat, often turning their attention to other matters. These episodes have been referred to as moral panics.

THE CANUDOS MASSACRE: BRAZIL, 1893–7

For twenty years, a religious mystic who came to be known as Antonio Conselheiro wandered the northeast backlands of Brazil, "preaching against ungodly behavior and rebuilding rural churches and cemeteries that had fallen into disrepair in the forbidding, semiarid interior" (Levine, 1992, p. 2). In 1893, Conselheiro led a pious group of disciples into an inaccessible mountain valley in Bahia; there, on the site of an abandoned ranch, he founded a religious community—Canudos. Thousands were attracted to it, drawn "by Conselheiro's charismatic madness. He promised only sacrifice and hard work and asked residents to live according to God's commandments and await the coming of the Millennium, when would come redemption, the Day of judgment" (p. 2). Conselheiro's vision was that the weak would inherit the earth; the order of nature itself would be overturned, with rainfall blessing the customarily arid region, ushering in an era of agricultural abundance. Within two years the settlement became the second largest city in the state of Bahia; at its height, Canudos's population was more than a tenth of that of the city of Sao Paulo at the time (p. 2).

Landowners did not take kindly to the loss of their labor-force; they demanded government intervention. The Catholic church, struggling against what it saw as heterodoxy, apostasy, and the influence of Afro-Brazilian cults, likewise demanded immediate action. The army dispatched soldiers to capture Conselheiro. The task proved to be far more formidable than any official had dreamed. The first three assaults were repulsed by tenacious resistance from Conselheiro's followers. The campaign stretched out over two years. Finally, in October 1897, Canudos was encircled by 8,000 troops serving under three generals and Brazil's Minister of War, and was bombarded into submission by heavy artillery. The repression of the community had been violent and bloody. Thousands of Conselheiro's followers were killed; the captured survivors numbered only in the hundreds. The wounded were drawn and quartered or "hacked to pieces limb by limb" (p. 190). Soldiers "killed children by smashing their skulls against trees" (p. 190). Conselheiro's head was cut off and displayed on a pike. (It turns out that he had already died two weeks before the final assault, probably of dysentery.) All 5,000 houses in the settlement were "smashed, leveled and burned" (p. 190); the grounds of Canudos were torched and dynamited. "The army systematically eradicated the remaining traces of the holy city as if it had housed the devil incarnate" (p. 190).

The resistance of Canudos had generated a crisis in Brazilian society:

> Highlighted by the universal fascination with stories about crazed religious fanatics, the Canudos conflict flooded the press, invading not only editorials, columns, and news dispatches, but even feature stories and humor. For the first time in Brazil, newspapers were used to create a sense of public panic. Canudos accounts appeared daily, almost always on the front page; indeed, the story was the first ever to receive daily coverage in the Brazilian press. More than a dozen major newspapers sent war correspondents to the front and ran daily columns reporting events.... Something about Canudos provoked anxiety, which would be soothed only by evidence that Canudos had been destroyed. (Levine, 1992, p. 24)

In order to understand the intensity of the public concern in Brazil in the 1890s over the existence of a religious community consisting of a few thousand souls who, as far as anyone could tell, were not violating any of the country's criminal statutes, it is necessary to turn the calendar back a century and examine the events of the time. The abolition of slavery had been achieved in Brazil in 1888; the monarchy had been overthrown in 1889. A standard, uniform system of weights and measures had been introduced, and the Portuguese language was being standardized on a nationwide basis by decree. Brazil, it seemed, was poised on the very brink of modernity. By forming a fanatical, millennial community, Conselheiro was defying government authority, which was attempting to extend its reach into every hamlet in Brazil. Indeed, Canudos rejected the very civilizing process itself; the millenarians threatened to plunge Brazilian society back into a state of darkness and superstition. The backlanders had defied "the progressive and modern benefits of civilized life" (p. 155). "Urban Brazilians were proud of their material and political accomplishments and felt only shame at the dark, primitive world of the hinterlands" (p. 155). Only one possible solution to the challenge posed by Canudos existed: The movement must be crushed, the community obliterated, and Conselheiro and his followers exterminated.

THE BOYS OF BOISE

On November 2, 1955, the citizens of Boise, Idaho, woke up to a headline in *The Idaho Daily Statesman*, which read: "Three Boise Men Admit Sex Charges." Charles Brokaw, a freight worker, Ralph Cooper, a shoe-store employee, and Vernon Cassel, a clothing-store clerk, were charged, the news-paper story said, with "infamous crimes against nature" (Gerassi, 1966, p. 1), which referred to various homosexual practices. An investigation "was being launched" into allegations of "immoral acts involving teen-age boys" (p. 1). Although the authorities "had barely scratched the surface," the article con-tinued, there was incomplete evidence that similar acts were committed by other adults against about a hundred boys (p. 2). That day, conversation in Boise revolved around the arrests and their disturbing implications. Was it possible that "a vast secret organization of perverts" had been operating in Boise and that "every kid in high school" had been corrupted (p. 3)? Citizens called the (then, only) high school, police headquarters, the *Statesman*—and one another—"stressing the acute seriousness of the whole matter" (p. 3).

On the next day, November 3, in an editorial entitled "Crush the Monster," the *Statesman* demanded that the "whole sordid situation" be "completely cleared up, and the premises thoroughly cleaned and disinfected" (p. 4). Such an editorial "was bound to generate panic, and it did" (p. 4). However, when the *Statesman* called for all agencies to "crush the monster," one thing was certain: "there was no such thing" (p. 5). Three "rather unimportant, unassuming, unpolitical individuals had been arrested for doing something either infamous or lewd with some minors," and a probate-court officer claimed that some other adults had done the same thing with as many as a hundred teenagers. "On that kind of evidence, most newspapers would only demand more information" (p. 5).

A week later, one of the defendants, Ralph Cooper—who had a long record of arrests and convictions—received an astounding life sentence for his crimes. (He was released after nine years.) The other two men received 15-year sentences. Four days after Cooper's imprisonment, Joe Moore, vice-president of the Idaho First National Bank, was arrested on felony charges of committing, once again, an "infamous crime against nature" (p. 12). Another *Statesman* editorial appeared the next day which warned Boise parents "to keep an eye on the whereabouts" of their children because "a number of boys have been victimized by these perverts.... No matter what is required, this sordid mess must be removed from this community" (p. 13).

Men who stopped to talk to adolescent boys, men who paused to look at football practice, even men "who were not good, kind, obedient husbands," were denounced (pp. 13–14). The county's prosecuting attorney, Blaine Evans, became a local hero. He vowed to "eliminate" all homosexuals from Boise. Though this sort of talk made the town's citizens alarmed, at least, they reasoned, "something was being done" about the problem (p. 13). On the morning of November 15, a young teacher, an admitted homosexual, while eating his breakfast of eggs, toast, and coffee and reading his morning *Statesman*, came upon the news item of Moore's arrest, accompanied by Blaine's promise to "eliminate" all homosexuals. He never finished his breakfast. "He jumped up from his seat, pulled out his suitcases, packed as fast as he could, got into his car, and drove straight to San Francisco, never even bothering to call up the school to let it be known that he would be absent. The cold eggs, coffee and toast remained on his table for two days before someone from his school came by to see what had happened" (p. 14).

On December 2, Charles Herbert Gordon, an interior decorator, pled guilty to "lewd and lascivious conduct," and was sentenced to 15 years imprisonment. On December 11, a dozen men, some prominent citizens, were arrested on homosexual charges. On December 12, the scandal reached national proportions; *Time* magazine ran a story claiming that "a widespread homosexual underworld that involved some of Boise's most prominent men and had preyed on hundreds of teen-age boys for the past decade" (p. ix). On December 19, a curfew was established in Boise for minors age 16 and younger. On December 22, the Boise City Council called for the conviction and sentencing of all arrested homosexuals. On December 23, five homosexuals were sentenced to periods ranging from six months to ten years. In April, the mayor announced that nearly 1,500 persons had been interviewed concerning the investigation. Over the next year, the arrests and sentences continued; by January 1957, the scandal was regarded as having come to an end (pp. xv–xviii).

Why the panic over homosexuality in Boise in 1955 and 1956? Why the ludicrous and almost literally impossible assertion that a "ring" or "organization" of adult men were preying on scores, possibly hundreds, of local boys? Was the issue homosexuality in the first place? And to whom was it an issue?

One journalist (Gerassi, 1966) claimed that the investigation which launched the panic was undertaken by the city's power elite, the "Boise gang," a circle of rich, powerful, and conservative executives, entrepreneurs, and politicians, to discredit City Hall—"which was then in the hands of a fairly decent, reformist administration" (p. 21)—and one council member in particular whose son had been involved in the homosexual activity under investigation. In addition, the intention was to flush out and discredit a member of that powerful inner circle, a man referred to publicly as the "Queen." The irony of the scandal was that the individuals who were the real target of the scandal were never named, while the unintended victims, many humble and powerless, were punished. Moreover, not all of the individuals who were named had sex with underage minors; several, in fact, engaged in homosexual acts with consenting adults (though still a crime in the state of

Idaho in 1955). Even those who technically violated the state's laws against sex with minors were involved in activity with a small number of 15-, 16-, and 17-year-old juvenile delinquents and male prostitutes who hustled adult homosexuals for pay and engaged in blackmail against them. The Boise sex scandal proved to be a proverbial "tempest in a teapot."

When questioned a decade later, the prosecuting attorney responsible for the cases defended his role in investigating and arresting homosexuals: we had to get "these guys," he said, "because they strike at the core of society, I mean the family and the family unit. And when you get these guys crawling around the streets, you've got to prosecute to save the family" (p. 25). When asked why such a fuss was made at this particular time and why the sentences at this time were so harsh, he replied, "I guess we didn't know that there were so many of them in the community. You know, when it's going on in the basement of the Public Library, and in the hotels, and these guys are soliciting business all over town, you've got to do something about it, don't you?" (p. 24). A Boise Valley farmer put the matter even more simply; when interviewed ten years after the scandal, he said: "We grow them tough out here...and that's the way we want to grow them. None of this hanky-panky and city stuff for us. Our kids have to be men, just like their forefathers....There's no room for these queers. We don't want them. They should be run out of the state" (p. 129).

RUMOR IN ORLEANS, FRANCE, MAY 1969

In May 1969, in Orleans, France, a rumor began to spread to the effect that six women's dress shops in town were involved in what was referred to at the time as the "white slave traffic." Young women, it was said, were forcibly drugged by injection while trying on dresses in fitting-rooms, and spirited away under the cover of darkness to foreign locales and forced into prostitution. All six of the shops that were the focus of the rumor were owned by Jews. At one stage of the development of this rumor, it was claimed that all the shops were connected by means of underground tunnels that met in a main sewer which flowed into the Loire River, where a boat (in one version, a submarine) picked up its "cargo," again, under the cloak of darkness (Morin, 1971).

Of course, no women were drugged or abducted, and none disappeared from Orleans. The story was—it hardly needs to be stated—a complete invention, a rumor utterly lacking in substance. Why did it arise where and when it did? Fantastic stories of the enforced prostitution of young women, especially in exotic foreign locales, has been a theme in western literature for well over two centuries. But why Orleans and why 1969?

Early in 1969, a French translation of a supposedly journalistic book, entitled *Sex Slavery*, was published. One of the stories in this book detailed an attempted clothing-store fitting-room abduction by means of a drug injection.

In the second week of May 1969, a translation of the attempted fitting-room kidnaping account appeared in a French magazine, *Noir et Blanc* under the title, "White Slavery Tricks." No source was attributed, the event was said to have occurred "not long ago," and erotic photographs accompanied the article. The rumor in Orleans began to circulate the week after the magazine hit the newsstands; clearly, the *Noir et Blanc* article had launched the rumor.

Still, *Noir et Blanc* was a national magazine, sold all over France. Why did the white slavery story crop up in Orleans and not throughout the country? A second event almost certainly provided another catalyst. On May 10, a new department of a boutique celebrated its opening. Called "The Dungeon," its fitting-rooms were located in a cellar; the decor was mysterious, medieval, and dungeon-like. (Significantly, no rumors circulated about "The Dungeon," whose owner was not Jewish.) Thus, while the article in *Noir et Blanc* provided the "script," the opening of "The Dungeon" provided the "appropriate stagesetting" (Morin, 1971, p. 22). Both events acted as catalysts in launching the white slavery rumor in Orleans in May 1969.

But why were Jewish boutique owners selected as the perpetrators of this nefarious activity? More specifically, the rumor did not circulate about elderly Jews with foreign accents or recent Jewish immigrants from North Africa. "It concentrated exclusively on a group of shop owners who had nothing exotic about them, who looked just like anyone else but through that very fact contrived to conceal the one mysterious difference which the whole world knew: their Jewishness" (Morin, 1971, p. 28). Thus, it was not so much the fact of their difference from the rest of the French population that was significant, but their similarity. They had assimilated into French society but they had remained different—and exotic—by virtue of being Jewish.

The rumor mobilized no police action, and not a single line in the press endorsed it. Indeed, the story was so fantastic and unbelievable that no mainstream organization or institution gave any credence to it whatsoever. However, to the story's true believers, these facts simply demonstrated its validity—they did not challenge it: "More and more girls were disappearing. Yet why was it that the police...somehow failed to arrest these white slavers?" Moreover, how can we "explain the total silence of the newspapers?" Anxiety and hysteria, "soon sought and found an...explanation.... Everyone had been bribed, bought—the police, the Prefect, the Press—by the Jews. The authorities had sold [out] and were now acting as agents for these hidden powers, operating from their underground hideout" (Morin, 1971, p. 28).

On May 30, after one store owner received anonymous phone calls—one requesting "fresh meat," another addresses in Tangier—representatives of the Jewish community got together and decided to take action. However, the police told them that nothing could be done until after the weekend, that is, after Monday, when the first round of the upcoming presidential elections took place. On Saturday, normally the week's biggest shopping day, crowds gathered outside several of the more centrally located shops, but very few customers entered them. The owners sensed hostile glances from members of the crowd. One heard, "Don't buy anything from the Jews," uttered outside his shop. On a bus, returning home that night, an assistant in one of the shops was told, "You work for the Jews—you must know all about it!" (Morin, 1971, p. 32). The night before, an assistant was dragged out of the store in which she worked by her husband, who shouted, "I'm not going to let you stay in this place a moment longer!" (p. 32). All the store owners felt threatened and apprehensive; they believed that elements in the community were beginning to mobilize against them.

On June 2, two local daily newspapers (one left of center, the other right of center) vigorously denounced the rumor. Within ten days, statements were released by several parents' associations, several professional educational institutions, chambers of commerce, manufacturers' organizations, the local Communist Party, and the Bishop of Orleans. In short order, editorials and articles appeared in a number of prestigious Paris newspapers and magazines, again, attacking the rumor and those who propagated it, emphasizing its anti-Semitic theme. While the principal rumor was quashed by this barrage of denunciation, nonetheless, the suspicion remained on the part of some Orleans residents that something fishy was going on. "Someone's hiding something from us" and "There's no smoke without fire" were two commonly heard phrases at the time (Morin, 1971, p. 40). A "mishmash of mini-myths" (p. 40), "subrumors" (p. 38), and "minirumors" (p. 42) continued to circulate in the wake of the collapse of the principal rumor. Some believed that "a German" (that is, a Nazi) was behind the fabrication in order to discredit the Jews; as evidence, the name of a German chain store was invoked. Perhaps the Jews started the whole thing, some said, to discredit competitors. Some blamed the communists. Or others, the left generally. Some retained portions of the rumor but discarded others. Some suspected even more sinister activities for which white slavery was only a cover story. "A purely fabulous tale turned into a historical pseudo-event, stirred up scandal, all but started a panic, then became a bizarre and shady enigma" (Morin, 1971, p. 43). Within a matter of two months, even the mini-rumors began to dissipate.

MORAL PANICS

In each of these cases—the furor over Canudos in Brazil at the end of the nineteenth century, the fear and persecution of homosexuals in Boise, Idaho, in the 1950s, and the rumor that young women were being abducted from clothing stores in Orleans, France, in 1969—we have a moral panic on our hands. In each, there is strong, widespread (although not necessarily universal) fear or concern that evil doings are afoot, that certain enemies of society are trying to harm some or all of the rest of us. In each of these three cases, this fear or concern is referred to by the author describing and analyzing it as a "panic" (Levine, 1992, p. 24; Gerassi, 1966, p. 4; Morin, 1971, p. 43). In each, evidence suggests, the fear or concern that was generated was all out of proportion to the threat that was, or seemed to be, posed by the behavior, or the supposed behavior, of some. In one case, the basis for the threat was completely nonexistent and in two, the basis existed, but the threat was, in all likelihood, imaginary. And in each case, the panic was not simply the product of the over-active imaginations of a number of unconnected individuals scattered around a city or a society. Rather, in each case, the fear and concern had a social foundation, a dynamic that revealed the inner workings of the society in which it took place.

While the moral panics concept is fairly recent, the concrete manifestations of moral panics have been described and analyzed for some time in a more or less implicit fashion. The development of the concept, however, has focused a spotlight on its causes, accompaniments, variations, and consequences. Having a specific concept to classify and capture the phenomena enables us to notice elements and dynamics that we would have otherwise missed.

REFERENCES

Gerassi, John 1966. *The Boys of Boise: Furor Vice, and Folly in an American City*. New York: Macmillan.

Levine, Robert M. 1992. *Vale of Tears: Revisiting the Canudos Massacre in Northeastern Brazil, 1893–1897*. Berkeley: University of California Press.

Morin, Edgar 1971. *Rumor in Orleans* (Peter Green, trans.) New York: Pantheon Books.

THE CLASSIC MORAL PANIC

Mods and Rockers

KENNETH THOMPSON

Below, Thompson summarizes one of the first systematic accounts of a moral panic, the case of the Mods and Rockers in 1960s England. Some processes from previous theoretical articles come into play in the creation of a moral panic. For one thing, the creation of a moral panic is likely to occur in the midst of social change and serves to clarify the moral boundaries of a society. For another, it was not so much the behavior of the Mods and Rockers that triggered the panic as it was the needs of various interest groups (i.e., the "audience"), including the media. Note the important role of the media in "amplifying" deviance and creating "folk devils."

A panic about what was happening to British youth in the 1960s was the occasion for the first sociological analysis of a moral panic (S. Cohen, 1972) and this is significant for [at least two] reasons: first, because concerns about the moral condition of youth have been the object of periodic episodes of moral panic and so they may enable us to pinpoint a major and recurrent source of social anxiety about risk; [and] second, because the moral panic about Mods and Rockers in 1960s Britain provides a good example of the signification spiral by which the interaction of claims-makers, moral entrepreneurs and the mass media results in the establishment of a discourse in which certain groups are demonized as the source of moral decline....

The initial episode of deviant behavior that gave rise to a moral panic and the elevation of a section of British youth to the status of folk devils began in the small seaside town of Clacton in 1964. The rather mundane nature of the event is captured in Cohen's description:

> Easter 1964 was worse than usual. It was cold and wet, and in fact Easter Sunday was the coldest for eighty years. The shopkeepers and stall owners were irritated by the lack of business and the young people had their own boredom and irritation fanned by rumors of cafe owners and barmen refusing to serve some of them. A few groups started scuffling on the pavements and throwing stones at each other. The Mods and Rockers factions—a division initially based on clothing and lifestyles, later rigidified, but at that time not fully established—started separating out. Those on bikes and scooters roared up and down, windows were broken, some beach huts were wrecked and one boy fired a starting pistol in the air. The vast number of people crowding into the streets, the noise, everyone's general irritation and the actions of an unprepared and undermanned police force had the effect of making the two days unpleasant, oppressive and sometimes frightening. (S. Cohen, 1972/80: 29)

THE ROLE OF THE MEDIA

Adapting a model of stages of development of certain forms of collective behavior derived from studies of disaster behavior, S. Cohen called this the *initial deviation* or *impact* phase. This was followed by the *inventory* stage, in which observers take stock of what they believe has happened. The most important factor was the way in which the situation was initially interpreted and presented by the mass media, "because it is in this form that most people received their pictures of both deviance and disasters. Reactions take place on the basis of these processed or coded images" (S. Cohen, 1972/80: 30).

Cohen shows that the media presentation or inventory of the Mods and Rockers events was crucial in determining the later stages of reaction:

> On the Monday morning following the initial incidents at Clacton, every national newspaper, with the exception of *The Times* (fifth lead on the main news page), carried a leading report on the subject. The headlines are self-descriptive: "Day of Terror by Scooter Groups" (*Daily Telegraph*), "Youngsters Beat Up Town—97 Leather Jacket Arrests" (*Daily Express*), "Wild Ones Invade Seaside—97 Arrests" (*Daily Mirror*). The next lot of incidents received similar coverage on the Tuesday and editorials began to appear, together with reports that the Home Secretary was "being urged" (it was not usually specified by whom) to hold an inquiry or to take firm action. Feature articles then appeared highlighting interviews with Mods and Rockers. Straight reporting gave way to theories especially about motivation: the mob was described as "exhilarated," "drunk with notoriety," "hell-bent on destruction," etc. (S. Cohen, 1972/80: 30)

The media inventory of the initial incident was analyzed by Cohen under three headings:

- exaggeration and distortion;
- prediction;
- symbolization.

The type of distortion in the inventory lay in exaggerating the seriousness of events in terms of criteria such as the number taking part, the number involved in violence and the amount and effects of any damage or violence. Further distortion took place in the mode and style of presentation characteristic of most crime reporting: the sensational headlines, the melodramatic vocabulary and the deliberate heightening of those elements in the story considered as news. There was frequent use of words and phrases such as "riot," "orgy of destruction," "battle," "attack," "siege," "beat up the town" and "screaming mob." Of the total number of arrests (ninety-seven) at Clacton, only one-tenth were charged with offenses involving violence, and twenty-four were charged with "non-hooligan" sorts of offenses: stealing a half a pint of petrol, attempting to steal drinks from a vending machine and "obtaining credit to the amount of 7d by means of fraud other than false pretenses" (an ice cream) (S. Cohen, 1972/80: 37). The total estimated cost of damage at Clacton was £513. One newspaper reported that "all the dance halls near the seafront were smashed" (ibid: 37); but, in fact, the town had only one dance hall and it had some of its windows broken. Similarly, there was use of the generic plural (if a boat was overturned, reports read "boats were overturned" (ibid: 39)) and the technique, familiar to war correspondents, of reporting the same incident twice to make it look like two different incidents.

Another element in the inventory was that of constant prediction that the event would be followed by more such events involving even worse consequences, and the assertion this was all part of a pattern due to underlying causes that were gathering pace. Subsequently, similar events to those at Clacton were reported during the following holiday period of Whitsun 1964 at Bournemouth, Brighton and Margate, but all of them were in fact of smaller magnitude than those at Clacton. However, the media coverage suggested that they were getting worse, and it is true that the media publicity had led to heightened expectations of dramatic events, which then attracted spectators eager to witness the drama.

The publicity given to the events entailed a form of symbolization in which key symbols (differences in fashion, lifestyle and entertainment) were stripped of their favorable or neutral connotations until they came to evoke unambiguously unfavorable responses:

> There appear to be three processes in such symbolization: a word (Mod) becomes symbolic of a certain status (delinquent or deviant); objects (hairstyle, clothing) symbolize the word; the objects themselves become symbolic of the status (and the emotions attached to the status). (S. Cohen, 1972/80: 40)

Studies of moral panics associated with the Mods and Rockers and other forms of deviance, as well as research on the mass communication process itself (Halloran et al., 1970), suggest that two interrelated factors determine the presentation of deviance inventories: the first is the institutionalized need to create news and the second is the selective and inferential structure of the news-making process. The mass media operate with certain definitions of what is newsworthy:

> It is not that instruction manuals exist telling newsmen that certain subjects (drugs, sex, violence) will appeal to the public or that certain groups (youth, immigrants) should be continually exposed to scrutiny. Rather, there are built-in factors, ranging from the individual newsman's intuitive hunch about what constitutes a "good story," through precepts such as "give the public what it wants" to structured ideological biases, which predispose the media to make a certain event into news. (S. Cohen, 1972/80: 45)

For example, disturbances of various sorts, variously called "hooliganism," "rowdyism" or "gang fights," had been a regular occurrence during the late 1950s and early 1960s in English coastal towns, but it was only with the labeling of the Clacton event as an example of a widespread deviant phenomenon that it became news. "The Mods and Rockers didn't become news because they were new; they were presented as new to justify their creation as news" (S. Cohen, 1972/80: 46). The process of news manufacture is described by Halloran et al. by reference to the development of an inferential structure: this is not intentional bias or simple selection by expectation but rather "a process of simplification and interpretation which structures the meaning given to the story around its original news value" (Halloran et al., 1970: 215–16). The conceptual framework used to locate this process, and one which was taken over by Cohen, is that of Boorstin's notion of the event as news. That is to say, the question of "is it news" becomes as important as "is it real?" The argument is that:

> events will be selected for news reporting in terms of their fit or consonance with pre-existing images—the news of the event will confirm earlier ideas. The more unclear the news item and the more uncertain or doubtful the newsman is in how to report it, the more likely it is to be reported in a general framework that has already been established. (Halloran et al., 1970: 215–16)

In the light of this, Cohen concludes:

> It is only when the outlines of such general frameworks have been discerned, that one can understand processes such as symbolization, prediction, the reporting of non-events and the whole style of presentation. The predictability of the inventory is crucial. So constant were the images, so stylized was the mode of reporting, so limited was the range of emotions and values played on, that it would have been perfectly simple for anyone who had studied the Mods and Rockers coverage to predict with some accuracy the reports of all later variations on the theme of depraved youth: skinheads, football hooligans, hippies, drug-takers, pop-festivals, the Oz trial. (S. Cohen, 1972/80: 47)

However, although the media coverage may have created an interpretative framework for the events, the media did not operate in a vacuum; there were other actors involved—social control agents such as the police and judges, and moral entrepreneurs, particularly politicians.

SOCIAL CONTROL AGENTS AND MORAL ENTREPRENEURS

One of the effects of the symbolization contained in the media reports of deviance is that it sensitizes people to signs of a threat. Incidents and events that might otherwise not be regarded as connected come to be seen as symptoms of the same threatening form of deviance. After the reports of the first disturbances, all kinds of youth misbehavior were interpreted in terms of the same symbolic framework. As a result of sensitization, incidents that might have been written off as "horseplay" or a "dance hall brawl" were interpreted as being part of the Mods and Rockers phenomenon. Public nervousness increased and there was pressure for more police vigilance and stronger action from the forces of law and order. The police then reacted by stepping up patrols and increasing their interventions in potential trouble spots—seaside towns, dance halls, fairs and other public events. Court proceedings reflected the sensitization. In the northern town of Blackburn, many miles from the seaside resorts where the Mods and Rockers disturbances had taken place, a police officer prosecuting two youths for using threatening behavior (they had been in a crowd of twenty flicking rubber bands at passersby) said in court:

> This case is an example of the type of behavior that has been experienced in many parts of the country during the last few weeks and it has been slowly affecting

Blackburn. We shall not tolerate this behavior. The police will do everything within their power to stamp it out. (*Lancashire Evening Telegraph*, 29 May 1964; quoted in S. Cohen, 1972/80: 80)

According to Cohen, the reaction of the control culture was distinguished by three common elements: diffusion, escalation and innovation. Diffusion could be seen in the way in which control agents distant from the original incidents were drawn in, either by regional and national police collaboration, or by defining their own local activities as coping with the same deviant phenomenon. Escalation of measures to deal with the problem was reflected in calls to "tighten up," "take strong measures," "don't let it get out of hand," which were legitimized by invoking the images of those who had to be protected as innocent holiday-makers," "old people," "mums and dads," "little children building sand castles" and "honest tradesmen." The final aspect of the control culture was that it extended not only in degree but also in kind through the actual or suggested introduction of new methods of control, e.g. new powers for the police and new penalties. Confiscation of bikes was one suggested punishment, and one magistrate went further in suggesting that offenders should be given hammers to smash up their own bikes: "a childish action should be met with a similar punishment" (quoted in S. Cohen, 1972/80: 91).

Perhaps the most important interface in the control culture is that where state control in the form of legislation and legislators meets pressures of public opinion as channeled by claims-makers and moral entrepreneurs. This is particularly important where the moral entrepreneurs are themselves politicians. The initial reaction in the case of Clacton and the other seaside resorts was shaped by local spokespersons, who defined the hooliganism as a threat to local commercial interests. However, they knew that nothing would be done if the problem was defined in purely local terms—the event had to be magnified to national proportions and the responsibility for it shifted upwards. Calls were made for a government inquiry, for the laws to be "tightened up," for the courts and the police to be given more powers. At some point, in order to have a wider impact, such sporadic general appeals from individuals and local organizations as were reported in the press needed to become formalized into fully fledged action groups. Cohen analyzed the process in terms of Neil Smelser's (1963) theory of collective behavior and the development of social movements. The action groups corresponded to what Smelser calls "norm-oriented movements," and they developed through a sequence of cumulative stages: strain (deviance); anxiety; an identification of the agents responsible; a generalized belief that control was inadequate; a belief that the trouble could be cured by reorganizing the normative structure itself ("there ought to be a law"); and, finally, the formulation of specific proposals to punish, control or destroy the agent. Cohen also provided a detailed profile of one of the typical moral entrepreneurs, a Mr. Blake, who formed an action group, gained publicity for his cause and drew in local politicians and other representatives of authority. This culminated in a resolution in the House of Commons:

> That this House in the light of the deplorable and continual increase in juvenile delinquency and in particular the recent regrettable events in Clacton urges the Secretary of State for Home Department to give urgent and serious consideration to the need for young hooligans to be given such financial and physical punishment as will provide an effective deterrent. (15 April 1964, House of Commons; quoted in S. Cohen, 1972/80: 134)

Legislation was rushed through to deal with "Malicious Damage," justified by explicit reference to the dangers from Mods and Rockers, although the Minister responsible had admitted in the first debate that "Some of the reports of what happened at Clacton over the Easter weekend were greatly exaggerated." Nevertheless, the process had been completed by which a mythology had been created and stereotypes about folk devils had taken hold.

In addition to the control culture, which amplified the deviance, there was also the phenomenon of what Lemert (1952) calls "deviance exploitation." Lemert referred to the "socioeconomic symbiosis between criminal and noncriminal groups" (1952: 310), pointing to the direct or indirect profit derived from crime by persons such as bankers, criminal lawyers, policemen and court officials. There was also *commercial exploitation* of folk devils such as Mods and Rockers by those engaged in marketing teenage consumer goods, who advertised using the groups' style images. The symbiotic relationship between the condemners and the condemned, the "normal" and the "deviant" was shown in the media treatment of the Mod-Rocker differences, as in the *Daily Mail* quiz "Are you a Mod or Rocker?," published immediately after Clacton. There was also *ideological exploitation*, which involves a similar ambivalence in the sense that the exploiter "gains" from the denunciation of deviance and would "lose" if the deviance proved to be less real or serious. Such ideological exploitation is not confined to politicians and moral crusaders, but includes a wide variety of groups who could use the symbolic connotations to justify their positions, e.g., "The men in the BBC who feed violence, lust, aimlessness and cynicism into millions of homes nightly must squarely consider their responsibility" (Resolution passed at the Moral Rearmament Easter Conference, 30 March 1964; quoted in S. Cohen, 1972/80: 141).

SOCIAL CONTEXT

The moral panic about Mods and Rockers did not arise in a social vacuum. The media, control agents and moral entrepreneurs required social circumstances conducive to the amplification and willing reception of their message about moral danger. As Cohen explains:

> The Mods and Rockers symbolized something far more important than what they actually did. They touched the delicate and ambivalent nerves through which

post-war social change in Britain was experienced. No one wanted depressions or austerity, but messages about "never having it so good" were ambivalent in that some people were having it too good and too quickly: "We've thrown back the curtain for them too soon." Resentment and jealousy were easily directed at the young, if only because of their increased spending power and sexual freedom. When this was combined with a too-open flouting of the work and leisure ethic, with violence and vandalism, and the (as yet) uncertain threats associated with drug-taking, something more than the image of a peaceful Bank Holiday at the sea was being shattered. (S. Cohen, 1972/80: 192)

Cohen suggests that ambiguity and strain was greatest at the beginning of the 1960s. The lines had not yet been clearly drawn and the reaction was part of this drawing of the line. He sees the period as constituting what Erikson (1966), in his study of witchhunts in puritan Massachusetts, had termed a "boundary crisis"—a period in which a group's uncertainty about itself was resolved in ritualistic confrontations between the deviant and the community's official agents. Cohen maintains that it is not necessary to make conspiratorial assumptions about deviants being deliberately "picked out" to clarify normative contours at times of cultural strain and ambiguity to detect in the response to the Mods and Rockers declarations about moral boundaries, about how much diversity can be tolerated. With respect to moral panics, as with the so-called "crime waves," they dramatize the issues at stake when boundaries are blurred and provide a forum to articulate the issues more explicitly. The social and physical mobility of the Mods and Rockers—relatively affluent teenagers who could dress in new styles and travel on their bikes outside working-class areas—provoked unease and hostility:

> Traditionally the deviant role had been assigned to the lower class urban male, but the Mods and Rockers appeared to be less class tied; here were a group of impostors, reading the lines which everyone knew belonged to some other groups. Even their clothes were out of place; without leather jackets they could hardly be distinguished from bank clerks. The uneasiness felt about actors who are not quite in their places can lead to greater hostility. Something done by an out-group is simply condemned and fitted into the scheme of things, but in-group deviance is embarrassing, it threatens the norms of the group and tends to blur its boundaries with the out-group. (S. Cohen, 1972/80: 195)

This analysis of boundary confusion is particularly relevant in the case of the Mods, whose style and social status did not easily fit established norms. The Mod's appearance was different from the stereotypical hooligan personified by the earlier fashion of the Teddy Boy or the leather-jacketed Rockers, who were thought to be imitating the American motor-bike gangs. The Mods seemed to offer some kind of snub to traditional values through their air of distance and ingratitude for what society had given them. Although there can be no doubt that the Mods' and Rockers' behavior did seem to pose a threat to the material interests of local traders and property owners in the resorts where disturbances occurred, the sense of moral outrage they evoked cannot be explained in those terms alone. The statements of the moral crusaders who demonized these youth cultures portrayed them as prematurely affluent, aggressive, permissive and challenging the ethics of sobriety and hard work. Psychologists have attempted to explain such responses in terms of the envy and resentment felt by the lower middle classes, supposedly the most frustrated and repressed of groups, who condemn behavior which they secretly crave. There may be some truth in this, but the fuller sociological explanation that we have suggested needs developing is multifactoral, stressing the interaction of structural conditions, cultural signs and symbols, the actions of key actors and movements, and processes by which typical forms of collective behavior develop.

REFERENCES

Cohen, S. (1972/80) *Folk Devils and Moral Panics: The Creation of the Mods and Rockers*, London: MacGibbon & Kee; new edition with Oxford: M. Robertson, 1980.

Erikson, K. (1966) *Wayward Puritans: A Study in the Sociology of Deviance*, New York: Wiley.

Halloran, J. D. *et al.* (1970) *Demonstrations and Commnications: A Case Study*, Hammondsworth: Penguin.

Lemert, E. M. (1952) *Social Pathology*, New York: McGraw Hill.

Smelser, N. J. (1963) *Theory of Collective Behaviour*, London: Routledge and Kegan Paul.

THE DEVIL GOES TO DAY CARE

McMartin and the Making of a Moral Panic

MARY DEYOUNG

While many may think that we have come a long way since the Salem witch trials, that we are far too sophisticated to let such a thing happen today, much more recent events suggest otherwise. As in previous articles, we see in the following account how deviance is constructed in the public imagination to encompass folk deviltry on an remarkable scale. Again, we see the role of the media in creating a moral panic. And again we see how the public is "primed" for such a panic by acute, but amorphous, anxieties brought about by social change. Students of the sociology of deviance should try to remain circumspect and examine the evidence when the next moral panic emerges. If the allegations seem preposterous, then there is a good chance that they are either unfounded or exaggerated.

A new type of sex crime was discovered during the 1980s—the abuse of very young children in rituals performed by robed and hooded satanists who also happened to be their day care providers. Satanic ritual abuse, as this new sex crime quickly came to be termed, appeared to be epidemic during the 1980s, and the McMartin Preschool was its first *locus delicti*.

The cultural response to the McMartin case had all of the characteristics of what sociologists call a moral panic:[1] it was widespread, volatile, hostile, and overreactive (Goode and Ben-Yehuda, 156–59). From Texas to Tennessee, New Jersey to North Carolina, Maine to Michigan, hundreds of local day care centers were investigated for satanic ritual abuse and scores of day care providers, as many males as females, were arrested and put on trial. From the witness stand, their accusers, the three- and four-year-old children once entrusted to their care, accused them of sexual abuse during satanic cere- monies that included such ghastly practices as blood-drinking, cannibalism, and human sacrifices. Despite the absence of evidence corroborating the chil- dren's accounts, many of the day care providers were convicted, and to the cheers and jeers of their deeply divided communities, were sentenced to what often were draconian prison terms.

In the accusatorial post-McMartin climate, day care providers, surrogate parents to this country's youngest children, took measures to protect themselves from their false allegations (Bordin, 80–81). They installed video cameras to record all of their activities, opened up private spaces to public view by taking down doors to bathrooms and closets and, fearing the act now could be misinterpreted, stopped hugging and holding their young charges. State legislatures also took measures. They hurriedly passed laws that mandated the fingerprinting and criminal records check of all current and prospective day care providers; state licensing agencies tightened regulations and by legislative fiat were given more teeth to enforce them. Yet insurance liability premiums soared, forcing many small day care centers out of business and many more, unlicensed and uninsured, to go under- ground.

Heralded at the start of the decade as playgrounds for children, day care centers were feared at its end as playthings of the devil. The aim of this pre- sent article is to analyze the moral panic about satanic day care centers that spread across this country during the 1980s. First, it examines the cultural context of the moral panic by focusing on the social forces and strains pecu- liar to that decade that not only gave rise to it, but that made what at first blush must appear to be the most innocuous of social institutions, the local day care center, the scene of the most horrific of sex crimes. Second, it inter- prets the McMartin Preschool case as the trigger that set off the moral panic, and then analyzes the roles that interest, grassroots, and professional groups played in spreading it across the country. Third, the article explains why, after nine long and bitter years, the moral panic finally ended and what "moral," if any, can be derived from it.

CULTURAL CONTEXT OF THE MORAL PANIC

An insightful examination of the social change most critical to the rise of the satanic day care center moral panic during the 1980s is provided by David Bromley and Bruce Busching who examine the changing relation between what they call the covenantal sphere and the contractual sphere of social life at the beginning of that decade. The covenantal sphere is that of the family. Within it, relations are built upon mutual commitment, bonding, and emotional expressiveness, and are articulated through the logic of moral involvement and unity. The contractual sphere, in contrast, is that of the market economy where relations are based upon mutual agreement, negotiation, and exchange, and are articulated through the logic of vested interest and shrewd involvement. By historic necessity, the covenantal and contractual spheres have been always, and uneasily, interdependent. As the locus of socialization, the family always has prepared children for successful participation in the market economy which, in turn, always has provided the legitimate opportunities for gaining the resources needed to sustain the family. In the early 1980s, however, the tension between these two spheres of social life intensified and that most innocent of social institutions, the local day care center, ended up being situated right on the faultline. This heightened tension between family and market economy was largely the result of cultural forces and strains peculiar to that decade. Significant among them were the ideological force of the women's movement that made participation in the market economy an attractive and increasingly accessible alternative to unpaid housework, and the economic strains that made it a necessity.[2] In 1980, in fact, 45% of women with young children had entered the labor market, and because the forces and strains that compelled their doing so had the same impact on their extended families, they had to turn away from relatives as a source of child care, and to public and private day care centers (Hofferth and Phillips, 560–63).

And they did so with more than a little ambivalence. Although day care centers packaged themselves as attractive alternatives to family care, with their use of educational toys to stimulate the mind, playground equipment to develop the body, excursions to cultivate aesthetic taste and, only when needed, just the right kind of discipline administered by trained professionals to shape socially correct behavior, most working parents considered this alternative a change for the worse from their parents' generation (Hutchison, 73–74).

Economic strains of a different type only reinforced that view. For one thing, as the baby-boomer generation went out to look for day care for its own children, it was confronted with a harsh reality: there simply were not enough reputable, licensed, affordable day care centers to meet its needs. Deep cuts in federal funding that over half of the public day centers had received just a few years before now resulted in high costs to working parents, overcrowded facilities, low wages for child care providers, and high staff turnover (Hofferth and Phillips 563–67). Dramatizing this dilemma was a blitz of day care horror stories in popular parents' magazines. Their images of toddlers in soiled diapers forlornly waiting for attention from overworked day care providers in overcrowded centers did little to assuage the anxiety or the guilt of working parents. Trapped as they were between necessity and risk, working parents reluctantly began transforming the covenantal duty of caring for their young children into contractual arrangements with day care providers. And many feared that in doing so they were relinquishing some control over the socialization of their children. . . .

So, here is the essence of the dilemma experienced by working parents in the early 1980s: on the one hand, the time and energy they were investing in the covenantal sphere of the family was jeopardizing their economic success in the contractual sphere of the market economy; on the other hand, the time and energy they were investing in the contractual sphere of the market economy was diminishing their control over the socialization of their children in the covenantal sphere of the family. And situated on the faultline of this dilemma, where these two once separate spheres of social life were now uncomfortably overlapping, was the local day care center. The tension produced by this imbrication of covenantal and contractual spheres made the local day care center a target of conflict. But a trigger was needed to set off a moral panic, some kind of spark that in the words of Jeffrey Adler "would link ethereal sentiment to focused activity" (262). That spark was ignited in 1983 at the McMartin Preschool.

TRIGGER OF THE MORAL PANIC

Hardly the dark satanic mill of cultural imagination, the McMartin Preschool was a rambling building on the main boulevard of the southern California town of Manhattan Beach where, if the Chamber of Commerce brochure were to be believed, residents enjoy "small town living, friendly neighbors, and community spirit." Established in the mid-1960s by Virginia McMartin, the family-owned and run day care center had a certain cachet among young, upwardly mobile parents and it filled early each year. So when Judy Johnson[3] went to enroll her two-year-old son in the spring of 1983, there were no openings. She dropped him off anyway. The day care providers arrived early one morning to find him in the yard of the center, and taking pity on the woebegone little boy and his recently separated mother, took him in.

Over the next several months, and without incident, the boy occasionally attended the center. But one day in August of that year, he came home with a reddened anus. His mother, stressed, emotionally unstable, and drinking heavily, immediately suspected that he had been sexually abused (Hubler, A1). She questioned him relentlessly, but to no avail, before she decided on a different tact. Having noticed how her son often pretended to be a doctor like the one who was tending his terminally ill older brother who was living at home, she asked if Raymond Buckey, the only male staff member and grand-son of the day care center's founder, had ever given him an injection. The boy said no, but when the question was asked again and again, he finally told his mother that what Buckey really had done was take his temperature. Judy Johnson concluded that the "thermometer" her son described was actually Buckey's penis, and that he had been sexually abused after all (Nathan and Snedeker, 67–70).

The medical exam performed the following day, however, was inconclusive for sexual abuse and the boy disclosed nothing at all to the detective his mother had contacted. But the matter was far from over. Several days later, Judy Johnson called the detective again and informed him that in the privacy of their own home her son was talking about sexual acts of the most perverse kind perpetrated not only on himself, but on other children enrolled at the day care center as well. So convincing was she that the detective demanded she get a second medical opinion. This physician, inexperienced in perform-ing sexual exams and finding nothing of significance anyway in the one she did perform, nonetheless erred on the side of caution and gave the diagnosis that finally confirmed what Judy Johnson was insisting had happened: her son had been sexually abused. Detectives now took a new interest in what the boy allegedly was telling his mother. They telephoned parents with chil-dren enrolled in McMartin and asked them to question their young sons and daughters about whether they, too, had been sexually abused. None answered in the affirmative. But in the wake of those telephone contacts that same "small town living, friendly neighbors, and community spirit" that made Manhattan Beach a desirable place to live also assured that rumors would gather and roll. So when the detectives pressed on and later sent the following letter to two hundred families whose children were current or recent enrollees at McMartin, the rumors were reified:

> Please question your child to see if he or she has been a witness to any crime or if he or she had been a victim. Our investigation indicates that possible criminal acts include: oral sex, fondling of genitals, buttocks or chest area, and sodomy, pos-sibly under the pretense of "taking the child's temperature." (Cited in Nathan and Snedeker, 72)

The letter also named Buckey as the prime suspect. Over the next several weeks as terrified and outraged parents questioned their children, met with each other to exchange facts and rumors, and questioned their children again, more and more of them answered in the affirmative. The assistant prosecutor appointed to oversee what too many already believed would turn out to be the case of the century, called a community meeting and encour-aged parents to take their sons and daughters to the Children's International Institute (CII), a non-profit diagnostic and treatment facility, for evaluation. Over the next year, the CII social workers, already caught up in the fad and folly about satanic sex cults that was still rolling over southern California in the wake of the Bakersfield case,[4] interviewed over 400 McMartin children and determined that 369 of them had been victims of a new and ghastly sex crime—satanic ritual abuse.

In February 1984, the same month that the prosecuting attorney quietly asked the grand jury to issue indictments against Raymond Buckey, as well as his grandmother, mother, sister, and three other McMartin staff members, a KABC reporter broke the story, plunging the local and the national news into what media critic David Shaw describes as "a feeding frenzy" (A1). Bent on proving satanic ritual abuse, the CII social workers kept relentlessly grilling the children who, despite their tender years, soon figured out that "round, unvarnish'd tales" were not what their inquisitors wanted to hear. And so they told other tales—tales about the ritualistic ingestion of feces, urine, blood, semen, and human flesh; the disinterment and mutilation of corpses; the sacrifices of infants; and the orgies with their day care providers, costumed as devils and witches, in the classrooms, in tunnels under the center, and in car washes, airplanes, mansions, cemeteries, hotels, ranches, gourmet food stores, local gyms, churches, and hot air balloons. And they named not only the seven McMartin day care providers as their satanic abusers, but their soccer coaches, babysitters, next-door neighbors, and even their own parents, as well as local businesspeople, the mayor's wife, who was said to drive around town with the corpses of sacrificed infants in the back of her stationwagon, news reporters covering the story, television and film stars, and members of the Anaheim Angels baseball team (Nathan and Snedeker, 78–91).

In 1986, the same year that *Los Angeles Times* reporter Lois Timnick revealed that 80% of the surveyed residents of Los Angeles County were convinced that all seven of the McMartin day care providers were guilty of satanic ritual abuse, the criminal charges against five of them were dismissed for lack of evidence. Now only Raymond Buckey and his mother, Peggy McMartin Buckey, were left to stand trial.

That trial began the following year and lasted twenty-eight months, the longest and, at a cost of $13 million, the most expensive criminal trial in the history of the country (Shaw, A1). The jury listened to 124 witnesses, fourteen of them children, examined 974 major exhibits, and reviewed 64,000 pages of transcripts before returning its verdict after nine weeks of deliberation (DeBenedictis, 29). It acquitted Peggy McMartin Buckey of all of the fifty-two charges against her, and acquitted Raymond Buckey of thirty-nine of the charges, but deadlocked on the remaining thirteen. His second trial on eight of those dead-locked charges ended with a hung jury after two weeks of deliberation. A month later, despite the vehement protests of the parents and many others across the country, the prosecutor dismissed all of the charges against him.

And what of Judy Johnson? The mother of the little boy who never shared his dark secrets with anyone, and who never could even pick out Raymond Buckey's picture from a photo lineup, was institutionalized for a while with the diagnosis of paranoid schizophrenia after she told detectives that her ex-husband also had sodomized her son, and that an intruder had broken into her house and sodomized the family dog. By the time of her death in 1986 from massive liver failure brought on by alcoholism, there had been at least fifty "little McMartin's" across the country; by the fifth anniversary of her death, there were fifty more (Sauer, D1).

SPREAD OF THE MORAL PANIC

The "moral" of the moral panic is now accounted for: the disturbing overlap between the covenantal and contractual spheres of social life had made local day care centers a site of conflict; the McMartin case set the moral boundaries of that conflict by casting day care providers into the role of evil satanists, their young charges into innocent victims, and the parents, social workers, prosecutors, and police into heroes. The "panic" that ensued, however, must be accounted for by yet another set of factors.

First, a clarification of the word "panic." While it tends to conjure up images of frenzied folks frantically fighting more devils than hell can hold, its sociological meaning is different. Panic refers to what Jeffrey Victor describes as a "collective stress reaction in response to a belief in a story about immediately threatening circumstances" (59). For the McMartin Preschool case to set off that collective reaction, that panic, it first had to be narrated, and here the role of interest, grassroots, and professional groups in telling, re-telling, and spreading the McMartin satanic day care story is important to consider.

The major interest group was the news media. After the KABC reporter broke the McMartin story early in 1984 during the local "sweeps week," other press, radio, and television reporters scrambled to surpass his exclusive. "The story had a life of its own," recalled one of them. "We didn't even think at the time about what we were doing. It was, 'We gotta get something new on McMartin; look how big this thing is getting' " (Shaw, A1).

Splattered with words like "grotesque," "bizarre," "chilling," "horrific," and "nightmarish," the early local news stories set the hysterical tone that would be mimicked by the national media and that would resound for nearly a decade throughout the country. And that tone hyperbolized the moral dimensions of the case through the process of what sociologists refer to as role amplification: in each re-telling of the story, the day care providers became more evil; the young children more innocent; the parents, social workers, police, and prosecutors more heroic.

The mass media certainly did nothing to temper that hysterical tone. *People* magazine titled its first feature on the case, "California's Nightmare Nursery"; *Time* magazine's headline was a single, sinister word: "Brutalized!" And on the primetime news magazine, *20/20*, the McMartin Preschool was dubbed "the sexual house of horrors" and the reporter, appearing deeply affected by his own reportage, somberly predicted that the children would never psychologically recover from what they were saying they had experienced.

McMartin had become a household word, synonymous with evil, by the end of 1984. But a household word does not a moral panic make. What yet was needed was that sense of imminent threat that Jeffrey Victor described, that shuddering fear that the mischief the devil had found in a day care center in southern California also was going on in centers in Oregon, Florida, Massachusetts, Iowa, and all places in between. What dissolved the boundaries on the map of imagination was the 1984 Congressional testimony of the CII social worker who had diagnosed satanic ritual abuse for the largest number of the McMartin children. In a widely quoted statement, she told Congress that the McMartin Preschool actually was an "organized operation of child predators" that "serves as a ruse for a larger, unthinkable network of crimes against children" that has "greater financial, legal, and community resources than any of the agencies trying to uncover it" (Brozan, A21). A touch of conspiracy was added to the story.

The plot thickened with its introduction. Not only did the conspiracy theory neatly explain why local and federal investigators were never able to find any evidence of satanic ritual abuse in the McMartin case, but it primed the larger culture's compact and conspiratorial imagination. Now the threat of satanic day care centers was real and exigent, and no community could consider itself immune from it.

That became the message of the grassroots group that also played a significant role in the telling, retelling, and spreading of the McMartin story. "Believe the Children" was formed in 1984 by a coterie of McMartin parents whose activism grew in sophistication from wearing buttons and carrying hand-painted signs to establishing a clearinghouse on satanic ritual abuse, replete with a speakers' bureau, a support network for parents, police, and prosecutors involved in other satanic day care cases, and a referral list of sympathetic professionals ("Believe the Children" n.d.).

Those sympathetic professionals also played a notable role in spreading the moral panic about satanic day care centers across the country. During the bitter years of McMartin, they not only received a great deal of local, national, and international news attention, but also appeared on television talk shows and primetime news magazines. They took to the lecture circuit, gave testimony in government-sponsored hearings, addressed conferences of child abuse professionals, consulted with other professionals as other satanic day care cases began cropping up across the country, and testified as experts in the criminal trials of day care providers. And in each interview, each presentation, each consultation, the story of McMartin was told and re-told in communities that were being primed for the moral panic by the telling.[5]

Originating in cultural anxieties about the socialization and protection of young children, triggered by the McMartin Preschool case, and spread across the country by interest, grassroots, and professional groups, the satanic day care center moral panic swept across the country. It lasted just a year short of a decade. Its longevity, actually quite remarkable by historical standards, is explained not by any corroborative evidence of satanic ritual abuse in day care, there never was any of that, but by its continuing resonance with the prevailing cultural conflict.

MAKE A MORAL OF THE DEVIL

The moral panic ended in 1992 when the last of the alleged satanic day care providers, a wife and her husband, were led off in handcuffs to begin a nearly half-century-long prison sentence.[6] Any temptation to celebrate its end as proof that the forces of good finally and forever triumphed over the forces of evil is best resisted. Instead, its dissolution is better explained in sociological terms: the cultural conflict that spawned and sustained it finally was somewhat ameliorated by it.

But only somewhat. The cultural conflict in question, of course, is that disconcerting overlap between the covenantal and contractual spheres of social life, and that conflict was not at all altered by the satanic day care center moral panic, if any measure of alteration can be found in the rate of public and private day care usage during the years of its duration. The number of working mothers increased both steadily and rapidly between 1983 when the McMartin case started and 1992 when the moral panic finally subsided, and so did the number of young children who were enrolled in public and private day care centers (Hofferth and Phillips, 561). Even with its dramatization, even demonization, of the tension between these two spheres, the moral panic could not thwart the steady encroachment of the contractual sphere into the covenental. But it could, and did, reduce the irritation of its intrusion.

It did so by provoking fear-based changes that had the interesting effect of smoothing the sharp edges of the contractual sphere's penetration into the covenantal sphere by replicating in the former some of the ever so familiar and much valued characteristics of the latter. More to the point, these changes made day care centers more like families, and thus more subject to parental control. Several examples are particularly noteworthy. In reaction to the moral panic, many states hurriedly passed legislation that required the screening of all prospective day care providers not only for criminal and psychiatric histories, but for "good moral character." The intent behind the legislation was almost transparent: it assured that day care providers would have the kind of right-mindedness and trustworthiness of the very best of the working parents who were contracting with them for the care of their children. The care of their children still may be a matter of contract, but it also was being carried out by people with character.

On a more local level, many day care centers reacted to the moral panic by adopting open-door policies. Parents were invited to drop in any time to chat with the staff and administration, observe their children, or even spend time with them. This policy had the effect of replicating within the local day care center the kind of easy informality of interaction that characterized the families from which their young charges had come. Accustomed to that style, and practiced in it, parents could monitor, even supervise to some extent, the care of their children by the agents whom they paid to provide it. And they could control that care as well. Day care centers invited parents to play more active roles in the centers, by sitting on their boards of directors, volunteering their time as classroom aides, chaperoning outings, and recruiting other parents to enroll their young children into the happy family that local day care centers fast were becoming.

One less obvious, but certainly sociologically significant, change that occurred in day care during the satanic day care center moral panic was its refeminization. In 1983, the year Judy Johnson's paranoid delusion transmogrified Raymond Buckey into an evil satanist, only 5% of day care providers were male (Weinback, 32). During the nine years of the moral panic, an alarming number of those male providers were accused of that new and horrific sex crime, satanic ritual abuse.[7] As a result of these allegations, males left the profession in droves, seeking the comparative safety of male sex-role stereotyped employment. Day care was refeminized. Once again, and in the time-honored and very familiar tradition of the family, the primary responsibility for the care and socialization of young children was placed on the shoulders of low-paid women.

The satanic day care center moral panic is a fascinating slice of cultural history. Yet in so many ways, this moral panic is really no different from all of the others that have preceded it, and all of the others that inevitably will follow. It originated in an unsettling cultural conflict peculiar to its era and was sustained by that same conflict over time. It set the moral boundaries of that conflict by casting antagonists into the role of evil satanists, and then spread the fear that casting generated. And it ended when it ameliorated that cultural conflict. If there is a moral to this or any other moral panic, it is perhaps nothing more than this: for a little sense of familiarity, a touch of order, a bit of control, the culture always seems willing to pay a most exacting price.

NOTES

1. There is a rich sociological literature on moral panics. Ben-Yehuda (1980), for example, treats the European witchhunts as a moral panic; Cohen (1972) uses the concept to analyze the the British reaction to juvenile gangs in the early 1960s; Sindall (1987) uses it to explain the London garroting panics of the 1800s, and Adler (1996) the Boston garroting panics just few years later; and Victor (1993) treats the anti-satanism movement of the 1980s as a moral panic.

2. For an extended discussion on the changing relationship between family and economy, see Negrey (1993), Rubin (1994), and Stacey (1990).

3. Judy Johnson is her real name. Both her name, and the name of her young son, have been widely reported in the media from the very beginning of the McMartin case.

4. Eight child sex rings were uncovered in the greater Bakersfied area in the early 1980s. The largest would come to be known as the Satanic Church case, and would implicate more

than sixty adults and seventy-seven children. Virtually every conviction in all eight of the cases has since been overturned. See Nathan and Snedeker (53–66) for an analysis of the Bakersfield cases.

5. Communities really were primed by conferences and workshops conducted by professionals. That priming effect is particularly evident in the Little Rascals Day Care Center case in Edenton, North Carolina, where seven adults, five of them day care providers and the other two unaffiliated with the center, were charged with sexually abusing nearly a hundred children in satanic rituals. Just a few months before the case began, the detective who would go on to investigate the Little Rascals case, the prosecutor who tried it, and the social workers who repeatedly interviewed the children, had attended a three-day conference on satanic ritual abuse in day care centers.

6. That case was Fran's Day Care in Austin, Texas. Day care owner Fran Keller and her husband Dan were each convicted of one count of aggravated sexual assault on a child and were sentenced to 48 years in prison, where they remain today. For a thorough examination of this controversial case, see Gary Cartwright's investigative report, "The Innocent and the Damned."

7. In a sample of 35 major satanic day care center cases, 30 (49%) of the 61 criminally charged day care providers were male.

WORKS CITED

Adler, Jeffrey S. "The Making of a Moral Panic in 19th Century America: The Boston Garroting Hysteria of 1865." *Deviant Behavior* 17 (1996): 259–78.

"Believe the Children." (Brochure). Cary, IL: Author, n.d.

Ben-Yehuda, Nachman. "The European Witch Craze of the 14th and 17th Centuries: A Sociological Perspective." *American Journal of Sociology* 86 (1980): 1–31.

Bordin, Judith A. "The Aftermath of Nonsubstantiated Child Abuse Allegations in Child Care Centers." *Child and Youth Care Forum* 25 (1996): 73–87.

Bromley, David, and Bruce C. Busching. "Understanding the Structure of Contractual and Covenantal Social Relations." *Sociological Analysis* 49 (1989): 15–32.

Brozan, N. "Witness Says She Fears 'Child Predator' Network." *New York Times* 18 Sept. 1984: A21.

Cartwright, Gary. "The Innocent and the Damned." *Texas Monthly* April 1994: 100–05+.

Cohen, Stanley. *Folk Devils and Moral Panics.* London: MacGibbon and Kee, 1972.

DeBenedictis, Don J. "McMartin Preschool's Lessons." *ABA Journal* 55 (1990): 28–9.

Goode, Erich, and Nachman Ben-Yehuda. "Moral Panics: Culture, Politics, and Social Construction." *Annual Review of Sociology* 20 (1994): 149–71.

Hofferth, Sandra L., and Deborah A. Phillips. "Child Care in the United States: 1970–1995." *Journal of Marriage and the Family* 49 (1987): 559–71.

Hubler, Shawn. "Driven to Her Death." Los Angeles Herald Examiner 8 Mar. 1987: A1.

Hutchison, Elizabeth D. "Child Welfare as a Woman's Issue." *Families in Society* 73 (1992): 67–77.

Nathan, Debbie, and Michael Snedeker. *Satan's Silence: Ritual Abuse and the Making of a Modern American Witchhunt.* New York: Basic, 1995.

Negrey, Cynthia. *Gender, Time, and Reduced Work.* Albany, New York: State University of New York Press, 1993.

Rubin, Lillian. *Families on the Fault Line.* New York: Harper, 1994.

Sauer, Mark. "Decade of Accusations: The McMartin Preschool Child Abuse Case Launched 100 Others." *San Diego Union Tribune* 29 Aug. 1993: D1.

Shaw, David. "Reporter's Early Exclusives Triggered a Media Frenzy." *Los Angeles Times* 20 Jan. 1990: A1.

Sindall, Rob. "The London Garrotting Panics of 1856 and 1862." *Social History* 12 (1987): 351–58.

Stacey, Judith. *Brave New Families.* New York: Basic, 1990.

Timnick, Lois. "McMartin Attorneys to Seek Relocation of Trial." *Los Angeles Times* 23 Feb. 1987: A1.

Victor, Jeffrey. *Satanic Panic.* Chicago, IL: Open Court, 1993.

Weinbach, Robert W. "Refeminization of Child Care: Causation, Costs and Cures." *Journal of Sociology and Social Welfare* 14 (1987): 31–40.

PENIS PANICS

ROBERT E. BARTHOLOMEW

While not technically a moral panic, the following article describes a well-documented phenomenon with similar mechanics of a moral panic—in terms of the dispersion of poorly premised alarm in a population—without the "moral" character of a moral panic. In particular, what the "penis panics" that occasionally crop up in parts of Asia have in common with the previous articles— and many of the subsequent articles in this volume—is found in the applicability of the "Thomas Theorem." The theorem, named after sociologist W. I. Thomas, states that things that are perceived as real are real in their consequences. In other words, for example, whether or not satanic ritual abuse actually pervaded American day care centers (see previous article), the belief that it did had real consequences for those accused of such, for the children alleged to have been victims, and for child care centers throughout the United States. Likewise, according to labeling theory, those who are labeled "deviant" suffer very real consequences regardless of the verity of the label.

Similarly, the "victims" of penis panics suffer real consequences, regardless of the absurdity of the phenomenon to Western observers.

It sounds like something from a poor B movie. It might even make the 1978 cult film *Attack of the Killer Tomatoes* seem plausible. I'm referring to scares where communities are swept up in the fear that their sex organs are rapidly shrinking. In parts of Asia entire regions are occasionally overwhelmed by terror-stricken men who believe that their penises are shriveling up or retracting into their bodies. Those affected often take extreme measures and place clamps or string onto the precious organ or have family members hold the penis in relays until an appropriate treatment is obtained, often from native healers. Occasionally women are affected, believing their breasts or vaginas are being sucked into their bodies. Episodes can endure for weeks or months and affect thousands. Psychiatrists are divided as to the cause of these imaginary scares. Some believe that it is a form of group psychosis triggered by stress, while others view it as mass hysteria. How can groups of people come to believe that their sex organs are shrinking? We will try to unravel this mystery by briefly describing several genital-shrinking scares, their similarities, and the factors involved in triggering them.

While genitalia-shrinking is known by a variety of names in different cultures, psychiatrists refer to it with the generic term "koro." A Malay word of uncertain derivation, koro may have arisen from the Malay word "keruk," meaning to shrink (Gwee, 1968, 3), although it is more likely a reflection of the Malaysian-Indonesian words for "tortoise" (kura, kura-kura, and kuro). In these countries, the penis, especially the glans or tip, is commonly referred to as a tortoise head. This led Dutch scientist P.M. Van Wulfften-Palthe to conclude that this is how the modern term "koro" most likely got its name: "The fact that a tortoise can withdraw its head with its wrinkled neck under its shell literally into its body, suggested...the mechanism...in 'koro' ('kura') and gave it its name" (1936, 536).

THE ANATOMY OF A MASS HYSTERIA

The first well-documented outbreak in modern times occurred in October and November, 1967, when hospitals on the tiny Southeast Asian island nation of Singapore were inundated by frantic citizens who were convinced that their penises were shrinking and would eventually disappear, at which time, many believed, death would result. "Victims" used everything from rubber bands to clothes pins in desperate efforts to prevent further perceived retraction. These methods occasionally resulted in severe organ damage and some pretty sore penises. At the height of the scare the Singapore Hospital treated about 75 cases in a single day. The episode occurred amid rumors that eating pork vaccinated for swine fever prior to slaughter could trigger genitalia shrinkage. One erroneous report even claimed that a pig dropped dead immediately after inoculation when its penis suddenly retracted!

The panic abruptly ended when the Singapore Medical Association and Health Ministry held public news conferences to dispel fears. Writing in the prestigious *British Journal of Psychiatry*, Singaporean doctor C.T. Mun described two typical cases. In one, a pale 16 year-old boy rushed into the clinic accompanied by his parents and clutching his penis. After providing reassurance and a sedative, there was no recurrence. The frightened boy said that he had heard the rumors of contaminated pork at school, had eaten pork that morning, and upon urinating, his penis appeared to have shrunk. At that point he hung on for all he was worth and shouted for help. In a second case, a mother dashed into the clinic clutching the penis of her 4-month-old baby frantically seeking help. Dr. Mun said that:

The child had not been well for two days with cold and a little diarrhea. The mother was changing his napkin...when the child had colic and screamed. The mother saw the penis getting smaller and the child screamed and [she] thought he had koro. She had previously heard the rumors. The mother was first reassured, and the baby's cold and diarrhea treated. The child was all right after that.

Most Singaporeans are of Chinese origin where there is a common belief in the reality of shrinking genitalia. Chinese medical texts from the 19th century even describe such cases as caused by an actual disease. Pao Sian-Ow's book, *New Collection of Remedies of Value* published in 1834, states that episodes occur when "the penis retracts into the abdomen. If treatment is not instituted at once and effective, the case [patient] will die. The disease is due to the invasion of cold vapors and the treatment is to employ the 'heaty' drugs."

At least 5,000 inhabitants in a remote area of southern Guangdong province, China, were affected by a genital-shrinking panic between August 1984 and the summer of 1985 (Jilek, 1986, 273). Male residents of the region are reared to practice restraint in matters of sexual desire and activity, as excessive semen discharge is believed to cause poor physical and mental health, even death. If that wasn't enough to worry about, many residents believe that certain spirits of the dead, especially female fox maidens, wander in search of penises that will give them powers. Each of the 232 'victims' surveyed by University of Hawaii psychiatrist Wen-Shing Tseng and his colleagues, was convinced that an evil female fox spirit was the culprit, while 76 percent of those affected had witnessed others being "rescued." Most of these cases occurred at night following a chilly sensation which would appear before a feeling of penile shrinkage. Tseng and his researchers reported: "Thinking this [chill] to be a fatal sign and believing that they were affected by an evil ghost, they [koro 'victims'] became panic stricken and tried to pull at their penises, while, at the same time, shouting for help" (Tseng et al., 1988, 1540). Interestingly, several children reported shrinkage of their tongue, nose and ears, reflecting the prevalent ancient Chinese belief that any male (yang) organs can shrink or retract. Tseng investigated a separate episode in 1987, affecting at least 300 residents on the Leizhou Peninsula of Guangdong province. Genital-shrinking panic is well-known in southern China, with episodes recorded in 1865, 1948, 1955, 1966, and 1974, all involving at least several hundred residents (Bartholomew, 1998).

Dr. Tseng has sought to determine why episodes repeatedly occur in the vicinity of Leizhou Peninsula and Hainan Island, but never spread to the principal section of Guangdong province or other parts of China, and why it is that only certain residents in a region report koro, while others do not. It was found that those affected held the more intense koro-related folk beliefs relative to a control group from the adjacent nonaffected area (Tseng et al. 1992, 122), helping to explain "why each time the koro epidemic spread from the Peninsula, it would cease when it reached the urban area of Guangzhou, where the people are more educated and hold less belief in koro." While recognizing the importance of rumors and traditional beliefs in precipitating episodes, Tseng considers koro outbreaks in southern China to be a psychiatric disorder ("genital retraction panic disorder") which primarily affects susceptible individuals, such as the poorly educated and those possessing below normal intellectual endowment who are experiencing social crisis or tension (1988, 1542; 1992, 117).

Another koro episode happened in northeast Thailand between November and December, 1976, affecting about 2,000 people, primarily rural Thai residents in the border provinces of Maha Sarakham, Nakhon Phanom, Nong Khai, and Udon Thani. Symptoms included the perception of genitalia shrinkage and impotence among males, while females typically reported sexual frigidity, with breast and vulva shrinkage. Other symptoms were panic, anxiety, dizziness, diarrhea, discomfort during urination, nausea, headaches, facial numbness, and abdominal pain. Some patients temporarily lost consciousness, and many were fearful of imminent death. Of 350 subjects studied in detail, irrespective of whether they sought treatment from native healers or physicians, "most patients had recovered within one day and all within one week" (Suwanlert and Coates, 1979, 65).

The episode began at a technical college in Udon Thani province, with rumors that Vietnamese immigrants had deliberately contaminated food and cigarettes with a koro-inducing powder. During this period, there was a strong anti-Vietnamese sentiment throughout Thailand following communist victories in Southeast Asia in 1975, the growing influence of the Communist Party of Thailand, and the perceived control of Cambodia and Laos by the Vietnamese. Anti-Vietnamese sentiments in the region were especially strong in the month before the episode (Andelman, 1976a, 1976b), with allegations by Thailand's Interior Minister that there was "solid evidence" of a plot whereby "Vietnamese refugees would incite rioting in northeast Thailand, providing Vietnam with an excuse to invade" on February 15 (Andelman, 1976c). As the episode continued, the poisoning rumors became self-fulfilling as numerous Thai citizens recalled that previously consumed food and cigarettes recently purchased from Vietnamese establishments had an unusual smell and taste. However, an analysis of suspected sources by the Government Medical Science Department "detected no foreign substance that could possibly cause sexual impotence or contraction of the male sex organ" (Jilek and Jilek Aall, 1977a, 58).

Koro rumors, combined with pre-existing awareness of the "disease," served to foster and legitimate its plausible existence. Suwanlert and Coates (1979,65) found that 94 percent of "victims" studied "were convinced that they had been poisoned." Negative government analysis of alleged tainted substances was undermined by contradictory statements issued by authority figures in the press. Security officials attributed the tainting substances believed responsible for causing the koro in food to a mixture of vegetable sources undetectable by medical devices (1977a, 58).

Another outbreak occurred in northeastern India from July to September, 1982. Cases numbered in the thousands, as many males believed their penises and testicles were retracting while women felt their breasts "going in." Indian psychiatrist Ajita Chakraborty said the panic reached such proportions that medical personnel toured the region, reassuring those affected with loud speakers (Chakraborty et al., 1983). Some parents tied string to their sons' penises to reduce or stop retraction, a practice that occasionally produced penile ulcers. Authorities even went to the extent of measuring penises at intervals to allay fears. A popular local remedy was to have the "victim" tightly grasp the affected body part, drink lime juice and be dowsed with buckets of cold water, (Sachdev and Shukla, 1982, 1161). While there was evidence of pre-existing koro-related beliefs among some residents, the episode spread across various religious and ethnic groups, social castes, and geographical areas by way of rumors. Based on interviews with 30 "victims," investigating physicians were unable to identify obvious signs of psychological disturbance (Sachdev and Shukla, 1982)....

UNRAVELLING THE MYSTERY

..."Victims" of genitalia-shrinking panics recover within hours or days after being convinced that the "illness" is over or never existed, and most clearly lack any psycho-sexual problems. Episodes also share similar symptoms: anxiety, sweating, nausea, headache, transient pain, pale skin, palpitations, blurred vision, faintness, insomnia, and a false belief that body parts are shrinking. These symptoms are normal body responses to extreme fear. The penis, scrotum, breasts, and nipples are the most physiologically plastic external body parts, regularly changing size and shape in response to various stimuli from sexual arousal to temperature changes. Studies also reveal that stress, depression, illness, and urination can cause small but discernible penis shrinkage (Oyebode et al., 1986; Thase et al., 1988). Another key factor is the nature of human perception, which is notoriously unreliable (Ross et al., 1994). Perception is also preconditioned by a person's mental outlook and social and cultural reference system. In each of the countries reporting epidemic koro, there were preexisting beliefs that genitalia could shrivel up under certain circumstances.

Far from exemplifying group psychosis, disorder or irrationality, penis-shrinking panics are a timely reminder that no one is immune from mass delusions, and that the influence of culture and society on individual behavior is far greater than most of us would like to admit. This is a valuable lesson to remember at the dawn of a new millennium. It is all too easy to think of past or non-Western delusions with a wry smile as if we are somehow now immune or those involved were naive and gullible. Yet, the main reason for the absence of penis-shrinking epidemics in Western societies is their incredible nature. It is simply too fantastic to believe. But any delusion is possible if the false belief underlying it is plausible. So while we may laugh at the poor "misguided" Indian or Chinese for believing in penis and breast-shrinking panics, we are haunted by our own unique delusions of crashed saucers, alien abductors, and CIA cover-ups of just about everything.

BIBLIOGRAPHY

Andelman, D. 1976a. "Thai Junta Re-Examines Relations With Neighbor Nations and U.S." *New York Times*, October 18, 1976.

———. 1976b. "Vietnam Accuses Thai Regime And Demands That It Free 800." *New York Times*, October 28, p. 30.

———. 1976c. "Campaign Grows Against Vietnamese in Thailand Region." *New York Times*, December 12, p. 3.

Bartholomew, R. E. 1998. "The Medicalization of Exotic Deviance: A Sociological Perspective on Epidemic Koro." *Transcultural Psychiatry* 35 (1):5–38.

———. 1994."The Social Psychology of 'Epidemic' Koro." *The International Journal of Social Psychiatry* 40 (1):46–60.

Berrois, G. E., and Morley, S. J. 1984. "Koro-like Symptoms in a Non-Chinese Subject." *British Journal of Psychiatry* 145:331–334.

Chakraborty, A., Das, S., and Mukherji, A. 1983. "Koro Epidemic in India." *Transcultural Psychiatric Research Review* 20:150–151.

Devan, G. S., and Hung, O. S. 1987. "Koro and Schizophrenia in Singapore." *British Journal of Psychiatry* 150:106–107.

Cremona, A. 1981. "Another Case of Koro in a Briton" Letter. *British Journal of Psychiatry* 138:180.

Edwards, J. G. 1970."The Koro Pattern of Depersonalization in an American Schizophrenic Patient." *American Journal of Psychiatry* 126 (8):1171–1173.

Emsley, R. A. 1985. "Koro in Non-Chinese Subject." Letter. *British Journal of Psychiatry* 146:102.

Gittelson, N. L. and S. Levine. 1966. "Subjective Ideas of Sexual Change in Male Schizophrenics." *British Journal of Psychiatry* 112:1171–1173.

Gwee, A-L. 1968. "Koro—Its Origin and Nature as a Disease Entity." *Singapore Medical Journal* 9 (1):3–6.

Ilechukwu, S. T. C. 1992. "Magical Penis Loss in Nigeria: Report of a Recent Epidemic of a Koro-Like Syndrome." *Transcultural Psychiatric Research Review* 29:91–108.

———. 1988. "Letter from S.T.C. Ilechukwu, M.D." (Lagos, Nigeria) which describes interesting koro-like syndromes in Nigeria. *Transcultural Psychiatric Research Review* 25:310–314.

Jilek, W. G. 1986. "Epidemics of 'Genital Shrinking' (Koro): Historical Review and Report of a Recent Outbreak in Southern China." *Curare* 9:269–282.

——— and Jilek-Aall, L. 1977. "A Koro Epidemic in Thailand." *Transcultural Psychiatric Research Review* 14:56–59.

Kendall, E. M., and Jenkins, P. L. 1987. "Koro in an American Man." *American Journal of Psychiatry* 144 (12):1621.

Mun, C. I. 1968. "Epidemic Koro in Singapore." Letter. *British Medical Journal* i: 640641, March 9.

Oyebode, F., Jamieson, M. J., and Davison, K. 1986. "Koro: A Psychophysiological Dysfunction." *British Journal of Psychiatry* 148:212–214.

Ross, D. F., Read, J. D., and Toglia, M. P. 1994. *Adult Eyewitness Testimony: Current Trends and Developments*. Cambridge: Cambridge University Press.

Sachdev, P. S. and Shukla, A. 1982. "Epidemic Koro Syndrome in India." *The Lancet*: 161.

Suwanlert, S. and Coates, D. 1979. "Epidemic Koro in Thailand—Clinical and Social Aspects." Abstract of the report by F. R. Fenton appearing in *Transcultural Psychiatric Research Review* 16:64–66.

Thase, M. E., Reynolds, C. F., and Jennings, J. R. 1988. "Nocturnal Penile Tumescence is Diminished in Depressed Men." *Biological Psychiatry* 24:33–46.

Tseng, W. S., Mo, K. M., Hsu, J., Li, L. S., Ou, L. W., Chen, G. Q., and Jiang, D. W. 1988. "A Sociocultural Study of Koro Epidemics in Guangdong, a." *American Journal of Psychiatry* 145 (12):1538–1543.

Tseng, W. S., Mo, K. M., Li, L. S., Chen, G. Q., Ou, L. W., and Zheng, H. B. 1992. "Koro Epidemics in Guangdong, China: A Questionnaire Survey." *The Journal of Nervous and Mental Disease* 180 (2):117–123.

Van Wulfften-Palthe, P. M. 1936. "Psychiatry and Neurology in the Tropics" p. 525–547. In C. de Langen and A. Lichtenstein (eds.), *Clinical Textbook of Tropical Medicine*. Batavia: G. Kolff and Company.

PART 3

Sex and Sexuality

THE COCHÓN AND THE HOMBRE-HOMBRE IN NICARAGUA

ROGER N. LANCASTER

In the United States, conceptions of sexual orientation are dichotomized. That is, Americans tend to view sexuality in an either-or mode: either you're heterosexual or you're homosexual. If you are homosexual, then you are not heterosexual, and vice versa. If you enjoy sexual relations with the same sex, then you are homosexual and not heterosexual. Many other cultures (and some subcultures within the United States) do not force their members to fit into such mutually exclusive categories. That is, they permit a person to engage in homoerotic behavior without compromising his or her heterosexual status. However, there are rules that such a person must follow in order to maintain their status as "normal." The following article describes the situation in Nicaragua.

THE SOCIAL CONSTRUCTION OF SEXUAL PRACTICES

The *cochón*, at first glance, might be interpreted as a Nicaraguan "folk category." The noun itself appears in both masculine (*el cochón*) and feminine (*la cochón, la cochona*) genders; either case typically refers to a male. The term is loosely translated as "queer" or "faggot" by English-speaking visitors; educated Nicaraguans, if they are fluent in international terminologies, are apt to translate the term in a similar (but more polite) fashion, giving "gay" or "homosexual" as its English equivalents. It becomes clear on closer inspection, however, that the term differs markedly from its Anglo-American counterparts of whatever shade. (And therein lies the danger of treating it as a folk category, which suggests that it is simply the rural version of some larger cosmopolitan concept.) In the first place, the term is not always as derogatory as the slanderous English versions are. Of course, it can be derogatory, and it almost always is. However, it can also be neutral and descriptive. I have even heard it employed in a particular sort of praising manner by ordinary Nicaraguan men: for instance, "We must go to Carnaval this year and see the cochones. The cochones there are very, very beautiful."[1]

Second, and more important, the term marks and delimits a set of sexual practices that partially overlaps but is clearly not identical to our own notion of the homosexual. The term specifies only certain practices in certain contexts. Some acts that we would describe as homosexual bear neither stigma nor an accompanying identity of any special sort whatsoever; others clearly mark their practitioner as a cochón.

If homosexuality in the United States is most characteristically regarded as an oral phenomenon, Nicaraguan homosexual practice is understood in terms of an anal emphasis. The lexicon of male insult clearly reflects this anal emphasis in Nicaraguan culture, even as the North American lexicon generally reflects an oral orientation. Cocksucker is the most common sexually explicit pejorative in the United States. Although equivalents to this term are sometimes used in Nicaragua, men there are more likely to be insulted in reference to anal intercourse. The dominant assumptions of everyday discourse, too, reflect the assumption of privileged, primary, and defining routes of intercourse in each case. That is, in Anglo-American culture, orality defines the homosexual; whatever else he might or might not do, a gay man is understood as someone who engages in oral intercourse with other men. In Nicaragua, anal intercourse defines the cochón; whatever else he might or might not do, a cochón is tacitly understood as someone who engages in anal intercourse with other men. But more is involved here than a mere shifting of the dominant sites of erotic practice or a casting of stigma with reference to different body parts. With the exception of a few well-defined contexts (e.g., prisons) where the rule may be suspended, homosexual activity of any sort defines the Anglo-American homosexual. In Nicaragua, by contrast, it is the passive role in anal intercourse that defines the cochón. Oral or manual practices receive scant social attention; everyday speech does not treat them in great detail, and non-anal practices appear far less significant in the repertoire of actually practiced homosexual activities.

The term *cochón* itself appears to indicate the nature of that status and role. None of my informants was certain about the origin of the term; it is *Nica*, a word peculiar to the Nicaraguan dialect of Spanish. Moreover, one encounters different pronunciations in various neighborhoods, classes, and regions, so there can really be no agreed spelling of the word: I have heard it rendered *cuchón*, *culchón*, and even *colchón*.[2] The last suggests a possible origin of the word: *colchón* means "mattress." As one of my informants suggested when prompted to speculate on the origin of the word, "You get on top of him like a mattress."

In neighboring Honduras, the point is made with even greater linguistic precision. There, "passive" partners in anal intercourse are known as *culeros*, from the term *culo*, meaning "ass," with the standard ending *-ero*. A *zapatero* is a man who works with shoes (*zapatos*); a culero is a man whose sexual activity and identity are defined as anal. As in Nicaragua, the act of insertion carries with it no special identity, much less stigma.

"You get on top of him like a mattress" summarizes the nature of the cochón's status as well as any phrase could, but it also points to the question, *Who* gets on top of him like a mattress? The answer is, Not only other cochones. Indeed, relationships between cochones seem relatively rare and, when they occur, are generally short-term. It is typically a noncochón male who plays the active role in sexual intercourse: a machista or an *hombre-hombre*, a "manly man." Both terms designate a "masculine man" in the popular lexicon; cochones frequently use either term to designate potential sexual partners. Relationships of this type, between cochones and hombres-hombres, may be of any number of varieties: one-time-only affairs; purchased sex, with the purchase running in either direction (although most typically it is the cochón who pays); protracted relationships running weeks or months; or full-scale emotional commitments lasting years.

The last sort is preferred but carries its own type of difficulties, its own particular sadness. As one of my informants related, "I once had a lover for five continuous years. He was a sergeant in the military, an hombre-hombre. During this period of time he had at least fifteen girlfriends, but I was his only male lover. He visited me and we made love almost every day. You have asked me if there is love and romance in these relations; yes, there is. He was very romantic, very tender, and very jealous. But he is married now and I rarely see him."

. . . In spite of my research strategy, and in settings as diverse as the marketplace and the school, I did meet and interview a number of men classified as cochones.[3] In our discussions, many of them told me that they were really comfortable only in the anal-passive position. Others alternate between active and passive roles, depending on whether they are having relations with an hombre-hombre (almost always passive) or with another cochón (passive or active). Some reported practicing oral sex, though not as frequently as anal intercourse. Several of my noncochón informants denied having any knowledge of oral techniques. Nicaraguans in general express revulsion at the idea of oral intercourse, whether heterosexual or homosexual. "Oral sexual relations? What's that?" was a common response to my queries about varied sexual positions in heterosexual intercourse. *"Me disgusta"* (That's disgusting) was the typical response to my descriptions of cunnilingus and fellatio. A series of (not necessarily sexual) aversions and prohibitions concerning the mouth seems to be involved here. The mouth is seen as the primary route of contamination, the major path whereby illness enters the body, and sex is quintessentially *sucio* (dirty). This conception is socialized into children from infancy onward. Parents are always scolding their small children for putting things in their mouths. This oral prohibition curbs the possibilities of oral intercourse.

The resultant anal emphasis suggests a significant constraint on the nature of homoerotic practices. Unlike oral intercourse, which may lend itself to reciprocal sexual practices, anal intercourse invariably produces an active partner and a passive partner. It already speaks the language of "activity" and "passivity," as it were.[4] If oral intercourse suggests the possibility of an equal sign between partners, anal intercourse in rigidly defined contexts most likely produces an unequal relationship: a "masculine" and a "feminine" partner, as seen in the context of a highly gendered ordering of the world. But this anal emphasis is not merely a negative restraint on the independent variable (homosexuality); positively, it produces a whole field of practices and relations.

THE SPECIFIC ROUTES OF STIGMA

There is clearly stigma in Nicaraguan homosexual practice, but it is not a stigma of the sort that clings equally to both partners. Only the anal-passive cochón is stigmatized. His partner, the active hombre-hombre, is not stigmatized at all; moreover, no clear category exists in the popular language to classify him. For all purposes, he is just a normal Nicaraguan male. The term *heterosexual* is inappropriate here. First, neither it nor any equivalent of it appears in the popular language. Second, it is not really the issue. One is either a cochón or one is not. If one is not, it scarcely matters that one sleeps with cochones, regularly or irregularly. Indeed, a man can gain status among his peers as a vigorous machista by sleeping with cochones in much the same manner that one gains prestige by sleeping with many women. I once heard a Nicaraguan youth of nineteen boast to his younger friends: "I am very sexually experienced. I have had a lot of women, especially when I was in the army, over on the Atlantic coast. I have done everything. I have even done it with cochones." No one in the group thought this a damning confession, and all present were impressed with their friend's sexual experience and prowess. This sort of sexual boasting is not unusual in male drinking talk.

For that matter, desire is not at issue here, and it is irrelevant to what degree one is attracted sexually to members of one's own sex, as long as that attraction does not compromise one's masculinity, defined as activity. What matters is the manner in which one is attracted to other males. It is expected that one would naturally be aroused by the idea of anally penetrating another male. (In neighboring Honduras, it is sometimes said that to become a man, one must sleep with a culero and two women.)

This is not to say that active homosexual pursuits are encouraged or even approved in all social contexts. Like adultery and heterosexual promiscuity, the active role in homosexual intercourse is seen as an infraction. That is, from the point of view of civil-religious authority, and from the point of view of women, it is indeed a "sin" (*pecado* or *mal*). But like its equivalent forms of adultery and promiscuity, the sodomizing act is a relatively minor sin. And in male-male social relations, any number of peccadillos (heavy drinking, promiscuity, the active role in same-sex intercourse) become status markers of male honor.

Nicaraguans exhibit no true horror of homosexuality in the North American style; their responses to the cochón tend rather toward amusement or contempt. The laughter of women often follows him down the street—discreet derision, perhaps, and behind his back, but the amusement of the community is ever present for the cochón. For men, the cochón is simultaneously an object of desire and reproach—but that opprobrium knows tacit limits, community bounds. A reasonably discreet cochón—one who dresses conservatively and keeps his affairs relatively discreet—will rarely be harassed or ridiculed in public, although he may be the target of private jokes. If he is very discreet, his status may never even be publicly acknowledged in his presence, and his practices will occupy the ambiguous category of a public secret....

[T]he hombre-hombre's exemption from stigma is never entirely secure. He might find his honor tainted under certain circumstances. If an hombre-hombre's sexual engagement with a cochón comes to light, for example, and if the nature of that relationship is seen as compromising the former's strength and power—in other words, if he is seen as being emotionally vulnerable to another man—his own masculinity would be undermined, regardless of his physical role in intercourse, and he might well be enveloped within the cochón's stigma. Or if the *activo's* attraction to men is perceived as being so great as to define a clear preference for men, and if this preference is understood to mitigate his social and sexual dominion over women, he would be seen as forgoing his masculine privileges and would undoubtedly be stigmatized. However, the Nicaraguan hombre-hombre retains the tools and strategies to ward off such stigma, both within and even *through* his sexual relationships with other men, and his arsenal is not much less than that which is available to other men who are not sleeping with cochones.

This is a crucial point. These kinds of circumstances are perhaps not exceptions at all but simply applications of the rules in their most general sense. Such rules apply not only to those men who engage in sexual intercourse with other men but also to men who have sex only with women. The sound of stigma is the clatter of a malicious gossip that targets others' vulnerabilities. Thus, if a man fails to maintain the upper hand in his relations with women, his demeanor might well be judged passive, and he may be stigmatized, by degrees, as a *cabrón* (cuckold), *maricón* (effeminate man), and cochón. Whoever fails to maintain an aggressively masculine front will be teased, ridiculed, and, ultimately, stigmatized. In this regard, accusations that one is a cochón are bandied about in an almost random manner: as a jest between friends, as an incitement between rivals, as a violent insult between enemies. Cats that fail to catch mice, dogs that fail to bark, boys who fail to fight, and men who fail in their pursuit of a woman: all are reproached with the term. And sometimes, against all this background noise, the charge is leveled as an earnest accusation.

That is the peculiar and extravagant power of the stigmatizing category: like Nietzsche's "prison-house of language" (Jameson, 1972), it indeed confines those to whom it is most strictly applied; but ambiguously used, it conjures a terror that rules all men, all actions, all relationships.

NOTES

1. Called "the festival of disguises," Carnaval is a religious celebration held annually in the large agricultural market town of Masaya. It marks the climax of a series of religious festivals

in that town, and not the approach of Lent. An important presence among the elaborate masks and disguises of Carnaval is that of the cochones, who don female attire and parade alongside other participants in the day's procession.

2. My spelling throughout conforms to the only spelling I have ever seen in print, in a *Nuevo diario* editorial (6 Dec. 1985).

3. I was not "out"—openly gay—in Erasmus Jimenez. At first, this strategy was to ensure that I could establish good relations with my informants, who, I imagined, would not approve. Later, it became problematic to me just how I would articulate my own understanding of my own sexuality to my informants—as this chapter demonstrates. Covertly, and through various circumlocutions, a few men from the neighborhood attempted to establish sexual liaisons with me; more generally, I encountered cochones in "neutral" and relatively "anonymous" settings such as the marketplace. In either case, for the most part these men assumed that I was an hombre-hombre. If I described myself to them as homosexual or gay, their sexual interest was generally diminished greatly.

4. As Boswell observes (1989, 33–34), fellatio can be considered an "active" behavior; if anything, it is the fellated who is "passive."

REFERENCES

Boswell, John. 1989. "Revolutions, Universals, and Sexual Categories." In Duberman et al., *Hidden from History*, 17–36. New York: NAL Books.

Jameson, Frederic, 1972. *The Prison-House of Language: A Critical Account of Structuralism and Russian Formalism.* Princeton: Princeton University Press.

WOMEN IN LESOTHO AND THE (WESTERN) CONSTRUCTION OF HOMOPHOBIA

K. LIMAKATSO KENDALL

The previous article and the one below both deal with the importance of language in the social construction of deviant categories. A label is a word and without the word in one's vocabulary, one cannot affix the label. John Lofland referred to these words or labels as "pivotal categories," or concepts in our minds around which we organize our perceptions. Put figuratively, a pivotal category is a socket in our brains into which we plug our perceptions. No socket for deviance, no perceptions of deviance. In Lesotho, they do not have a salient category for lesbianism and when women engage in homoerotic behavior, it is not considered "sex"; so women who engage in such behavior are not labeled lesbians. The author is reasonably concerned, however, that with globalization and the spread of Western beliefs around the world, today's "normal" Basotho women risk being tomorrow's "deviant" Basotho women.

Globalization could indeed cause radical shifts in the construction of deviant categories in countries throughout the world.

My search for lesbians in Lesotho began in 1992, when I arrived in that small, impoverished southern African country and went looking for my own kind. That was before the president of nearby Zimbabwe, Robert Mugabe, himself mission-educated, declared moral war on homosexuality and insisted that homosexuality was a "Western" phenomenon imported into Africa by the colonists.[1] When I left Lesotho two and a half years later, I had not found a single Mosotho[2] who identified herself as a lesbian. However, I had found widespread, apparently normative erotic relationships among the Basotho women I knew, in conjunction with the absence of a concept of this behavior as "sexual" or as something that might have a name. I learned not to look for unconventionality or visible performance of sex role rejection as indicators of "queerness." Most Basotho women grow up in environments where it is impossible for them to learn about, purchase, or display symbols of gay visibility, where passionate relationships between women are as conventional as (heterosexual) marriage, and where women who love women usually perform also the roles of conventional wives and mothers. I have had to look again at how female sexualities express themselves, how privilege and lesbianism intersect (or do not), and whether what women have together—in Lesotho or anywhere else—should be called "sex" at all. I have concluded that love between women is as native to southern Africa as the soil itself, but that homophobia, like Mugabe's Christianity, is a Western import.

BACKGROUND: LESOTHO AND ITS HISTORY

Surrounded on all sides by South Africa, Lesotho, with no natural resources except population, squirms in an ever-tightening vise. Only 10 percent of the land in Lesotho is arable, but 82 percent of its population of over two million is engaged in subsistence agriculture (Internet World Factbook 1995). Most Basotho have no source of cash income at all, while a few are wealthy even by U.S. standards. Under these circumstances "mean national income per household member" means little, but in 1994 it was [about $13 per month](Gay and Hall 1994:20). The conclusion of international experts is that Lesotho is experiencing a "permanent crisis" (Gay and Hall 1994:9) exacerbated by unemployment, population growth, decline in arable land, reduction in soil fertility, desertification, and hopelessness....

All women are legally "minors" in Lesotho under customary law. Under common law women are minors until the age of twenty-one, but they revert to minor status if they marry, attaining majority status only if single or widowed (Gill 1992:5). Women cannot hold property; they have no custody rights in the case of divorce; they cannot inherit property if they have sons; they cannot borrow money, own or manage property or businesses, sign contracts, buy and sell livestock, land, or "unnecessary" goods. Nor can a woman obtain a passport without a husband's or father's consent (Gill 1992:5). Although women do now vote, the franchise is one of the few areas in which women have gained legal rights since independence in 1966. A few well-educated middle-class women are fighting for greater equity. The Federation of Women Lawyers has "mounted an awareness campaign on the rights of women" and is trying to secure legal rights for women, but with three legal codes operative in Lesotho (customary law based on tradition and the chieftaincy, common law based on the Roman-Dutch system of South Africa, and constitutional law) the going is difficult, to say the least, for Basotho feminists (Thai 1996:17)....

[An] important aspect of the background of this study is that women in Lesotho endure physical abuse almost universally. Marriage is compulsory by custom, and divorce is very expensive; the divorce rate is only 1 percent for this reason (Gill 1992:5). However, women manage up to 60 percent of the households on their own, in small part because of male migrant labor, but in larger part because of de facto separation and divorce occasioned by couples never having been married and then separating, by male abandonment, or by women leaving abusive mates (Gill 1992:21).

In the two years I lived in Lesotho, I met only one woman who said she had never been beaten by a husband or boyfriend, and she said she was the only woman she knew who had been so fortunate. According to precolonial tradition, a man claimed a woman as a wife by raping her, and this custom is still common in the mountain areas. One scholar notes the "apparent tolerance of a man's unbridled right to exploit women sexually" (Epprecht 1995:48). Men are conditioned to abuse women; women are conditioned to accept abuse. In this context, women often seek comfort, understanding, and support from other women. In addition, the homosocial nature of Basotho society, both before and after colonization, separates boys and girls from early childhood and conditions members of one gender group to regard members of the other gender group as a distinct "other." Thus, whatever her sexual desires and impulses may be, a Mosotho woman is likely to establish significant emotional bonds only with other women and with children and to become accustomed to expressing affection toward members of her own sex. Indeed, it is common all over Lesotho to see people of the same sex walking hand-in-hand or arm-in-arm, but it is so rare as to be remarkable to see public displays of affection between males and females. In this context, it is not surprising that some women who experience sexual desire for other women find it easy to express that desire, and it is also not surprising that the lines between what is affection and what is sex or desire blur.

PROBLEMATIZING THE AUTHOR

I cannot claim to have conducted an objective scientific study of Basotho women and sexuality, nor would I want to make such a claim. In every respect, what I see or understand of Basotho women's experience is filtered through my own range of perceptions and beliefs and is colored by my own experience of what is sexual, what is affectional, and what is possible between women. My experience as a lesbian shapes my interpretation of behavior I perceive as being "erotic" or "lesbianlike."[3] My experience as a white working-class woman, who has made it into academe and thereby lost her class connections and identity, shapes my understanding of privilege and its relationship to "lesbianism" as a lifestyle. I have now been "out" for thirty-one years, but I prefer not to share a household with my partner and resent definitions of lesbianism that reify the tidy domestic arrangement that features two middle-class women under one roof, so popular in lesbian communities in the U.S. My personal experience strongly influences my perception of the intersections of class privilege (or the lack of it) and sexual choices in Lesotho. My informants were all black women, Basotho friends, neighbors, and acquaintances, mostly residents of the Roma Valley, an area of Lesotho steeped in and named for the Roman Catholic religion. Although many of the women with whom I discussed women's sexuality had migrated to the Roma Valley from the mountains and can tell about rural women's lives firsthand, nonetheless there is a distance and separation of their experiences from those of the mountain women who have not migrated. The very fact that they were talking to a white woman about bodily functions set them apart from women in the mountains who have never done so. Their lenses, like mine, are unique, and not ideally representative, if indeed such a thing as ideal representativity exists. I speak Sesotho, but not fluently, and I am not an anthropologist. Much of what I have learned about women, class, and sexuality in Lesotho has come to me through lucky coincidences....

WOMEN IN LESOTHO

Probably the most important accident in my quest for lesbians in Lesotho was that on my arrival at the university I was housed at the guest house, where I befriended 'M'e Mpho Nthunya,the cleaning woman.[4] I learned before long that 'M'e Mpho had actually, in a sense, married another woman (more about that later). When I asked her if she knew of any women-loving women in Lesotho, she was puzzled. "Many of us love each other," she said, laughing. Thinking she had misunderstood me, I said I meant not just affectionate loving, but, well, I stammered, "Women who share the blankets with each other," that being the euphemism in Lesotho for having sex.

'*M'e* Mpho found that uproariously funny. "It's impossible for two women to share the blankets," she said. "You can't have sex unless somebody has a *koai* (penis)." This concise, simple observation led me to two different but related trains of thought.

First, '*M'e* Mpho's "impossible" brought to mind one of Greenberg's remarks in *The Construction of Homosexuality*, to wit, "the kinds of sexual acts *it is thought possible to perform*, and the social identities that come to be attached to those who perform them, vary from one society to another" (1988:3, italics mine). Greenberg continues:

> Homosexuality is not a conceptual category everywhere. To us, it connotes a sym-
> metry between male-male and female-female relationships.... When used to
> characterize individuals, it implies that erotic attraction originates in a relatively
> stable, more or less exclusive attribute of the individual. Usually it connotes an
> exclusive orientation: the homosexual is not also heterosexual; the heterosexual is
> not also homosexual.
>   Most non-Western societies make few of these assumptions. Distinctions of age,
> gender, and social status loom larger. The sexes are not necessarily conceived
> symmetrically. (1988:484)

Lesotho is one such non-Western society, and Basotho society has not constructed a social category "lesbian." Obviously in Lesotho the sexes are not
conceived symmetrically. Nor is "exclusive orientation" economically feasible for most Basotho women. There is no tradition in Lesotho that permits
or condones women or men remaining single; single persons are regarded as
anomalous and tragic. Thus women have no identity apart from that of the
men to whom they are related; only comparatively wealthy divorced or widowed women could set up housekeeping alone or with each other. As in
many other African societies, including that of Swahili-speaking people in
Mombasa, Kenya, "a respectable adult is a married adult" (Shepherd
1987:243). However, there is much less wealth in Lesotho than in Mombasa.
The lesbian unions Shepherd describes as common and "open" among married and formerly married Swahili-speaking women are based, as she notes,
on the constructions of rank and gender in that society, as well as upon the
existence of a considerable number of women with sufficient economic
power to support other women (1987:262–265). Even more important,
Swahili-speaking women, according to Shepherd, do have a concept of the
possibility of sexual activity between women. In Swahili the word for lesbian
is *msagaji*, which means "a grinder" and has obvious descriptive meanings
for at least one variety of lesbian sexual activity. Although I found no evidence of any comparable use of words in the Sesotho language, what is more
significant is that Basotho women define sexual activity in a way that makes
lesbianism linguistically inconceivable; it is not that "grinding" does not take
place, but it is not considered "sexual."

The second train of thought '*M'e* Mpho Nthunya's "impossible" led me to
is the great mass of scientific sex studies. From Kraft-Ebbing through Kinsey

and Hite and on up to the present, these studies repeatedly show that lesbians "have sex" less frequently than heterosexuals or gay men. Marilyn Frye (1992) cites one study by Blumstein and Schwartz that shows that "47% of lesbians in long-term relationships 'had sex' once a month or less, while among heterosexual married couples only 15% had sex once a month or less" (110). Frye is amused by how the sexperts count how many times people have sex. She notes that the question "how many times" they "had sex" is a source of merriment for lesbians. For what constitutes "a time"? Frye continues, "what 85% of long-term heterosexual married couples do more than once a month takes on the average eight minutes to do" (1992:110). In contrast, what lesbians do so much less frequently takes anything from half an hour to half a day to do and can take even longer if circumstances allow. Frye concludes: "My own view is that lesbian couples...don't 'have sex' at all. By the criteria that I'm betting most of the heterosexual people used in reporting the frequency with which they have sex, lesbians don't have sex. There is no male partner whose orgasm and ejaculation can be the criterion for counting 'times'" (1992:113).

Or as *'M'e* Mpho Nthunya put it: no *koai*, no sex. Diane Richardson writes on a similar tack,

> How do you know you've had sex with a woman? Is it sex only if you have an orgasm? What if she comes and you don't?...What if what you did wasn't genital, say you stroked each other and kissed and caressed, would you later say you'd had sex with that woman? And would she say the same? The answer, of course, is that it depends; it would depend on how you and she interpreted what happened. (1992:188)

Since among liberated Western lesbians it is difficult to determine when one has had "sex" with a woman, it is not at all surprising that in Roman Catholic circles in Lesotho, "sex" is impossible without a *koai*. Among Basotho people, as among those surveyed in numerous studies in the U.S. and the U.K., sex is what men have—with women or with each other. The notion of "sex" or the "sex act" is so clearly defined by male sexual function that *'M'e* Mpho Nthunya's view of it should not surprise any of us. However, women in Lesotho do, as *'M'e* Mpho said, love each other. And in expressing that love, they have *something*.

Judith Gay (1985) documents the custom among boarding school girls in Lesotho of forming same-sex couples composed of a slightly more "dominant" partner, called a "mummy," and a slightly more "passive" partner called a "baby." The girls do not describe these relationships as sexual, although they include kissing, body rubbing, possessiveness and monogamy, the exchange of gifts and promises, and sometimes, genital contact (112). Gay also describes the custom among Basotho girls of lengthening the labia minora, which is done "alone or in small groups" and "appears to provide opportunities for auto-eroticism and mutual stimulation among girls" (1985:101). Certainly there are ample opportunities for Basotho women of various ages to touch each other, fondle each other, and enjoy each other physically. The fact that these activities are not considered to be "sexual" grants Basotho women the freedom to enjoy them without restraint, embarrassment, or the "identity crises" experienced by women in homophobic cultures like those of the U.S. and Europe. Margaret Jackson writes convincingly that the valorization of heterosexuality and the "increasing sexualization of western women [by sexologists] which has taken place since the nineteenth century should not be seen as 'liberating' but rather as an attempt to eroticize women's oppression" (1987:58).

I have observed Basotho women—domestic workers, university students, and secretaries (but not university lecturers)—kissing each other on the mouth with great tenderness, exploring each other's mouths with tongues and this for periods of time of more than sixty seconds—as a "normal," even daily expression of affection. The longest kisses usually take place out of view of men and children, so I presume that Basotho women are aware of the eroticism of these kisses and are protective of their intimacy, yet never have I heard any Mosotho woman describe these encounters as "sexual." When I called attention to this activity by naming it in speaking with a Mosotho professional researcher who was educated abroad, she told me, "Yes, in Lesotho, women like to kiss each other. And it's nothing except—." She seemed at a loss for words and did not finish the sentence but skipped, with some obvious nervousness, to "Sometimes-I-I-I-don't like it myself, but sometimes I just do it."

It is difficult to discuss women's sexuality in Lesotho because of the social taboos (both precolonial and postcolonial) against talking about it. Even now, it is socially taboo in Lesotho for a woman who has borne children to discuss sex with girls or women who have not. (Fortunately for my research, I have borne children; a childless American colleague also doing research in Lesotho found it difficult to have discussions about sexuality with adult Basotho women.) My Basotho women friends would not dream of explaining menstruation to their daughters; rather, they expect girls to learn the mysteries of their developing bodies and of sexual practices from other girls, perhaps a year or two older than themselves. Like everything else in Lesotho, this is changing—very slowly in more remote rural areas and rather quickly in the towns. Sex education two or three generations ago took place in "initiation schools" for boys and girls, but these traditional schools were a major target of missionary disapproval and have now just about disappeared in all but the most remote areas. The taboo on talking about sex certainly hampered the efforts of family planning advocates to institute sex education during the 1970s. The Roman Catholic Church did little to change that, but as a result of concerted efforts of a number of nongovernmental agencies and of the Lesotho government itself, birth control information, drugs, and other pregnancy-prevention techniques are now widely available in health clinics. For the most part, the Church now seems to look the other way when women line up at the clinics for pills, IUDs, and injections to prevent pregnancy. More recently, government-sponsored AIDS education workers have been at pains to dispel dangerous myths kept alive by groups of prepubescent teenagers, to popularize the use of condoms, and to encourage young people to learn about and talk about "safe sex." Over time this may have profound and lasting affects on sexual behavior in Lesotho.

A number of difficulties remain. The Sesotho language was first written down by missionaries, who compiled the first Sesotho-English and Sesotho-French dictionaries; not surprisingly, these dictionaries include few words to describe sexuality or sex acts. If there ever were words for "cunnilingus," "g-spot," or "Do you prefer clitoral or vaginal orgasm?" in Sesotho, they certainly did not make it into the written records of the language nor do translations of these terms appear in phrase books or dictionaries.

My attempts to "come out" to rural women and domestic workers were laughable; they could not understand what I was talking about, and if I persisted, they only shook their heads in puzzlement. Despite this, I had some long conversations with Basotho women, especially older university students and domestic workers, who formed my social cohort in Lesotho and who trusted me enough to describe their encounters in as much detail as I requested. From these I learned of fairly common instances of tribadism or rubbing, fondling, and cunnilingus between Basotho women, with and without digital penetration. This they initially described as "loving each other," "staying together nicely," "holding each other," or "having a nice time together." But not as having sex. No *koai*, no sex.

Lillian Faderman's observation that "A narrower interpretation of what constitutes eroticism permitted a broader expression of erotic behavior [in the eighteenth century], since it was not considered inconsistent with virtue" (1981:191) makes sense here. If these long, sweet Basotho women's kisses or incidences of genital contact were defined as "sexual" in Lesotho, they could be subject to censure both by outside observers who seem to disapprove of sex generally (nuns, visiting teachers, traveling social workers) or by the very women who so enjoy them but seek to be morally upright and to do the right thing. If the mummy/baby relationships between boarding-school girls were defined as "sexual," they would no doubt be subject to the kind of repression "particular friendships" have suffered among nuns.

Since "sex" outside of marriage in Roman Catholic terms is a sin, then it is fortunate for women in this mostly Catholic country that what women do in Lesotho cannot possibly be sexual. No *koai*, no sex means that women's ways of expressing love, lust, passion, or joy in each other are neither immoral nor suspect. This may have been the point of view of the nineteenth-century missionaries who so energetically penetrated Lesotho and who must have found women-loving women there when they arrived. Judith Lorber writes, "Nineteenth-century women were supposed to be passionless but arousable by love of a man; therefore, two women together could not possibly be sexual" (1994:61).

'*M'e* Mpho Nthunya dictated her entire autobiography to me over the two years I lived in Lesotho, a book called *Singing Away the Hunger: The*

Autobiography of an African Woman (1997). In it she describes, in addition to a loving and affectionate (though compulsory) heterosexual marriage, a kind of marriage to a woman that included an erotic dimension. According to Judith Gay (1985), these female marriages were common among women of Nthunya's generation. Gay writes, "elderly informants told me that special affective and gift exchange partnerships among girls and women existed 'in the old days' of their youth" (1985:101).

Nthunya describes how the woman she calls 'M'alineo chose her as her *motsoalle* (special friend) with a kiss. Nthunya writes: "It's like when a man chooses you for a wife, except when a man chooses, it's because he wants to share the blankets with you. The woman chooses you the same way, but she wants love only. When a woman loves another woman, you see, she can love with her whole heart" (1997:69).

Nthunya describes the process of their relationship, the desire that characterized it, the kisses they shared, their hand-holding in church, their meetings at the local cafe. And she describes the two ritual feasts observed by themselves and their husbands, recognizing their relationship. These feasts, held one year apart, involved ritual presentation and slaughter of sheep as well as eating, drinking, dancing, singing, exchanges of gifts, and general merriment and validation of the commitment they made to each other by all the people they knew. "It was like a wedding," Nthunya writes (1997:70). This ritual, which she describes as taking place around 1958, was widespread and well-known in the mountains where she lived. She describes the aftermath of her feast this way:

> So in the morning there were still some people drinking outside and inside, jiving and dancing and having a good time.
>
> Alexis [my husband] says to them, "Oh, you must go to your houses now. The joala [home-made beer] is finished."
>
> They said, "We want meat."
>
> He gave them the empty pot to show them the meat is all gone. But the ladies who were drinking didn't care. They said, "We are not here to see you; we are coming to see [your wife]."
>
> They sleep, they sing, they dance. Some of them are motsoalle of each other. (1997:71)

It would appear from Nthunya's story that long-term loving, intimate, and erotic relationships between women were normative in rural Lesotho at that time and were publicly acknowledged and honored. Gay (1985) describes an occasion when she was discussing women's relationships with three older women when a twenty-four-year-old daughter-in-law interrupted the discussion by clapping her hands. "Why are you clapping so?" asked the straightforward ninety-seven-year-old woman. "Haven't you ever fallen in love with another girl?" (1985:102). Both Nthunya's and Gay's accounts emphasize the fact that while such relationships were common and culturally respected up to the 1950s, they no longer seem to exist, or at least young women of the 1980s and 1990s are unaware of this cultural activity so central to their grandmothers' lives. What remains are the affectionate relationships among girls and women, the public kissing and hand-holding, and the normativity of homosocial and homoerotic relationships among working-class or poor women....

HOMOPHOBIA

After an earlier version of this article was published in Lesotho, I received a letter from a young professional woman with whom I had worked closely in writing workshops. She had read my article, came out to me in the letter, observed that she had not deduced that I was a lesbian either, and confirmed, "Life goes on in this place and like you said, we conform, smile and flirt with the male *homo sapiens* that we desperately wish to do without" (Anonymous 1997). She concluded her letter, "You cannot imagine the confusion and loneliness that drove me deeper into myself just wishing all the time I was raised in a different, freer society" (ibid.). This young Mosotho woman found the information about motsoalle relationships an interesting bit of history, and yet clearly, homophobia has now intervened in the lives of professional women to such an extent that she feels she has no permission to express her own sexuality.

In examining the question of options or choices it may be useful to clarify to what extent women in Lesotho have social or sexual options. Five years before Judith Gay wrote her article "Mummies and Babies," she wrote a Ph.D. dissertation at Cambridge called "Basotho Women's Options: A Study of Marital Careers in Rural Lesotho" (1980). In that paper she examined the lives of married women whose husbands are migrant workers and those whose husbands remain at home, of widows, and of separated or divorced women. Gay does not even mention the possibility of single, independent women living alone, or of lesbianism as an option for Basotho women. Instead she states, "marriage is the principal means whereby these women attain adult status and gain access to the productive resources and cash flows which are essential to them and their dependents" (1980:299). She predicts with accuracy the likelihood of growing unemployment among men in Lesotho and conjectures, "It is possible also that the resulting marital conflict and economic difficulties will lead to increasing numbers of independent women who become both heads of matrifocal families and links in matrilateral chains of women and children" (1980:312). That is certainly happening, and perhaps in another decade the lesbian option, as it is experienced in the northern hemisphere (or the "West"), will have come to Lesotho. But its shadow, homophobia, has already preceded it.

'M'e Mpho Nthunya concludes the story of her "marriage" to 'M'e Malineo as follows: "In the old days [note that here she refers to a period up to the late 1950s] celebrations of friendship were very beautiful—men friends and women friends. Now this custom is gone. People now don't love like they did long ago" (1995:7). As Nthunya and I were preparing her autobiography for publication, I asked her if she could add something to the conclusion of that chapter, to perhaps explain why people do not love like they did long ago. She added the following: "Today the young girls only want men friends; they don't know how to choose women friends. Maybe these girls just want money. Women never have money, so young girls, who want money more than love, get AIDS from these men at the same time they get the money" (1996:72). Perhaps that is all there is to it, though I would have thought that women in the "old days" needed money too. And the young professional woman who came out to me via the mail, who does not need money as desperately as the girls in Nthunya's experience, experiences homophobia in what she describes as a "soul-destroying" way (Anonymous 1997).

I believe that one pressure leading toward the demise of the celebration of batsoalle[5] is the increasing westernization of Lesotho and the arrival, at least in urban or semi-urban areas and in the middle class, of the social construction "homophobia" with and without its name. Gay noted in her study of lesbianlike relationships in Lesotho that women who live "near the main road and the South African border" were "no longer involved in intimate female friendships" (1985:102). Living near a "main road" or a South African border would expose a woman to imported ("Western") ideas and values, as would formal education. Women in rural areas would be less likely to suffer the pollution of homophobia.

By scrutinizing homophobia as the "queer" thing it is, given examples of healthy lesbian activity in indigenous cultures in Lesotho and elsewhere, we might conclude that homophobia is an "unnatural" vice, that homophobia is far more likely to qualify as "un-African" . . . than homosexuality, that homophobia is the product of peculiar (Western or northern-hemisphere) cultures.

As Michel Foucault writes in his groundbreaking *History of Sexuality*, it is useful to view sexuality not as a drive, but "as an especially dense transfer point for relations of power" (1981:103). No *koai*, no sex. In that case the loving and egalitarian erotic friendships of Basotho women would not be "sexual" at all, which is exactly what Basotho women have been saying whenever anyone asked them. The freedom, enjoyment, and mutual respect of Basotho women's ways of loving each other, occurring in a context in which what women do together is not defined as "sexual" suggests a need to look freshly at the way Western constructions of sexuality and of homophobia are used to limit and oppress women. Having a (sexualized) "lesbian option" may not be as liberating as many of us have thought.

NOTES

1. Mugabe was quoted in the South African newspaper Mail and Guardian declaring homosexuality "immoral," "repulsive," "an 'abhorrent' Western import" (p. 15, August 4–10, 1995).

2. Lesotho is the country; Sesotho is the language; one person from Lesotho is a Mosotho; two or more are Basotho.

3. If by "lesbian" we mean an identity that emerged in the twentieth century in certain Western cultures, then by definition the word cannot be applied to the Basotho situation. Some scholars are using the term "lesbianlike" to describe erotic and deeply affectional relationships among women who do not have the option of identifying themselves as lesbian. See, among others, Vicinus (1994) and Jenness (1992).

4. 'M'e is the honorific or Sesotho term of address for a mature woman. It literally means "mother" and is used with the woman's first name. It is an insult to speak of her without the honorific or to speak of her by her surname only. In submission to Western academic custom, I sometimes refer to 'M'e Mpho as "Nthunya" in this paper, but I would never address her in that form. One Mosotho woman said to me, "to speak of a grown woman without using 'M'e is the same as stripping off all her clothes."

5. Plural of motsoalle, special friend.

REFERENCES

Cleland, John. 1749. *Fanny Hill*. London: Fenton.

Epprecht, Marc. 1995 "'Women's Conservatism' and the Politics of Gender in Late Colonial Lesotho." *Journal of African History* 36:29–56.

Faderman, Lillian. 1981. *Surpassing the Love of Men: Romantic Friendship and Love Between Women from the Renaissance to the Present*. New York: William Morrow.

Foucault, Michel. 1981. *The History of Sexuality*. Harmondsworth: Penguin.

Frye, Marilyn. 1992. *Willful Virgin: Essays in Feminism, 1976–1992*. Freedom, CA: The Crossing Press.

Gay, John and David Hall 1994. *Poverty in Lesotho, 1994: A Mapping Exercise*. Lesotho: Sechaba Consultants.

Gay, Judith. 1980. "Basotho Women's Options: A Study of Marital Careers in Rural Lesotho." Ph.D. diss., University of Cambridge.

———. 1985. "'Mummies and Babies' and Friends and Lovers in Lesotho." *Journal of Homosexuality* 2 (3–4): 97–116.

Gill, Debby. 1992. *Lesotho, a Gender Analysis: A Report Prepared for the Swedish International Development Authority*. Lesotho: Sechaba Consultants.

Greenberg, David E. 1988. *The Construction of Homosexuality*. Chicago: University of Chicago Press.

Internet World Factbook. 1996.: http\www\world.

Jackson, Margaret. 1987. "'Facts of Life' or the Eroticization of Women's Oppression? Sexology and the Social Construction of Heterosexuality." In Pat Caplan, ed., *The Cultural Construction of Sexuality*, pp. 52–81. London: Tavistock.

Jenness, Valerie. 1992. "Coming Out: Lesbian Identities and the Categorization Problem." In Ken Plummer, ed., *Modern Homosexualities: Fragments of Lesbian and Gay Experience*, pp. 65–74. London: Routledge.

Kendall [Kathryn]. 1993. "Ways of Looking at Agnes de Castro." In Ellen Donkin and Susan Clement, eds., *Upstaging Big Daddy: Directing Theatre as if Race and Gender Matter*, pp. 107–120. Ann Arbor: University of Michigan Press.

———. 1990. "Finding the Good Parts: Sexuality in Women's Tragedies in the Time of Queen Anne." In Mary Ann Schofield and Cecilia Macheski, eds., *Curtain Calls: An Anthology of Essays on Eighteenth-Century Women in Theatre*, pp. 165–176. Columbus: Ohio University Press.

———. 1986. "From Lesbian Heroine to Devoted Wife: Or, What the Stage Would Allow." *Journal of Homosexuality* 12 (3/4): 9–22.

Lorber, Judith. 1994. *Paradoxes of Gender*. New Haven: Yale University Press.

Nthunya, Mpho 'M'atsepo. 1995. "'M'alineo Chooses Me." In K. Limakatso Kendall, ed., *Basali! Stories by and about Basotho Women*, pp. 4–7. Pietermaritzburg: University of Natal Press.

———. 1997. *Singing Away the Hunger: Stories of a Life in Lesotho*. Ed. K. Limakatso Kendall. Pietermaritzburg: University of Natal Press, 1996. Reprint, Bloomington: Indiana University Press.

Richardson, Diane. 1992. "Constructing Lesbian Sexualities." In Ken Plummer, ed., *Modern Homosexualities*, pp. 187–199. London: Routledge.

Shepherd, Gill. 1987. "Rank, Gender, and Homosexuality: Mombasa as a Key to Understanding Sexual Options." In Pat Caplan, ed., *The Cultural Construction of Sexuality*, pp. 240–270. London: Tavistock.

Thai, Bethuel. 1996. "Laws Tough on Basotho Women." *Sowetan* 17.

Vicinus, Martha. 1994. "Lesbian History: All Theory and No Facts or All Facts and No Theory?" *Radical History Review* 60:57–75.

PARAPHILIAS ACROSS CULTURES

DINESH BHUGRA

As with the previous articles, the layperson's belief that human sexuality is dictated by our genes is called into serious question by a cross-cultural examination of sexual behavior. Likewise, the belief that some paraphilas (or "perversions," as some see them) are caused by some dysfunction (or "sickness") in society is also called into doubt by cross-cultural examination. It should come as no surprise that different cultures react differently to different sexual behaviors. That is, the behavior of the "audience" is culturally relative and so too is the nature of deviance.

Literature on the cultural relativity of sexual deviance is not hard to find. The following article, though, is somewhat unusual in the way it blends sociological, anthropological, and psychiatric perspectives.

INTRODUCTION

A range of "abnormal" sexual behaviors is observed and reported in the Western industrialized societies. Deviance is behavior that contravenes the norms of society. Such deviance can be defined by a number of parameters. Of these, statistical or psychopathological norms are two ways of defining abnormality or deviance. These norms usually combine the institutionalized norms or laws and the internalized or shared norms. Deviation from these norms can sometimes be easily defined, as with excessive sexual desire or "nymphomaniac" behavior, and are sometimes difficult to define, as with cross-dressing on social occasions or for party going. It is obvious that such variations are dictated by societal norms.

Psychopathological norms are much more difficult to quantify because often sociological norms are being used and medical or diagnostic norms may well follow these. This is illustrated by the inclusion of homosexuality in the medical diagnostic categories—as societies have changed their attitudes, physicians have followed suit and the diagnosis (except ego-dystonic) has been removed from the classificatory systems.

Sexual deviance is often used as a term for individuals whose sexual preferences or mores do not fall into mainstream sexual behavior. However, this remains a pejorative term so that, by definition, a negative value is being expressed. Bancroft (1989) suggests using sexual minority behavior as a term. *Paraphilia* is the current preferred term in the psychiatric literature, and will be used in the present paper.

Gagnon and Simon (1967) classified sexual deviance as normal, subcultural or individual deviance. Normal deviance includes behavior like masturbation, oral sex and premarital intercourse which, while legally or socially proscribed in some parts of the world, is practiced by large numbers of people, thereby falling within the statistical norm. Subcultural deviance is associated with particular subcultures (for example, homosexual) and will include categories of fetishism, sadomasochism, transvestism and transsexualism. These are often consensual behaviors, and their incidence is difficult to establish because individuals may not acknowledge these patterns and may well not seek help....

Sex and Societies by Bullough (1976) provides a classic account of sexual variance and society across different time periods, religions and geographical areas. He argues that male and female patterns of sexual orientation and behavior (i.e. sex roles) are attributable to acquired learning, therefore, to social and cultural factors. For example, Ford and Beach (1965) found that there was a wide variation in sexual behavior in people and cultures and, although there are many similarities, there existed differences too. For example, different societies have had widely different rules and attitudes about masturbation but, regardless of whether the attitude was one of approval or condemnation, at least some adults in all or nearly all societies appear to have masturbated.

Homosexual behavior was not found to be predominant among adults in any of the societies studied, although some homosexual behavior took place in a significant proportion of the population. In many societies, homosexuality was acceptable only in certain age groups and not others. In societies where women and men are not expected to be seen together or could appear in mixed company only under carefully controlled conditions, the need for companionship and entertainment was often served either by professional outcasts such as prostitutes or by men who acted the part of women. Some of these men-women were transvestites, others were homosexuals and, for others, the line was blurred. In addition, double standards often apply to the sexes. Men are encouraged to be promiscuous or, at least, expected to be so, whereas women are not expected to have any sexual desire at least till marriage and, even then, it may be subsumed. This is by no means a universal view.

Some societies, according to Bullough (1976), were sex-positive (that does not mean that they condoned promiscuity, only that their attitudes to sex are relatively free) and others sex-negative. These attitudes towards sex-related behavior were not static and often changed in response to religion and changing political climates. For example, early Hinduism was strongly sex-positive because sex was seen as a mystic and magical activity. Contrary to prevalent beliefs elsewhere, the Hindus believed that women enjoyed sex much more than men and, in their sex manuals, considerable attention was devoted to other non-procreative purposes of sex, and a range of sexual behaviors was considered normal. The sexual act, according to various sex manuals, was to be seen as a refined form of combat. The male attacks, the woman resists and, amid the subtle interplay of advance, retreat, assault and defense, the desires are built up. However, the final result is a delightful victory for both parties. Women are said to be aroused by a show of strength and men by a show of resistance. At the height of passion, consciousness is enhanced by intensive stimulation, often through sadistic acts, because the senses have become so dulled to the unpleasantness of pain that they find sharp delight in it. During such a combat it is possible to bite, scratch, pull the hair of the partner and beat or slap with the palm of the hand, the back of the hand, the side of the hand, a half-open fist or a closed fist on the shoulders, back, bosom and buttocks (Kalyanamalla, 1964). Various types of nail marks and teeth marks are described with observations that certain kinds of marks on women are supposed to be responded to in return with only specific types of marks. These practices are discussed later when discussing various paraphilias. From such a liberal view of sex, sexual behavior and sexual activity, where temples were constructed for celebration and worship of activity, things changed with the invasions of Muslim rulers. Hindu women went into purdah and the openness of sexual mores started to change dramatically; over the past few centuries India has become relatively conservative.

Similarly in China, although the world was seen in dualistic terms, this duality was not about the conflict between the spiritual and the material, rather it looked to the inherent unity of opposing forces with the individual. Sexual union of the male and female was like the intermingling of heaven and earth—essential to achieving harmony as well as a happy and healthy sex life. Several manuals described the secrets of intercourse, though most of them have been destroyed (Bullough, 1976). Of various sexual positions described, a few included a third party; thus polygamy or multi-partner sexual activity was acceptable. Males were expected to satisfy more than one wife without ejaculating. For this purpose, clear guidelines were given on the frequency of intercourse as well as its timing. Initially, women were seen as superior or equal to men, but gradually their status was lowered. Foreplay was encouraged and oral sex was permitted. Sexual intercourse with prostitutes was accepted, although semen loss was not encouraged. Manipulation of sexual organs without orgasm was encouraged. Balls were placed inside the vagina to heighten the pleasures of sexual intercourse or masturbation. Special instruments, soaked mushrooms and other materials were also placed inside the vagina to achieve sexual pleasure.

Eunuchs fulfilled a valuable function in China, being allowed free access to the palaces and yet not being a threat because they were seen as incomplete men. They were also known to engage in homosexual activity, especially passive activity, because the anus was supposed to have a highly developed sense of touch which made the activity pleasurable. Women changing into men and men changing into women were described. It is difficult to say whether this change was anatomical or psychological. However, transvestitism was institutionalized on stage. From this relatively open and positive attitude to sexual variations in ancient China, the country has certainly become less positive today: for example, in the Chinese diagnostic system, homosexuality is still recorded as a mental illness....

Sex-negative societies are likely to encourage individuals to see sexual behavior as duty, secretive and something to be shunned or indulged in only for specific purposes.... Ford and Beach (1965) reported that, of 78 relatively primitive societies, 49 approved or tolerated homosexuality in some form. Of the total 190 societies studied, they observed that heterosexual coitus was the prevalent form of sexual behavior for the majority of adults in all human societies, but this is rarely the only sexual activity indulged in. Although the actual sexual position may be different in some societies, the initiation of sexual intercourse in some cultures is encouraged to be by the female partner.

There are several societies in Ford and Beach's sample where couples indulge in a minimum of sexual foreplay. Kissing is a ubiquitous item in the sex play in most societies. However, there are some peoples among whom kissing is unknown and it is equated with a dirty practice of eating saliva and dirt. Thus it would appear that some cultures pay little attention to foreplay which includes kissing. There were at least some cultures where penetration was the key factor and no foreplay or afterplay was described. These were largely preliterate societies where obviously sexual behavior was for the purposes of procreation only.

For nearly every human society, sexual intercourse is usually preceded by some degree of sensory stimulation and is often accompanied by stimulation, often visual or tactile. Visual stimulation is often of the individual partner, but sometimes this stimulation is related to a body part or part of clothing in achieving sexual excitement. Among societies where a minimum of such activity is carried out, it is possible that fetishistic sexual activity may well be lower. In the absence of concrete data, it is difficult to ascertain whether individual fetishistic behaviors are affected by the proliferate nature of the society or the socio-centrism of the individual. Within each culture and society there are variations too, both in pre-intercourse stimulation and foreplay. Some couples may well practice elaborate forms of genital manipulation, whereas others who may have bad feelings about sex or their partner may wish to skip the preliminaries. Breast stimulation and kissing as forms of sexual stimulation are more or less restricted to the human species, whereas preliminary stimulation of genital organs has more ancient phylogenetic origin (Ford & Beach, 1965).

The infliction of physical pain is often associated with sexual excitement, and this process is regular and characteristic in many human societies. In many cultures, individuals whose stereotype of intense lovemaking includes scratching, biting and pulling of the hair of the partner in sexual excitement are seen. There are also societies in which these forms of sexual stimulation are totally absent. Ford and Beach (1965) observe that societies which incorporate painful stimulation in the approved forms of foreplay also provide ample opportunity for individuals to develop and learn the facilitative effects of the resulting sensations. These behaviors are not indiscriminate but occur at certain times, in certain places and under certain circumscribed conditions. In most societies, sexual intercourse takes place in seclusion, although in some cultures it could be in public but not in front of children and not in places where children might come across the copulating couple. Societies living in unpartitioned multiple dwellings are more likely to have outdoor sex.

Some societies will have sex only at night (irrespective of individuals' preferences) because to be seen copulating is a source of great shame and day time coitus is too risky. Only a few societies prefer sex only during the day because children conceived in darkness may be born blind.

SEXUAL ATTRACTION

There are few, if any, universal standards of sexual attractiveness. The physical characteristics which are regarded as sexually stimulating vary appreciably from one society to another. In most societies, the physical beauty of the female receives more explicit consideration than that of the male. This may go some way towards explaining why men get turned on by objects. These selected female traits include plump body build, small ankles, elongated labia majora, large clitoris or pendulous breasts.

In some societies, bestiality is tolerated (even though seen as unnatural, silly and disgusting, and inferior to normal sexual activity) in the absence of more appropriate sexual behavior. Such contact is often seen as inadequate and is sometimes allowed for teenage males. There are at least four societies in which animal contacts are practiced and do not meet with condemnation (Ford & Beach, 1965). Such a variation reflects the influence of learning and social channelization.

Similarly, adult masturbation is tolerated in some societies and encouraged in others, but the double standards in response to male and female masturbation remain. The relative infrequency of adult masturbation in some societies is said to be the result of socialization (Ford & Beach, 1965). In societies which are restrictive in their attitudes to sex, teenagers may suppress their sexual desire but it is unlikely that no sexual activity takes place. Where boys are less carefully watched than girls, it appears that youths are able to circumvent the barriers. In semi-restrictive societies, formal prohibitions exist but are apparently not very serious, and are not enforced. Sexual experimentation may take place in secrecy but without incurring punishment. Permissive societies have a permissive and tolerant attitude towards sex expression in childhood. Girls are expected to remain virgins until marriage in restrictive societies, whereas in the other two types, such expectations, if they exist at all, are not obvious. Actual sexual behavior develops somewhat more rapidly in certain societies than in others.

CULTURE AND BEHAVIOR

Intracultural and intercultural behaviors are affected to a degree by learning behaviors. With increasing globalization, industrialization and the spread of global media, very few societies and cultures have been left isolated. Attitudes of a society towards certain sexual activities and behaviors are key factors in the way individuals adopt and enjoy a passive or an active role in the sexual relationship. The emphasis on the feminine means that females are encouraged not to take the lead in sexual intercourse and to be passive; they are less likely to experience clear-cut sexual orgasm. Although some patterns of sexual behavior are reflexive incorporation of painful stimulation (sadomasochistic activity), the culturally accepted patterns of precoital play and the type of response to such stimulation are strongly influenced by learning. In societies where sexual excitement is associated with the experience of being scratched or bitten, these feelings become eroticized, and it is possible that no or limited enjoyment occurs without such actions. Similar foreplay techniques in other cultures may not produce similar results.

PARAPHILIAS ACROSS CULTURES

The field of paraphilias across cultures is severely limited. Although a fetish is defined as a magical erotic or love icon, its existence across cultures is by no means confirmed in the sense that individuals can out-perform sexually in its presence. Of the four paraphilias to be considered here, fetishism is probably quite common, although the rates are derived from those who attend clinics. There is general agreement that fetishism is rare in women. The principal categories of sexual signal or stimulus have been considered by Bancroft (1989). These are a part of the body or an intimate extension of the body, e.g. a piece of clothing and a source of specific tactile stimulation. The determinants of fetishism are many, and social learning theory must be seen to play an important role. There is virtually no literature reporting fetishism from non-industrialized countries....

Bancroft (1989) argues a majority of fetishes can be understood as an extension of the loved one which acquires special importance if there are other factors or causes of anxiety blocking the development of a more appropriate sexual relationship. Under these circumstances it makes sense that, in societies where sexual love may have amorphous meaning and the individual's concept of the self is socio-centric rather than egocentric, the likelihood of being attracted to high heels, leather, rubber or boots may be low. In cases where fetishes are extremely bizarre and cannot be understood as extensions of the body, but are more likely to be associated with some neurological abnormality such as temporal lobe epilepsy, the stimulus may be random, and it is possible that cases may occur across cultures. As discussed, sado-masochistic behavior is more likely to occur across cultures especially if it develops as part of sexual foreplay and individuals accept it.

Of the remaining two paraphilias, transvestism and transexualism are quite interesting. Cross-dressing occurs in most societies and throughout history, and is also less likely to be a true paraphilia. Bhugra and de Silva (1996) postulate that for uniforms to work as fetish or individuals to dress in uniforms for sexual performance can be a reflection of fashion or fantasy. The sexual significance of cross-dressing is incredibly complex. Bancroft (1989) divides this group into four types; the fetishistic transvestite, the transsexual, the double-role transvestite and the homosexual transvestite. The sexual relationships of cross-dressers vary accordingly.

In their cross-cultural study of the sexual thoughts of children, Goldman and Goldman (1982) found that 50% of boys and 9.5% of girls expressed aversion to their biological sex. This reaction peaked in adolescence, with 30% of 13-year-old boys in Australia and 20% in the USA expressing such feelings which, by contrast, were virtually absent in Sweden. Bancroft (1989) suggests that the more rigid the sex role stereotypes in a society, the greater the likelihood of this gender dysphoria. Thus, rigid expectations could produce anxiety and insecurity about gender identity, for which transsexual ideas would offer one method of coping. Consequently, Australia has a greater number of transsexuals seeking help than does Sweden. Similarly, Australian gay males see themselves as more strongly feminine than their counterparts in Sweden (Ross et al., 1981; Ross, 1983).

The heterogeneity of sexual behavior and societies in which they occur suggests that males are more likely to have fetishistic tendencies and that the development of sexual identity is dictated by social and cultural factors, thereby producing variation in rates of different fetishistic behaviors.

Several authors (Caplan, 1987; Herdt, 1990a, 1990b; Herdt & Stoller, 1990) have argued that intersexes may not be discomfited by issues of sex and gender identity. Yet across cultures this identity may not conform to that coinciding with the Western binary mode of gender assignment. Herdt (1990b), in contrast to the Western notion of binary gender (male vs. female), calls for a three-sex code system because some societies are more flexible about the fit between gender identity and gender classification and emphasize the social context, ideology, socialization and gender development. Such an individual in this cultural milieu is neither a man nor a woman, nor a man wanting to be a woman (or vice versa) but belongs to a distinct third category. Other similar categories based on social and cultural categories have been described (David & Whitten, 1987). Jacobs and Roberts (1989) suggest that (even) three genders may not be enough to capture the complexity of the ethnographic material. Different gender designations are reflected in some Latin American settings (Parker, 1991).

It must be emphasized that gender identity may not bear any relation to sexual arousal. Sexual identity, cross-dressing and sexual orientation are not on a direct continuum but discrete independent categories (Callender & Kochens, 1986). There remain several problems in this classification and, as noted, the binary model is not necessarily applicable to many other societies.

CULTURE-BOUND SYNDROMES

Davis (1996) highlights the fact that these syndromes have implications for understanding fertility concerns and concerns with sexual performance in certain cultures and certain ethnic groups. She argues that there is a danger inherent in the psychiatric fascination with these exotic syndromes, through which clinicians and researchers alike reduce considerations of cultural sensitivity and turn these sexual disorders into colorful high-profile conditions, overlooking the extent to which all the sexual disorders of DSM-IV are culture-bound.

Bhugra and Jacob (1997) describe the pitfalls inherent in this preoccupation. A better term may be culture-specific syndromes. These syndromes are more often than not associated with sexual disorders of desire and performance. The debate over whether these are universalist or relativist syndromes is by no means over, and another complication is the lack of a clear set of definitions or inclusion criteria. There is some evidence that *dhat* (or the semen-loss anxiety syndrome) symptoms do occur in different cultures, though the presentation for help is quite variable. Quite often, these syndromes also cover underlying anxiety and mood disorders, and this overlay may color the physician's perceptions and methods of assessment as well.

The cultural constructions of these symptoms and syndromes is of interest to clinicians. Cultural constructionists insist that, to develop culturally sensitive understandings of human sexuality and sexual behavior, one must move beyond the simple assumptions and simplistic assessment of how select features of sexuality of other cultural and ethnic groups fit into or vary from that propounded by Western society as reflected by Western medicine (Davis, 1996). It would therefore make sense to move away from a classificatory-based system to an emphasis on questioning and analyzing the constructions of these categories as culture-bound. Foucault (1978) argues for a reassessment of the nature and applicability of these categories across historical, ethnic and ethnographic tenets. Thus sexuality has to be viewed not as a fixed or given biological or psychic entity—instead sexualities are constantly practiced, altered, modified and amended, as are the meanings and categories attributed to them. Davis (1996) suggests that the critique of the concept of paraphilias is culture-bound and based on outdated constraints of Western medicine. In Papua New Guinea, Herdt and Stoller (1990) found that man-boy sex was common and oral sex and swallowing of the semen were part of the rites of passage, and yet this concept does not reflect Western concepts of pedophilia. It has been argued that pedophilia is a Western culture-bound syndrome and reflects Western views of sex as an (egocentric) individual personal responsibility, with some emphasis on biological reductionism (Rubin, 1984), since Western sexualities are structured within an extremely punitive social framework, where an excess of significance is associated with differences in sexual acts and unfit forms of sexual desire (especially those that deviate from practices with reproductive potential). Similar arguments can be directed at the classificatory categories of sexual dysfunction and functions of sexual desire. More importantly, however, similar observations can he made about the treatment packages being made available based on Western (eurocentric) models.

Davis (1996) argues that Kraft-Ebing was the person responsible for the categorization of paraphilias (and also for their medicalization). The search for cultural relativity among these norms and values may well have done a disservice to patients and those seeking help. For "paraphiliac" sexual disorders may not have a parallel in all countries (Kendell, 1991). Most standard paraphilias are unique to Western societies. They have been linked to the non-availability of sexual partners and the primacy of masturbatory behavior (Meikle, 1982; Weatherford, 1986). However we know masturbatory behavior is almost universal—as is the lack of sexual partners up to a certain age—so how is it that they are so common in Western societies. Gebhard (1971) explains this as a result of living in complex societies where individuals can evade social sanctions through anonymous behaviors. It is also likely that, as these activities are egocentric and individualistic, social sanctions are few and far between and, where they exist, are part of a legal framework.

Clinical studies of culture, ethnicity, race and paraphilias are rare. The critique of the categories of paraphilias is wide and comes from a variety of sources such as feminists (Irvine, 1990; Teifer, 1998), historians (D'Emilio & Freedman, 1989; Weeks, 1985), social scientists (Reiss, 1996; Puieroba, 1988), and members of sexual minorities (Ullerstam, 1966; Weeks, 1985).…

CONCLUSIONS

There is little doubt that paraphilias are, by and large, a Western culture-specific syndrome, although transsexualism is more likely to be reported from other societies. However, this reporting depends upon the availability of certain services and how individuals use these services. The exact rates have to be established. It is highly unlikely that non-industrialized societies where sexual behavior is procreative will have many cases of paraphilias. Social, rather than biological, factors are more likely to play a key role in the etiology of paraphilias.

REFERENCES

Bancroft, J. (1989) *Human Sexuality and its Problems* (Edinburgh, Churchill Livingstone).

Bughra D. & De Silva, P. (1996) Uniforms: fact, fashion, fantasy and fetish, *Sexual and Marital Therapy*, 11, pp. 393–406.

Bhugra, D. & Jacob, K. S. (1997) Culture bound syndromes, in: D. Bughra & A. Munro (Eds), *Troublesome Disguises* (Oxford, Blackwell).

Bullough, V. I. (1976) *Sexual Variance in Society and History* (Chicago, II, University of Chicago Press).

Callender, C. & Kochens, L. (1986) Men and non men: male gender mixing statuses and homosexuality, in: E. Blackwood (Ed.) *Anthropology and Homosexual Behaviors* (New York, Howarth).

Caplan, P. (Ed.) (1987) *The Cultural Construction of Bisexuality* (London, Tavistock).

David, D. L. & Whitten, R. G. (1987) The cross-cultured study of human sexuality, *Annual Review of Anthropology*, 16, pp. 69–98.

Davis, D. L. (1996) Cultural sensitivity and the sexual disorders of DSM-IV, in: J. E. Mezzich, A. Kleinman, H. Fabraga & D. L. Parson (Eds), *Culture and Psychiatric Diagnosis* (Washington, DC, APA Press).

D'Emilio, J. & Freedman, E. (1989) *Intimate Matters* (New York, Harper and Row).

Ford, C. F. & Beach, F. (1965) *Patterns of Sexual Behavior* (London, Eyre and Spottiswoode).

Foucault, M. (1978) The History of Sexuality, Vol. 1 (New York, Pantheon).

Gagnon, J. & Simon, W. (1967) *Sexual Deviance* (New York, Harper & Row).

Gebhard, P. H. (1971) Human sexual behavior, in: H.S. Marshall & R. C. Suggs (Eds) *Human Sexual Behaviors* (New York, Basic Books).

Goldman, R. & Goldman, J. (1982) *Children's Sexual Thinking* (London: Routledge & Kegan Paul).

Herdt, G. H. (1990a) Mistaken gender, *American Anthropologist*, 92, pp. 433–446.

Herdt, G. H. (1990b) Development discontinuities and sexual orientation across cultures, in: D. McWhirter (Ed.) *Homosexuality/Heterosexuality* (New York, Oxford University Press).

Herdt, G. H. & Stoller, R. (1990) *Intimate Communications* (New York, Columbia University Press).

Irvine, L. M. (1990) *Disorders of Desire: Sex and Gender in Modern American Sexology* (Philadelphia, PA, Temple University Press).

Jacobs, S. & Roberts, C. (1999) Sex, sexuality and variance, in: S. Morgan (Ed.) *Gender and Anthropology* (Washington, DC, APA Press).

Kalyanamalla (trans. T. Ray) (1964), *Ananga Raga.* (New York, Citadel Press).

Kendell, R. (1991) Relationship between DSM-IV and ICD-10, *Journal of Abnormal Psychology*, pp. 297–301.

Meilke, S. (1982) Culture and sexual deviation, in: I. AL-ISSA (Ed.) *Culture and Psychopathology* (Baltimore, University Park Press).

Parker, R. (1991) *Bodies, Pleasures and Passions* (Boston, Beacon Press).

Puieroba, J. (1988) *Antropologia Sexual: Lectuaros de Antropologi Sexual* (Madrid, Universidad Nacional de Education Distancia).

Reiss, H. (1996) *Journey into Sexuality* (Englewood Cliffs, NJ, Prentice Hall).

Ross, M. W., Walinder, J., Lindstrom, B. & Thuwe, L. (1981) Cross-cultural approaches to trans-sexualism: a comparison between Sweden and Australia, *Acta Psychiatrica Scandinavica*, 63, pp. 75–82.

Ross, M. W. (1983) Societal relationships and gender roles in homosexuals, *Journal of Sex Research*, 19, pp. 273–288.

Rubin, G. (1984) Thinking sex: notes for a radical theory of the politics of sexuality, in: C. Vance (Ed.) *Pleasure and Danger* (Boston, MA, Routledge & Kegan Paul).

Teifer, I. (1988) A feminist critique of the sexual dysfunction nomenclature, in: E. Cole (Ed.), *Women and Sex Therapy* (New York, Haworth).

Ullerstam, I. (1966) *The Erotic Minorities* (New York, Grove Press).

Weatherford, J. M. (1986) *Porn Row* (New York, Arbor House).

Weeks, J. (1985) *Sexuality and its Discontents* (London, Routledge).

PART 4

Prostitution

PROSTITUTION AND THE STATUS OF WOMEN IN SOUTH KOREA

ROBERT HEINER

One of the reasons why people conform to the norms is their fear of being labeled deviant. That is, the potential stigma of a label serves as a powerful form of social control, of maintaining the status quo. The following article demonstrates how labeling helps to maintain the patriarchal status quo in South Korea. Note how the deviant label has a powerfully negative effect on prostitutes in Korea; but note also how the fear of being labeled has an effect on all Korean women and serves to keep them in their submissive roles.

INTRODUCTION

Functionalists have argued that if an allegedly undesirable phenomenon permeates a culture, and if it has always permeated the culture, and if it permeates other cultures as well, then it must exist for a reason. It must serve some useful function for the society. For Durkheim (1947), consensual moral aversion to crime unites a society; and therefore, crime functions to enhance social solidarity. For Erikson (1966), reactions to deviance serve as a means of publicizing those things that are not tolerated in the community; and therefore, the deviant is necessary for maintaining moral boundaries. For Davis (1937), prostitution provides a sexual outlet for the male that does not interfere with his responsibilities to his family; that is, a man utilizing the services of a prostitute is less likely to have an affair and leave his wife for another woman. In this article, it will be argued that prostitution in South Korea does indeed fulfill a function. It functions to perpetuate an extraordinarily patriarchal social structure. Namely, the fear of being labeled a prostitute keeps women dutiful and submissive. This argument will be developed once the situation regarding prostitution and the status of women in South Korea have been discussed.

This examination is based on my experiences and observations having lived for a year in South Korea, having made it a point to visit a large variety of prostitution districts, having badgered a wide variety of Korean citizens with questions about the trade, and having made contacts with "managers" (pimps) who allowed me to interview their "girls" (in all, nineteen women were interviewed). It should be noted that, due to various cultural, political, and methodological constraints, this research is largely impressionistic in nature. Prostitution is a phenomenon not openly discussed in Korea. Though rampant, it is regarded as shameful; and it is technically illegal. As anyone who has studied Korean culture knows, "Koreans are preoccupied with appearances, especially with foreigners" (Gibbons, 1988:234). While in Western cultures it is acceptable to study and write about the seamier side of society, it is much less acceptable in Korean culture. Just as the individual has face that must be guarded at all times, so does the nation; and it is considered somewhat of a betrayal to reveal to an outsider those things that might bring shame to the country.

THE HISTORY AND EXTENT OF PROSTITUTION

Prostitution is rampant in many Asian countries today. Other than being Asian and rife with prostitution, what these countries have in common is that they can trace many of their customs back to Chinese civilization which has been fiercely patriarchal and has a long tradition in prostitution. In Chinese history, and in the history of many of its "relative" cultures, infanticide, the selling, pawning, and enslavement of women were all common practices for centuries. Women were of little economic value in these cultures. When they married, they left their parents' home; and they usually married before they could contribute much to the family in terms of their labor. It was, therefore, in the interest of the family (poorer families especially) to rid themselves of the burden of raising female children. Attitudes towards women can also be traced to Confucianism which established a very strict hierarchy of authority between government and subjects, parents and children, and men and women. Writes one Koreanist, "Anyone familiar with China reads Korean ethnography with a smothering sense of deja vu" (Kendall, 1985:25). Remarkably, Korea has been more strongly influenced by Confucianism than even China (Iyer, 1988). The same history of infanticide, selling, pawning, enslavement, and prostitution of women belongs to Korea.

Also, Korea and China have in common extensive histories of tremendous economic and political unrest and social dislocation—conditions often associated with the prevalence of prostitution (cf. Cohen, 1958; Gronewold, 1982). There have been very few periods of economic and political stability throughout the thousands of years of Korean history. The 20th century was particularly tumultuous with the brutal Japanese occupation, the Korean War, the bifurcation of north and south, and the American "occupation."

Prostitution proliferates virtually every sector of Korean society. Every city has a prostitution district. Some have a street devoted to the trade. Some have a neighborhood. Some have many streets scattered throughout. Some have many neighborhoods scattered throughout. Virtually every bus and train station has a series of brothels nearby. There are even small towns devoted to the trade, especially those that cater to the American military bases—such as "Silver Town" outside of Kunsan in the south, and Sunyo-ri near the DMZ in the north—that are known as "villes." (However, the impression of those who believe that the presence of the American military is responsible for the majority of prostitution in Korea is simply incorrect. Probably more prostitutes serve Japanese tourists; and most clients are Korean nationals—cf. Kim, 1987.)

There are streets and neighborhoods where the prostitutes wait outside and approach all male passersby. More typically, there are streets and neighborhoods where the women, dressed in traditional formal attire, wait together inside rooms with a big window that opens onto the street so men can look in and choose which one they want. There are prostitutes that work all of the large and not-so-large hotels. There are prostitutes who work on the cleaning staffs of innumerable inns. There are prostitutes who work out of the bars. There are prostitutes who work in the restaurants and coffee shops. There are manicurists who ply another trade in dimly lit barbershops. There are prostitutes who work in the many Korean massage parlors. There are even prostitutes who work in the massage parlors located on the American bases. And, most likely, there are other locales where they work of which I have not been informed.

PATRIARCHY AND THE CULT OF THE MALE

The Korean female lives in a society in which it is most advantageous to be male. Sexism and sex discrimination permeate the entire culture. Males are given the best jobs, the better part of the family's inheritance, and the benefit of the doubt. The birth of a son in Korea is always a joyous event, whereas "the birth of a daughter occasions lament" (Kendall, 1980:12). In fact, "given the pressure placed on couples to produce a male heir and the ability to have legal abortions, the [Korean National] assembly [has considered] legislation forbidding doctors from performing tests capable of determining [the sex] of an unborn child" (McBeth, 1987:38). When a male baby is born, its first formal baby picture will likely be of him sitting spread-eagle, displaying the "family jewels," of which the parents are so proud. As he is growing up, relatives and friends of the family will greet and compliment him by a brisk fondling of the genitals as a way of expressing "my what a man you are!" and of signifying respect for the family for their having a male child. (Koreans planning to travel abroad must spend a day at "passport school" where, among other things, they are strongly advised not to pay their compliments to Western families by fondling their little boys' genitals.)

The female will grow up in this cult of the male—in a society where it is considered bad luck if a shopkeeper's first customer in the morning is a woman. She will quickly learn that her role is to serve men. Eventually, she will probably marry. The routes to marriage are varied: perhaps she will marry out of love; perhaps her marriage will be arranged; perhaps she will marry because her older sisters cannot marry until she is married off; or she may marry because she is approaching her thirties and will soon be over the hill. When she marries, she will find herself subservient to her husband. Traditionally, the man's world is a public one, while the wife's is private. Korean folklore venerates the woman who refuses to flee her burning home. Today, a frequently used expression referring to "wife" is *annae*, meaning "the one inside." Her husband will quite possibly go out every weekend and get rip-roaring drunk. He is very likely to make use of a prostitute on occasion. And there is more than a slight possibility that he will beat his wife with some regularity. In a national survey, "61 percent of the men queried readily admitted that they beat their wives" (Kim, 1987).

In light of this backdrop, it is probably superfluous to say that sexism plays a major role in Korean prostitution. This phenomenon simply cannot be explained without reference to the patriarchal social structure. Prostitution provides an alternative, though a painful one, to the subjugation imposed by marriage. It also provides an alternative to the subjugation imposed by the legitimate labor market. Writes Elaine Kim:

> The female entertainment industry is particularly attractive to women workers in South Korea, where employment opportunities are limited even for educated women....Women's jobs are predominantly in low-wage factory and service occupations....Women in South Korea work ten hours a month more than men, averaging 59 hours a week, the longest in the world (Kim, 1987:135).

In fact, the widespread employment of women in the factories for menial wages is one of the factors associated with Korea's current economic success. Their history of being exploited, their willingness to accept low wages, and "the Confucian expectations of a woman—that she be morally strong, self-sacrificing and submissive to men—[have] played and continue to be significant factor[s] in the economic development of the nation" (Yoo, 1985:840).

It is hardly surprising, then, that many young women are drawn to prostitution. While the average monthly salary for working women in Korea was less than 150,000 won (about $170), the average salary for the prostitutes I interviewed was about 800,000 won (about $900). Kim writes, "It is said that it is hard to find pretty bus girls or housemaids any longer, since the good-looking women are all working in the hospitality trade" (1987:136).

FACE AND FAMILY

The most striking paradox of Korean prostitution is that it is so rampant in a society where the worst of all human existences is one involving shame, where there is so much emphasis on keeping face, and where prostitution is seen as such a cause of shame and loss of face. We might expect that a cultural priority emphasizing honor would keep most people honorable;

however, such a strong demand for honor has the opposite effect. It provides a standard that is often unrealistic, and those who do not meet this standard are cast out. As labeling theory holds, once labeled and cast out, an honorable existence becomes all the more problematic.

The concept of face is inextricably connected to the Korean concept of *kibun*, perhaps best translated as "harmony of self and others." Paul Crane describes this concept:

> Perhaps the most important thing to an individual Korean is recognition of "selfhood." The state of his inner feelings, his prestige, his awareness of being recognized as a person—all these factors determine his morale, his face, or self-esteem, essentially his state of mind, which may be expressed in Korean by the word kibun (Crane, 1978:25).

If everyone in a social interaction can keep their face intact (honor), then there is kibun (harmony). Koreans will go out of their way to preserve harmony.

This emphasis on honor and harmony very often has a destructive influence on family relations. It is truly remarkable to live in Korea and hear the continuous litany on the importance of the family, and yet find that family members almost never confide in one another. Things that people are likely to confide are also things that are likely to threaten the family's honor and disrupt the family harmony. Many of the women who find their way into prostitution are women who have already felt themselves to be shamed, who could not confide in their families or who did so with disastrous consequences. A norm that is only recently beginning to change is the one requiring women to be virgins on their wedding night. (The extent to which this expectation has changed is unclear; it almost certainly depends upon the family and their place of residence.) But many of the women I interviewed, at least half (many chose not to answer my questions on the subject), were women who were sexually involved before they left home. They left because they were ashamed to admit it; or because they were prohibited from seeing their lover again; or because the tension created by their indiscretion had become unbearable. As in American society (but more so), when the child does something shameful, she or he brings shame onto the whole family. Many of these women were disowned before they turned to prostitution; and many have been disowned after they turned to prostitution.

THE SPOILED IDENTITY OF THE PROSTITUTE

To be a prostitute is to lose face; to lose face is to be an "unperson." Because of the loss of face associated with prostitution, to have a background in prostitution is to have a spoiled identity. If those with whom she interacts know of her background, then her identity is discredited; if they are not aware of her background, then her identity is discreditable (Goffman, 1974). Worse yet, in Korea to associate with an "unperson" is to compromise one's own face, one's own personhood. It is, therefore, important to the Korean to be always on guard, ready to discredit the discreditable.

It is difficult to overstate how attuned Koreans are to the social background of another. As big as the United States is, having once been a dumping ground for England's criminals, and with as much social mobility that has taken place here, it is difficult for Americans to imagine a country in which one cannot escape one's background. In Korea, it is not so easy. Crane addresses this problem of no-escape in his discussion of social relationships gone sour:

> In a tight little country surrounded by water and a hostile boundary to the north, there is no place to escape from the wrath of the enemy. For most people, this means that they must endure when they are under attack or go and hide until the heat subsides.... Rarely does a foreigner get more than a peep into the seething, bubbling cauldron of hates and fears and subtle attacks that pressure the average person in Korea, who lacks the mobility of most Americans (Crane, 1978:31).

Even in the large and populous country of China a hundred years ago, Gronewold (1982) says that it was almost impossible to escape one's background. Communities were tight-knit; and the newly arrived stranger, whose true background was unknown, was assumed to have the worst of backgrounds.

Koreans are acutely aware of any signs of suspect status. The labeling of deviance is easily facilitated under such conditions. As Lofland points out (1969), when there are a "large number of alternatively sufficient indicators," people can be successfully labeled when they meet one of any number of criteria. Flashy dress, employment on an American base, employment as an actress or in other fields of entertainment, employment in certain neighborhoods, living alone without family coming to visit, unfeminine behavior—these are just a few of the conditions that might eventuate in the label of "prostitute." As labeling theory holds, whether or not one engages in deviant behavior is less important than whether or not one is labeled deviant, because once one is labeled, he or she *is* deviant (Schur, 1971).

Prostitutes in Korea suffer all the conditions associated with stigma described by Goffman (1974). The more salient of these include the following. First, they are regarded as less than human by those who are aware of their spoiled identity. Second, their discreditability drives a wall between them and their family and their past. Separating them from their past, their stigma, in effect, means the reconstitution of their entire identity. Third, they live in fear that one day in the future, after they have left the "business" and thought they had "passed" as normal, someone will denounce them. (Many of the women I interviewed expressed hopes of one day getting married, but explained that they were terrified that one day their past would be discovered by their future husbands.) Finally, when they are interacting with someone who does not know of their discreditability, they are aware of the unsettling fact that this person would shun them if he or she knew the truth about their background.

AND THE PATRIARCHY GOES ON

There are, of course, an intricate variety of means by which patriarchal domination is maintained and enhanced in Korea, as in all other patriarchal societies. One of these means in Korea is through the institution of prostitution. Prostitution involves the exploitation of women in the service of men. This position has been well established. However, prostitution in Korea is also a means of subjugating *all* women, not just those involved in the trade. The fact that so many women are involved makes it all the more feasible that any particular woman is or has been involved. In order to stave off the suspicion of their involvement, it becomes necessary for women to strictly adhere to their assigned (submissive) roles in society. To stray from this role is to invite the label of "prostitute," which means reconstitution of herself for the worst. If she divorces her husband, he will probably get the kids, and she will have to reestablish herself by herself. A woman living alone invites suspicion. If a woman works on an American base or as an entertainer, she might be exposed to ideas that would challenge male domination; but she will also be inviting the label. If she behaves in an "unladylike" manner, she will, by definition, be challenging the norms governing relations between men and women; but she will also be inviting the label. Aside from prostitution, most of the things a woman could do that might eventuate in the label "prostitute" are things that, in one way or another, pose a challenge to patriarchal relations between men and women.

If prostitution is critical in maintaining the moral/patriarchal boundaries in society as I have argued, then, according to Erikson (1966), reactions to deviance that allegedly discourage it may, in actuality, encourage it. Indeed, this is the case. Many might suppose that the defamatory nature of the label "prostitute" would act to discourage prostitution. However, the ease with which this label is meted out acts as a propellent rather than a repellant. Korean culture has set a vicious cycle in motion. Insistence on adherence to strict ethical principles has led to the "fall" of multitudes of women. The existence of multitudes of fallen women has given rise to a situation in which all women are possibly suspect. When all women are possibly suspect, people become even more attuned to moral strictures in order to identify the status of another, or to demonstrate their own virtuous status. The result is an insistence on adherence to strict ethical principles, which leads to the fall of multitudes of women. And thus, a steady supply of deviant women is insured. To paraphrase Erikson: the prostitute is not a bit of debris spun out by faulty machinery, but an integral component of patriarchal domination.

REFERENCES

Cohen, Yehudi (1958). "The sociology of commercialized prostitution in Okinawa." *Social Forces*, 37, December, 160–168.

Crane, Paul (1978). *Korean Patterns* Seoul, South Korea; The Royal Asiatic Society and Kwangjin Publishing Co.

Davis, Kingsley (1937). "The sociology of prostitution." *American Sociological Review*, 2, 744–755.

Durkheim, Emile (1947). *The Division of Labor in Society.* trans. by G. Simpson. New York: Free Press.

Erikson, Kai (1966). *Wayward Puritans.* New York: John Wiley.

Gibbons, Boyd (1988). "The South Koreans." *National Geographic,* 174 (August), 232–257.

Goffman, Erving (1974). *Stigma: Notes on the Management of Spoiled Identity.* New York: Prentice Hall.

Gronewald, Sue (1982). *Beautiful Merchandise: Prostitution in China, 1860–1936.* Institute for Research in History and Haworth Press.

Iyer, Pico (1988). "The yin and the yang of paradoxical, prosperous Korea." *Smithsonian,* 19 (August). 45–58.

Kendall, Laurel (1980). "Suspect saviors of Korean hearths and homes." *Asia,* 3 (May/June). 12+.

Kendall, Laurel (1985). *Shamans, Housewives, and other Restless Spirits: Women in Korean Ritual Life.* Honolulu: University of Hawaii Press.

Kim, Elaine (1987). "Sex tourism in Asia: A reflection of political and economic inequality." In E. Yu and E. Phillips. eds. *Korean Women in Transition.* pp. 127–144. Los Angeles: Center for Korean-American and Korean Studies, California State University.

Lofland, John (1969). *Deviance and Identity.* Englewood Cliffs, N.J.: Prentice-Hall.

McBeth, John (1987). "A family feud for Confucians and women." *Far Eastern Economic Review,* 135 (26) February. 38–41.

Schur, Edwin (1971). *Labeling Deviant Behavior: Its Sociological Implications.* New York: Harper and Row.

Yoo, Ok-Za (1985). "Korean women in the home and the work place." *Korea and World Affairs,* 9 (Winter). 820–872.

BIG SISTER IS WATCHING YOU!

Gender Interaction and the Unwritten Rules of the Amsterdam Red-Light District

MANUEL B. AALBERS

Everyday social interactions are governed by rules. Nowhere are these rules written down, yet almost all of us know them and follow them intuitively. While we might expect that deviant behaviors are less likely to be guided by these unwritten rules, sociologists who study people who provide substances or services that are either illegal or of questionable legitimacy—such as prostitutes and drug dealers—have found that the transactions between these providers and their customers are often highly stylized and ritualized. So stylized are these interactions that they are often analogous to a theatrical performance. Note how these concepts of interaction rules and performance appear in the following observations of the red-light district in Amsterdam.

Windows offer the sensation of great openness: culture flows through these windows, as it were, from private to public spaces and vice versa. It may be a conspicuous claim that "I have something to trade," made by a scantily dressed young woman in a window framed by red neon lights.... Through the window the market displays its goods, and forms of life other than one's own can be inspected, at least surreptitiously, in passing. And this is a two-way flow, for windows allow you to keep an eye on the street scene. (Hunnerz, 1993, pp. 154–155.)

Habermas (1962) views public space foremost as the domain of communication, and in the red-light district, voyeurism concentrates preeminently on the communicative function of windows. Window prostitution is the ultimate example of "invited voyeurism." According to Brunt (1996), urban public life revolves mainly around watching and being watched. This is even more the case in a red-light district than in other urban public areas.

Prostitutes are watched by visitors to the area, but the prostitutes themselves also watch the people who pass by their windows. In this case, voyeurism is executed not only in its most extreme but also in its purest form: Nowhere else is "people watching" as important as here.

As Tani (2002, p. 349) argues. "Usually, the media and the literature on prostitution emphasize the subject/object relationship between men and women, representing men as active sex-hunters and women as passive victims." In other words, life in a red-light district reinforces the ideas many people still have of the man as hunter and the woman as gatherer (cf. Brunt, 1996). After all, men roam around looking for their "prey" while the women behind the windows are the ones who allow themselves to be hunted. These women's purpose is to gather men. After all, if they do not gather any men, they do not earn any money. Furthermore, the women are not mobile, while the men must track down the women and thus take initiative.

Is the situation as simple as it seems? How do men and window prostitutes communicate with each other? Are the men the only ones who hunt, or do the women hunt too? Are the men all tough hunters, or do they also allow themselves to be hunted? In other words, to what extent is the image of the man as hunter and the woman as gatherer in a red-light district correct? How do men choose a woman and in what ways do women pick a man? Who is watching and who is being watched? Also, we may ask how people protect their privacy in a place where securing privacy is highly regarded but complete anonymity is not guaranteed. Arising from all these questions is the core issue of this study: What social rules apply in a red-light district? The answers to these questions paint a picture of one component of the structure of urban life and of its inhabitants and their culture, which is part of this life. Window prostitution should in this respect not be viewed as something that is outside social reality, but as an aspect of it (see Aalbers, Bodaar, Kloosterman, and Pinkster, 2004): "We must then accept these 'moral regions' and the more or less eccentric and exceptional people who inhabit them, in a sense, at least, as part of the natural, if not the normal, life of a city" (Park, 1952, p. 51).

OVERVIEW

I addressed study questions within the context of an empirical case study and through a discussion drawing on the insights of several disciplines, including urban anthropology, social psychology, geography, gender studies, and urban sociology. In the next section I discuss the importance of privacy in public space and in particular in a red-light district with a view to the work of Lyn Lofland and Erving Goffman. Next, the structure of the research is discussed, followed by the results of the research project, based on Lodewijk Brunt's discussion on the different styles of hunting. In the subsequent sections, I discuss these styles of hunting in light of the work of Goffman and Lofland, as it relates to the assumed passive sexual role of women and assumed active role of men. In this segment, I use the work of Phil Hubbard, among others, to argue that the presence of prostitution disrupts sexual and spatial orders. In the final subsection of the Discussion section, I argue that life in a red-light district is regulated by unwritten rules and implicit social regulation.

SETTING

The setting for this study was the red-light district "De Wallen" in Amsterdam. It is important to note that in The Netherlands, prostitution has been legalized since 2000. However, legalization does not mean that prostitution is left completely to the free market: In The Netherlands, it is currently more regulated than it was prior to legalization. Examples include the use of brothel licensing to control illegal immigration and taxation of registered prostitutes, which also enables legal action against nonlicensed prostitutes offering their services (cf. Brants, 1998: Outshoorn, 2004). Contrary to the impressions of many foreigners, Dutch citizens in general do not support or encourage prostitution and sexual commerce (Wonders, 2004). Nonetheless, in The Netherlands, prostitution is much more accepted as a social fact than elsewhere. Brants calls this "regulated tolerance": Even before being codified in legislation, it involved "self-regulation, enforced if necessary through administrative rules, but always with the criminal law as a threat in the background," although, "it is not an offense to make use of the services of a prostitute" or to offer services as a prostitute (Brants, 1998, pp. 624–625). Because of the unique situation in The Netherlands, Amsterdam's major red-light district De Wallen is not just associated with danger, immorality, drugs, and crime (Hubbard. 1997), but also with tolerance, excitement, and freedom, making De Wallen one of Amsterdam's major tourist attractions.

> In Amsterdam, the commodification of bodies has been perfected to an art form. The red-light district resembles the modern open-air shopping mall in the United States. Relatively clean streets, little crime, and neon atmosphere and windows and windows of women to choose from—every size, shape, and color (though not in equal amounts). The red-light district seems designed to be a tourist's Mecca. The range of services for the leisure traveler includes sex clubs, sex shows, lingerie and S&M clothing shops, condomeries, and a sprinkling of porno shops. But the character of Amsterdam's red-light district is different from most other sex tourist locations because it is centered in a historic district…and surrounded by a well-established residential neighborhood. (Wonders and Michalowski, 2001, p. 553)

The commodification of sex is not very hidden in the De Wallen, and commerce is indeed open to everyone…. Unlike other red-light districts, De Wallen is not visited only by heterosexual men seeking sexual pleasure and members of groups that are usually seen as "undesirables"—although there are indeed many of these people—but also by locals there for other purposes. The crowd on the street includes locals passing through on walks as well as couples, women, homosexual men, business people, and families with grandparents and children in tow (Wonders, 2004). The Amsterdam red-light district announces itself slowly. Both physically and socially, the area is not very strictly separated from its surroundings, and borders appear relatively porous. The occasional sex shop can be found on the adjacent streets among cultural institutions, respectable cafes, child-care facilities, and residential housing (often located above the window brothels and the sex shops). This does not imply, however, that De Wallen is no different from the rest of the city. As I will show in this paper, the Amsterdam red-light district is characterized by its own set of socially and spatially defined rules.

PRIVACY IN PUBLIC SPACE

People have different strategies to "survive" in public space. The more threatening a situation is, the more people will use these strategies. Goffman (1971) names eight territories of the self. These territories are determined according to place and situation, and their importance also varies situationally. Firstly, there is a distinction between public space and private space. The protection of privacy is more important in public space (frontstage in Goffman's terminology) than in private space (backstage in Goffman's terminology). Additionally, the preservation of a certain territory can be more important in some places in public space than in others (Goffman, 1971). In certain situations—for instance, on a crowded subway train—people are forced to drop their claim to a certain territory. The question is, to what extent do these territories of the self play a role in human behavior in a red-light district? And which territories play the most important roles in this environment?

Lofland (1973) also addresses the ways in which people protect their privacy in public space. People react to the unordinary by becoming familiar with it, giving it a place, or ignoring and excluding it (Deben & Rings, 1999; Lofland, 1973). According to Lofland, living with strangers is possible because we have stripped some of them of their strangeness. We have to protect ourselves from others. We do this by, among other things, creating a symbolic shield of privacy in public spaces. Lofland describes six ways in which this shield is created. Two of these tactics are of great importance to the gender interaction in a red-light district. The first is to minimalize expression. A neutral facial expression will not provoke irritation in others and it also protects one's privacy by not revealing emotion. On the other hand, singing and speaking to oneself in public spaces are seen as a taboo in Western society.

The second tactic is to minimalize eye contact, as focusing on someone in public space might invade his or her privacy. This does not mean that observing others is forbidden. On the contrary, it is often pleasing to some people to be observed because it acknowledges their self-esteem (Lofland, 1973). However, social interaction is contingent not only on the individuals involved but also on the sexualized nature of the surroundings (Hubbard, 2000). The question is whether the principles described by Lofland are discernible when prostitutes and (potential) clients make contact, or if they must drop these privacy shields to be able to make contact. Especially in a red-light district, many people may be reluctant to give up their privacy shield, but dropping it may be essential to making contact.

METHODS

To answer this question. I observed prostitutes and potential visitors at different times and at different locations in the biggest and most famous red-light district of Amsterdam, locally known as "De Wallen."

...After choosing De Wallen as the location. I needed to select the technique for observation. By remaining in one location. I could quietly observe. However, such standing still would clearly distinguish me from the other men in the redlight district. Thus I chose participant observation: "just" walking about much like the other people. Had I, for example, observed only the alley called "Trompetsteeg," I might have concluded that the initiative was mainly taken by men, while observing only "Boomsteeg" would have suggested that the initiative was for the most part taken by women. Therefore, I made observations throughout the red-light district as a whole instead of in only one specific area....

Logically, participation in the group of prostitutes was...difficult for me (a male) than it might be for female researchers.... To access the women as well, I also made contact with about 30 prostitutes after several days of simple observation. This involved brief informal conversations with the women about their attitudes regarding the men who pass by their windows. Contrary to my expectations, a strikingly high number of women did not object to such conversations, as long as they did not take too long. I presented myself as a passerby who was interested in their opinion and did not introduce my status as a researcher. This position of anonymous researcher, both with regard to the prostitutes and to the visitors of the red-light district, can be easily justified: Neither prostitutes nor clients are identified by name or other personal details in this study, nor were they compromised in any other way during this research project or by the results of it....

RESULTS

Styles of Hunting

Observations in De Wallen did not support the hunter-gatherer characterization. I found that there was not just one method of initiating encounters in the red-light district. In some cases the man clearly took the initiative, in others the woman. Often it was not crystal clear who was leading the initiative, and a shared initiative occurred. More useful than two or three categories is a scale of taking initiative on which every position is possible. The forms of "solitary hunting" described in the next subsection are the ones closest to the extremes, while the forms of "hunting together" in the subsequent subsection are the ones located more in the middle of this scale. This classification serves as a heuristic device, a way of looking at reality, rather than reality itself.

The Dutch sociologist/anthropologist Brunt (1996) described three different styles of hunting: the encirclement, the direct approach, and the natural approach. The discrete and cautious encirclement occurs mostly in the shared initiative: "The hunter positions himself strategically in the scope of the prey, in order to enable nonverbal communication in the form of body language, and especially eye contact. Were this to result in any encouragement, the hunter moves up [or the roles of hunter and gatherer/prey are switched], until the ultimate step is taken and the prey is approached directly" (Brunt, 1996, p. 66, my translation). The direct approach occurs with both the man and woman as initiator. "In this strategy, the hunter does not hide his intentions and goes straight after his goal" (Brunt, 1996, p. 66, my translation). Both these styles of hunting are mostly used in combination with the natural approach. "In the natural approach deliberation is made use of, it is all about a stylized form of not being committed. The hunter puts the emphasis on being 'spontaneous,'...taking surroundings and context into consideration" (Brunt, 1996, p. 67, my translation).

Even though the empirical case in this research project was limited to one of two red-light districts in Amsterdam, the different styles of hunting and ways to take initiative are found beyond Amsterdam. In other red-light districts one can also find different strategies in which the man is not always the hunter, nor the woman always the gatherer. A good example of this is Wonders and Michalowski's (2001) description of the interaction between a male tourist and a female prostitute in Havana's (sex) tourist district. Although Wonders and Michalowski used the following observation to contrast the soft-sell sex trade in Havana to the hard-sell sex trade in Amsterdam, their research also shows that female initiative is common in two very different cultural and spatial contexts. In fact, they show that prostitutes in Havana approach men using a combination of two of the three styles of hunting-encirclement and the natural approach:

> A woman, usually decades younger than the object of her immediate interest, approaches a foreign tourist. Brandishing a cigarette, she asks for a light, or maybe points to her wrist and asks for the time. The opening gambit leads to other questions: Where are you from? Where are you going? For a walk? Would you like me to walk with you? Have you been to such-and-such disco? Would you like me to take you there? If the mark seems interested, the woman turns the subject to sex, describing the pleasures she can give, often with no mention of price unless the man asks. If they agree to go off to a disco or for a drink, the subject of sex may not even be openly discussed. (Wonders and Michalowski, 2001, p. 559)

Solitary Hunting: The Direct Yet Natural Approach

In this study, when men took the initiative, they were straightforward in their approach to the women behind the windows. Sometimes the prostitute then opened the window herself, other times she waited until the man tapped on the window. The man often addressed the woman in English—probably because it was often unknown whether or not the woman spoke Dutch, but maybe also because the man himself spoke better English than Dutch. Men did not begin by listing desires and inquiring about prices; few had an involved introduction. Something like a plainly pronounced "Hey...how are you? Fine?" was a common and also accepted opening. Not all introductions could be understood because of the (lack of) volume, but the reaction, body language, and facial expression clearly showed that it was rare for men to immediately start out by negotiating the price. Such an introductory sentence was hardly ever replied to, and yet seemed to be part of the unwritten rules of De Wallen. Whether a neutral opening sentence was meant to make the woman or the man himself feel at ease was unclear, but it seemed that the man wanted to express something like "I am okay, you can trust me." If the introduction was too long, the man may have been sent away. "Pay first, then talk" was (literally) the women's motto. The negotiations over price often took place partly in the doorway and did not last very long. Not only the men who quietly approached the women but also the ones who were more obvious about it negotiated the price in very soft voices. When men continued haggling, most women closed their windows before long. Sometimes the men looked indignant, but generally they gave up and moved on.

But the prostitutes were far from passive: "it is common for women to hover near the doorways of their small window booths, hooting and calling at men to 'come here!' in a number of different languages" (Wonders & Michalowski, 2001, p. 553). A woman taking the initiative would tap on her window or call out to men passing by. It was notable that there were plenty of women hunting for men who seemed to be disinterested in them. The men's attention had to be drawn by tapping on windows, exuberantly twisting breasts and other body parts, and shouting out phrases like "Hey lover boy," or "One minute, one minute...come inside." Most men did look up for a moment at the women shouting for their attention, but then moved on.

Some women took up an active role at more quiet moments of the day. The female enticement was probably prompted not only by commercial motives but also by boredom. At the same time it could be a matter of "construction worker mentality" (cf. Feigelman, 1974). The same way "tough" construction workers are almost obliged to whistle at nice-looking women, scantily clad women might also whistle at nice-looking men out of habit. It was notable that some women selectively employed this enticing behavior. Most women reported clearly preferring young men.... But there were also other prostitutes who appeared to make no distinction. This was confirmed by brief conversations with prostitutes. Young men were preferred not only because they ejaculate sooner (and therefore do not take up as much work time) but also because they were more often capable of giving the women sexual pleasure or because they were cleaner. Moreover, prostitutes often had regulars.... Some women also indicated that they would more easily lower their prices for men they found attractive than for men they did not find attractive.

Hunting Together: A Natural Encirclement Approach

Aside from hunting by men and hunting by women, another common form of initiating is carefully hunting for each other one step at a time. This shared initiative presented in many forms. Following are four examples from fieldnotes:

> The man walks by the windows and smiles at the woman of his choice. As soon as she smiles back, he approaches her. The woman opens the window and after a brief introduction a calm negotiation begins. Within 30 seconds the man enters.

> At the Sint Annedwarsstraat a man suddenly stops at a window. The woman behind the window notices this and opens her window. After a very brief

introduction, the negotiations commence. They do not go well and the woman tells the man to leave. He moves on. Carefully, I follow him. The man ducks into an alley. He casually looks at the women. A woman taps her window. He smiles back, hesitates for a moment and then walks along, to the end of the alley, around the corner and immediately into the next alley. He is now walking slower while looking at the women more carefully. Right before the end of the alley, he once again stops quite abruptly. The woman behind the window notices this and smiles at him. Carefully, he smiles back, causing the woman to show a big smile. He motions her to open the window, which she does instantly. He greets her and asks her how she is doing. "Okay" is the answer and the man partly steps inside. The woman raises her hand as if she is trying to say "Until here and no further." "What do you want?" The answer cannot be made out. She whispers the prices into his ear. He hesitates for a moment and then agrees by nodding. He enters and, while he is reaching for his wallet, she closes the curtain.

While the two examples above seem similar to situations in which a man is the initiator, the two following examples appear to be closer to the woman taking the initiative.

At the Oudezijds Achterburgwal an elderly man has been pacing back and forth for a while. He seems to be indecisive. Most women pay no attention to him. Even more so, they ignore him. After a while, one of the women taps on her window. She motions him to come to her. Which he immediately does. "Do you wanna look or do you wanna fuck?" He looks as if he does not understand her. "Come inside" she says and motions him to enter. He does. She closes the door and talks to him. Soon after that the curtains are being closed.

Another man walks past the windows and is smiled at by a woman behind the window. He looks at her attentively, but does not smile back. When the woman also taps the window, he smiles back but moves on. I follow him. He walks down the street, pays no more attention to the other women and walks back to the woman who drew his attention. He waits for another one of her smiles and then walks up to her. She has opened the window even before he reaches her and, friendly, wishes him a "Good afternoon." He mumbles something, after which the woman names her price. The man agrees by nodding and enters.

As argued above, hunting together takes a position between the man as a hunter and the woman as a hunter. It is a less direct way of approaching and of being approached. But like the two styles of solitary hunting, the natural style of hunting is applied to keep from disrupting or discrediting the position of the other. Prostitutes also use this technique to make preliminary checks of the man who approaches: The time used to discuss the wishes of the man and those of the prostitute allow the prostitute to check any dangerous signs and determine what type of client the man is (Sanders, 2004). As I show in the next section, this type of behavior by both prostitutes and men can be explained through the work of Goffman and Lofland.

DISCUSSION

Out of the eight territories of the self-within which one "retains" and protects oneself from intruders, described by Goffman, two are clearly visible in the conduct of people in a red-light district. First, we can see people keeping information to themselves. Goffman (1971, pp. 38–39) claims that "the set of facts about himself to which an individual expects to control access while in the presence of others" varies according to environment and culture. In a red-light district one wants more privacy than elsewhere. But especially here, the "right not to be stared at or examined" (Goffman, 1971, p. 39) is violated. A red-light district, after all, cannot exist without the notions of watching and being watched. Second, there is "conversational presence." This is "the right of an individual to exert some control over who can summon him into talk and when he can be summoned; and the right of a set of individuals once engaged in talk to have their circle protected from entrance and overhearing by others" (Goffman, 1971, p. 40). Here, the women involved also may have to use ways to fend off the advances of unwanted men (cf. Snow, Robinson & McCall, 1991). A prostitute is not obliged to respond to a man if she—for whatever reason—does not feel like it, and a man is not obliged to react if a woman calls out to him. In other situations one would be surprised if someone did not respond when called, but in a red-light district this is acceptable. If a prostitute and a man do have a conversation, it is considered normal that they speak softly to one another so others do not hear them and to secure the privacy of both parties. It is important for not only the prostitute that the "deal making" takes place in circumspection, but also for the man. Both parties apply interactional strategies to soften the humiliation or dampen the prospect of aggressive compensatory behavior that often follows on the heels of rejection or failure (Goffman, 1952; Snow et al., 1991).

The tactics of privacy preservation in public spaces of minimalizing expression and eye contact (Lofland, 1973) are applied alternately in the red-light district. Most men avoided eye contact for as long as possible. Once they wanted to make contact with a woman, eye contact was inevitable. Men in the red-light district always avoided expression. The behavior of the men fits in with the principles of Lofland. For women the situation is different. Some women minimalized expression and eye contact; others made a deliberate decision to attract men. The fact that not all women opt for minimal expression and minimal eye contact can have various explanations. Naturally, they may want to attract clients, but perhaps they also want to feel more at ease in the space. To them, the red-light district might rarely be an all-controlling reality, but it is indeed their everyday reality, while it is only a small part of the reality of most men—a reality which they often prefer to deny. Moreover, men find themselves in a public space while the women are in a semi-private space. Obviously they are being watched, but they are accustomed to that. Most men are not. They feel watched by the women behind the windows and also by other visitors to the red-light district. As one man commented after a walk through the Amsterdam red-light district, "I've never felt so objectified in my life. I felt like a piece of meat walking through there" (Wonders & Michalowski, 2001, p. 553). Feeling ashamed and uncomfortable, many men give up on their hunter role. In this way, they become the gatherers and women the hunters....

CONCLUSION

As Goldenberg, Cox, Pyszrczynski, Greenberg, and Solomon (2002) demonstrate, sex can be a source of anxiety, shame and disgust for humans, and is always subject to cultural norms and social regulation. Thus, although the Amsterdam red-light district has the image of a place in which anything should be possible (e.g., Van Straaten, 2000), life there is in fact bound together by unwritten rules. This research has shown that Lofland's principles of privacy preservation in public spaces (minimalizing expression and eye contact) as well as Goffman's territories of the self and his rules of securing personal information...can be used to explain socially and spatially specific unwritten rules.... In the prostitute-man communication in a red-light district, an introduction is desired, provided that it does not take too long. Not until the introduction is complete do price negotiations, which occur quietly, commence. The men are expected to behave modestly and calmly, while the prostitutes have more freedom in their behavior. A shouting man is looked upon with disapproval, while a woman shouting is completely acceptable. Understanding and discretion regarding the need for others' privacy are required but must sometimes be broken down in order to get down to business. In this the man can take the initiative, but so can the woman. Frequently, a prostitute and a client get down to business one step at a time. These unwritten rules apply specifically to the social situation as well as to the geographical location. Although it may be assumed that men in a red-light district are the ones watching and prostitutes the ones being watched, the socially and spatially specific rules of a red-light district may turn things upside down: "Big Sister" is watching you!

REFERENCES

Aalbers, M., Bodaar, A., Kloosterman, R., & Pinkster, F. (2004). Seks en de stad [Sex and the city]. *Rooilijn*, 37, 316–318.

Bancroft, J. (Ed.). (2000). *The role of theory in sex research*. Bloomington: Indiana University Press.

Brants, C. (1998). The fine art of regulated tolerance: Prostitution in Amsterdam. *Journal of Law and Society*, 25, 621–635.

Brunt, L. (1996). *Stad* [City]. Meppel. The Netherlands: Boom.

Deben, L., & Rings, P. (1999). Reglenientering cn disciplinering van het gebruik van de openbare ruimte [Regimentation and discipline in the use of public space]. *Sociologische Gids*, 46, 245–256.

Feigelman, W. (1974). Peeping: The pattern of voyeurism among construction workers. *Urban Life and Culture*, 3, 35–49.

Goffman, E. (1952). On cooling the mark out: Some aspects of adaptation to failure. *Psychiatry: Journal for the Study of Interpersonal Relations*, 15, 451–463.

Goffman, E. (1971). *Relations in public: Microstudies of the public order*. New York: Basic Books.

Goldenberg, J. L., Cox, C. R., Pysczynski, T., Greenberg, J., and Solomon, S. (2002). Understanding human ambivalence about sex: The effects of stripping sex of meaning. *The Journal of Sex Research*, 39, 310–320.

Habermas, J. (1962). *Strukturwangel der Offentlichkeit* [The structural transformation of the public sphere]. Frankfurt, Germany: Suhrkamp.

Hannerz, U. (1993). Thinking about culture in cities. In L. Deben, W. Heinemeijer, & D. van der Vaart (Eds.). *Understanding Amsterdam: Essays on economic vitality, city life and urban form* (pp. 141–156). Amsterdam: Centrum poor Grootstedelijk Onderzoek/Het Spinhuis.

Hubbard, P. (1997). Red-light districts and toleration zones: Geographies of female street prostitution in England and Wales. *Area*, 29, 229–237.

Hubbard, P. (2000). Desire/disgust: Mapping the moral contours of heterosexuality. *Progress in Human Geography*, 24, 191–217.

Lasker, S. (2002). Sex and the city: Zoning "pornography peddlers and live nude shows." *UCLA Law Review*, 49, 1139–1185.

Lofland, L. H. (1973). *A world of strangers: Order and action in urban public space*. New York: Basic Books.

Outshoorn. J. (2004). Pragmatism in the polder: Changing prostitution policy in The Netherlands. *Journal of Contemporary European Studies*, 12, 165–176.

Park, R. E. (1952). *Human communities: The city and human ecology*. Glencoe, IL: The Free Press.

Sanders, T. (2004). The risks of street prostitution: Punters, police and protesters. *Urban Studies*, 41, 1703–1717.

Snow, D. A., Robinson, C., & McCall, P. L. (1991). "Cooling out" men in singles bars and nightclubs: Observations on the interpersonal survival strategies of women in public places. *Journal of Contemporary Ethnography*, 19, 423–449.

Tani, S. (2002). Whose place in this space? Life in the street prostitution area of Helsinki, Finland. *International Journal of Urban and Regional Research*, 26, 343–359.

Van Straaten, S. (2000). *De Walletjes als themapark voor volwassenen* [De Wallen as a themapark for adults]. Rooilijn, 33, 438–443.

Wonders, N. A. (2004). Seks en de aandacht van de toerist in Amsterdam [Sex and the tourist gaze in Amsterdam]. *Rooilijn*, 37, 325–331.

Wonders, N. A., & Michalowski, R. (2001). Bodies, borders, and sex tourism in a globalized world: A tale of two cities—Amsterdam and Havana. *Social Problems*, 48, 545–571.

PART 5

Drugs

Rx DRUGS
60 MINUTES (TRANSCRIPT)

There's a certain paradox in our understanding of, and efforts to deal with, drug offenders. On the one hand, we often tend to see drug users as having an addiction; that is, they are unable to resist the compulsion to consume the drug of their choice; and we often pity the addict. On the other hand, we often deal with addicts through the criminal justice system, punishing rather than treating them. Neither treatment nor punishment seems to have much success in reforming the addict.

The following is a transcript of a broadcast of the television 'newsmagazine' 60 Minutes. It describes a program in Liverpool, England, in which addicts are prescribed the drug of their choice by a physician. It represents a form of limited legalization: certain addicts may use certain drugs that would otherwise be illegal; but they are kept under medical supervision. What is notable about this program is that addicts can be stabilized, continue their drug consumption, and yet lead otherwise normal lives in terms of both job and family. This phenomenon certainly goes against the popular view of drug effects as being absolutely debilitating. As indicated in the following article, it seems that the very illegality of certain drugs causes their debilitating effects.

ED BRADLEY: Can Britain teach us anything about dealing with drug addicts? That remains to be seen, but one thing seems certain, there's little or nothing we can teach them. They tried our hard-line methods back in the '70s and '80s and all they got for their trouble was more drugs, more crime and more addicts. So they went back to their way, letting doctors prescribe whatever drug a particular addict was hooked on. Does it work? If they're ever going to know, Liverpool, where drugs are out of control, is the place to find out.

This is a gram of 100 percent pure heroin. It's pharmaceutically prepared. On the streets, it would be cut 10 to 15 times and sell for about $2,000. But take it away from the black market, make it legal and heroin's a pretty cheap drug. The British National Health Service pays about $10 for this gram of heroin and for an addict with a prescription, it's free.

(Footage of Dr. John Marks sitting at his desk)

BRADLEY: *(Voiceover)* In Britain, doctors who hold a special license from the government are allowed to prescribe hard drugs to addicts. Dr. John Marks, a psychiatrist who runs an addiction clinic just outside Liverpool, has been prescribing heroin for years.

DR. JOHN MARKS *(Runs Addiction Clinic in Liverpool)*: If they're drug takers determined to continue their drug use, treating them is an expensive waste of time. And really the choice that I'm being offered and society is being offered is drugs from the clinic or drugs from the Mafia.

(Footage of a woman dispensing a drug and a patient talking to Dr. Marks, a nurse and a social worker)

BRADLEY: *(Voiceover)* To get drugs from the clinic rather than from the Mafia, addicts have to take a urine test to prove they're taking the drugs they say they are. And unlike most other addiction clinics, where you have to say you want to kick the habit before they'll take you in, addicts here have to convince Dr. Marks, a nurse, and a social worker that they intend to stay on drugs come what may. But doesn't Dr. Marks try to cure people?

DR. MARKS: Cure people? No. Nobody can. Regardless of whether you stick them in prison, put them in mental hospitals and give them electric shocks—we've done all these things—put them in a nice rehab center away in the country; give them a social worker; pat them on the head. Give them drugs; give them no drugs. Doesn't matter what you do. Five percent per annum, one in 20 per year, get off spontaneously. Compound interested up, that reaches about 50 percent. Fifty-fifty after 10 years are off. They seem to mature out of addiction regardless of any intervention in the interim. But you can keep them alive and healthy and legal during that 10 years if you so wish to.

BRADLEY:. By giving them drugs?

DR. MARKS: It doesn't get them off drugs. It doesn't prolong their addiction either. But it stops them offending; it keeps them healthy and it keeps them alive.

(Footage of Julia pushing her daughter on a swing)

BRADLEY: *(Voiceover)* That's exactly what happened to Julia. Although she doesn't look it, Julia is a heroin addict. For the last three years, the heroin she injects every day comes through a prescription. Before she had to feed her habit by working as a prostitute, a vicious circle that led her to use more heroin to cope with that life.

JULIA *(Heroin Addict):* And once you get in that circle, you can't get out. And I didn't think I was ever going to get out.

BRADLEY: But once you got the prescription...

JULIA: I stopped straight away.

BRADLEY: Never went back?

JULIA: No, I've never. I went back once just to see, and I was almost physically sick just to see these girls doing what I used to do.

(Footage of Julia talking to her daughter)

BRADLEY: *(Voiceover)* Julia says she's now able to have normal relationships, to hold down a job as a waitress and to care for her three-year-old daughter.

Without that prescription, where do you think you'd be today?

JULIA: I'd probably be dead by now.

DR. MARKS: OK.

UNIDENTIFIED MAN: OK.

DR. MARKS: One sixty then...

MAN: If I can, yes.

DR. MARKS: ...of heroin.

(Footage of a man sitting in Dr. Marks' office)

BRADLEY: *(Voiceover)* Once they've got their prescriptions, addicts must show up for regular meetings to show they're staying healthy and free from crime. But how can anyone be healthy if they're taking a drug like heroin?

MR. ALLAN PARRY *(Former Drug Information Officer):* Pure heroin is not dangerous. We have people on massive doses of heroin.

(Footage of Parry talking to Bradley)

BRADLEY: *(Voiceover)* Allan Parry is a former drug information officer for the local health authority and now a counselor at the clinic. So how come we see so much damage caused by heroin?

MR. PARRY: The heroin that is causing that damage is not causing damage because of the heroin in it. It's causing the damage because of brick dust in it, coffee, crushed bleach crystals, anything. That causes the harm. And if heroin is 90 percent adulterated, that means only 10 percent is heroin; the rest is rubbish. Now you inject cement into your veins, and you don't have to be a medical expert to work out that's going to cause harm.

OK, George, let's put your leg up. Let's have a look.

(Footage of George having his leg looked at)

BRADLEY: *(Voiceover)* Many at the clinic, like George, still suffer from the damage caused by street drugs. Allan Parry believes you can't prescribe clean drugs and needles to addicts without teaching them how to use them.

(Footage of George in the office)

MR. PARRY: *(Voiceover)* The other major cause of ill health to drug injectors is not even the dirty drugs they take; it's their bad technique, not knowing how to do it.

I've seen drug users in the States with missing legs and arms, and that is through bad technique.

Can I have a look at your arms. Have you been...

(Footage of George in the office)

BRADLEY: *(Voiceover)* George's legs have ulcerated and the veins in his arms have collapsed. To inject, he must use a vein in his groin which is dangerously close to an artery.

MR. PARRY: Now when you go in there, you getting any sharp pains?

GEORGE *(Addict)*: No.

MR. PARRY: If you hit the artery, how would you recognize it?

GEORGE: If I hit the artery?

MR. PARRY: Yeah.

GEORGE: By me head hitting the ceiling.

MR. PARRY: So we show people how to—not how to inject safely, but how to inject less dangerously. We have to be clear about that. You know, stoned people sticking needles into themselves is a dangerous activity, but the strategy is called "harm minimization."

(Footage of a billboard with the words: Heroin screws you up; police entering a building and a man under arrest)

BRADLEY: *(Voiceover)* In the '70s, the British weren't content with minimizing the harm of drug abuse. They adopted the American policy of trying to stamp it out altogether. Prescription drugs were no longer widely available, and addicts who couldn't kick the habit had to find illegal sources. The result? By the end of the '80s, drug addiction in Britain had tripled. In Liverpool, there was so much heroin around it was known as smack city. And then came a greater threat.

More than anything else, it's been the threat of AIDS that has persuaded the British to return to their old policy of maintaining addicts on their drug of choice. In New York, it's estimated that more than half of those who inject drugs have contracted the AIDS virus through swapping contaminated needles. Here in Liverpool, the comparable number—the number of known addicts infected—is less than 1 percent.

(Footage of a pharmacist Jeremy Clitherow dispensing cigarettes containing heroin)

BRADLEY: *(Voiceover)* In an effort to get addicts away from injecting, Liverpool pharmacist Jeremy Clitherow has developed what he calls "heroin reefers." They're regular cigarettes with—heroin in them. Whatever you feel about smoking, he says, these cigarettes hold fewer risks than needles for both the addicts and the community.

MR. JEREMY CLITHEROW *(Pharmacist)*: So we then use this to put in a known volume of pharmaceutical heroin into the patient's cigarette. And there we are, one heroin reefer containing exactly 60 milligrams of pharmaceutical heroin.

BRADLEY: So the National Health Service will pay for the heroin, but not for the cigarettes.

MR. CLITHEROW: Oh yes. Yes, of course. It's the patient's own cigarette, but with the National Health prescription put into it.

(Footage of the outside of Clitherow's pharmacy and people waiting in line inside the store)

BRADLEY: *(Voiceover)* Addicts pick up their prescriptions twice a week from his neighborhood pharmacy. And how does this affect his other customers?

MR. CLITHEROW: *(Voiceover)* The patient who comes in to pick up a prescription of heroin in the form of reefers would be indistinguishable from a patient who picks up any other medication.

PAUL *(Heroin Addict):* Good morning.

MR. CLITHEROW: Hello, Paul. How are you doing?

PAUL: Fine.

MR. CLITHEROW: All right.

PAUL: Cigarettes next-next week?

MR. CLITHEROW: That's my sheet. Anything else we can do for you?

PAUL: No, that's fine…

MR. CLITHEROW: The prescription is ready and waiting, and they pick it up just as they would pick up their Paracetamol, aspirin or bandages.

BRADLEY: But with all of these drugs available to—to—to most people, plus the hard drugs which you have here, what's your security like?

MR. CLITHEROW: Like Fort Knox. But we keep minimal stocks. We buy the stuff in—regularly, frequently. It comes in, goes out.

(Footage of Clitherow filling a prescription)

BRADLEY: *(Voiceover)* And heroin isn't the only stuff to come in and out of here. Clitherow also fills prescriptions for cocaine, and that's 100 percent pure freebase cocaine—in other words, crack.

So in fact when you're putting cocaine in here…

MR. CLITHEROW: Yes.

BRADLEY: …you're actually making crack cigarettes?

MR. CLITHEROW: Yes.

BRADLEY: In America that has a very negative connotation…

MR. CLITHEROW: Mm-hmm.

BRADLEY: …but not for you?

MR. CLITHEROW: It depends which way you look at it. If they continue to buy on the street, whether it's heroin, methadone, crack or whatever, sooner or later they will suffer from the—the merchandise that they are buying. I want to bring them into contact with the system. And let's give them their drug of choice—if the physician agrees and prescribes it—in a form which won't cause their health such awful deterioration.

BRADLEY: And you don't have any problems giving people injectable cocaine or cocaine cigarettes.

DR. MARKS: No, not in principle. I mean, there are—there are patients to whom I've prescribed cocaine and to whom I've then stopped prescribing the cocaine because their lives do not stabilize. They continue to be thieves or whatever. But there are equally many more to whom we prescribe cocaine who've then settled to regular, sensible lives.

(Footage of Mike)

BRADLEY: *(Voiceover)* Mike is one of those who has settled into a regular, sensible life on cocaine. He has a prescription from Dr. Marks for both the cocaine spray and the cocaine cigarettes. Before he got that prescription, the cocaine he bought on the street cost him $1,000 a week, which at first he managed to take from his own business. But it wasn't long before it cost him much more than that.

So you lost your business.

MIKE *(Cocaine Addict):* Yeah.

BRADLEY: You lost your—your wife.

MIKE: Yeah.

BRADLEY: You lost the kids.

MIKE: Yeah.

BRADLEY: And the house.

MIKE: Yeah.

BRADLEY: But you kept going after the cocaine.

MIKE: Yeah. That's what addiction is. That's the whole—the very nature of addiction is the fact that one is virtually—chemically and physically—forced to continue that way.

(Footage of Mike sitting in a chair writing)

BRADLEY: *(Voiceover)* Now after two years of controlled use on prescription cocaine, Mike has voluntarily reduced his dose. He's got himself a regular job with a trucking company and is slowly putting his life back together again.

Where do you think you would be now if—if Dr. Marks had not given you a—a prescription for cocaine?

MIKE: I wouldn't be here now talking to you, and you probably wouldn't be interested in talking to me, either. I'd be on the street.

BRADLEY: Dr. Marks, how would you reply to critics who would say that you're nothing more than a legalized dealer, a pusher?

DR. MARKS: I'd agree. That's what the state of England arranges, that there's a legal, controlled supply of drugs. The whole concept behind this is control.

(Footage of Bradley talking to Parry while they're walking outside)

BRADLEY: *(Voiceover)* And there are signs that control is working. Within the area of the clinic, Allan Parry says the police have reported a significant drop in drug-related crime. And since addicts don't have to deal anymore to support their habit, they're not recruiting new customers. So far fewer new people are being turned on to drugs.

What do the dealers around the area of the clinic think about it all?

MR. PARRY: *(Voiceover)* Well, there aren't any around the clinic.

BRADLEY: *(Voiceover)* You—you've taken away their business.

MR. PARRY: Exactly. There's no business there. The scene is disappearing. So if you want to get rid of your drug problem, which presumably all societies do, there are ways of doing it, but you have to counter your own moral and political prejudice.

BRADLEY: What would you say to people who would ask, "Why give addicts what they want? Why give them drugs?"

JULIA: So they can live. So they have a chance to live like everyone else does. No one would hesitate to give other sorts of maintaining drugs to diabetics. Diabetics have insulin. In my mind it's no different. It's the same. I need heroin to live.

(Show motif)

(Announcements)

HEALTHY NIGHTCLUBS AND RECREATIONAL SUBSTANCE USE

From a Harm Minimization to a Healthy Settings Approach

MARK A. BELLIS, KAREN HUGHES, AND HELEN LOWEY

The drug treatment program described in the previous article provides us with one example of a harm minimization. The following article describes a healthy settings approach. Both approaches recognize that criminalization is either an ineffective or insufficient means of control—if the goal of control is to safeguard the health of drug users and/or the public. Both approaches take a realistic perspective, recognizing that some people are going to use drugs come what may; but many of the associated risks of drug-taking can be reasonably reduced. The following article demonstrates how the health of drug users is compromised by many factors—beyond the biochemical effects of a given substance—that can be controlled without criminalization.

INTRODUCTION

In the UK alone, approximately 3.5 million individuals go to nightclubs each week (Mintel International Group, 2000). Most of these are younger people and a large proportion of them consume illegal drugs often in combination with alcohol (Measham, Aldridge, & Parker, 2001). The relationship between recreational drug use and dance music events is now well established (Release, 1997; Winstock, Griffiths, & Stewart, 2001). In the UK, for instance, estimates of ecstasy, amphetamine, and cocaine use in regular clubbers (i.e. attendees at nightclubs) or those travelling abroad to visit international nightclub resorts (e.g. Ibiza) far exceed average levels of consumption by individuals in the general population (Bellis, Hale, Bennett, Chaudry, & Kilfoyle, 2000) (Table 1).

The acute and long-term problems relating to recreational (i.e. ecstasy, amphetamine, and cocaine) drug use are the subject of a wide range of studies (Parrott, Milani Parmar, & Turner, 2001; Reneman et al., 2001) and form the rationale for a variety of health interventions (Niesnk, Nikken, Jansen, & Spruit, 2000; Page, 2000). Thus, ecstasy use has been linked to short-term health effects such as hyperthermia (Henry, Jeffreys, & Dawning, 1992) as well as long-term effects such as memory problems (Reneman et al., 2001). Interventions addressing recreational drug use have often been outreach based (Crew 2000, 2001) and focused on disseminating information on adverse effects of drugs and how to avoid them, problems around combining substances (often drugs and alcohol), and courses of action necessary when acute adverse effects are experienced. However, there is now a growing recognition that the adverse effects of club drugs are strongly related to the environment in which they are used rather than resulting solely from the toxic properties of substances themselves (Calafat et al., 2001). Often, reports of ecstasy-related deaths refer to the temperature of the environment: [t]he most likely cause of death is heatstroke. The temperature inside [a] club had reached $40°$ C [$104°$ F](Burke, 2001) or in other instances the lack of basic

Table 1 Levels of drug use in three UK surveys

	BRITISH CRIME SURVEY[a] (%)	IBIZA UNCOVERED SURVEY[b] (%)	DANCING ON DRUGS SURVEY[c] (%)
Cannabis	22	51	69.5
Ecstasy	5	39	51.4
Amphetamine	5	27	53.5
Cocaine	5	26	27.1

[a] 16–29-year-olds in the general population; drugs used in last 12 months (Ramsay, Baker, Goulden, Sharp, & Sondhi, 2001).
[b] 16–29-year-olds who visited Ibiza during Summer 2000; drugs used in last 6 months (Bellis et al., 2000).
[c] 15–57-year-olds attending dance events; drugs used in last 3 months (Measham et al., 2000).

facilities to redress the effects of dancing and substance use (a number of people complained about lack of water—Bowcott, 2001).

In this paper, we argue that the relationship between the health effects of substance use and the environment in which they are used is much wider than temperature control and access to water and extends across the entire nightlife setting. We explore the wide range of factors that contribute to risk in nighttime environments and describe initiatives that effectively address these issues without curtailing fun. Consequently, we argue that by adopting a broad settings approach (World Health Organization, 1997) to nightclubs, inclusive solutions to reducing harm in clubs (including that caused by drugs) can be better developed and disseminated.

Furthermore, the same approach can also facilitate multidisciplinary involvement in nightlife health, taking health issues solely from health departments and placing the responsibility also in the hands of organizations such as local authorities, police, voluntary organizations, club owners and managers, door staff, and clubbers themselves. Finally, we suggest that with worldwide growth in dance music tourism, this multidisciplinary approach needs to be extended to include travel and tourism organizations and requires collaboration on an international level.

HEALTHY SETTINGS AND NIGHTCLUBS

A healthy settings approach (World Health Organization, 1997) recognizes that the effects of any particular setting on an individual's health are related to the general conditions within that setting, perhaps more than they are to provision of health or other care facilities. The nightclub setting at its most basic is a building that provides loud music, often with a repetitive beat, a dance area that usually has low background light and intermittent bright lighting effects and a licensed bar. Developing this environment as a healthy setting must recognize that large numbers of clubbers regularly consume substances such as alcohol, drugs, and tobacco (often in combination) and consequently experience a variety of psychological and physiological effects. Furthermore, the criminal nature of some drug use and environmental factors such as poor ventilation mean substance consumption can directly affect staff, for example, pressure of door staff to allow drugs into clubs (Morris, 1998) and passive smoking affecting bar staff, respectively (Jones, Love, Thomson, Green, & Howden-Chapman, 2001).

Some settings approaches to club health are well established. Harm minimization messages advising sipping water, avoiding mixing alcohol with ecstasy, and taking periods of rest provide the essential information for individuals to protect their health (London Drugs Policy Forum, 1996). However, without cool areas within the club, often referred to as chill out areas (London Drug Policy Forum, 1996) and access to free cold water, such advice cannot be implemented. Equally, when adverse reactions to drugs are experienced, a separate appropriately stocked first-aid room, trained staff, and access [to] emergency services are all required to allow the best chance of recovery. However, other often more deleterious effects on health are also related to nightlife and substance use. In the UK in 1999, 19% of all violent acts (n = 3,246,000) occurred outside a pub or club. Overall, 40% of violent incidents were related to alcohol use and 18% to drugs (Kershaw et al., 2000). The paraphernalia of alcohol use also contributes to harm, with 5000 people being attacked with pint glasses every year of whom many are scarred for life (Deehan, 1999). Thus, both the promotion of aggression by, for instance, alcohol (Institute of Alcohol Studies, 2001) and the paraphernalia of substance use play parts in the harm caused by violence.

Less frequently addressed issues, which are important to a settings approach to club health, include the risk of smoking and in particular fire. Large amounts of electrical equipment, the use of old converted premises, low lighting, and a high proportion of smokers (Measham et al., 2001) all contribute to making nightclubs high-risk environments. Additionally, substance use can mean that patrons can be disorientated, leading to further implications particularly if an emergency evacuation of the building is required. A healthy setting should promote well-marked fire exits (some have been known to be camouflaged to fit in with club decor), crowd control training (Newcombe, 1994), and strict compliance with fire limits on the building's capacity (Ministry of Health, 1999). The effects of fires in clubs can be horrific, as graphically illustrated by the loss of life associated with recent incidents (*BBC News*, 2000; CNN, 2000; *The Guardian*, 2001). However, the effects of smoking alone may also be significant. Dancing while holding a cigarette can result in damage to eyes of those nearby (Luke, 1999), whilst nonsmoking bar staff are subject to heavy exposure to environmental tobacco smoke while at work (Jarvis, Foulds, & Feyerabend, 1992).

Noise levels in clubs can also pose a substantial risk to health. UK guidance on protection at work suggests earplugs are used when levels regularly exceed 90 dB (Health and Safety Executive, 1999). However, noise levels in many nightclubs reach 120 dB (Royal National Institute for Deaf People, 1999) and at some points noise can approach the pain threshold (140 dB) (Walsh, 2000). However, those utilizing the nighttime environment are unlikely to recognize the effects on their hearing. The clubbing experience, especially in conjunction with substance use, distracts from concerns about health effects and in the case of some drugs (e.g. ketamine or cocaine) may even anaesthetize the user against pain (European Monitoring Center for Drugs and Drug Addiction, 2000). As increasing numbers of young people are exposed to loud music in dance clubs, it would be expected that more young people would develop hearing problems. In fact, a survey by the Medical Research Council Institute of Hearing Research found that 66% of club goers reported temporary hearing problems after attending a nightclub (Smith & Davis, 1999). Policies about maximum noise levels in clubs can address some of these issues. However, noise is not just a concern within the club but may also affect the surrounding environment, either through loud music contaminating nearby residential areas or through the noise of inebriated clubbers appearing on the street when clubs finally close (BBC Devon, 2001). Such noise may also be associated with violence (often related to alcohol and drug use), lack of appropriate access to public transport (leaving long waits or drink/drug driving as the only alternatives), and difficulties in coordinating an adequate police presence when clubs close (Calafat et al., 2001).

Furthermore, any comprehensive approach to a healthy club setting should recognize the close relationship between substance use and sexual health. A variety of studies identify the relaxation of safe sex measures (particularly condom use) associated with alcohol and drug-taking (e.g. Poulin & Graham, 2001). One study has identified individuals using drugs, particularly GHB, specifically in order to temporarily forget safe sex messages they have previously heard (Clark, Cook, Syed, Ashton, & Bellis, 2001). Addressing such issues means providing safe sex information within the club setting and combining this with easy access to condoms. Fire, noise, sex, and other areas for health promotion and protection in the nighttime environment as well as their relationship with substance use are summarized in Table 2.

DISSEMINATING KNOWLEDGE AND DEVELOPING SOLUTIONS

The use of substances often contributes to the dangers presented within the nighttime environment. Previously, harm minimization has tended to focus on direct effects of drug use. However, basic measures to alter the environment can substantially reduce substance-related harm. Measures to reduce violence in and around clubs include training and registration of door staff, good lighting around the main entrance, and public transport integrated into the nighttime environment so that individuals can quickly and easily leave city centers (London Drug Policy Forum, 1996; Calafat et al., 2001). Specific measures to reduce spillage of bottles from bars and clubs onto streets can also reduce the risk of glass-related injuries (The Kirklees Partnership, 1999). Inside, club design should anticipate and acknowledge the exuberant behavior and intoxicated state of patrons by restricting access to any areas where falls are likely and ensuring exits are well lit and distinctive (London Drug Policy Forum, 1996).

Importantly, the process of tackling harm reduction across the entire nightlife setting legitimizes the inclusion of a wide variety of organizations and individuals who may have felt that they could not engage in dialogue solely on a drug use agenda. These groups may include club and bar owners, club goers and club staff, event promoters, local authorities and politicians,

Table 2 Some wider club health issues, their relationship with substance use, and developing a setting response

HEALTH RISK	RELATIONSHIP TO SUBSTANCE USE	SETTING RESPONSE	GROUPS INVOLVED
Dehydration and hyperthermia	Ecstasy alters thermoregulation (McCann, Slate, & Ricaurte, 1996) Increased energetic dancing Alcohol consumption causes dehydration	Prevent overcrowding Well ventilation and temperature control Cool and quieter *chill out* areas or ability to leave and reenter Access to cool, free water Information on effects of taking drugs Pill testing First-aid room and staff training	Club owners/staff Drug outreach workers Health promotion groups Licensing authority Club goers Local A&E
Fire	High levels of smoking among club goers Intoxication leads to disorientation when exiting clubs Flammable clubbing clothes (e.g. PVC)	Prevent overcrowding High visibility and accessible emergency exits Availability and maintenance of all fire equipment Ensure electrical equipment is safe Encourage use of noncombustible material	Club owners/staff Fire authorities Building inspectors Licensing authority Club goers
Damage to hearing	Alcohol and drugs reduce awareness of potential hearing damage Greater exposure to noise due to prolonged dancing	Set maximum levels on systems Restricted areas around speakers Make earplugs available Information on the effects of excessive noise Information on signs of hearing damage	Club owners/staff Club goers Environmental inspectors Licensing authority Health promotion Club goers
STIs and unwanted pregnancies	Alcohol and drugs reduce inhibitions (Calafat, 2001) Substances help forget safe sex message (Clark et al., 2001)	Easy availability of condoms Information on safer sex	Health promotion groups Public health department Contraception services Club owners Club goers

Category			
Accident	Disorientation	Toughened glass or plastic bottles	Club owners/staff
Glass	Anaesthetising effect of substances	No drinking/smoking on dance floor	Public health departments
Burns	(European Monitoring Centre for Drugs and Drug Addiction, 2000)	Provide places to dispose of cigarettes	Health promotion groups
Falls	Lack of fear and increased confidence	Well-lit and clear stairwells	Licensing authority
General	Increased risk-taking	Restricted access to potentially dangerous areas	Club goers
		Secure fixtures and fittings are secure	
		On-site first-aid	
Violence	Alcohol and drugs increase aggression	Stagger closing times	Club owners/staff
	Drug dealing (Morris, 1998)	Increase public transport availability	Police
	Steroid and cocaine use by door staff	throughout night	Licensing authority
	(Lenehan & McVeigh, 1998)	Plastic/toughened glass	Club goers
	Increased risk-taking, lower inhibitions	Registration and training of door staff	Transport authority
		Complaints procedures and Policing	
Drink/drug driving	Increased confidence	Provide cheap soft drinks	Club owners/staff
	Lack of coordination	Public transport: taxis, buses, and trains available	Health promotion group
	Increased risk-taking, lower inhibitions	Information of safety issues	Club goers
	(Crowley & Courney, 2000)	Special club buses provided by clubs	Police
			Transport authority
Passive smoking	Increased smoking when out	Adequate ventilation (especially behind the bar)	Club owners
	Many "occasional" smokers	Adequate "break areas" for staff	Outreach workers
	Link between smoking and other	No smoking areas	Smoking prevention groups
	substance use	Information on dangers of smoking	Health promotion groups
	(Lewinsohn, Rohde, & Brown, 1999)		Licensing authority
			Club goers

environmental health officials, and travel and tour operators as well as youth services, health services, police, and other emergency services. Furthermore, sometimes, this mix of individuals produces novel solutions. For example, to reduce night crime and increase public safety, the owners of a number of neighboring venues have supported the employment of a uniformed police officer dedicated to patrolling outside their premises (Greater Manchester Police, 2001). Also, in North Devon, a police initiative involved handing out free lollipops as clubbers left nightclubs in order to reduce noise in the surrounding areas (BBC Devon, 2001).

INTERNATIONAL CONSIDERATIONS

The recent clubbing phenomenon probably has its roots in Ibiza where the mix of music (known as the Balearic Beat) and concurrent use of ecstasy rose to popularity (Calafat et al., 1998). Today, traveling in the form of dance music tourism (individuals specifically traveling abroad to attend dance events or choosing to holiday in destinations renowned for their nightlife) is more popular than ever. Major international clubbing resorts include Ibiza in Spain, Rimini in Italy, and Ayia Napa in Cyprus. Clubbing has additional elements of risk when undertaken in an unfamiliar country. Thus, geography abroad is often unfamiliar, and combined with a different language, this can mean health services or other forms of help are difficult to locate and access. Furthermore, accessing items such as condoms or emergency contraception may also prove more difficult. Legislation can be different and poorly understood, leading to unexpected confrontations with judicial services. If drugs are purchased, the supplier will often be untested, raising the possibility of counterfeits. Equally, alcohol measures may vary in size and purity from standard measures within individuals' home countries. When alcohol and drugs are consumed, a combination of hotter climates, longer periods of dancing, and possible gastrointestinal infections increase the risk of severe dehydration. Importantly, however, along with environmental change, individuals abroad are often free from the social constraints of work and family that restrict their substance use and sexual behavior (Ryan and Kinder, 1996). Thus, an individual may go clubbing one night per week while at home, whereas during a 2-week trip abroad the same individual may visit a club every night. This in turn can significantly alter an individual's exposure to substances. For instance, around a third of all young people from the UK who visited Ibiza in 1999 used ecstasy while on the island. The vast majority of these also used ecstasy in the UK (Bellis et al., 2000). However, the way in which people used ecstasy while abroad was significantly different. Of ecstasy users, only 3% used the drug 5 or more days a week in the UK while 45% of the same group used the drug 5 or more days a week while in Ibiza. Similar trends in increased frequency of use were also seen for alcohol, amphetamine, and cocaine.

Little is currently known about the health effects of such periods of intense substance use. Clearly, the opportunities for adverse reactions are substantially increased where multiple drugs are being regularly consumed along with alcohol on a nightly basis. Furthermore, intense periods of consumption provide at least the possibility that more frequent drug use could continue when individuals return home, potentially moving individuals' habits further towards problematic use.

In order to address the health needs of the increasingly large numbers of young people who regularly travel to experience international nightlife, new approaches to health promotion and protection are required. New literature and campaigns are needed that provide international information on substance use and nightlife health for those traveling abroad. They should tackle the broad range of risks to health, including environmental considerations, but should also address the changes in substance use that occur while abroad (Bellis et al., 2000). Access to such information can utilize new technologies affiliated with club culture (e.g. the Internet) and popular with the major clubbing age groups (Hughes & Bellis, in press). Good examples of such sites are already available (www.dancesafe.org and www.ravesafe.org).

CONCLUSIONS

Around the world, clubbing is now well established as a major feature of the nighttime environment. It provides a social outlet for millions of individuals every week and developing a popular club scene has reinvigorated many cities, bringing money and employment. Substance use in clubs is strongly affiliated with relaxation, exercise (Gaule, Dugdill, Peiser, & Guppy, 2001), and meeting new sexual partners. Whether these pastimes lead to increased well-being or ill health depends on the environment and the specific behavior of individuals. Developing clubs as a healthy setting requires interventions that protect and promote health while retaining fun as a central feature. Where interventions or regulations substantially reduce fun, young people may look elsewhere for their entertainment (e.g. illegal parties). Consequently, organizations need to recognize the importance of involving young people in the development of nighttime health interventions.

Substance use is one of the major risks to health in the nighttime environment both through its direct effects on individuals' health and through the alterations in behavior and perception that it causes. However, many organizations and individuals do not feel either comfortable or equipped to engage in drug-specific interventions or even discussions. By developing a healthy settings approach to clubs, the emphasis of health interventions can be diverted away from solely drug use to include a wider range of issues. This means key individuals and organizations (including club owners, staff, promoters, and major industries) can be engaged in a harm minimization agenda that includes drug use along with alcohol, tobacco, transport, security, and other environmental issues. Furthermore, tackling a broad range of issues in the nighttime environment reaches groups that are difficult to reach through education or occupational settings, such as those who play truant or are unemployed.

Some countries have already engaged in this more holistic approach to nighttime health by generating broader guidelines on safer clubs and clubbing (e.g. London Drug Policy Forum, 1996; Ministry of Health, 1999; Newcombe, 1994). However, with cheaper air travel and young people having greater expendable income (Calafat et al., 2001) combined with the international nature of the clubbing phenomenon, a significant proportion of an individual's annual clubbing nights can be spent in nightclubs abroad where risks to health may be even greater. As a result, guidelines are required to provide basic standards for nightclubs on an international basis and different interventions need to be developed to address local and international needs. Efforts to develop international guidelines on club health are already underway (www.clubhealth.org.uk). However, empirical evidence on changes in individuals' behavior when abroad (Bellis et al., 2001) and the resultant effects on health are both rare and urgently needed. Without such intelligence, the appropriate structure of health interventions to minimize harm for millions of dance music tourists remains unclear and the burden of ill health carried especially by younger people may unnecessarily be increasing.

REFERENCES

BBC Devon News (2001). Lollipops gag late-night revellers. *BBC News* (online).

BBC News (2000). Mexico club blaze kills 19. *BBC News*, Friday, 20 October 2000.

Bellis, M. A., Hale, G., Bennett, A., Chaudry, M., & Kilfoyle, M. (2000). Ibiza uncovered: changes in substance use and sexual behaviour amongst young people visiting an international night-life resort. *International Journal on Drug Policy*, 11, 235–244.

Bellis, M. A., Hughes, K., Bennett, A., & Chaudri, M. (2001). *Three years of research on risk behaviour in Ibiza* (in preparation).

Bowcott, O. (2001). Ecstasy deaths may have been called by heat, not a bad batch. *The Guardian*, Saturday, 30 June 2001.

Burke, J. (2001). Ecstasy's death toll "set to go on rising." *The Guardian*, Sunday, 1 July 2001.

Calafat, A., Fernandez, C., Juan, M., Bellis, M. A., Bohrn, K., Hakkarainen, P., Kilfoyle-Carrington, M., Kokkevi, A., Maalste, N., Mendes, F., Siamou, I., Simojn, J., Stocco, P., & Zavatti, P. (2001). *Risk and control in the recreational drug culture: SONAR project*. Spain: IREFREA.

Calafat, A., Stocco, P., Mendes, F., Simon, J., van de Wijngaart, G., Sureda, M., Palmer, A., Maalste, N., & Zapatti, P. (1998). *Characteristics and social representation of ecstasy in Europe*. Valencia: IREFREA and European Commission.

Clark, P., Cook, P. A., Syed, Q., Ashton, J. R., & Bellis, M. A. (2001). *Re-emerging syphilis in the North West: lessons from the Manchester outbreak*. Liverpool: Public Health Sector, Liverpool John Moores University.

CNN (2000). Christmas fire kills at least 309 at China shopping center. *CNN*, 27 December 2000.

Crew 2000 (2001). Development of strategies for secondary prevention in drug use. Patterns of drug use amongst young people at clubs and pre-club bars in Edinburgh. *Project Report*. Edinburgh: Crew 2000.

Crowley, J., & Courney, R. (2000). The relation between drug use, impaired driving and traffic accidents. *The results of an investigation carried out for the European Monitoring Center on Drugs and Drug Addictions* (EMCDDA), Lisbon. Proceedings of Road Traffic and Drugs, Strasbourg, 19–21 April 1999. Council of Europe Publishing.

Deehan, A. (1999). *Alcohol and crime: taking stock.* Policing and Reducing Crime Unit, Crime Reduction Research Series Paper 3. London: Home Office.

European Monitoring Center for Drugs and Drug Addiction (2000). *Report on the risk assessment of ketamine in the framework of the joint action on new synthetic drugs.* Portugal: EMCDDA.

Gaule, S., Dugdill, L., Peiser, B., & Guppy, A. (2001). *Moving beyond the drugs and deviance issues: rave dancing as a health promoting alternative to conventional physical activity.* Proceedings of club health 2002. Liverpool John Moores University and Trimbos Institute. Available at: www.clubhealth.org.uk.

Greater Manchester Police (2001). *Manchester City Center venues team up with police to reduce night crime.* Press release.

Health and Safety Executive (1999). *Introducing the noise at work guidelines: a brief guide to the guidelines controlling noise at work.* INDG75 (rev) C150 11/99. Suffolk: HSE Books.

Henry, J. A., Jeffreys, K. J., & Dawling, S. (1992). Toxicity and deaths from 3,4-methylene-dioxymethamphetamine ("Ecstasy"). *Lancet*, 340, 384–387.

Hughes, K., & Bellis, M. A. (2002). *Disseminating public health information and the public health evidence base: assessing the current and future potential for the Internet and e-mail.* Health Development Agency and North West Public Health Observatory (in press).

Institute of Alcohol Studies (2001). Alcohol and crime. *IAS factsheet.* Cambridgeshire: Institute of Alcohol Studies.

Jarvis, M. J., Foulds, J., & Feyerabend, C. (1992). Exposure to passive smoking among bar staff. *British Journal of Addiction*, 87, 111–113.

Jones, S., Love, C., Thomson, G:, Green, R., & Howden-Chapman, P. (2001). Second-hand smoke at work: the exposure, perceptions and attitudes of bar and restaurant workers to environmental tobacco smoke. *Australian and New Zealand Journal of Public Health*, 25, 90–93.

Kershaw, C., Budd, T., Kinshott, G., Mattinson, J., Mayhew, P., & Myhill, A. (2000). *The 2000 British crime survey.* Home Office Statistical Bulletin 18/00. London: Home Office.

Lenehan, P., & McVeigh, J. (1998). *Anabolic steroids: a guide for professionals.* The Drugs and Sport Information Service, University of Liverpool.

Lewinsohn, P. M., Rohde, P., & Brown, R. A. (1999). Level of current and past adolescent cigarette smoking as predictors of future substance use disorders in young adulthood. *Addiction*, 94, 913–921.

London Drug Policy Forum (1996). *Dance till dawn safely: a code of practice on health and safety at dance venues.* London: Drug Policy Forum.

Luke, C. (1999). A little nightclub medicine. In M. Kilfoyle, & M. A. Bellis (Eds.), *Club health: the health of the clubbing nation.* Liverpool: Department of Public Health, Liverpool John Moores University.

McCann, U. D., Slate, S. O., & Ricaurte, G. A. (1996). Adverse reactions with 3,4-methylene-dioxymethamphetamine (MDMA: "ecstasy"). *Drug Safety*, 15, 107.

Measham, F., Aldridge, J., & Parker, H. (2001). *Dancing on drugs: risk, health and hedonism in the British club scene.* London: Free Association Books.

Ministry of Health (1999). *Guidelines for SAFE dance parties: the big book.* New Zealand: Ministry of Health.

Mintel International Group (2000). *Nightclubs and discotechques: market size and trends.* Report Code 11/2000, London.

Morris, S. (1998). *Clubs, drugs and doormen.* Crime Detection and Prevention Series Paper 86, Police Research Group, London: Home Office.

Newcombe, R. (1994). *Safer dancing: guidelines for good practice at dance parties and nightclubs.* Liverpool: 3D Pub.

Niesnk, R., Nikken, G., Jansen, F., & Spruit, L. (2000). *The drug information and monitoring service (DIMS) in the Netherlands: a unique tool for monitoring party drugs.* Proceedings of club health

2002. Liverpool John Moores University and Trimbos Institute. Available at: www.club health.org.uk.

Page, S. (2000). *Death on the dancefloor*. Proceedings of club health 2002. Liverpool John Moores University and Trimbos Institute. Available at: www.clubhealth.org.uk.

Parrott, A. C., Milani, R. M., Parmar, R., & Turner, J. D. (2001). Recreational ecstasy/MDMA and other drug users from the UK and Italy: psychiatric problems and psychobiological problems. *Psychopharmacology*, 159, 77–82.

Poulin, C., & Graham, L. (2001). The association between substance use, unplanned sexual intercourse and other sexual behaviours among adolescent students. *Addiction*, 96, 607–621.

Ramsay, M., Baker, P., Goulden, C., Sharp, C., & Sondhi, A. (2001). *Drug misuse declared in 2000: results from the British crime survey*. Home Office Research Study 224. London: Home Office.

Release (1997). *Drugs and dance survey: an insight into the culture*. London: Release.

Reneman, L., Lavalaye, J., Schmand, B., de Wolff, F. A., van den Brink, W., den Heeten, G. J., & Booij, J. (2001). Cortical serotonin transporter density and verbal memory in individuals who stopped using methylenedioxymethamphetamine (MDMA or "ecstasy"): preliminary findings. *Archives of General Psychiatry*, 58, 901–906.

Royal National Institute for Deaf People (1999). *Safer sound: an analysis of musical noise and hearing damage*. London: RNID.

Ryan, C., & Kinder, R. (1996). Sex, tourism and sex tourism: fulfilling similar needs? *Tourist Management*, 17, 507–518.

Smith, P., & Davis, A. (1999). Social noise and hearing loss. *Lancet*, 353, 1185.

The Guardian (2001). Dutch fire toll climbs to 10 with 17 fighting for life. *The Guardian*, Wednesday, 3 January 2001.

The Kirklees Partnership (1999). *Boiling point preventer: a code of practice for dealing with drugs and violence in pubs and clubs*. Yorkshire: The Kirklees Partnership.

Walsh, E. (2000). *Dangerous decibels: dancing until deaf*. San Francisco: The Bay Area Reporter, Hearing Education and Awareness for Rockers.

Winstock, A. R., Griffiths, P., & Stewart, D. (2001). Drugs and the dance music scene: a survey of current drug use patterns among a sample of dance music enthusiasts in the UK. *Drug and Alcohol Dependence*, 64, 9–17.

World Health Organization (1997). *The Jakarta declaration on leading health promotion into the 21st century*. Fourth international conference on health promotion, Jakarta, 21–25 July 1997.

WHY RITALIN RULES

MARY EBERSTADT

From their parents' perspective, children have been too distractable since the beginning of humanity. Today, such distractability is frequently classified as a medical disorder and treated chemically. Even though scientific explanations for the disorder are sketchy and the science of identifying patients who have the disorder is very imprecise, thousands of medical practitioners have very few qualms about prescribing a relatively potent drug for children's long-term consumption. As you are reading this article, take note of the politics of classifying drugs.

There are stories that are mere signs of the times, and then there are stories so emblematic of a particular time and place that they demand to be designated cultural landmarks. Such a story was the *New York Times'* front-page report on January 18 appearing under the tame, even soporific head line, "For School Nurses, More Than Tending the Sick."

"Ritalin, Ritalin, seizure drugs, Ritalin," in the words of its sing-song opening. "So goes the rhythm of noontime" for a typical school nurse in East Boston "as she trots her tray of brown plastic vials and paper water cups from class to class, dispensing pills into outstretched young palms." For this nurse, as for her counterparts in middle- and upper-middle class schools across the country, the day's routine is now driven by what the *Times* dubs "a ticklish question," to wit: "With the number of children across the country taking Ritalin estimated at well over three million, more than double the 1990 figure, who should be giving out the pills?"

"With nurses often serving more than one school at a time," the story goes on to explain, "the whole middle of the day can be taken up in a school-to-school scurry to dole out drugs." Massachusetts, for its part, has taken to having the nurse deputize "anyone from a principal to a secretary" to share the burden. In Florida, where the ratio of school nurses to students is particularly low, "many schools have clerical workers hand out the pills." So many pills, and so few professionals to go around. What else are the authorities to do?

Behold the uniquely American psychotropic universe, pediatrics zone—a place where "psychiatric medications in general have become more common in schools" and where, in particular, "Ritalin dominates." There are by now millions of stories in orbit here, and the particular one chosen by the *Times*— of how the drug has induced a professional labor shortage—is no doubt an estimable entry. But for the reader struck by some of the facts the *Times* mentions only in passing—for example, that Ritalin use more than doubled in the first half of the decade alone, that production has increased 700 percent since 1990, or that the number of schoolchildren taking the drug may now, by some estimates, be approaching the 4 million mark—mere anecdote will only explain so much.

Fortunately, at least for the curious reader, there is a great deal of other material now on offer, for the explosion in Ritalin consumption has been very nearly matched by a publishing boom dedicated to that same phenomenon. Its harbingers include, for example, Barbara Ingersoll's now-classic 1988 *Your Hyperactive Child*, among the first works to popularize a drug regimen for what we now call Attention Deficit Disorder (ADD, called ADHD when it includes hyperactivity). Five years later, with ADD diagnoses and Ritalin prescriptions already rising steeply in the better-off neighborhoods and schools, Peter D. Kramer helped fuel the boom with his best-selling *Listening to Prozac*—a book that put the phrase "cosmetic pharmacology" into the vernacular and thereby inadvertently broke new conceptual ground for the advocates of Ritalin. In 1994, most important, psychiatrists Edward M.

Hallowell and John J. Ratey published their own best-selling *Driven to Distraction: Recognizing and Coping with Attention Deficit Disorder from Childhood to Adulthood*, a book that was perhaps the single most powerful force in the subsequent proliferation of ADD diagnoses; as its opening sentence accurately prophesied, "Once you catch on to what this syndrome is all about, you'll see it everywhere."

Not everyone received these soundings from the psychotropic beyond with the same enthusiasm. One noteworthy dissent came in 1995 with Thomas Armstrong's *The Myth of the ADD Child*, which attacked both the scientific claims made on behalf of ADD and what Armstrong decried as the "pathologizing" of normal children. Dissent also took the form of wary public pronouncements by the National Education Association (NEA), one of several groups to harbor the fear that ADD would be used to stigmatize minority children. Meanwhile, scare stories on the abuse and side effects of Ritalin popped out here and there in the mass media, and a national controversy was born. From the middle to the late 1990s, other interested parties from all over—the Drug Enforcement Administration (DEA), the Food and Drug Administration (FDA), the medical journals, the National Institutes of Health (NIH), and especially the extremely active advocacy group CHADD (Children and Adults with Attention Deficit Disorder)—further stoked the debate through countless reports, conferences, pamphlets, and exchanges on the Internet.

To this outpouring of information and opinion two new books, both on the critical side of the ledger, have just been added: Richard DeGrandpre's iconoclastic *Ritalin Nation: Rapid-Fire Culture and the Transformation of Human Consciousness* (Simon and Schuster, 1999), and physician Lawrence H. Diller's superbly analytical *Running on Ritalin: A Physician Reflects on Children, Society and Performance in a Pill* (Bantam Books, 1998). Their appearance marks an unusually opportune moment in which to sift through some ten years' worth of information on Ritalin and ADD and to ask what, if anything, we have learned from the national experiment that has made both terms into household words.

Let's put the question bluntly: How has it come to pass that in *fin de siecle* America, where every child from preschool onward can recite the "anti-drug" catechism by heart, millions of middle- and upper-middle class children are being legally drugged with a substance so similar to cocaine that, as one journalist accurately summarized the science, "it takes a chemist to tell the difference"?

WHAT IS METHYLPHENIDATE?

The first thing that has made the Ritalin explosion possible is that methylphenidate, to use the generic term, is perhaps the most widely misunderstood drug in America today. Despite the fact that it is, as Lawrence

Diller observes in *Running on Ritalin*, "the most intensively studied drug in pediatrics," most laymen remain under a misimpression both about the nature of the drug itself and about its pharmacological effects on children.

What most people believe about this drug is the same erroneous character-ization that appeared elsewhere in the *Times* piece quoted earlier—that it is "a mild stimulant of the central nervous system that, for reasons not fully under-stood, often helps children who are chronically distractible, impulsive and hyperactive settle down and concentrate." The word "stimulant" here is at least medically accurate. "Mild," a more ambiguous judgment, depends partly on the dosage, and partly on whether the reader can imagine describ-ing as "mild" any dosage of the drugs to which methylphenidate is closely related. These include dextroamphetamine (street name: "dexies"), metham-phetamine (street name: "crystal meth"), and, of course, cocaine. But the chief substance of the *Times'* formulation here—that the reasons why Ritalin does what it does to children remain a medical mystery—is, as informed writers from all over the debate have long acknowledged, an enduring public myth.

"Methylphenidate," in the words of a 1995 DEA background paper on the drug, "is a central nervous system (CNS) stimulant and shares many of the pharmacological effects of amphetamine, methamphetamine, and cocaine." Further, it "produces behavioral, psychological, subjective, and reinforcing effects similar to those of d-amphetamine including increases in rating of euphoria, drug liking and activity, and decreases in sedation." ... To put the point conversely, as Richard DeGrandpre does in *Ritalin Nation* by quoting a 1995 report in the *Archives of General Psychiatry*, "Cocaine, which is one of the most reinforcing and addicting of the abused drugs, has pharmacological actions that are very similar to those of methylphenidate, which is now the most commonly prescribed psychotropic medicine for children in the U.S."

Such pharmacological similarities have been explored over the years in numerous studies. DeGrandpre reports that "lab animals given the choice to self-administer comparative doses of cocaine and Ritalin do not favor one over another" and that "a similar study showed monkeys would work in the same fashion for Ritalin as they would for cocaine." The DEA reports another finding—that methylphenidate is actually "chosen *over* cocaine in preference studies" of non-human primates (emphasis added). In *Driven to Distraction*, pro-Ritalin psychiatrists Hallowell and Ratey underline the interchangeable nature of methylphenidate and cocaine when they observe that "people with ADD feel focused when they take cocaine, *just as they do when they take Ritalin* [emphasis added]." Moreover, methylphenidate (like other stimulants) appears to increase tolerance for related drugs. Recent evidence indicates, for example, that when people accustomed to prescribed Ritalin turn to cocaine, they seek higher doses of it than do others. To summarize, again from the DEA report, "it is clear that methylphenidate substitutes for cocaine and d-amphetamine in a number of behavioral paradigms."

All of which is to say that Ritalin "works" on children in the same way that related stimulants work on adults—sharpening the short-term attention span when the drug kicks in and producing equally predictable valleys ("coming down," in the old street parlance; "rebounding," in Ritalinese) when the effect wears off. Just as predictably, children are subject to the same adverse effects as adults imbibing such drugs, with the two most common— appetite suppression and insomnia—being of particular concern. That is why, for example, handbooks on ADD will counsel parents to see their doctor if they feel their child is losing too much weight, and why some children who take methylphenidate are also prescribed sedatives to help them sleep. It is also why one of the more Orwellian phrases in the psychotropic universe, "drug holidays"—meaning scheduled times, typically on weekends or school vacations, when the dosage of methylphenidate is lowered or the drug temporarily withdrawn in order to keep its adverse effects in check—is now so common in the literature that it no longer even appears in quotations.

Just as, contrary to folklore, the adult and child physiologies respond in the same way to such drugs, so too do the physiologies of *all* people, regardless of whether they are diagnosed with ADD or hyperactivity. As Diller puts it, in a point echoed by many other sources, methylphenidate "potentially improves the performance of anyone—child or not, ADD-diagnosed or not." Writing in the *Public Interest* last year, psychologist Ken Livingston provided a similar summary of the research, citing "studies conducted during the mid seventies to early eighties by Judith Rapaport of the National Institute of Mental Health" which "clearly showed that stimulant drugs improve the performance of most people, regardless of whether they have a diagnosis of ADHD, on tasks requiring good attention." ("Indeed," he comments further in an obvious comparison, "this probably explains the high levels of 'self-medicating' around the world" in the form of "stimulants like caffeine and nicotine.")

A third myth about methylphenidate is that it, alone among drugs of its kind, is immune to being abused. To the contrary: Abuse statistics have flourished alongside the boom in Ritalin prescription-writing. Though it is quite true that elementary schoolchildren are unlikely to ingest extra doses of the drug, which is presumably kept away from little hands, a very different pattern has emerged among teenagers and adults who have the manual dexterity to open prescription bottles and the wherewithal to chop up and snort their contents (a method that puts the drug into the bloodstream far faster than oral ingestion). For this group, statistics on the proliferating abuse of methylphenidate in schoolyards and on the street are dramatic.

According to the DEA, for example, as early as 1994 Ritalin was the fastest-growing amphetamine being used "non-medically" by high school seniors in Texas. In 1991, reports DeGrandpre in *Ritalin Nation*, "children between the ages of 10 and 14 years old were involved in only about 25 emergency room visits connected with Ritalin abuse. In 1995, just four years later, that number had climbed to more than 400 visits, which for this group was about the same number of visits as for cocaine." Not surprisingly, given these and other measures of methylphenidate's recreational appeal, criminal entrepreneurs have responded with interest to the drug's increased circulation. From 1990 to 1995, the DEA reports, there were about 2,000 thefts of methylphenidate, most of them night break-ins at pharmacies—meaning that the drug "ranks in the top 10 most frequently reported pharmaceutical drugs diverted from licensed handlers."

Because so many teenagers and college students have access to it, methylphenidate is particularly likely to be abused on school grounds. "The prescription drug Ritalin," reported *Newsweek* in 1995, "is now a popular high on campus—with some serious side effects." DeGrandpre notes that at his own college in Vermont, Ritalin was cited as the third-favorite drug to snort in a campus survey. He also runs, without comment, scores of individual abuse stories from newspapers across the country over several pages of his book. In *Running on Ritalin*, Diller cites several undercover narcotics agents who confirm that "Ritalin is cheaper and easier to purchase at playgrounds than on the street." He further reports one particularly hazardous fact about Ritalin abuse, namely that teenagers, especially, do not consider the drug to be anywhere near as dangerous as heroin or cocaine. To the contrary: "they think that since their younger brother takes it under a doctor's prescription, it must be safe."

In short, methylphenidate looks like an amphetamine, acts like an amphetamine, and is abused like an amphetamine. Perhaps not surprisingly, those who value its medicinal effects tend to explain the drug differently. To some, Ritalin is to children what Prozac and other psychotropic "mood brightening" drugs are to adults—a short-term fix for enhancing personality and performance. But the analogy is misleading. Prozac and its sisters are not stimulants with stimulant side effects; there is, ipso facto, no black market for drugs like these. Even more peculiar is the analogy favored by the advocates in CHADD: that "Just as a pair of glasses help the nearsighted person focus," as Hallowell and Ratey explain, "so can medication help the person with ADD see the world more clearly." But there is no black market for eyeglasses, either—nor loss of appetite, insomnia, "dysphoria" (an unexplained feeling of sadness that sometimes accompanies pediatric Ritalin-taking), nor even the faintest risk of toxic psychosis, to cite one of Ritalin's rare but dramatically chilling possible effects.

What is methylphenidate "really" like? Thomas Armstrong, writing in *The Myth of the ADD Child* four years ago, probably summarized the drug's appeal best. "Many middle and upper-middle class parents," he observed then, "see Ritalin and related drugs almost as 'cognitive steroids' that can be used to help their kids focus on their schoolwork better than the next kid." Put this way, the attraction to Ritalin makes considerable sense. In some ways, one can argue, that after-lunch hit of low-dose methylphenidate is much like the big cup from Starbucks that millions of adults swig to get them through the day, but only in some ways. There is no dramatic upswing in hospital emergency room visits and pharmacy break-ins due to caffeine abuse; the brain being jolted awake in one case is that of an adult, and in the other that of a developing child; and, of course, the substance doing the jolting on all those children is not legally available and ubiquitous as caffeine, but a substance that the DEA insists on calling a Schedule II drug, meaning that it is subject to the same controls, and for the same reasons of abuse potential, as related stimulants and other powerful drugs like morphine.

WHAT IS CHADD

This mention of Schedule II drugs brings us to a second reason for the Ritalin explosion in this decade. That is the extraordinary political and medical clout of CHADD, by far the largest of the ADD support groups and a lobbying organization of demonstrated prowess. Founded in 1987, CHADD had, according to Diller, grown by 1993 to include 35,000 families and 600 chapters nationally. Its professional advisory board, he notes, "includes most of the most prominent academicians in the ADD world, a veritable who's who in research."

Like most support groups in self-help America, CHADD functions partly as clearing-house and information center for its burgeoning membership— organizing speaking events, issuing a monthly newsletter (*Chadderbox*), putting out a glossy magazine (named, naturally enough, *Attention!*), and operating an exceedingly active website stocked with on-line fact sheets and items for sale. Particular scrutiny is given to every legal and political development offering new benefits for those diagnosed with ADD. On these and other fronts of interest, CHADD leads the ADD world. "No matter how many sources of information are out there," as a slogan on its website promises, "CHADD is the one you can trust."

One of CHADD's particular strengths is that it is exquisitely media-sensitive, and has a track record of delivering speedy responses to any reports on Ritalin or ADD that the group deems inaccurate. Diller quotes as representative one fund-raising letter from 1997, where the organization listed its chief goals and objectives as "conduct[ing] a proactive media campaign" and "challeng[ing] negative, inaccurate reports that demean or undermine people with ADD." Citing "savage attacks" in the *Wall Street Journal* and *Forbes*, the letter also went on to exhort readers into "fighting these battles of misinformation, innuendo, ignorance and outright hostility toward CHADD and adults who have a neurobiological disorder." The circle-the-wagons rhetoric here appears to be typical of the group, as is the zeal.

Certainly it was with missionary fervor that CHADD, in 1995, mounted an extraordinary campaign to make Ritalin easier to obtain. Methylphenidate, as mentioned, is a Schedule II drug. That means, among other things, that the DEA must approve an annual production quota for the substance—a fact that irritates those who rely on it, since it raises the specter, if only in theory, of a Ritalin "shortage." It also means that some states require that prescriptions for Ritalin be written in triplicate for the purpose of monitoring its use, and that refills cannot simply be called into the pharmacy as they can for Schedule III drugs (for example, low-dosage opiates like Tylenol with codeine, and various compounds used to treat migraine). Doctors, particularly those who prescribe Ritalin in quantity, are inconvenienced by this requirement. So too are many parents, who dislike having to stop by the doctor's office every time the Ritalin runs out. Moreover, many parents and doctors alike object to methylphenidate's Schedule II classification in principle, on the grounds that it makes children feel stigmatized; the authors of *Driven to Distraction*, for example, claim that one of the most common problems in treating ADD is that "some pharmacists, in their attempt to comply with federal regulations, make consumers [of Ritalin] feel as though they are obtaining illicit drugs."

For all of these reasons, CHADD petitioned the DEA to reclassify Ritalin as a Schedule III drug. This petition was co-signed by the American Academy of Neurology, and it was also supported by other distinguished medical bodies, including the American Academy of Pediatrics, the American Psychological Association, and the American Academy of Child and Adolescent Psychiatry. Diller's account of this episode in *Running on Ritalin* is particularly credible, for he is a doctor who has himself written many prescriptions for Ritalin in cases where he has judged it to be indicated. Nevertheless, he found himself dissenting strongly from the effort to decontrol it—an effort that, as he writes, was "unprecedented in the history of Schedule II substances" and "could have had a profound impact on the availability of the drug."

What happened next, while CHADD awaited the DEA's verdict, was in Diller's words "a bombshell." For before the DEA had officially responded, a television documentary revealed that Ciba-Geigy (now called Novartis), the pharmaceuticals giant that manufactures Ritalin, had contributed nearly $900,000 to CHADD over five years, and that CHADD had failed to disclose the contributions to all but a few selected members.

The response from the DEA, which appeared in the background report cited earlier, was harsh and uncompromising. Backed by scores of footnotes and well over 100 sources in the medical literature, this report amounted to a public excoriation of CHADD's efforts and a meticulous description, alarming for those who have read it, of the realities of Ritalin use and abuse. "Most of the ADHD literature prepared for public consumption and available to parents," the DEA charged, "does not address the abuse liability or actual abuse of methylphenidate. Instead, methylphenidate is routinely portrayed as a benign, mild stimulant that is not associated with abuse or serious effects. In reality, however, there is an abundance of scientific literature which indicates that methylphenidate shares the same abuse potential as other Schedule II stimulants."

The DEA went on to note its "concerns" over "the depth of the financial relationship between CHADD and Ciba-Geigy." Ciba-Geigy, the DEA observed, "stands to benefit from a change in scheduling of methylphenidate." It further observed that the United Nations International Narcotics Control Board (INCB) had "expressed concern about non-governmental organizations and parental associations in the United States that are actively lobbying for the medical use of methylphenidate for children with ADD." (The rest of the world, it should be noted, has yet to acquire the American taste for Ritalin. Sweden, for example, had methylphenidate withdrawn from the market in 1968 following a spate of abuse cases. Today, 90 percent of Ritalin production is consumed in the United States.) The report concluded with the documented observations that "abuse data indicate a growing problem among school-age children," that "ADHD adults have a high incidence of substance disorders," and that "with three to five percent of today's youth being administered methylphenidate on a chronic basis, these issues are of great concern."

PUMPED-UP PANIC

DAYN PERRY

Identifying a moral panic is precarious business because, while everyone else seems swept up in moral outrage, skeptics stand the risk of being accused of heresy, or of being amoral sympathizers who are out of touch with reality. In fact, it is often only after the moral panic has subsided and the evidence has been collected that the social analyst can identify it as such with some certainty.

In the following article, Dayn Perry is taking some risk in identifying an anti-steroid panic. At the time this book is being compiled, such a position amounts to heresy. Only time will tell whether he was "out of touch" or one of only a few level-headed critics around at the time of the "panic."

Had Ken Caminiti been a less famous ballplayer, or had he merely confessed his own sins, then it would have been a transient controversy. But it wasn't. Last May, Caminiti, in a cathartic sitdown with Tom Verducci of *Sports Illustrated*, became the first major league baseball player, current or retired, to admit to using anabolic steroids during his playing days. Specifically, he said he used them during the 1996 season, when he was named the National League's Most Valuable Player. And his truth session didn't stop there.

"It's no secret what's going on in baseball. At least half the guys are using [steroids]," Caminiti told *SI*. "They talk about it. They joke about it with each other .... I don't want to hurt fellow teammates or fellow friends. But I've got nothing to hide."

The suggestion that steroids are a systemic problem in professional athletics is hardly shocking, but such candor from players—particularly baseball players, who until recently weren't subject to league-mandated drug testing—was virtually unheard of. Before the Caminiti flap had time to grow stale, Jose Canseco, another high-profile ex-ballplayer, upped the ante, declaring that a whopping 85 percent of current major league players were "juicing."

The estimates were unfounded, the sources unreliable, and the implications unclear. But a media orgy had begun. The questions that are being asked of the players—Do you think it's worth it? How many are using? Why did the players union wait so long to adopt random testing? Why won't you take a test right now?—are mostly of the "Have you stopped beating your wife?" variety. The accusation is ensconced in the question.

This approach may be satisfying to the self-appointed guardians of baseball's virtue, but it leaves important questions unexplored. Indeed, before the sport can solve its steroid problem, it must determine whether it even has one.

From those sounding the clarion call for everything from stricter league policies to federal intervention, you'll hear the same two-pronged concern repeated time and again: Ballplayers are endangering their health and tarnishing baseball's competitive integrity. These are defensible, if dogmatic, positions, but the sporting media's fealty to them obscures the fact that both points are dubious.

A more objective survey of steroids' role in sports shows that their health risks, while real, have been grossly exaggerated; that the political response to steroids has been driven more by a moral panic over drug use than by the actual effects of the chemicals; and that the worst problems associated with steroids result from their black-market status rather than their inherent qualities. As for baseball's competitive integrity, steroids pose no greater threat than did other historically contingent "enhancements," ranging from batting helmets to the color line. It is possible, in fact, that many players who use steroids are not noticeably improving their performance as a result.

There are more than 600 different types of steroids, but it's testosterone, the male sex hormone, that's most relevant to athletics. Testosterone has an androgenic, or masculinizing, function and an anabolic, or tissue-building, function. It's the second set of effects that attracts athletes, who take testosterone to increase their muscle mass and strength and decrease their body fat. When testosterone is combined with a rigorous weight-training regimen, spectacular gains in size and power can result. The allure is obvious, but there are risks as well.

HEALTH EFFECTS

Anecdotal accounts of harrowing side effects are not hard to find—everything from "roid rage" to sketchy rumors of a female East German swimmer forced to undergo a sex change operation because of the irreversible effects of excess testosterone. But there are problems with the research that undergirds many of these claims. The media give the impression that there's something inevitably Faustian about taking anabolics—that gains in the present will undoubtedly exact a price in the future. Christopher Caldwell, writing recently in The *Wall Street Journal*, proclaimed, "Doctors are unanimous that [anabolic steroids] increase the risk of heart disease, and of liver, kidney, prostate and testicular cancer."

This is false. "We know steroids can be used with a reasonable measure of safety," says Charles Yesalis, a Penn State epidemiologist, steroid researcher for more than 25 years, and author of the 1998 book *The Steroids Game*. "We know this because they're used in medicine all the time, just not to enhance body image or improve athletic performance." Yesalis notes that steroids were first used for medical purposes in the 1930s, some three decades before the current exacting standards of the Food and Drug Administration (FDA) were in place.

Even so, anabolic steroids or their derivatives are commonly used to treat breast cancer and androgen deficiencies and to promote red blood cell production. They are also used in emerging anti-aging therapies and to treat surgical or cancer patients with damaged muscle tissue.

Caldwell cites one of the most common fears: that anabolics cause liver cancer. There is dubious evidence linking oral anabolics to liver tumors, but athletes rarely take steroids in liquid suspension form. Users almost uniformly opt for the injectable or topical alternatives, which have chemical structures that aren't noxious to the liver. And as Yesalis observes, even oral steroids aren't causally linked to cancer; instead, some evidence associates them with benign liver tumors.

More specifically, it's C-17 alkylated oral steroids that are perhaps detrimental to liver function. But the evidence is equivocal at best. A 1990 computer-assisted study of all existing medical literature found but three cases of steroid-associated liver tumors. Of those three cases, one subject had been taking outrageously large doses of C-17 oral anabolics without cessation for five years, and a second case was more indicative of classic liver malignancy. It's also C-17 orals, and not other forms of steroids, that are associated with decreased levels of HDL, or "good" cholesterol. But, again, C-17s are almost never used for athletic or cosmetic purposes.

Another commonly held belief is that steroid use causes aggressive or enraged behavior. Consider the case of San Francisco Giants outfielder Barry Bonds, whose impressive late-career home run hitting and built-up physique have long raised observers' eyebrows. Last season, Bonds, long known for being irascible, had a dugout shoving match with teammate Jeff Kent. A few columnists, including Bill Lankhof of *The Toronto Sun* and Jacob Longan of the *Stillwater NewsPress*, obliquely diagnosed "roid rage" from afar. "There's very inconsistent data on whether 'roid rage' even exists," says Yesalis. "I'm more open to the possibility than I used to be, but its incidence is rare, and the studies that concluded it does exist largely haven't accounted for underlying factors or the placebo effect."

Scientists are nearly unanimous that excessive testosterone causes aggression in animals, but this association begins to wither as you move up the evolutionary ladder. Diagnosing such behavior in athletes is especially tricky. "There's a certain degree of aggression that's not only acceptable but necessary in competitive sports," Yesalis says. "What's perhaps just the intensity that's common to many athletes gets perceived as steroid-linked outbursts."

Fears about steroid use also include other cancers, heart enlargement, increased blood pressure, elevated cholesterol levels, and musculoskeletal injuries. Upon closer examination, these too turn out to be overblown. Reports associating heart enlargement, or cardiomegaly, with steroid use often ignore the role of natural, nonthreatening enlargement brought on by prolonged physical exertion, not to mention the effects of alcohol abuse. The relationship is unclear at best. Evidence supporting a link between steroids and ligament and tendon damage is weak, since steroid-related injuries are virtually indistinguishable from those occurring normally. And blood pressure problems, according to Yesalis, have been exaggerated. There is some associative evidence that steroid use can increase the risk of prostate cancer, but this link has yet to be borne out in a laboratory setting. No studies of any kind link the use of anabolics to testicular cancer.

Addiction is a legitimate concern, and Yesalis says a quarter to a half of those who use steroids solely to improve their body image exhibit signs of psychological dependence. "But in all my years of research," Yesalis continues, "I've only known three professional athletes who were clinically addicted to steroids." The distinction, he explains, is that professional athletes see steroids as little more than a tool to help them do their job—the way "an office worker views his computer." Once their playing days are over, almost all the athletes within Yesalis' purview, "terminate their use of the drug."

One reason the health effects of steroids are so uncertain is a dearth of research. In the almost 65 years that anabolic steroids have been in our midst, there has not been a single epidemiological study of the effects of long-term use. Instead, Yesalis explains, concerns about extended usage are extrapolated from what's known about short-term effects. The problem is that those short-term research projects are often case studies, which Yesalis calls the "lowest life form of scientific studies." Case studies often draw conclusions from a single test subject and are especially prone to correlative errors.

"We've had thousands upon thousands [of long-term studies] done on tobacco, cocaine, you name it." Yesalis complains. "But for as much as you see and hear about anabolic steroids, they haven't even taken that step."

What about the research that has been done? At least some of it seems to yield engineered results. "The studies linking steroid use to cancer were performed by and large on geriatric patients," notes Rick Collins, attorney, former bodybuilder, and author of the book *Legal Muscle*, which offers an exhaustive look at anabolic steroid use under U.S. law. The hazard of such research is that side effects observed in an older patient could be the result of any number of physiological problems unrelated to steroid intake. Moreover, the elderly body is probably more susceptible to adverse reactions than the body of a competitive athlete.

Collins believes that some studies were performed with a conclusion in mind at the outset. "Their hearts were in the right place," says Collins. "Curtailing nonessential steroid use is a good and noble goal, but they undermined their efforts by exaggerating the dangers." Call it the cry-wolf effect.

For instance, it's long been dogma that use of anabolic steroids interferes with proper hepatic (liver) function and causes thickening of the heart muscle. However, a 1999 study at the University of North Texas found that it's not steroid use that causes these medical phenomena; rather, it's intense resistance training. Weight-lifting causes tissue damage, and, at high extremes, can elevate liver counts and thicken the left ventricular wall of the heart. Both disorders were observed in high-intensity weight-lifters irrespective of steroid use. The researchers concluded that previous studies had "misled the medical community" into embellishing the side effects of use.

TESTOSTERONE-FUELED PANIC

The cry-wolf effect may have as much to do with the boom in steroid use as anything else. Athletes were inclined to be skeptical of warnings about steroids because their own experience contradicted what critics were saying. When use of Dianabol and other anabolics began to surge in the 1960s and '70s, opponents decried them as ineffective. The message was: They don't work, so don't take the risk. But steroids did work, and users knew it. Once weight-lifters, bodybuilders, and other athletes realized they were being lied to about the efficacy of steroids, they were less likely to believe warnings about health hazards, especially when the evidence backing them up was vague or anecdotal.

One of the chief drum-beaters for the steroids-don't-work movement was Bob Goldman, author of the hysterical anti-steroids polemic *Death in the Locker Room*. Goldman, a former competitive power-lifter turned physician and sports medicine specialist, was an early, and shrill, critic of performance pharmacology. In his 1984 exposé, Goldman attributes steroids' tissue-building qualities almost entirely to the placebo effect. His agenda may have been morally sound, but his conclusions ran counter to the preponderance of scientific evidence at the time. Today, his claims are even less supportable. Goldman is working on a new edition of the book, one that he says will better crystallize current scientific thought on the subject. Of his 1984 edition and its seeming histrionics, Goldman says the book was intended "as an educational tool to warn high school students of the possible hazards of drug use, but then it became something else."

Whatever his intentions at the time, Goldman's views played well in the media, which cast the book as a sobering empirical assault on performance-enhancing drugs. Its warnings soon gained traction with lawmakers. Although the Anti-Drug Abuse Act of 1988 had already made it illegal to dispense steroids for nonmedical reasons, Congress, ostensibly out of concern over reports of increasing steroid use among high school athletes, revisited the matter in 1989.

Congressional hearings convened to determine whether steroids should become the first hormone placed on Schedule III of the Controlled Substances Act, reserved for drugs with substantial abuse potential. Such legislation, if passed, would make possession of anabolic steroids without a prescription a federal offense punishable by up to a year in prison. Distributing steroids for use, already prohibited by the 1988 law, would be a felony punishable by up to five years in prison. What's usually forgotten about these hearings, or perhaps simply ignored, is the zeal with which many regulatory agencies, research organizations, and professional groups objected to the proposed changes.

The American Medical Association (AMA), the FDA, the National Institute on Drug Abuse, and even the Drug Enforcement Administration all opposed the reclassification. Particularly adamant was the AMA, whose spokespersons argued that steroid users did not exhibit the physical or psychological dependence necessary to justify a change in policy.

Nevertheless, Congress voted into law the 1990 Anabolic Steroids Control Act, which reclassified steroids as Schedule III controlled substances, placing them on legal par with barbiturates and narcotic painkillers such as Vicodin, just one step down from amphetamines, cocaine, and morphine. Now even first-time steroid users faced possible jail time.

BLACK-MARKET "ROIDS"

Prohibition naturally produced a black market, and unintended consequences followed. Besides creating yet another economic niche for the criminal underworld, the legislation scuttled any hope of using steroids as a legitimate and professionally administered performance enhancer.

Criminalization of steroids created dangers more serious than any that had prompted the ban. Once steroids became contraband, many athletes bought black-market anabolics that, unbeknownst to them, were spiked or cut with other drugs or intended solely for veterinary use. Physicians were forbidden to prescribe steroids for promoting muscle growth and thus were not able to provide steroid users with responsible, professionally informed oversight. New league policies even ban the use of steroids for recovery from injuries.

Combine the lack of medical supervision with the mind-set of the garden-variety steroid user, and you have a potentially perilous situation. "Many of those using anabolic steroids," says Penn State's Yesalis, "have the attitude that if one [dose] works, then five or ten will work even better. That's dangerous."

Athletes who acquire steroids on the black market are loath to consult with their physician after they begin using regularly. If they do disclose their habit and ask for guidance, the physician, for fear of professional discipline or even criminal charges, may refuse to continue seeing the patient. For professional athletes, another deterrent to proper use is that all responsible doctors keep rigorously accurate records of their dealings with patients. The fear that those records might be leaked or even subpoenaed makes pro athletes even less likely to seek medical guidance.

Since many of the observed side effects of steroids—anecdotal, apocryphal, or otherwise—most likely result from excessive or improper use of the drug, one wonders: Can steroids be used for muscle building with a reasonable degree of safety? "The candid answer is yes, but with caveats," says Collins, the attorney who specializes in steroid law. "It would need to be under the strict direction of a physician and administered only after a thorough physical examination, and it would need to be taken at reasonable and responsible dosages."

It's a statement that even Goldman, once the bellwether scaremonger, says is "something I could probably agree with."

Herbert Haupt, a private orthopedist and sports medicine specialist in St. Louis, is "absolutely, unequivocally, positively opposed" to steroid use as a training or cosmetic tool. But he concedes that properly supervised use of the drug for those purposes can be reasonably safe. "The adverse side effects of steroids typically subside upon cessation of use," says Haupt, "and use over a short span, say a six-week duration, probably carries nominal risk."

Moreover, the official attitude toward steroid use seems anomalous when compared to the treatment of other methods that people use to improve their bodies. "People die from botched liposuctions," Collins notes. "We're also allowed to inject botulism into people's faces [in botox therapy], but no one is allowed to use steroids for similar cosmetic reasons."

Collins is quick to add that adolescents, whose bodies are already steeped in hormones, cannot use steroids safely. But the fact remains that the illegality of steroids makes responsible professional oversight virtually impossible.

Another puzzling distinction is the one made between steroids and other training supplements. Many baseball players have openly used androstenedione, a muscle-building compound that major league baseball hasn't banned even though it's merely a molecular puddle-jump from anabolic steroids. Androstenedione is a chemical precursor that is converted to testosterone by the liver. Creatine monohydrate, another effective supplement, is far more widely used than androstenedione and is virtually free of stigma. Creatine is chemically unrelated to anabolic steroids or androstenedione and also differs in that it does not manipulate hormone levels; rather, creatine allows muscle cells to recover from fatigue more quickly. But all three substances—creatine, androstenedione, and anabolic steroids—increase a naturally occurring substance in the body to promote the building of muscle tissue. Anabolic steroids simply accomplish this end more quickly and dramatically.

The list of "artificial" enhancements doesn't stop there. Indeed, the boundaries of what constitutes a "natural" modern athlete are increasingly arbitrary. Pitchers benefit from computer modeling of their throwing motions. Medical and pharmacological technologies help players to prevent and recover from injuries better than ever before. Even laboratory-engineered protein shakes, nutrition bars, and vitamin C tablets should theoretically violate notions of "natural" training. Yet no one claims these tools are tarnishing the competitive integrity of the game.

MUSCLE BEACH ZOMBIES

Rangers pitcher Kenny Rogers has said, in a bizarre admission, that he doesn't throw as hard as he can because he fears that the line drives hit by today's players, if properly placed, could kill him on the mound. And you need not read the sports pages for long to find someone complaining that today's "juiced" ballplayers are toppling the game's sacrosanct records by the shadiest of means. This sentiment began percolating when Roger Maris' single-season home run record tottered and fell to Mark McGwire in 1998. Since the Caminiti and Canseco stories broke, sportswriters have been resorting to preposterous rhetorical flourishes in dismissing the accomplishments of the modern hitter. Bill Conlin of the *Philadelphia Daily News*, for example, writes: "To all the freaks, geeks android zombies who have turned major league baseball into a Muscle Beach version of the Medellin Cartel: Take your records and get lost."

Yet baseball statistics have never existed in a vacuum. Babe Ruth became the sport's chief pantheon dweller without ever competing against a dark-skinned ballplayer. Chuck Klein of the Philadelphia Phillies posted some eye-popping numbers in the 1930s, but he did it in an era when runs were scored in bundles, and he took outrageous advantage of the Baker Bowl's right field fence, which was a mere 280 feet from home plate. Detroit pitcher Hal Newhouser won two most valuable player awards and a plaque in Cooperstown in part by dominating competition that had been thinned out by World War II's conscription. Sandy Koufax crafted his run of success in the '60s with the help of a swollen strike zone. Also a boon to Koufax was the helpfully designed Dodger Stadium, which included, according to many, an illegally heightened mound. Gaylord Perry succored his Hall of Fame career by often calling upon an illegal spitball pitch. Take any baseball statistic, and something is either inflating or depressing it to some degree.

Beginning in the mid-'90s in the American League and the late '90s in the National League, home runs reached unseen levels. This fact has encouraged much of the present steroids conjecture. But correlation does not imply causation, as the deductive reasoning platitude goes, and there are more likely explanations for the recent increase in homers.

Home runs are up, in large part, because several hitter-friendly ballparks have opened in recent years. Coors Field, home of the Colorado Rockies since 1995, is the greatest run-scoring environment in major league history. Until the 2000 season, the Houston Astros played in the Astrodome, a cavernous, run-suppressing monstrosity with remarkably poor visuals for hitters. They replaced it with Enron Field (now renamed Minute Maid Park), which is second only to Coors Field in terms of helping hitters and boasts a left field line that's so short it's in violation of major league rules. The Pittsburgh Pirates, Milwaukee Brewers, and Texas Rangers also have recently replaced their old ballparks with stadiums far more accommodating to hitters. The Arizona Diamondbacks came into being in 1998; they too play in a park that significantly inflates offensive statistics. The St. Louis Cardinals, Baltimore Orioles, and Chicago White Sox have all moved in their outfield fences in the last few years. Add to all that the contemporary strike zone, which plainly benefits hitters, and it's little wonder that home runs are at heretofore unimaginable levels.

And then there is Barry Bonds and the momentous season he had in 2001. In the midst of Bonds' siege on McGwire's still freshly minted single-season home run record, Bob Klapisch of the Bergen County, *New Jersey Record* made a transparent observation-cum-accusation by writing, "No one has directly accused Bonds of cheating—whether it be a corked bat or steroids.... "

Bonds is plainly bigger than he was early in his career. That fact, considered in tandem with his almost unimaginable statistical achievements, has led many to doubt the purity of his training habits. But Bonds had bulked up to his current size by the late '90s, and from then until 2001 his home run totals were in line with his previous yearly levels. So there's obviously a disconnect between his body size and his home runs. Last season, bulky as ever, Bonds hit "only" 46 homers, which isn't out of step with his pre-2001 performance. More than likely, Bonds had an aberrant season in 2001—not unlike Roger Maris in 1961.

STEROIDS VS. THE PERFECT SWING

This is not to suggest that no ballplayers are taking advantage of modern pharmacology. Rick Collins says he knows some major league ballplayers are using steroids but can't hazard a guess as to how many. And Yesalis believes that at least 30 percent of major league ballplayers are on steroids.

But then there are skeptics like Tony Cooper of the *San Francisco Chronicle*, a longtime sportswriter and 20-year veteran of the weightlifting and body-building culture. During the 2001 season, as Bonds was assailing McGwire's freshly minted home run record, Cooper responded to the groundswell of steroid speculation by writing that he saw no evidence of steroid use in baseball. Cooper had seen plenty of steroid users and plenty of "naked baseball players" and he couldn't name one obvious juicer in the entire sport. As for Bonds, Cooper called the accusations "ludicrous," writing that the Giants' slugger "merely looks like a man who keeps himself in condition."

Canseco, of course, claims 85 percent of players are on steroids. Caminiti initially said half, then backpedaled to 15 percent. Other players have dotted the points in between with guesses of their own. Whatever the actual figure, such widely divergent estimates suggest that not even the ballplayers themselves know the extent of the problem. And if they don't know, the pundits assuredly don't either.

A more reasonable (and answerable) question is: If players are on steroids, how much of a difference is it making?

Not much of one, according to Chris Yeager, a human performance specialist, private hitting instructor, and longtime weightlifter. Yeager's argument is not a replay of Bob Goldman's assertion that steroids function merely as placebos. Yeager posits that the engorged arms, chests, and shoulders of today's ballplayers could well be the result of steroid use—but that they aren't helping them hit home runs.

Upper body strength doesn't increase bat speed, he explains, "and bat speed is vital to hitting home runs. The upper body is used in a ballistic manner. It contributes very little in terms of power generation." Yeager likens the arms, in the context of a hitter's swing, to the bat itself: simply a means to transfer energy. A batter's pectoral muscles, says Yeager, "are even less useful."

Yeager isn't saying steroid use couldn't increase a batter's power. He's saying most ballplayers don't train properly. "There's a difference between training for strength and training for power," he says, "and most baseball players train for strength." If hitters carefully and specifically trained their legs and hips to deliver sudden blasts of power, then steroids could be useful to them, but by and large that's not what they do. "Mark McGwire hit 49 home runs as a 23-year-old rookie," Yeager says. "And, while I think he probably used steroids at some point in his career, he hit home runs primarily because of his excellent technique, his knowledge of the strike zone, and the length of his arms. Barry Bonds could be on steroids, but his power comes from the fact that he has the closest thing to a perfect swing that I've ever seen."

MUCH ADO ABOUT NOTHING

In what at first blush seems counterintuitive, Yeager asserts that steroid use may have decreased home run levels in certain instances. Specifically, he points to Canseco. "I'm almost positive Canseco used steroids, and I think it hurt his career," says Yeager. "He became an overmuscled, one-dimensional player who couldn't stay healthy. Without steroids, he might have hit 600, 700 home runs in his career."

In short, steroids are a significant threat to neither the health of the players nor the health of the game. Yet the country has returned to panic mode, with both private and public authorities declaring war on tissue-building drugs.

The chief instrument in that war is random drug testing, which major league baseball adopted in September 2002 with the ratification of the most recent collective bargaining agreement. Players can be tested for drugs at any time, for any reason whatsoever. Leaving aside what this implies for players' privacy, testing is easily skirted by users who know what they're doing.

Sprinter Ben Johnson tested positive for steroids at the 1988 Summer Olympics and forfeited his gold medal, but subsequent investigation revealed that he'd passed 19 drug tests prior to failing the final one at the Seoul games. Yesalis says most professional athletes who use steroids know how to pass a drug test. Whether by using masking agents, undetectable proxies like human growth hormone, or water-based testosterone, they can avoid a positive reading. At the higher levels of sports, Yesalis believes, drug testing is done mostly "for public relations." Image protection is a sensible goal for any business, but no one should be deluded into thinking it eliminates drug use.

Nevertheless, lawmakers are lining up to push the process along. California state Sen. Don Perata (D-East Bay) has introduced a bill that would require all professional athletes playing in his state to submit to random drug testing. Federal legislation could be forthcoming from Sen. Byron Dorgan (D-N.D.). It's unlikely that any bill calling for this level of government intrusion will pass. But the fact that such legislation is even being considered suggests how entrenched the steroid taboo is. Meanwhile, baseball's new collective bargaining agreement has firmly established drug testing in the sport. The Major League Baseball Players Association, contrary to what some expected, agreed to the testing program with little resistance.

The measure won't do much to prevent the use of performance-enhancing drugs in baseball, but it may serve as a palliative for the media. At least until the next cause celebre comes along.

PART 6
Corporate Deviance

REGULATION, WHITE-COLLAR CRIME AND THE BANK OF CREDIT AND COMMERCE INTERNATIONAL

BASIA SPALEK

Perhaps one reason why corporate criminals are frequently treated relatively leniently by the criminal justice system (with the exception of some recent high-profile scandals in the United States) is because there is little under- standing of who the victims are and of the degree of harm done to the victims. The recent Enron scandal in the United States was exceptional in that it did indeed bring to light the victimization of employees, their loss of employment and of their rightful pensions.

The following article also focuses on employees as victims of a corporate scandal some years earlier. As a multinational corporation, BCCI victimized employees (and investors and taxpayers) in many countries. Their losses were great, but rarely considered by the press and the public. These include financial losses, their lost reputations, their diminished employability, and their loss of faith in corporate, media, and governmental institutions.

Over the last three decades researchers and policy makers have shown an increasing interest towards the victims of crime (Mawby and Walklate, 1994; Zedner, 1994). An important dimension to victimization which has been considered is that of the impact of criminal justice responses to victims' plight. There has been an acknowledgment that negative treatment by, and experiences of, the police and courts may adversely affect victims and there- fore may constitute their "secondary victimization" (Maguire and Pointing, 1988). As such, initiatives have been put into place which aim to ease victims' plight through attempting to ensure that their needs are satisfied. For example, Victim Support schemes offer practical advice, support and counseling to victims of homicide, sexual violence, assault, burglary, theft, and road death (Victim Support, 1998), while in 1997 the Home Office published a sec- ond Victims' Charter setting out the services that victims should expect from the criminal justice system. Victim satisfaction with various agencies and processes of the criminal justice system has also been examined (Shapland et al., 1985; Newburn and Merry, 1990; Mayhew et al., 1993; Kelly and Erez, 1997; Mirrlees-Black and Budd, 1997; Mirrlees-Black, Budd, Partridge and Mayhew, 1998).

However, despite the concern shown to victims of crime, it appears that this has been directed predominantly towards the victims (both adult and child) of physical and sexual violence and property crime. Individuals victimized by more hidden forms of crime, for example white-collar crime, have tended to be overlooked. In particular, the impact of criminal justice and regulatory responses to the plight of white-collar victims is largely unknown. Literature on white-collar crime often portrays victims as individuals who do not know that they have been victimized and therefore as individuals who do not have any contact with the criminal justice system or regulatory authorities. However, as Levi and Pithouse (1992) observe, this is a generalization which does not apply to all instances of white-collar crime. In a significant proportion of cases, victims of white-collar crime have some contact with agencies of the criminal justice system, as well as various regulatory bodies. It is crucial to examine the regulatory and criminal justice responses towards the victims of white-collar crime, as these may have a significant impact upon their plight.

This article presents the findings of a study exploring the impact of the closure of the Bank of Credit and Commerce International (BCCI) upon its former employees. BCCI was closed down by the Bank of England as a result of fraud and corruption occurring at the bank (Kochan and Whittington, 1991). Data gathered via interviews reveal that former employees incurred financial, emotional and physical costs as a consequence of having worked for a bank which was considered to be corrupt by regulatory authorities and which was closed down. Particularly interesting is the finding that the employees taking part in this study tended to view themselves as victims not only of fraudulent activities carried out by some staff members of BCCI, but also by the misjudged action of the Bank of England, an unsympathetic liquidator and the negative press coverage of the whole affair. The harm caused by the actions of employees is thus heightened by regulatory and media responses. This feature of white-collar victimization has rarely been documented, and suggests that "secondary victimization" may be particularly relevant in some instances of white-collar crime.

THE CASE STUDY

The Bank of Credit and Commerce International was registered in Luxembourg on 21 September 1972, and quickly expanded into an organization which contained over 400 branches in 73 different countries, employing approximately 11,000 people (Gauhar 1995). However, on 5 July 1991 the Bank of England closed down BCCI, alleging that this was a result of large scale fraud and corruption—the founder of BCCI and some high-ranking employees of the bank were accused of engaging in false accounting, drug money laundering, fraud and conspiracy (Kochan and Whittington, 1991). Branches were closed, deposits were frozen, and staff members were made redundant.

This study asked former employees of BCCI to relay their experiences. I targeted the BCCI Employees Action Group in order to gain access to individuals caught up in this event. The predominant method of research which was used consisted of semi-structured interviewing. I considered this to be a valid approach to documenting former employees' experiences, as it would enable me to explore in depth the substance of individuals' experiences. . . . Interviews were carried out with ten former employees of BCCI (I could not find any more persons who were willing to be interviewed). The ten individuals interviewed consisted of four Pakistani, one Iranian, one Spanish and four British individuals, between 42 and 60 years of age, with nine of them being male and one being female. All except one, whose husband worked for the BCCI, are former employees of the bank and have made banking their careers, often working in many different offices of BCCI based in different parts of the world. All except one now live in Britain. Fictional names have been used throughout this article.

What then was the impact of the closure on former employees of the Bank of Credit and Commerce International? Financial, emotional and physical costs were significant as a result of the scandal surrounding the bank.

THE FINANCIAL IMPACT

The financial impact upon former employees was severe and multi-faceted. When BCCI was closed on 5 July 1991, employees were made redundant. Although they received redundancy payments, these were considered to be too low by former employees. For example, Mr. Ahmed said:

> At least if there had been a decent redundancy many of these people would have started on their own and life would have carried on. But with the £8,000 they got most of them could not do anything. They're stuck, at 40/50 you're not going to get another job in a financial institution because effectively you are past it.

Many employees also had held bank accounts with BCCI which means that they had also lost access to their funds as well. Mr. Khan, for instance, spoke of how as soon as he had heard that the bank had been shut down he used a cash machine to try to withdraw as much money as he could from his account:

> When the news came out I went to the ATM and I withdrew I think four or five thousand, that was all the money I had in Abu Dhabi to last my family when they were there.

Unfortunately, however, Mr. Khan was not able to withdraw all of his money:

> —Did you manage to withdraw all of your money?
> No no it's still there in the bank.

Moreover, many of the employees held mortgage accounts with BCCI, which means that when the bank was closed down they effectively owed this money to the liquidator. The liquidator in turn charged a high rate of interest on mortgages, and in many cases former employees were unable to pay since they no longer had an income. Interviews suggest that the liquidator was unsympathetic to the plight of former employees, charging a high rate of interest on their mortgage accounts and threatening many with repossession. For instance, Mr. Ahmed spoke about his frustration with the liquidator for charging a high rate of interest:

> Instead of being understanding and sympathetic the liquidator had a very arrogant and high horse attitude which rubbed people the wrong way. Instead of saying look Mr. Ahmed, here it is, this is your redemption figure, we'll give you something like six weeks or one month or whatever and you try and work towards that, they would not tolerate that. There are areas where it's better to say there is a mortgage here that this person wants to pay off, we're getting the money in which we can pay to the creditors. What they did in my case, and in the case of many other people, is they started charging interest on my mortgage which is about base rate plus 5,6,7 and the base is not the base in the City of London; the base they were using was the one when the bank was closed, it was 12%, so effectively I'm paying 17% on my mortgage.

Similarly, Mr. Reed spoke about an unsympathetic response from the liquidator:

> There was a moratorium on loans, all loans, for a year I think so we didn't pay any mortgage repayments, well we couldn't we were all out of work. The year was up and then the liquidator came and that's when I had a series of letters and meetings with people at the liquidator. The girl who spoke to me, she put up my scheme to the chief liquidator and he came back with his answer saying they want the whole lot so that was it. I just wrote back and said how do you expect me to live on that? And that's the last I heard. I'm just resigned to the fact now that I'll probably never own my own house.

One interviewee argued:

> House loans are nearly double the value of my house, mainly due to ridiculously high interest rates (around 15%).

Mr Ahmed was also threatened with repossession:

> You're in a no-win situation. In '94 they employed a woman from XX mortgages section to sort out the mortgages. At that time they started bombarding everybody with repossessions and they say to you this is our agents, hand them the keys, they did it to me as well. . . . It was a lot of stress to a lot of people. I mean I'm strong and I showed them two fingers basically, I said you're not getting away with me like that. But a lot of people simply went, people are badly affected.

By October 1997 there were approximately 200 former employees in Britain who owed around 40 million pounds to the liquidator as a result of outstanding mortgages and loans. Keith Vaz MP condemned the response of the liquidator as being aggressive (*The Guardian*, 13 October 1997). In British law, when a business is in liquidation, it seems that creditors take priority over the employees. This means that creditors have a claim over the assets of the business before employees receive any form of compensation (Sorell and Hendry, 1999). In the case of BCCI, the liquidator was claiming the bank's outstanding mortgages and loans back from the former employees in order to pay the bank's creditors.

BCCI employees who had been working outside the United Kingdom, in countries such as India and Abu Dhabi, had been paying part of their salaries into a staff provident fund. This fund was a type of insurance scheme for non-United Kingdom staff members, whereby in cases of ill-health or upon retirement, employees would be entitled to a share of this money. However, upon the closure of BCCI the provident fund was no longer available to former members of staff, leaving them financially insecure. Mr. Smith said:

> The provident fund is in the control of the liquidators.

Similarly, Mr. Khan, who had been paying into the provident fund, revealed how he was unable to have his share of the fund:

> You see we had our own contribution to the provident fund that was, I got a statement from it. You contribute all of your life to it and now the liquidator is saying we can't give you that provident fund. I have a house loan outstanding so I have asked the liquidator to adjust it (provident fund) against my house which is absolutely normal and justified but they're not even willing to do that.

THE EMOTIONAL IMPACT

The closure of the Bank of Credit and Commerce International also wreaked an emotional toll upon former employees, in terms of depression, anxiety and anger.

Anxiety and Depression

"Frustration," "sadness," "anxiety" and "worry" were named by my informants as common. For instance, one former employee wrote about the sense of helplessness experienced as a result of the closure of BCCI:

> I experienced a sense of helplessness against institutions like the Bank of England and the rights that have been given to liquidators.

Mr. Reed spoke of his depression upon losing a job which he enjoyed:

> I was very depressed, losing a job I liked very much. We would have retired at 60, I'd be retired by now with a good pension probably, 'cos I was banging away loads of AVCs so I'd have been quite happy. There's the fact that I couldn't get another job and I was broke. If I hadn't had a working wife who was earning quite good money we'd have been in trouble and I'd have probably lost the house as well. That's enough to make anyone depressed.

And how the closure of the bank still continues to affect him today:

> Sometimes I still lie in bed at night and think what if I hadn't done this, if I hadn't bought that other house, if I'd done that. I blame my wife for buying that other house 'cos she liked it, I wasn't all that crazy about it so I tend to blame her. Especially when you see how other people have got their future sewn up and mine is so iffy.

Mr. Reed also revealed how he has felt suicidal in the past:

> I get bitter sometimes but it doesn't do any good. These guys who lost all this money at Lloyd's topped themselves. I've probably felt like it a few times but I don't think that's a solution to anything. I worry about the house sometimes, what's gonna happen. What they could do is sell those mortgage loans and if they sell them to somebody even nastier than the liquidator that could be a problem, probably end up in court. That's still at the back of my mind. And I'm in a job I don't enjoy very much, I want to retire but I can't. I don't like the liquidators, they're all bastards.

Anger

Many former employees of BCCI stated that "anger" and "bitterness" were common. Although former employees acknowledged that some of the staff members at the bank were partly to blame for its closure, it seems that anger was particularly meted out against the Bank of England for closing down BCCI, also towards the liquidator. Many former employees are angry that their bank was ever closed down, and argued that it should have been kept open. One employee asked:

> How come the Governor of the Bank of England was not lynched? Nobody has been accounted for it.

Another said:

> I think they (Bank of England) got it closed down where they shouldn't have done. They shouldn't have let it get to that stage.

Another argued:

> In case of frauds, only the individuals involved or responsible for frauds should be punished. BCCI should never have been closed in order to save other innocent members of staff and customers from any losses, for no fault of their own.

Mr. Brown maintained that shutting down BCCI was a "criminal waste":

> If the liquidators close down a bank they will remove any assets they possibly can out of your control. So they take away the means by which people can repay what they owe. There was a lack of forethought in closing down BCCI. It seemed such a criminal waste of a brilliant idea and initial growth.

Some employees suggested that there were racist undertones behind the Bank of England's decision to close down the Bank of Credit and Commerce

International. Former employees claimed that the bank was singled out by regulatory agencies and labeled deviant, even though many other banks also deal with drug money. Employees spoke about how they believed that BCCI challenged Western dominance over the financial sector, and the dominance of American aid agencies and international organizations such as the International Monetary Fund as being the sources of finance for Third World countries. Former employees claimed that the corruption at BCCI provided the Bank of England with an ideal reason for shutting down an expanding Asian bank. For example, Mr. Khan claimed that Mr. Abedi, the founder of the bank, viewed African and Asian countries as good potential for creating a bank:

> And then he (Abedi) being a very dynamic man he wanted to create something. He had a great presence, he was a real visionary and then he realized the lack of banking facilities in Third World countries in Africa, the potential of banking in Africa and all those Third World countries, Latin American countries, that is the reason which he had about making BCCI one of the best banks in the world.

Mr. Khan spoke of how BCCI lent money to people that Western banks would not:

> I met an Asian businessman in Zambia, he's a multi-millionaire now, he said whatever I am is to BCCI because generations of my family did banking with Barclays and these banks in Africa and whenever we went to borrow we couldn't get a penny from them, and when BCCI came they lent us money, they took the risk and that is why we established ourselves. BCCI provided the resources for honest hard-working people. Not one, there were quite a few people which I met and said the same thing. . . . Western banks did not lend to blacks or Asian communities in those countries, they took deposits from them, they were not as liberal as BCCI. BCCI could take risks.

. . . A recurring theme to emerge during interviews was that employees believed that the majority of people working for BCCI were honest, and had no idea of the white-collar violations which were being carried out. These subsequently led to the closure of the bank and affected everyone working for the bank. When asked whether employees were aware of money disappearing out of Bank of Credit and Commerce International accounts, Mr. Brown replied:

> No, I would say that probably 90% of the employees in the bank had no idea.

When asked about the drug money laundering which occurred at the bank, Mr. Parmar stated that the Bank of Credit and Commerce International as an organization never dealt with drug money, but that a few dishonest bank managers did:

> There may be one or two dishonest or eager managers who, in order to get more deposits, took this money, but BCCI as an organization never did.

While one former employee argued:

> There were very few people who knew about the fraud. I'd been in the bank and I didn't have the slightest clue about how its losses were hidden.

The above quotations illustrate how employees who work for organizations in which white-collar violations occur may not know that these are taking place, since both legitimate and illegitimate actions may occur within an organization, and therefore not every employee will necessarily be involved in white-collar crime (Punch, 1996).

The bank's connection with drugs was considered not to be a sufficient enough reason to close down the bank. . . . [A]ccording to Mr. Khan all banks deal with drug money, and the amount that BCCI laundered was only a small portion of this:

> And what happened their allegation was that BCCI, when BCCI were guilty in Panama the amount was 17 million dollars in 17 years which was peanuts compared to the number of transactions BCCI did. What is happening to 150 billion dollars drug money every year? Who is dealing with that? Has that stopped? When it is being done by western banks it's okay justified, but BCCI unintentionally or unknowingly they have done that which I think is wrong to take drug money but that wasn't done the way it is being presented to the media, that the most corrupt bank wasn't most corrupt.

According to statistics issued by the National Criminal Intelligence Service, £2.4 billion of drug money is laundered through the United Kingdom each year, of which an estimated £1.75 billion is laundered through the financial sector. Worldwide, more than £500 billion is laundered (Gilmore 1995, p. 25). It seems that BCCI was not the only bank to deal with drug money laundering, and yet it was labeled as a deviant bank by the press and regulators. This stigmatized former employees.

THE PSYCHOLOGICAL IMPACT

Stigma

Many of the former employees taking part in this study argued that they have been stigmatized, and as a result have found great difficulty in finding work, which has in turn caused them considerable distress. According to Mr. Ahmed:

> One of the chief liquidators said BCCI was rotten to the core and all the culture was criminal. How can you take a broom and wipe ten, eleven thousand people around the world and say we are all criminals?

Mr. Ahmed argued that:

> I don't think that BCCI was as corrupt as it has been presented in the media. I have never been ashamed for working for BCCI.

When asked if the BCCI label stigmatizes him, Mr. Ahmed replied:

> Oh absolutely. It's slowly fading because it's becoming old news, Barings and all that have taken over, but in areas. For example, a friend of mine wanted to work in IMRO and another colleague of mine who left the bank before the scandal he joined IMRO and he said yes there are jobs but being from BCCI they're not going to take you on.

Similarly, Mr. Khan found difficulty in finding work:

> When I was made redundant I came to the UK. However, you are aware that there has been so much bad publicity on us that we were stigmatized. I tried my best for six months to get a job. I sent my family to Pakistan. I couldn't visualize going on the dole. I think I claimed dole for three months. Then I looked for a job in Pakistan. I luckily found a job there.

Mr. Khan continued to tell of how a colleague of his has turned to decorating houses as a result of being made redundant at BCCI:

> I've seen an old BCCI friend, he's doing house decoration. You see most of us don't want to live on the dole.

Another former employee said:

> I have not seen any sympathy from the papers. The staff were presented as crooks and criminals.

Another revealed:

> Due to the closure of the bank and propaganda by the media, it is very difficult to secure any job in my own field like financial institutions, banks etc.

Another argued:

> Employees were branded as culprits and so I have had considerable difficulty in getting an alternative job.

THE BANK OF CREDIT AND COMMERCE INTERNATIONAL AS A DEMONIZED BANK

When examining the press reporting of BCCI and after looking at the comments which the Governor of the Bank of England and the liquidator made at the time, there seems to be evidence that this bank was being demonized. As a result, those associated with the bank were labeled as corrupt. BCCI was portrayed as a criminal bank, as the most corrupt bank in history (*The Times*, 28 September 1993). Headlines such as "Bank Shut in Massive Fraud" (*The Times*, 6 July 1991) and "The World's Sleaziest Bank" (*Time Magazine*, July 1991) appeared in the press. Careless remarks made by the Governor of the Bank of England and the liquidator suggested that BCCI was rotten to the core and corrupt from top to bottom, thereby attaching corruption to every person associated with the bank.[1] An official at the CIA had described the bank as "the bank of crooks and criminals international" (Adams and Franz 1992, p. 6).

Stigma may perhaps explain why so many former BCCI employees refused to speak with me: I encountered a wall of silence when trying to establish contact with former employees. This case study suggests that in the aftermath of a white-collar scandal, the public process of blaming which occurs may have a direct influence upon employees' experiences. Where blame is cast on one deviant individual (as in the case of Barings, Morgan Grenfell and Maxwell[2]) it seems likely that other employees working for the same organization will not be stigmatized. If, on the other hand, blame is placed upon an entire institution (as in the case of BCCI), then it is possible that former employees, and indeed any other persons associated with the institution (such as depositors for example), will also be blamed and therefore stigmatized. This in turn can mean that former employees of an organization labeled as deviant encounter great difficulty in finding work.

SECONDARY VICTIMIZATION, BCCI AND "WHITE-COLLAR CRIME"

. . . This case study illustrates the complexities involved when researching "victimization" by so-called "white-collar crime." The phrase "white-collar crime" is a general term which encompasses a wide variety of offenses, including price-fixing, fraud, embezzlement, the sale of faulty goods and services, health and safety law violations, and the emission of dangerous pollutants. The phrase "white-collar victimization" thus lacks specificity and may obscure the context within which a particular offense occurs, as well as the specific experiences of the victims. Establishing the crimes by which individuals are victimized may be problematic, particularly when individuals relate their negative experiences, not necessarily to any crimes which have been committed, but rather to regulatory and media responses.

Moreover, the issue of "secondary victimization" has been examined by policy makers and researchers predominantly in relation to street crime rather than white-collar offenses. Thus, secondary victimization has been defined as the inadequate treatment of victims by the criminal justice system through, for example, insensitive questioning by the police, delays or inadequate provision of information (Maguire and Pointing, 1988, p. 11). This study illustrates that "secondary victimization" may also be relevant to the area of "white-collar crime." With respect to the BCCI case study, regulatory processes and media reportage constitute part of the material conditions within which to assess the impact of the closure of BCCI upon former employees.

A pertinent question to ask is why did there appear to be so little consideration paid to the needs of former employees of BCCI by the regulatory authorities? Former employees' inadequate and insensitive treatment lies in stark contrast to the attention paid by policy makers and agencies of the criminal justice system to the needs of victims of street and property crime (Zedner 1994).

One aspect of the negative treatment received by the former BCCI employees is that of the ambiguous nature of "white-collar crime" when individuals caught up in "white-collar scandal" may not be viewed as "victims" by regulatory authorities (Elias 1990) and so their needs are not considered. In addition, the majority of former BCCI employees did not play an important role in the detection and prosecution of the crimes which occurred at BCCI, and it seems that this is a significant reason for their negative treatment. Evidence against BCCI was gathered through undercover operations carried out by customs officers, and through intelligence agencies such as MI5 and the CIA. Price Waterhouse was also asked by the Bank of England to gather evidence when auditing BCCI's accounts. When prosecutions were carried out against this bank and some of its former employees, only a very small proportion of employees were required to give evidence. Moreover, these employees occupied high-ranking positions, since less senior employees would not have had any evidence of corruption to present at court (Passas, 1996). This means that most former employees of BCCI, many of whom had not been aware of the illicit operations and surveillance that had been occurring over the years, were unimportant to the prosecutions carried out. Researchers have argued that the recognition amongst agencies of the criminal justice system that the reporting and prosecution of physical and sexual violence and burglary often requires the victim (McCabe and Sutcliffe, 1978; Kelly and Erez, 1997) has acted as a "bargaining tool" (Zedner, 1994, p. 1230) in gaining recognition of victims' needs. In the case of employees who have worked for organizations in which white-collar violations have taken place, however, this case study suggests that where employees are largely superfluous to the investigations and prosecutions carried out by regulatory authorities, their needs, it seems, are secondary to the process of regulation and prosecution. . . .

CONCLUSION

This article illustrates how former employees of BCCI experienced psychological emotional and financial impacts as a result of the bank being enveloped in scandal. The financial costs which former employees had to bear included losing money from deposits held at the bank, losing money from a staff provident fund, loss of earnings and being charged high rates of interest on mortgage accounts. The emotional impact included anxiety, depression and anger. The psychological impact was that of having stigma attached as a result of being associated with a bank labeled as corrupt. A significant dimension to the impact of the closure of BCCI upon former employees is that of "secondary victimization." Former employees attributed the losses that they had incurred to the regulatory responses made by the Bank of England and liquidator, and also the media reportage of the bank. This suggests that the major element of the victimizing experience of victim employees may be that of the responses of regulatory agencies, and also the media reportage of the case. However, it is unlikely that regulatory authorities will examine employees' satisfaction with the actions that they take since victim employees are in some cases, it seems, superfluous to the process of investigation and prosecution.

NOTES

1. The liquidator spoke of BCCI as being rotten to the core, and the Governor of the Bank of England pronounced that "the culture of the bank was criminal" (Kochan and Whittington 1991, p. 168).

2. In the Barings scandal, Nick Leeson was singled out as being the main perpetrator behind the crash, and the managerial structure which allowed him to expose the bank to such huge risks was debated only as a secondary issue. When three investment funds at Morgan Grenfell were suspended, Peter Young the investment manager was blamed. While Nick Leeson was labeled a "rogue trader" by the press, Peter Young was considered to be a "quiet loner" (*The Sunday Times*, 8 September 1996).

REFERENCES

Adams, J. and Frantz, D. (1992) *A Full Service Bank: How BCCI Stole Billions Around the World*, London: Simon and Schuster.

Atkins, R. (1995) "Ex-BCCI staff lose appeal for redress," *The Financial Times*, 10 March.

Atkinson, D. (1997) "BCCI staff fight to keep loans," *The Guardian*, 13 October.

Corbett, C. and Maguire, M. (1988) "The value and limitations of VSS," in: M. Maguire and J. Pointing (Eds.), *Victims of Crime: A New Deal?*, Milton Keynes: Open University Press.

Elias, R. (1990) "Which victim movement? The politics of victim policy," in: A. Lurigio, W. Skogan and R. Davis (Eds.), *Victims of Crime: Problems, Policies and Programs*, London: Sage.

Eve, S. (1985) "Criminal victimization and fear of crime among the non-institutionalised elderly in the United States: a critique of the empirical research literature," *Victimology*, 10, 397–408.

Gauhar, H. (1995) "The fall guy Agha Hasan Abedi—September 25, 1922–August 5, 1995," *Politics and Business*, August, 68–75.

Gilmore, W. (1995) *Dirty Money*, Netherlands: Council of Europe.

Investment Management Regulatory Organization (1997) *Protecting Investors*, London: HMSO.

Kane, F. and Olins, R. (1996) "Morgan 'criminality' uncovered," *The Sunday Times*, 8 September.

Kelly, D. and Erez, E. (1997) "Victim participation in the criminal justice system," in: R. Davis, A. Lurigio and W. Skogan (Eds.), *Victims of Crime*, 2nd ed., London: Sage.

Kochan, N. and Whittington, B. (1991) *Bankrupt: The BCCI Fraud*, London: Gollancz.

Levi, M. and Pithouse, A. (1992) "The victims of fraud," in: D. Downes (Ed.), *Unravelling Criminal Justice*, London: Macmillan.

Maguire, M. and Pointing, J. (Eds.) (1988) *Victims of Crime: A New Deal?*, Milton Keynes: Open University Press.

Mawby, R. and Walklate, S. (1994) *Critical Victimology*, London: Sage.

Mayhew, P., Aye Maung, N. and Mirrlees-Black, C. (1993) *The 1992 British Crime Survey*, London: HMSO.

McCabe, S. and Sutcliffe, F. (1978) *Defining Crime*, Oxford: Blackwell.

Mirrlees-Black, C., Budd, T., Partridge, S. and Mayhew, P. (1998) *The 1998 British Crime Survey*, London: HMSO.

Newburn, T. and Merry, S. (1990) *Keeping in Touch: Police-Victim Communication in Areas* (Home Office Research Study No. 116), London: HMSO.

Passas, N. (1996) "The genesis of the BCCI Scandal," *Journal of Law and Society*, 23, 57–72.

Punch, M. (1996) *Dirty Business: Exploring Corporate Misconduct*, London: Sage.

Shapland, J., Willmore, J. and Duff, P. (1985) *Victims in the Criminal Justice System*, Aldershot: Gower.

Sorell, T. and Hendry, J. (1999) *Business Ethics*, Oxford: Butterworth-Heinemann.

Victim Support (1998) *Annual Report 1998*, London: Victim Support National Office.

Zedner, L. (1994) "Victims," in: M. Maguire, R. Morgan and R. Reiner (Eds.), *The Oxford Handbook of Criminology*, Oxford: Clarendon Press.

CORRUPTION SCANDALS IN AMERICA AND EUROPE

Enron and EU Fraud in Comparative Perspective

CRIS SHORE

As Durkheim pointed out, crime is universal. As most people consider this statement, they are probably thinking about crimes most often committed by the lower class; however, it seems to apply as well to crimes committed by the upper class.

Poor countries are frequently blamed for their own poverty, and one of the causes most frequently cited is political corruption. On this basis, wealthy countries often withhold financial assistance to these countries, or make it contingent upon a host of austerity measures and a requirement that they clean up their political corruption. In light of the corruption that pervades the upper echelons of the First World, this smacks of ethnocentrism and hypocrisy.

When crimes committed by the lower class become rampant, the most common response is to crack down on crime and become more punitive. Interestingly, though, as crime becomes more rampant in the upper class, a common response is for the public to become inured to it and look the other way (often toward crimes committed by the poor).

The recent wave of corruption scandals has sent a shockwave through corporate America and beyond, but as the tremors subside there is still no consensus on what lessons have been learned, and what changes should be implemented to restore public trust in corporate governance and the accountancy profession. The only certainty is that people will think twice before making jokes about boring accountants.

What shocked people was not only the sophistication and complexity of the Enron/Anderson relationship that had so effectively masked Enron's true value, but the fact that most of the devious accounting tricks that had enabled it to happen were perfectly legal under existing U.S. accounting rules. In June 2002, as the list of companies mired in what has become the largest fraud scandal in American business history spread from Enron and WorldCom to Xerox and Tyco, U.S. Treasury Secretary Paul O'Neill called on people to be "outraged" and promised stringent legislation to tighten up accountancy rules.[1] President Bush, for his part, told the American people that "corporate misdeeds will be found and will be punished" and denounced the excessive "greed" of certain individuals (friends excluded) who had played fast and loose with accepted business norms and ethics. Never mind the fact that the rules themselves facilitated and encouraged such behavior, or that today's fraudsters, who have robbed thousands of employees of their savings and pensions, were yesterday's heroes and celebrities, idolized for their entrepreneurial acumen and lionized on the covers of American business magazines. Elsewhere we have witnessed the extraordinary spectacle of chief executives from many of America's largest companies rushing to sign notarized oaths attesting that "to the best of my knowledge" their latest quarterly or yearly returns neither contain "untrue statements" nor "omit any material facts."[2] While these modern company rituals are designed to reassure shareholders and public opinion of the integrity of corporate America, this new image of the CEO as pillar of moral rectitude contrasts starkly with the ruthless corporate raider so effectively portrayed in the figure of Gordon Gekko, the antihero of Oliver Stone's 1987 film, *Wall Street*, whose defense of avarice and the unbridled pursuit of profit still epitomize for many the rationale behind modern corporate ethics.

But how does this rash of ethical pledges look from a European perspective, and what comparisons, if any, can we draw between the two continents when it comes to narratives of corruption and anti-corruption practices? Although the Enron scandal has precipitated calls in some parts of Europe for accountancy rules and regulations to be overhauled, the general attitude here is that these kinds of corporate scandal are a peculiarly American problem, home of American rather than European values. Leaving aside the question of what exactly these distinctly "American" values might be (and the observation that politicians on both sides of the Atlantic have been at pains to stress the unity of Western values in the post–11 September "war on terror"), this is a dubious assumption, even if the *scale* of corporate corruption in Europe does not match that of America. The key difference, perhaps, is that

Europe's major financial scandals tend to occur in the public rather than private sector, and are less evident among European business leaders as among Europe's political elites or *classe politique*—the recent corruption scandals surrounding Helmut Kohl, Jacques Chirac and Silvio Berlusconi being prime examples of this.

The European Union provides an exemplary case in point. In March 1999 the entire political leadership of the European Commission—the EU's supranational civil service—resigned after a damning official Parliamentary report by a group of independent auditing experts revealed massive evidence of fraud, mismanagement and corruption throughout its services.[3] What the report brought to light, beyond the various small instances of contract fixing, nepotism, and petty graft within the institutions, was that large sums of money had gone missing from the EU's budget, and an estimated £17 billion in structural fund projects could not be accounted for because the Commission had failed to keep records of monies spent. As in the Enron scandal, however, many of the illicit practices exposed by the report were not strictly speaking "corruption" in a legal sense. For example, Commissioner Edith Cresson may have appointed her personal dentist and friend, Mr. Bertheler, to a highly paid job as scientific advisor on an EU HIV/AIDS research program (for which he was manifestly unqualified and did no work beyond running personal errands for her), and she may well have presided over what the report termed a "dysfunctional organizational climate," but as Cresson had not made any "personal financial gain" from her abuse of public office, this was not classified as "corruption" according to the standard definition. Indeed, Cresson gave a spirited defense of her actions, arguing that this so-called "nepotism" was justifiable, and really no different from what is "standard practice in French public administration." Furthermore, as she stated in a press conference, the whole EU anti-fraud campaign was part of a "right wing" conspiracy designed to damage France, and an "Anglo-Saxon crusade" against the southern culture of administration.[4] In short, an assault on French culture itself.

As with the Enron affair, political leaders expressed moral indignation and promised root and branch reform. With the inauguration of the new Commission under Romano Prodi, Vice President Neil Kinnock was given the job of cleaning up the administration—the "House," as Commission officials call it. Over the past five years, Commissioner Kinnock has introduced a raft of new "accountability" measures and new codes of conduct designed to rationalize staffing policy and modernize the Commission's baroque "organizational culture." Perhaps the most striking aspect of the reform process—some would say the only aspect—has been the wholesale import of new acronyms and jargon (such as "Activity Based Management" and "policy-driven spp frameworks") borrowed from management consultants. Five years on, however, it looks increasingly like *plus ça change*.[5] In August 2002, accounting controls over the EU's £98 billion budget were once again criticized as "insecure," and "unreliable" in a scathing leaked report from the

European Court of Auditors. In its indictment, the report states that "no account has been taken of generally accepted accounting standards, mainly double-entry book keeping."[6] In response, the Commission lamely argued that the report might never have been published because it contained inaccuracies and that the "tone of the language was inappropriate."

At the same time as the leaked report was made public, Marta Andreasen, the former Commission chief accountant who had been controversially removed from her post in May, gave a press conference in London in which she accused Mr. Kinnock of trying to cover up lax accounting standards in the EU budget. Andreasen also alleged that she was harassed and subjected to a campaign of character assassination by senior Commission officials who sought to prevent her from voicing her concerns.

How does all this compare with Enron? In many ways, EU fraud is worse. Marta Andreasen noted: "Unlike the issues surrounding Enron and WorldCom, where you can at least trace transactions, you cannot do so within EU accounts as there is no system in place for tracing adjustments. Fraud can therefore lie hidden within the system undetected and untraced."[7] In other words, we have no way of knowing how much money that goes into the Brussels machinery comes out the other end.

If we leave aside the Common Agricultural Policy which accounts for half of all EU money spent, and which many consider to be a criminal waste of money, the Court of Auditors estimates that five to eight percent of the EU's budget is lost to fraud each year, while another five percent is not spent in the way it was intended. This is a not insignificant sum by any reckoning, although no government official has yet echoed Paul O'Neill in calling upon citizens to be "outraged." As in the case of Arthur Andersen, the company that audited Enron's accounts and later instructed its employees to shred incriminating documents, no individual in the Commission has yet (at the time of writing) been prosecuted or punished for corruption. Indeed, the only person to be disciplined and sacked from his post was Paul Van Buitenen, the Dutch audit official and whistleblower whose weighty dossier of accumulated evidence precipitated the original enquiry into allegations of fraud and mismanagement in the Commission.

In both the Enron and EU scandals, the most serious complicity and fraud were perpetrated not by junior staff but by senior officials, thus vindicating the old Greek and Sicilian folk proverb that "the fish rots from the head downward." In both situations too, those responsible for checking the budget or holding their executive to account, signally failed to do so in part because it was not in their interests to do so. In the case of the EU, the dereliction of duty was on the part of the European Parliament (which, ironically, now claims credit for bringing the Commission to book). For seven years in succession, the Court of Auditors had refused to sign off the EU's accounts, and had warned of "grave irregularities" in the budget. Yet despite these admonitions, the European Parliament (for political reasons) had consistently approved them.

One of the key factors noted in both the Enron and Andersen scandals was the "incestuous relationship" between firm and client, which prevented the auditors from acting independently. But the relationship between the European Commission and European Parliament—the body that is supposed to act as its constitutional watchdog—is equally incestuous (note that the disgraced former President of the Commission, Jacques Santer, like many former Commissioners, is now a member of the European Parliament thanks to the Party-List system). The appointment of Neil Kinnock—a veteran of the Santer Commission—to oversee the clean up of the Commission's administration might also raise reasonable questions about conflict of interest.

A third parallel is that in corporate America, as in the EU, corporate pressure is placed upon employees to show loyalty to their organization. Despite the post-1999 introduction of an EU whistleblowers charter, those who do blow the whistle are likely to face a range of bureaucratic obstacles and sanctions, including vilification, harassment and dismissal (the fate of Marta Andreasen and Paul Van Buitenen are particularly instructive here). Some corporations use "gagging clauses" to prevent employees from disclosing sensitive or potentially embarrassing information about company policy and practice: this is not unheard of even in British Universities and the National Health Service. In the case of WorldCom, company executives resorted to outright bribery. By contrast, in the case of the EU, the Statutes themselves provided the most effective instrument for inhibiting insider disclosure of malfeasance. Articles 17 to 19 of the old Staff Statutes expressly forbade officials from divulging any information about the organization deemed sensitive or damaging, thereby functioning as a kind of "official secrets act." Loyalty to the "House" was thus enshrined in the EU's corporate ethics and prevailing *esprit de corps*.

Fraudulent accounting within the EU is not, however, confined to the European Commission. In 1998, there was a great deal of fiddling by those governments seeking to qualify for membership of the new single currency. To do this, applicant countries had to demonstrate they had successfully fulfilled the stringent deflationary Maastricht Treaty entrance requirements. Many did so by "creative accountancy" to which the Commission was happy to turn a blind eye. This flexible use of statistics continues. In the words of the head of the Commission's Eurostat statistical office, Yves Franchet, the situation is "a bit like Enron," as members of the eurozone maneuver to avoid breaching the Stability and Growth Pact or the rules on budget deficits and borrowing. For example, the Italian and Greek government both tried to borrow money against future sales of lottery tickets, while the German government successfully borrowed money against the future rents of state owned railway cottages. In the post-Enron environment, accountants have even invented a new piece of jargon to describe this practice of inflating a company's (or country's) worth and then vigorously underwriting it: "aggressive actuarial assumptions."[8] In yet a further twist in the saga of EU corruption, Yves Franchet was suspended in July 2003 following disclosure of major fraud and cronyism at the EU's Eurostat office in Luxembourg, including the disappearance of €5 million of taxpayers' money into secret accounts used to fund staff perks.[9]

CONCLUSION

For years, the attitude of Western governments to the problem of corruption and shoddy business ethics has been framed within Eurocentric assumptions that corruption is essentially a Third World disorder; a pathology endemic to "backward" developing countries with weak civil societies and bloated public sectors. According to this view, the only effective solution was to introduce painful, deflationary, neoliberal reforms, and the fiscal and moral disciplines of the market. Under the twin banners of "anti-corruption" and "good governance," the U.S. government, the IMF, and the World Bank have systematically bullied their weaker trading partners into accepting the rules and norms of modern corporate capitalism. It would be encouraging to think that Enron has injected a note of humility and caution on the part of those self-righteous moral crusaders who, until recently, saw the export of Western free market ethics and practices as the panacea to the world's problems. After all, "reflexivity" is supposedly one of the defining characteristics of Western modernity according to some sociologists. But so too are hypocrisy and Eurocentrism. Here again comparisons between Enron and "EU-ron" are instructive. In July 1999, a small article appeared in the inside pages of the *Financial Times*, so small it was barely noticeable. It reported that the European Union had warned seventy-one African, Caribbean, and Pacific (ACP) countries that "they must commit themselves to rooting out corruption and misspending of aid money," and to the principle of "good governance" if they wanted to renew the Lomé trade and development agreement. This came barely three months after the Commission was forced to resign because of its own documented corruption and mismanagement.

If public cynicism in the ability of political elites to tackle problems of political corruption and corporate sleaze is growing, it is hardly surprising. The close personal ties between the perpetrators of fraud, and those in office that are supposed to prevent such abuse are increasingly apparent. Many members of the Bush administration come from the same cozy world of crony capitalism as Enron's Ken Lay: like the EU's emergent technocratic elite, they share the same "habitus."[10] This might explain their reluctance to root out such sleaze. For example, under the cover of the "war on terror" and the general anxiety about Iraq, President Bush has quietly slashed most of the new funding allocated to the Securities and Exchange Commission (SEC), the agency that oversees the corporate finance world.[11] That agency has itself become embroiled in scandal. On 13 November 2002, its newly appointed head, William Webster—a former federal judge, FBI and CIA director, and the man brought in to restore integrity to the regulatory process—resigned, following the revelation that he had been the head of the audit committee of U.S. Technologies, a company whose finances and deal making are under federal investigation. Like his predecessor, Harvey Pitt, Mr. Webster had failed to pass that information on to the other SEC commissioners.[12]

All this begs one final question: should "corporate ethics" in business be comparable to those in public administration? Or to put it another way, should we expect the same standards of probity and accountability from public administrators as we do from those who manage our investments and pension funds? Among the public at large, there is today almost an expectation that large corporations put pursuit of profit before ethical considerations —or as Gordon Gekko put it, "greed is good" not only because it fuels progress and company profit, but because it continues to be the bedrock upon which corporate America has flourished. In public administration there is no such excuse. In modern democracies, administrations are supposed to exist to serve the public interest—and taxation and public spending lie at the heart of the relationship between citizens and the state. But here again is another interesting contrast: in the EU there is no *European public* or a European press that can meaningfully claim to represent the "public interest." Paradoxically, that is a role the Commission claims for itself. Perhaps that is why fraud and mismanagement have proved to be such intractable problems for the EU; the bodies created to solve the problem may actually be part of the problem. At least Enron shareholders have the possibility of voting out their discredited executives.

NOTES

1. O'Neill (2002) calls the accounting scandal an "outrage."

2. Leader article, *Economist.* 17 August 2002, 11.

3. Committee of Independent Experts. 1999. *First Report into Allegations of Fraud, Mismanagement and Corruption in the European Commission.*

4. For more detailed analyses of these events, see Macmullen (1999) and Shore (2000).

5. Significantly, this was also what some Commission analysts and insiders had predicted at the time. See, for example, Spence (2000).

6. *Financial Times.* 1 August 2002, 1.

7. Cited in Trefgarne (2002: 4).

8. "Enron Scandal—The Burning Issue." *Financial Times* (FT Expat.), 1 May 2002.

9. *BBC News*, 10 July 2003; *Times*, 26 September 2003.

10. See Bourdieu (1990).

11. See Borger (2002).

12. See Michaels (2002).

REFERENCES

Borger, Julian. 2002. "'Clean-Up' Swept Under the Carpet." *Guardian Weekly* 7–13 November.

Bourdieu, Pierre. 1990. "Structures, Habitus, Practices." pp. 52–65 in *The Logic of Practice*, trans. Richard Nice. Cambridge: Polity Press.

Committee of Independent Experts. 1999. *First Report into Allegations of Fraud, Mismanagement and Corruption in the European Commission*. Brussels, European Parliament.

Macmullen, A. 1999. "Political Responsibility for the Administration of Europe: The Commission's Resignation March 1999. *Parliamentary Affairs*, 52, no. 1:703–718.

Michaels, Adrian. 2002. "Webster Quits after Debacle at SEC." *Financial Times*, 13 November.

O'Neill, Paul. 2002. *Financial Times*. 24 June.

Shore, Cris. 2000. *Building Europe: The Cultural Politics of European Integration* London: Routledge.

Spence, David. 2000. "*Plus ça change, plus c'est la même chose?* Attempting to Reform the European Commission?" *Journal of European Public Policy* 7. no. 1 (March): 1–25.

Trefgarne, George. 2002. *Daily Telegraph*, 2 September.

PART 7

Deviance and Religion

NONES ON THE RUN

Evangelical Heathens in the Deep South

ROBERT HEINER

Not surprisingly, people who stray from the norm often seek the company of others who stray, forming what are often called in the literature "deviant sub-cultures." Often shunned by others, they can find comfort and companionship in the group. In the company of others like themselves, they frequently establish beliefs, practices, and rituals that aid them in neutralizing the stigma attached to them by outsiders. Following is a discussion of atheists and other non-believers who have banded together in a religious southern community in the United States.

INTRODUCTION

Despite the important role religion plays in the social life of the United States and the thousands upon thousands of books and articles published on the subject, relatively little has been written about atheism. Although atheism predates Christianity by millennia, in 1971 James Thrower could refer to the history of atheism as "the so far neglected and well-nigh unrecorded history of unbelief."[1] But the student of deviance should be well aware of the fact that historically the deviant is often neglected in the professional literature. Because religious beliefs prevail in virtually every culture, and religion dates back to prehistory, it is possible that atheism has existed as a deviant status in most cultures since the beginning of humankind.

But this study is not just about atheists; it is about atheists and other unbelievers (e.g., agnostics and deists), people sometimes referred to as *nones* because they check the word "none" on surveys that ask their religion. They are also referred to as apostates in the sociology of religion literature, referring to people who have turned away from religion.[2] The nones examined in this article are not ordinary nones; they are rather extraordinary (and deviant) because they are outspoken and *organized*. In the minds of the fervently religious, they are all atheists, but they like to call themselves "freethinkers." This term seems a bit immodest and self-congratulatory, and as a sociologist, I am inclined to doubt the very existence of such a thing as a freethinker. But the word has a history of almost 300 years and for lack of a better term, it will be used in this article to refer to the loosely connected nationwide group of unbelievers who call themselves freethinkers.

The dearth of writings on the subject of atheism and freethought in the deviance literature is especially notable considering the pervasive and extensive history of the persecution of unbelievers in Western civilization. Until 1610 in England, outspoken unbelievers could be burned as heretics. Legal codes prohibiting blasphemy continued beyond this date, and ecclesiastical courts could imprison heretics for as long as six months. Laws prohibited blasphemers from holding public office, owning land, or bringing suit in courts, and blasphemers who repeated their offenses could be imprisoned for as long as three years.[3] Persecutory measures, in one form or another, have been officially exercised throughout Christendom to the present century. The list of notable figures who have been so persecuted includes Denis Diderot (French philosopher and atheist who was imprisoned for three years for blasphemy), Thomas Paine (British deist, American Revolutionary hero, banished from England, shunned in America for his outspoken deistic ideas), Richard Carlile (American publisher who spent more than nine years in prison for publishing such heretical works as Paine's *The Age of Reason*), and Annie Besant (British social reformer, deemed unfit to maintain custody of her children because of her beliefs).

Today in the United States, some state constitutions still ban unbelievers from holding public office (e.g., South Carolina, Arkansas, and Pennsylvania), and unbelievers continue to experience a good deal of prejudice and discrimination (this will be discussed in further detail later). In fact, while some of the worst atrocities perpetrated against unbelievers occurred in Europe in previous centuries, in this century there probably has been "more de facto discrimination and prejudice [in the United States] than in any other Western country."[4]

Considering that the sociology of deviance has traditionally examined groups that are oppressed, the study of unbelievers is a chapter sorely lacking in the literature. This article is a preliminary effort to fill that void.

In a society such as our own in which religion plays an important role in the lives of so many, the transition from belief to unbelief is likely to be accompanied by a good deal of uncertainty, self-doubt, and anomie. The unbelievers examined in this study are organized at least to the extent that they hold regular meetings (many of them pay dues to a national organization of unbelievers). That they band together on the basis of their deviant status makes them similar to various other deviant subcultures described in the literature.[5] Belonging to such groups fulfills certain basic needs for its members. Writes Simmons:

> In response to society's disapproval and harassment deviants usually band together with others in the same plight. Beyond the ties of similar interests and views which lie at the base of most human associations, deviants find that establishing fairly stable relationships with other deviants does much to ease

procurement and coping problems and to provide a stable and reliable source of direct support and interaction.[6]

Among the more important functions of the group is providing its members with the situated morality necessary to neutralize their deviancy. According to Goode, "Deviance neutralization is an effort to render a positive image of oneself while engaging in behavior and accepting an identity one knows is odious and obnoxious to others."[7] In the case of these freethinkers, neutralization consists of a series of arguments that strongly suggest both an intellectual and a moral superiority of freethought over religious conviction. Natural byproducts of such neutralization tactics are hostility and disdain on the part of freethinkers toward those who hold religious beliefs. Such hostile feelings toward the majority can be problematic. Freethinkers are often estranged not only from the general society, but also from members of their own families and from their own upbringings. These are the issues that will be addressed in this article. It will further be argued that the unbeliever plays an integral role in boundary maintenance for the religious community. But first, we will begin with a description of the group and the environment— the prejudice and discrimination—that gave rise to its formation.

THE STUDY SETTING AND METHOD

Southland (pseudonym) is a city in the Deep South with a population of roughly 200,000. Church attendance is very high, fundamentalism thrives, and religious bookstores and media programming do a booming business. The unbelievers examined in this analysis are not deviant simply because they are unbelievers, but because they are organized unbelievers, often outspoken, in a city where religion has a prominent influence. This group of unbelievers meets once a month as the Southland Freethought Association (SFA). Between 10 and 25 people attend each meeting, with the average attendance being between 12 and 15 people. This is one of many freethought associations around the country that are a part of the Freedom from Religion Foundation (FFRF), headquartered in Madison, Wisconsin. The stated goals of FFRF are to defend the First Amendment guarantee of separation of church and state and to educate the public about nontheistic beliefs. It claims a nationwide membership of 3,800. Membership is between $30 and $35 per year. Each member receives a monthly newspaper, *Freethought Today*.

SFA is one of the two freethought associations in the state. The other one is in Big City (pseudonym), a city with a population of about 300,000 residents about 250 miles from Southland. Both of these groups are aligned with various other liberal interest groups in the state. They are well connected with the National Organization for Women and the American Civil Liberties Union. In addition to separation of church and state, SFA's main political cause, members also tend to take liberal positions regarding abortion rights and the environment. Many SFA members also attend the Unitarian Fellowship, another one of a very few liberal organizations in Southland.

The data in this study come from notes taken during eight of the monthly SFA meetings (where I continually introduced myself as a sociologist and observer). I also interviewed 10 people who regularly attended the meetings. I interviewed people in both Southland and Big City; the interviews lasted between 45 minutes and one and a half hours. Data also include passages from the FFRF publication *Freethought Today*.

Deviant subcultures have their own rituals that serve to reaffirm the situated morality of the group.[8] As part of one such ritual, many members of these two freethought associations apparently take great pleasure in having letters published in the local newspapers. These letters usually involve some kind of attack on religious doctrine or local religious leaders. Members often photocopy their letters for distribution at the monthly meetings. These letters were also used as a source of information.

I can make no claims as to the representativeness of the 10 respondents. Admittedly, I especially sought to interview those who were most outspoken, expressive, eloquent, politically active, and cantankerous. Excerpts from *Freethought Today* are used to give a little breadth, if not representativeness, to the data obtained from the meeting notes, interviews, and letters. Though the people I chose for my sample, those who write letters, and those who write for *Freethought Today* may or may not be typical members of FFRF, they are the most outspoken, and they appear to dominate the direction and nature of the activities of FFRF and its association meetings.

Of the respondents I interviewed, one identified herself as an agnostic, one identified himself as a deist, and the rest identified themselves as atheists. Three had college degrees, two were college students (nontraditional students, one age 48, the other age 36), one had his GED, the rest were high school graduates. Most came from parents who did not graduate from high school. They ranged in age from 33 to 87. Five were female, five were male. Their occupations were varied, including a journalist, a self-employed insurance salesman, an electrician, a secretary, a retired radar technician, and a retired mechanic. Included in the sample were the director of the Southland chapter and his wife, and the director of the Big City chapter and his wife (the wives in both cases were very active and might best be considered co-directors). One of the respondents was once a rural Southern fundamentalist minister. Another respondent has spent most of his adult life as an atheist activist (he drives a car that is covered in decals spelling out atheistic and antireligious slogans). His name is of some renown among various atheistic circles around the country.

The respondents also come from various religious backgrounds. None reported having two freethinking parents. Interestingly, though, most of the respondents reported that their mothers were very religious (Pentecostal, Assembly of God, Southern Baptist, Methodist, Roman Catholic) and insisted on a good deal of religious adherence, while their fathers were either agnostic, atheist, or completely uninvolved in religion.

R3: My dad was a closet heretic, I think. But because of his career [an undertaker], he couldn't be open about his beliefs.

R4: My dad was an atheist, but he only started to talk about it when he found out I was interested [in her late twenties]. He never would have brought it up on his own.

R8: I never heard my father mention the word "religion" other than when he was cussing preachers.

R10: My mother was a fanatic. My father made me go to church; but he didn't believe none of it no how.

PREJUDICE AND DISCRIMINATION

Atheism has often been associated with immorality, anarchy, and during the Cold War, communism; some fundamentalists are taught that atheists are in league with the Devil. Furthermore, atheists and unbelievers get very strong signals from some of our nation's leaders when they are trying to appeal to the religious right. A flyer distributed by SFA quotes presidential candidate George H.W. Bush as saying, "I don't know that atheists should be considered as citizens, nor should they be considered patriotic. This is one nation under God." They are often misunderstood, sometimes suspected, occasionally despised. A social distance survey reported by Stark and Bainbridge asked respondents if they "would feel friendly and at ease" with various kinds of people. Only 23% of Protestant respondents and 24% of Catholic respondents said that they would feel friendly and at ease with an atheist.[9] As mentioned earlier, the state constitutions of Arkansas, Pennsylvania, and South Carolina have clauses that prohibit atheists from holding certain public offices; this practice "grew out of the conviction that people who were not believers were not trustworthy."[10] According to Robertson,

> There is an implicit cultural assumption that Americans should be religious—not necessarily by attending church or synagogue, but at least by expressing a belief in God and in religious principles. A 1983 Gallup poll found that only 42 percent of Americans would be willing to vote for an atheist for president (compared with 66 percent who would vote for a Jew, 77 percent for a black, 80 percent for a woman, and 92 percent for a Catholic).[11]

Members of FFRF are acutely aware of prejudice and discrimination directed toward them. The passage below is from the *Freethought Today* "Letter Box."

> As freethinkers in this country, we are a despised minority fighting to maintain our Constitutional right to exist. Our program is primarily one of image. People don't hate us for what we are. They hate us for what they're being told we are by their preachers.[12]

A respondent expressed similar feelings of persecution.

> R10: They'd burn me at the stake if they thought they could get away with it. There's no God protecting me; there's only a Constitution protecting me.

Almost all of the respondents had stories of being victims of prejudice and discrimination that they were anxious to tell. Many of these accounts dealt with relations in their own families.

> R1: We have family who are ultra-religious who keep their children away from us.

> R2: My nephew is not allowed to be around me.

> R7: My family is less likely to be cooperative with my ideas now than when they thought I was a Christian.

> R7: My sister will not allow me to discuss freethought. Her children are very special to me, but we don't see them as much since we [the respondent and her husband] came out of the closet.

> R7: Our next-door neighbors don't knock on our door anymore. But one good thing about it is the preachers don't come knocking either.

Relations at the workplace are also strained when employers and co-workers become aware of their unbelief.

> R1: I would have to work on holidays so the good Christians could go home. . . . The Christians could take off for church business, but I couldn't take off for freethought.

> R2: [After an article came out in the local newspaper about his involvement in SFA] I got fired. I became an antichrist. Nobody would even get in a car with me.

> R5: [About being an atheist] I don't wear it on my sleeve; but I don't deny it either . . . . A guy at work harasses me; he enjoys putting me on the spot to make me look bad.

> R10: [Retired and confined to a wheelchair] I get very little pension for one thing. I think I would get a lot more if I weren't an atheist. I can't belong to the VFW or the American Legion, because I won't swear an oath to God. And so they're fighting against me and not for me.

One respondent expressed concern about her child facing prejudice because of her beliefs.

> R5: I worry about how to bring up my girl so she doesn't get beat over the head.

Another source of embitterment and feelings of persecution is the fact that various local businesses offer discounts to customers who present a church bulletin when paying for goods or services.

Several issues that came up frequently at SFA meetings were related to members' concerns about prejudice and public attitudes. First, they were concerned about how to "reach out" to atheists who were afraid to "come out of the closet."

R10: [Speaking out during a meeting] One out of every four of your neighbors is an atheist. But Christians are such a violent people, nobody don't dare speak their mind.

Likewise, some members were concerned that their involvement with SFA be kept from public knowledge. Also, some members emphasized the importance of the organization's being involved in community and charitable service in order to counteract the public image of the unbeliever as being immoral.

Ever-conscious of the unpopularity of their beliefs, these people seek refuge in FFRF groups. The groups provide a place where they can speak openly, a kind of group therapy.

R6: It's nice to be around people who think like you. There are so few freethinkers around.

R4: [Answer to the question "What do you get out of the Freethought meetings?"] The opportunity to express feelings you're not free to discuss in outside society . . . to be free of recriminations . . . to be with like-minded people.

Expressing similar sentiments are the following letters typical of those published in *Freethought Today*.

Thank you for being an oasis of reason in a desert of religious fanaticism.[13]

It is so helpful getting from one day to the next knowing that despite the way it often looks, I am not alone in my dedication to rationality.[14]

ANOMIE AND CONVERSION

Given the degree of prejudice and discrimination against the unbeliever in our society, it is rather remarkable that anyone would become an unbeliever, especially an acknowledged unbeliever. Lofland and Stark describe "conversion" in the following terms:

All men and all human groups have ultimate values, a world view, or a perspective furnishing them with a more or less orderly and comprehensive picture of the world. . . . When a person gives up one such perspective or ordered view of the world for another we refer to this process as conversion.[15]

The authors are referring, of course, to religious conversions. Formerly religious members of Freethought have been through religious *unconversions*, or perhaps more precisely, unreligious conversions, in that they have merely converted from one orderly and comprehensive picture of the world to an unreligious (they say "rational") picture. Given their religious upbringing, and the often fiercely negative attitudes in the religious community toward unbelievers, an important question is how did their conversion to unbelief come about. Fear of unbelief and the wrath of God is often instilled at very young ages.

R4: My mother told me the only sin you'll never be forgiven for is questioning whether or not there is a God.

Naturally, many traced the earliest stirrings of doubt to unanswered questions during their childhood.

R2: I got chewed out for asking the question, where did God come from? I asked another question about whether dinosaurs were on the Ark.

In between religiousness and conversion, there appear to be periods of experimentation with doctrinal ideas, fear, normlessness, self-doubt, and a grasping for meaning. When religion (1) does not measure up to its claims, (2) does not achieve empirical validity, (3) contradicts other expectations or values of the believer, or (4) threatens the believer or his or her family, the believer can be thrust into a state of anomie; that is, previously held beliefs lose their meeting. This is the beginning of a lengthy process whose result may be unbelief. Following are examples of situations that respondents claimed caused them to doubt the value of religion.

An example of religion not measuring up to its claims:

R5: [Took the fundamentalist path to hold her family together] I went to church and got saved. People told me that if you stay in church, he's [her alcoholic husband] gonna break. I went for a year, stopped wearing makeup, jewelry, the whole nine yards; but he didn't change.

An example of religion not achieving empirical validity:

R9: [Talking about his childhood when the children in the neighborhood would blaspheme and raise hell] Mother said I mustn't talk like that or the Devil would come out of a crack in the ground and drag me down to hell alive. But I doubted that, because he never dragged the other little bastards down.

An example of religion contradicting the believer's expectations or values:

R4: In my twenties, I was a religious nut, and I could get pretty preachy. But my earliest turn-off came when I tried to give testimony in church. I waved my hand in the air, but the preacher would never call on me. Later I asked him why, and he told me that women were not allowed to talk in church.

An example of religion threatening the believer:

R7: My son and husband would jokingly blaspheme. They would call each other "God" and "Jesus." And that would scare me. But I started thinking: They were good people, they had good values, what kind of God would send them to hell?

While conversion to unbelief is usually preceded by anomie, in a culture where people are sometimes called upon to affirm their religious beliefs, anomie may persist beyond conversion to freethought. Unbelievers are frequently put in the position of deciding whether or not to identify themselves to others as deviant. The following are excerpts from an autobiography by Neysa Dickey entitled "Grace: It's Not So Amazing" published in *Freethought Today*.

When friends invite my husband and me for dinner, I still bow my head for grace—sometimes. . . . You see it's like this: My life as an atheist is filled with fits and spurts. . . . [I wish I didn't] bow my head for grace. Sometimes I don't! I also don't hold my hand over my heart during the "Star-Spangled Banner." I continue to believe people have a right to burn the flag in protest. . . . I continue not having babies and trying to be more vocal on all points, but it's hard when your personality is such that acceptance feels like lifeblood, and rejection or controversy leads to panic attacks![16]

During the transition from religion to freethought, when they are losing faith in their religious upbringing, along with anomie comes self-doubt. Much like Dank's description of the gay male's coming out of the closet, the self-doubt comes from society's stereotype of the deviant.[17]

R2: For a long time I was lying to myself because my beliefs were too radical for anybody. I did not believe there were any nonbelievers out there. If you didn't believe in Jesus, you were un-American, and I considered myself a patriot.

And with conversion to freethought often comes resentment of past religious indoctrination.

R10: I didn't attend church—but my mother brainwashed me. She'd have neighbors over and hold church at home. I was brainwashed. . . believed in Jesus until I was 35 . . . never had a thought of my own until I was 35. . . . I was a parrot.

CLAIMS OF SUPERIORITY

Perhaps one has no control over whether one believes or not, but one does have some control over whether or not other people know that one is an unbeliever. People are not likely to publicly acknowledge their disbelief unless they are able to neutralize this deviant status. Through their organization, it is apparent that freethinkers are quite effective in neutralizing their deviance (at least among themselves). Judging by the way they present themselves, although they may be cynical, freethinkers appear to feel pretty good about themselves. They place a high value on rationality and obviously feel themselves to be superior to the devoutly religious, whom they believe to be irrational. They see themselves as having been duped, but take great pride in the fact that they have overcome their religious indoctrination, unlike many in their families, their neighborhoods, and their places of employment. As with other deviant subcultures,[18] they have their own cultural heroes. They take pride in the intellectual heritage of freethought. Many of them, even the lesser educated, are quite familiar with the works of Voltaire, Thomas Paine, Robert Ingersoll, and Bertrand Russell; Mark Twain seems to be a favorite of almost all of them. Most also see themselves as patriotic and take heart in the fact that many of the founding fathers of the United States were deists.

It is often thought that two of the most important functions of religion are to motivate people to follow the rules and to provide people with a sense of meaning in their lives. Both of these are accomplished in part by providing the promise of an afterlife, which is a reward for doing good and a reason to put up with the often miserable contingencies of earthly existence. Freethinkers strongly assert their moral superiority in that they do not need the promise of heaven or the threat of hell to conduct themselves in a moral fashion. They view Christians, especially fundamentalists, as hypocrites who are more concerned with their own self-aggrandizement or salvation than they are with the welfare of others. Even when their deeds are good, their motives are not.

> R8: I know a lot of good caring people, but they care for the wrong reason—because they're afraid not to.

By the same token, these unbelievers believe that freethinkers are more humanitarian than their Christian counterparts. They say they are concerned about the here and now and not the welfare of themselves and others in the hereafter. Lack of concern about the hereafter is liberating. But, though it liberates, unbelievers say, it also makes one aware of all the suffering in the here and now. Unbelievers do not wait for God to make things better.

> R1: Freethinkers have been the ones to advance humanitarian ideas in this country. Humanitarian people are doers. Religious people are prayers; they sit back and wait for God to do it. We focus on our lives right now, not on an afterlife.

> R7: I have to compare it to a visiting preacher who knocks on your door. I don't think he's as concerned about the individual as he is about the soul. . . . A freethinker knocks on the door and sees the human, the humane part of it. . . . A preacher sees a poor pregnant woman and doesn't think about her present needs.

> R8: I feel real concerned about protecting the environment, which I think kind of developed through freethought. . . . Once you start freethinking, you stop living in a fantasy world and start becoming aware of the world around you.

Furthermore, they argue that the idea that one can pray for forgiveness is destructive and leads to the rampant commission of misdeeds throughout the Christian world.

> R9: Atheists might be inclined to be more humanitarian because they have no God to go to for forgiveness.

> R10: The only ones who are like Christians are atheists. They're the only ones with good morals. Christians are all sinners.

They often go a step farther in arguing that unbelievers are humanists, while Christian doctrine is inherently misanthropic, especially the notion that we are all born in sin.

> R9: Atheists are humanists; Christians aren't. They hate the human race. All they believe is war. They were born in sin. They think the human race is no good. I say

everyone is born an atheist. They could have been taught something good, but instead they were taught evil Christianity.

HOSTILITY

As has already become quite apparent, freethinkers display a good deal of hostility in their communications. It is difficult to vehemently claim superiority without, at least, some disdain for the allegedly inferior group. A believer who showed up at one of these meetings would likely be quite offended. Without a doubt, one of the most pronounced characteristics of most of these unbelievers is their fervent distaste for religion, especially fundamentalism. Their monthly meetings provide members an opportunity to delight in their mutual abhorrence of religion. One favorite pastime is pointing out contradictions in the Bible. One regular section in *Freethought Today*, entitled "The Unreasoning Clergy," is written every month by sociologist Michael Hakeem. Below is an excerpt:

> He talked of seeing "spiritual" bodies. Generally by "spiritual" he meant "supernatural." In fact the resurrected Jesus that he claimed he saw was not a physical but a "spiritual body." (This oxymoron should cast suspicion on Paul's authenticity in the eyes of the vast numbers of Christians who insist that Jesus was resurrected in his physical form; but it doesn't because their capacity for embracing mutually exclusive ideas is without limit).[19]

And from the *Freethought Today* "Letter Box":

Easter Message to Christians
Jesus Christ was a fraud. He cannot "save" you! He couldn't even save himself! (Matt. 27:46, Mark 15:34).[20]

Another attraction is taking quotes from the Bible so as to indicate that Christianity is lewd, pornographic, cruel, hypocritical, or ridiculous. Below are some liberally interpreted excerpts from the Bible taken from an article in *Freethought Today* entitled "The X-Rated Book: Sex and Obscenity in the Bible" by Ashleigh Burke.

> **Genesis** 17:9–14 Circumcision mandated
> 19:1–8 Righteous man impregnates his daughters while drunk
> 32:25 God grabs Jacob's testicles
> **Kings I** 1:1–4 Virgin as therapy for sick old man unsuccessful.[21]

A more extreme example of this activity is found in a letter written by a member of the SFA and distributed at a meeting. Below are some excerpts.

Exodus 29:14 is speaking of burning the dung of a bullock. This is probably the first record on [sic] God telling how to get rid of the bullshit.
Leviticus 4:11, 8:17 and 16:27—More bullshit.

Numbers 19:5 Female (heifer) bullshit

I Kings 14:10 Yes, God declares that if you piss against the wall, you must tote the shit. Praise Jesus.

Job 20:7 Job he is worth a shit, but no more.

It should be noted that there is not always unanimity of opinion at these meetings. A few present expressed disgust and indignation at the above letter during the meeting.

Along the same lines, it is popular to recount Biblical stories of God's cruelty. One article in *Freethought Today* is entitled "Does Your God Kill Babies?" and is emblazoned with the passage "God's crimes against humanity make Hitler and Stalin look like flower children."[22]

Another repeated theme in their anti-Christian liturgy has to do with providing accounts of the harm done by Christianity. Such accounts include stories of Christian Scientists allowing their children to die because they refused to seek medical help, stories of faith healers duping their followers with illusions, stories of fundamentalist churches being sued by their parishioners for inflicting psychological trauma, and stories of priests sexually abusing children in their parish. Christianity is also blamed for racism.

R10: 1 remember when we didn't think nuthin' of it if they hung a black next door, because we were good Christians.

R8: When I was a Christian (or thought I was a Christian), I was a racist. And I feel I've grown out of that since I became aware of being an atheist.

One unbeliever who attends meetings on occasion summed up this sentiment, saying, "I think all religions are an abomination. It's the worst thing that ever happened to mankind."

Of course, this contempt for religion and the religious is often expressed as ridicule. Another regular section in *Freethought Today* is entitled "You Won't Believe You're Reading This." Following are a few entries:

Satan Works in Strange Ways
A naked family of three was charged with arson after taking off their demon-infested clothing and burning them in a Holiday Inn bathroom.

One Less Church in the World
Although lava from the Kilauea Volcano ignited and consumed the much-prayed-for church on Kalapana, Hawaii, it spared a nearby store.

Safer to Be a Freethinker

The disgruntled chairman of a church building committee shot two parishioners, held a bleeding church deacon hostage for six hours, then committed suicide at St. Sebastian By-the-Sea Episcopalian church in Melbourne Beach, Florida.[23]

DISCUSSION

In his study of the "nudist management of respectability," Weinberg found that, much like these freethinkers, nudists displayed a good deal of disdain for social convention. He found that nudists went out of their way to prove to themselves and others that they were free of society's stilted views regarding sex and nudity.[24] The key phrase here is that "they went out of their way." The very fact that they went out of their way to demonstrate their freedom from social conventions indicates that they were not free of them. They used as their point of reference the very conventions they said were meaningless to them. Likewise, though the term freethought would seem to be a declaration of independent thinking, these freethinkers seem to think in a rather formulaic way. They define themselves not so much in terms of what they are, but in terms of what they are not—Christians. Le Blond writes that atheism

> represents a reaction against religion and a negation which presupposes an antecedent affirmation. But, it is abundantly clear that current atheism, at least that of the Occident, draws its nourishment from Christianity and can only be fully understood in relation to Christianity.[25]

These unbelievers are ever-conscious of their deviant status, flaunting and defending it. Their group would be of no significance, would not even exist, if it were not for the Christians "all around them." Their beliefs, rather than being independent of religion, are a reaction to religion; and, in that sense, their beliefs are based on religious beliefs.

In their anticonformist activities, they cannot avoid taking on the characteristics of their religious counterparts; they cannot avoid using the same techniques. They spin anti-Christian liturgy with the same zeal Christians spin their liturgy. They exhibit the same degree of intolerance as their religious counterparts, of whom they are intolerant because of their intolerance. They get together and give "testimony" to their antireligious revelations and conversion, just as their fundamentalist counterparts give testimony to their revelations and conversion. Freethinkers may not use the word "sin," but they frequently and vehemently accuse their religious counterparts of the moral equivalent. It is often said among Christians that "there are no atheists in foxholes." Conversely, it is often heard among freethinkers that religious leaders are really closet atheists. Here again, freethinkers are resorting to the same rationale as their opponents. Both are saying of the other, "They can't really believe what they say they believe."

The profane is the antithesis of the sacred, and yet the profane could not exist without the sacred.[26] Likewise, freethought is the antithesis of religion, yet it could not exist without religion. It appears that neither belief system could exist without the other. As Erikson noted, a community cannot exist without boundaries; it is the presence of the other that gives each group its boundaries.[27] Their relationship is symbiotic. Christianity could not exist without sinners (in this case, freethinkers); nor could freethought exist without religion (in this case, Christians). It follows, then, that the hostility between the two groups contributes to the continued survival of each group. The hostility toward freethought exhibited by the religious community takes the form of prejudice and discrimination. This creates a need in the deviant freethinking subculture to neutralize their deviance. In neutralizing their deviance, they become haughty, self-righteous, and smug, much like their oppressors. This further alienates them from the religious community and thus further increases the likelihood of their oppression, contributing to the continued survival of the deviant subculture and, therefore, of the religious community. To paraphrase Erikson, a freethinker does not represent a failure of the religious community to encompass the entire citizenry; he or she, instead, plays a prominent role in the religious indoctrination of the rest of the community.

In summary, this article has examined a group of deviants who represent a subset of a larger group of deviants; that is, a group of organized unbelievers who are part of the much larger group of all unbelievers. Unbelief in our society represents a deviation from the recognized norm (the word "recognized" is used deliberately, because we cannot be sure of actual normative beliefs). Remarkably, very little research has been done in this area. In a society in which so many people profess religious belief (84% of Americans say they believe in God),[28] the sociology of deviance needs to look more closely at those who do not believe. To be sure, the organized unbelievers considered in this study represent the more extreme and deviant group of unbelievers; but to what extent do they represent other unbelievers? To what extent do other unbelievers experience anomie, hostility, or feelings of superiority? To what extent do they feel different? How do they neutralize their deviance, and how does their deviance impinge upon their lifestyles? To what extent are they hesitant to disclose their unbelief, and to whom and under what circumstances are they likely to make such disclosures? Is it important to them that they find other unbelievers with whom to associate? For what types of people and in what environments is unbelief likely to be most problematic? As for the theory of boundary maintenance, can the symbiotic relationship between freethought and religion be empirically demonstrated? Is there a point at which the religiosity of a community might preclude the evolution of unbelievers? Or would the development of such a religious community be impossible without the presence of unbelievers? These are some of the questions that could be advanced in future research. They are significant questions because, as students of deviance learn early in their studies, the best way to understand the norm is to study deviations from the norm. That is, we cannot fully understand belief without first understanding unbelief.

NOTES

1. Thrower, J. (1971), *A short history of Western atheism.* London: Pemberton.

2. See Hunsberger, B. & Brown, L. B. (1984), Religious socialization, apostasy, and the impact of family background. *Journal for the Scientific Study of Religion,* 23(3), 239–251; and Hadaway, C. K. (1989), Identifying American apostates: A cluster analysis. *Journal for the Scientific Study of Religion,* 28, 201–215.

3. Mossner, E. C. (1972), Deism. In P. Edwards (Ed.), *The Encyclopedia of Philosophy,* Vol. 2. (pp. 326–336). New York: Macmillan.

4. Edwards, F. (1972), Atheism. In *The Encyclopedia of Philosophy,* Vol. 1. New York: Macmillan; p. 175.

5. See Weinberg, M. S. (1981), The nudist management of respectability. In *Deviance: The interactionist perspective.* E. Rubington and M. Weinberg, eds. New York: Macmillan, 336–345; Simmons, J. L. (1969), *Deviants.* Berkeley: Glendessary Press; Schur, E. (1971), *Labeling deviant behavior: Its sociological implications.* New York: Harper & Row.

6. Simmons, J. L. (1969), *Deviants;* p. 88.

7. Goode, E. (1978), *Deviant behavior: An interactionist approach.* Englewood Cliffs, NJ: Prentice-Hall; p. 71.

8. Cf. Simmons, J. L. (1969), *Deviants.*

9. Stark, R. & Bainbridge, W. S. (1985), *The future of religion: Secularization, revival, and cult formation.* Berkeley: University of California Press.

10. *The Christian Century* (1990), Atheist Candidate. Vol. 107(20), 627.

11. Robertson, I. (1987), *Sociology.* New York: Worth; p. 410.

12. *Freethought Today,* September 1990, p. 15.

13. *Freethought Today,* April 1990, p. 3.

14. *Freethought Today,* March 1990, p. 14.

15. Lofland, J. & Stark, R. (1965), Becoming a world saver: Theory of conversion to a deviant perspective. *American Sociological Review,* 30, p. 862.

16. *Freethought Today,* March 1990, p. 11.

17. Dank, B. (1971), Coming out in the gay world. *Psychiatry,* 34, 180–197.

18. Cf. Simmons, J. L. (1969), *Deviants.*

19. *Freethought Today,* April 1990, p. 5.

20. Ibid., p. 2.

21. Ibid., p. 7.

22. *Freethought Today,* October 1990, p. 12.

23. *Freethought Today,* August 1990, pp. 19–20.

24. Weinberg, M. S. (1981), The nudist management of respectability. In *Deviance: The interactionist perspective.* E. Rubington and M. Weinberg, eds. New York: Macmillan, 336–345.

25. Le Blond, J. (1965), The contemporary status of atheism. *International Philosophical Quarterly*, 5(1), p. 39.

26. Durkheim, E. (1961), *The Elementary Forms of Religious Life.* (J. Swain, Trans.). Glencoe, IL: Free Press.

27. Erikson, K. T. (1966), *Wayward puritans: A study in the sociology of deviance.* New York: Wiley.

28. Stark, R. & Bainbridge, W. S. (1985), *The future of religion.*

CAUGHT UP IN THE CULT WARS

Confessions of a Canadian Researcher

SUSAN J. PALMER

They are typically called "cults" by the media and the lay public. But sociologists call them New Religious Movements (or NRMs). "Cult" has taken on such negative connotations; the word conjures up images of mass suicide, mass murder, and brainwashed young adults following the mesmerizing commands of a religious fanatic drunk on power.

"New Religious Movement," on the other hand, is far more accurate and less subjective. It puts these religious organizations in their historical context. All of the major religions in the world today were once new, and their adherents were frequently seen as deviants—deluded zealots, mindlessly following the bidding of their fanatical leaders.

The following article describes some of the joys and tribulations of a sociologist who has dedicated her career to the study of deviant subcultures.

> *"It would seem, Dr. Palmer, that you have acquired a bit of a reputation for being 'soft on the cults.' Are you indeed . . . a cult-lover?"*
>
> —High Solicitor

I was standing nervously in the carved oak witness box in the High Court, Lincoln's Inn in London, when the High Solicitor asked this question. It was in 1994, when I became embroiled in what the Children of God's lawyer described as "the longest and second most expensive custody battle in the history of the British Empire." I protested that I strove to be an objective, value-free social scientist when I studied new religions—but then admitted I also felt a sneaking aesthetic appreciation for "the cults." This made the judge smile, but it made me wonder are the two approaches really incompatible?

As a mature researcher, somewhat scarred from my forays into that embattled terrain known as the cult wars, I am now ready to make a confession. I do see myself as a *connoisseur*. For me, NRMs are beautiful life forms, mysterious and pulsating with charisma. Each "cult" is a mini-culture, a protocivilization. Prophets and heretics generate fantasy worlds that rival those of Philip K. Dick or L. Frank Baum. When I venture into the thickets of wild home-grown spirituality, and explore the rich undergrowth of what society rejects as its "weed" religions, I sometimes think of Dorothy's adventures in The Emerald City of Oz. Dorothy follows the yellow brick road that leads her through Utensia, A City whose inhabitants are kitchen utensils. Managing to escape King Kleaver (who threatens to chop her), she wanders into Bunbury where houses are made of crackers with bread-stick porches and wafer shingles and are inhabited by living buns with currant eyes. She ventures on to meet the evil headless Scoodles, then continues on down the yellow brick road.

New religions are no less phantasmagorical. Immersed in the Oz books as a malingering schoolgirl, I wanted to "have adventures" when I grew up. My wish came true. Today I find myself in the not-quite-respectable, morally problematic, and impecunious field of "cult" studies. Travelling the "yellow brick road" of social scientific research, I encounter oddly coherent worldviews constructed higgledy-piggledy out of the most incongruous elements: songs of Solomon, UFO lore, electric bulbs, biofeedback machines, gnostic creation myths—all welded into one seamless syncretism. I drop in on dreams of Utopia and discover quaint communes like Puritan villages, the brothers and sisters marching to a tasteful percussion of Bible-thumping. I have felt trapped in nightmares—racist compounds, parodies of Paradise, Nietzchean dystopias.

Each new religion I encounter evokes in me a sense of awe not unlike what my art historian mother feels when she beholds Greek ruins, German cathedrals, or Renaissance paintings. I see heretical religions as "totems" or testaments—not necessarily of Ultimate Truth, but rather of the creative power of the collective human imagination. Their prophets I approach cautiously, and with respect, as artists of the most radically experimental sort: unpredictable conceptual artists at best, semi-opaque con artists at worst.

This approach seems to aggravate almost everybody; they find it frivolous, irresponsible. One Sufi lady at the Abode of the Messenger stopped me mid-interview and said accusingly, "You're not *really* interested in the spiritual path. I get the impression you have more of a *literary* interest in what we're doing!"

Another time I was effervescing on the sheer *fun* of researching NRMs when a psychologist at a lunchtime lecture for the psychologists at the Montreal General Hospital interrupted: "So I suppose you think it's fun and OK for groups like the Solar Temple to go around killing each other!" I was irritated, since I had just spent ten minutes explaining that each "cult" is different, and statistics showed that only a tiny handful engaged in criminal acts, so I responded: "You must excuse me, I prepared this talk for the doctors; I didn't realize that the psychiatric patients would be invited here as well." I don't expect to be invited back.

When asked to define a cult, I explain that it is a baby religion. Personally, I find cults (and babies) attractive. Babies can be heartbreakingly adorable or intensely annoying, depending on the beholder's perspective—but also on the baby's mood and stage of development. So infant religions are not quite toilet-trained, like MOVE, a cult that annoyed neighbors by throwing garbage on the street; toddler NRMs, like the Rajneesh, run around naked in the park and knock over tea trays; and teenage missionary movements, like The Family, mooch off their parent society, refuse to get a job, and flaunt their pimply sexuality.

I have heard mothers excuse their obstreperous infants by saying, "It's only a *phase* he's going through!" (teething, bed-wetting, screaming). NRMs also go through phases, shutting out the surrounding culture to form their own identity. NRM scholars may sound like overindulgent mommies making excuses for their spoiled brats when they protest that communal experiments, sexual innovations, and apocalyptic expectations are merely developmental phases, and that society should grit its teeth and give these budding religions a chance to grow up.

Having confessed to singular tastes, perhaps I should explain how I got into "cult studies." My formal debut as a researcher of new religious movements commenced in the 1970s, when meditations—like 100 per cent cotton wear or silk—were Oriental imports, and most of my cool friends had already left for India to seek the right guru. At that time we were, of course, wary of false gurus who sold useless *sadhanas* (spiritual guidelines), or leched after American blondes, but the notion of the charismatic cult leader as obligatory pederast, oppressor of women, and designer of mass suicide had not yet been forged in the media.

Professor Fred Bird was my MA adviser at Concordia University when the department received a grant to study new religious movements in Montreal. I was one of four students hired as research assistants, and was actually paid $60 a week to choose a cult, spy on it, and write up field reports. When I look back on this period the word "halcyon" comes to mind; we researchers were light-hearted and naive, fancying ourselves spiritual PIs. We swapped bizarre anecdotes about our chosen groups and boasted of mild vicarious spiritual highs. As young, counter-cultural types we could easily pass as typical spiritualseekers and, indeed, that's what we were in our own wishy-washy ways.

Like many of my fellow scholars, I have been called a closet cultist. Perhaps there is a grain of truth to this allegation, for although I have never joined a group I've researched, I did start out hanging around meditation centers as a spiritual seeker, and only ended up in the microsociology of NRMs by default—as a failed meditator. I tried many systems, but never got the hang of it. I realize, of course, that the whole point is not to try to be "good" at meditating . . . but I kept trying.

So I began *doing* sociology of religion inadvertently, simply because I was bored with trying to concentrate on my mantra or third eye. Sitting in lotus posture at 4:00 A.M. on a scratchy grey woolen blanket in Swami Vishnu Devananda's quonset hut in Morin Heights, Quebec, I would peek around at my fellow meditators chanting "AUMMMMMM" and observe their subtle social interactions. Making beds and washing sheets, understood as karma yoga, I would question my fellow *chelas* regarding their conversions. At the visiting swamis' evening lectures, I paid more attention to the jocular rivalry between these shrewd old disciples of Swami Sivanada than I did to Hindu philosophy. Had I been able to make honest progress in my meditation practice, I would perhaps be living happily in the Himalayas—probably in Swami Shyam's Canadian enclave in Kulu—celibate, sattvic (pure), probably childless, my consciousness percolating up towards my seventh chakra.

Researching NRMs has its pleasures. I meet delightful people. I hear the intimate spiritual confessions of peaceful meditators, unselfish communalists, and disciplined ascetics. But there are disadvantages to taking on the public role of "cult scholar." Courted by the media as an offbeat academic who represents the "other view," TV stations have offered me free travel and luxurious sojourns in Canadian Pacific Railway hotels; but then they edit my interview so I come across as a caricature of a misguided civil libertarian. In anticult circles I am dismissed as a naive dupe, or a closet cultist. In France my name has been listed with the other "revisionists" who deny atrocities *dans les sectes*. As for my Mormon relatives, they urge me to return to the fold lest I end up in the "telestial sphere."

Many cults also look askance at me. Grossed out by the social-scientific method and sick of a sociologist's depressingly secular scrutiny, leaders have denounced me to their disciples as a hireling of a corrupt society. A Rajneesh therapist warned the other "supermoms" not to give me interviews because "she's coming from her head, not from her heart." E. J. Gold (the gnostic guru whose declared mission is "the education of the universe, one idiot at a time"), upon reading my MA thesis (about him), reportedly said, "This lady has the consciousness of a rubber duck!" When I asked a barefoot missionary from the Free Daist Communion for an interview, she explained she must first collect all my writings and send them to Fiji to be vetted. "Do you mean *Da Free John* is going to read my articles?" I asked, thrilled. "Not exactly," she replied. "He *handles* them, and whatever wisdom they contain he absorbs through his fingertips." Da Free John never got back to me.

Excluded from Black Hebrew assemblies as a "leprous pale-eyed Amorite," shunned by the Asatru (racialist Druids) for looking "slightly Jewish," and dismissed by *les sectes Quebecois* as a *carré tête* (square-head or anglophone), I continue the struggle to present myself in such a way that my research attentions will be welcome. But what can be even more disconcerting is when I am besieged by groups *overly eager* to be studied, and subjected to that special kind of "love bombing" that is a product of what sociologist Roland Robertson dubbed philomandarinism: "Susan, we just *love* you!

You're so *beautiful*—and so *objective*!" Aside from that sticky feeling of entering a fly-trap, I can foresee the day when they will all turn on me. In fifty years or so, after achieving the status of minority churches with the assistance of the dull ethnographics of academics like myself who function as alkaline neutralizers of the more acid anticult/media reports, these once controversial cults will loose their church historians on me and my peers, and they will condemn our careful writings—all because we tried to include reasonable but unflinching explanations for their bad news, and neglected to indulge in what my Mormon relatives call "faith-promoting incidents."

COVERT RESEARCHER—OR CLOSET CONVERT?

. . . [In some] ways my role as "cult scholar" impedes my research. The wide range of strange groups I have investigated appear in my books, and some straitlaced groups assume I must be immoral to hang out with the Rajneeshees, the Raelians, and The Family, whom they perceive as sinners and sex maniacs. Others feel a little queasy about my overly tolerant attitude towards atheistic or "heretical" groups who claim Jesus was a space alien, and wonder how I can bear to sit down and sup with a mystical pope or a vampire. I received a letter from a Krishna devotee complaining she felt "quite nauseous" that her interview appeared in the same book as a Moonie. Several core-group leaders have expressed jealousy and feelings of abandonment—that since I stopped researching their community I have flitted off to some silly UFO group that even I must realize does not possess the Truth.

When I meet young graduate students researching NRMs today, I envy them their freedom, their naive enthusiasm, their straightforward, unpoliticized curiosity. I recall how effortless it used to be to blend into a following. Even after declaring oneself a researcher, the response was often, "Oh well, you'll soon get over that!" I miss the intensity of real participant observation, the altered states, the grueling ordeals I was subjected to!

I recall how, in the late 70s, I was among a group of neo-gnostics who jumped out of a van at 8:15 A.M. in front of a suburban supermarket. We all wore skin-tight grey leotards, transparent plastic gloves, grey bathing caps, bare feet (painted grey)—and shaved-off eyebrows! We formed a huddle around our core group leader, who instructed us that we were all "hungry ghosts" and our mission was to enter the supermarket by following a customer through the revolving door—"Make sure you touch nothing. If any part of your body makes contact with anything or anybody, go back outside immediately and start over." Having fasted for three days we were hungry, but our exercise was to wander the aisles staring longingly at our favorite food, but to take nothing. After one hour we were meant to leave by shadowing a customer. We didn't last the hour, for one of the cashiers called the police. ("Who are all those weirdos?" we overheard the staff muttering. "They look like a biker gang . . . planning a robbery.") We leaped into the van and squealed off before the police arrived. We lay on the rusty floor, doubled up, holding onto each other as we lurched around corners, hysterical with laughter. The same group, a month before, had me crawling around a giant playpen wearing diapers, undershirt, and bonnet for an entire day, gurgling incoherently, sucking huge bottles of warm milk and playing with building blocks with my fellow "babies." Anticultists might be onto something when they claim an important stage of mind control is to "humiliate the victim" by "reinforcing childish behavior."

Today I am never invited to humiliate myself. I wear suits and shoulder pads and am taken on decorous tours, like visiting royalty. My eyebrows have grown in again, though they've never been quite the same!

Kai Erikson (1967: 373) has argued that "it is unethical for a sociologist to deliberately misrepresent his identity for the purpose of entering a private domain to which he is not eligible; and second, that it is unethical for a sociologist to deliberately misrepresent the character of the research in which he is engaged." I find it difficult not to misrepresent my identity, since most of my informants ignore my staunch protests that I am merely a dreary academic, a boring social scientist doing my job. They insist that, deep down, I am a lost soul desperately struggling towards the light. It is often counterproductive to protest too vigorously, so I just let them think I am on the brink of a conversion—and, indeed, part of me secretly hopes I am still capable of what C. S. Lewis called being "surprised by joy." . . .

WHY I DON'T CONSIDER MYSELF A "KEPT SCHOLAR"

In 1992 I received two grants to study children in new religions. I approached two different sects in Quebec and was refused permission to interview their members (they suspected I was a spy sent by the Catholic school board to undermine their home schooling). Then two international NRMs heard about me and called me up, offering plane tickets to "come on out and study our kids!" I turned them down. The situation made me nervous, for several reasons. First, I was concerned about preserving my "scholarly virginity." Second, I feared that if in the future I did not cooperate with their agenda, they might resort to blackmail (no doubt this is pure paranoia). Finally, I like to feel I am unhampered as a writer, free to poke fun at the group delicately if I feel like it, or mention stuff that is embarrassing. In short, I don't like being censored. I was aware that by choosing to study controversial child-rearing methods in NRMs, I would be vulnerable to criticism, but I didn't realize that I was stepping into the front line of a new battleground in the Cult Wars.

April 1994, I was standing in the witness box at the High Court, Family Division, in Lincoln's Inn to testify during the Turle vs. Turle custody battle over the grandson of a millionairess whose mother joined The Family. The same official solicitor who wanted to know if I were "soft on the cults" asked:

"Who paid for your trip to San Diego to study The Family's home-school?" Fortunately I was able to respond: "I paid for it out of my SSSR grant"—and could have produced the receipts if necessary.

I have never accepted money from an NRM to study them, but I have had to make deals with leaders who have curtailed the areas I was allowed to go into. I have managed to preserve my scholarly virginity, but have engaged in mutual flattery and love-bombing, if not heavy petting (figuratively speaking), with charismatic leaders and their top aides. Personally, I don't know of any kept scholars in real life, but I am unsuited for the job since I prefer my NRMs wild and virgin. I seek out groups that are almost inaccessible and unselfconscious, groups that know they are not a cult, but I naively swallow what the newspapers say about other cults—groups that have never heard of the term NRM, groups that are suspicious of researchers and assume a sociologist is just a pretentious variety of journalist. Once they start sending out PR reps to conferences wearing suits, groomed hair, and name tags, they're no fun anymore. Well, that's not true. They can still be interesting, but suddenly they seem tame, almost domesticated. Other scholars horn in and conduct schmaltzy interviews in the hotel breakfast nook and arrange visits.

If NRMs are baby religions, scholarly conferences provide the venues to set up *petting zoos*.

A CONDOMINIUM ON THE OUTSKIRTS OF HEAVEN

I have been offered bribes, so I keep all my receipts and correspondence to make it more convenient to sue anyone who suggests my research efforts or opinions can be bought. But I never turn down otherworldly rewards. Three different apocalyptic sects have awarded me a sort of last-minute squeezed-in salvation when the cosmic countdown comes. "We want you to know you will be blessed when Our Saviour returns," a bearded elder told me. Technically I deserve to be consigned to eternal oblivion or fall into the pit amidst other soulless beer-swilling sinners, but I have been promised a condominium on the outskirts of Heaven, according to "The Chosen People." I have been assured by another "biblically based" group that I will be beamed up before Armageddon gets too nasty. I was informed that Da Free John (currently known as Adidam) "meditated me" long before I appeared on their scene. An infamous "cult leader" prophesied I was "one of the three wise women sent by God to assist the Prophet in opening the seventh seal at the end of time." One Raelian guide suggested I might be eligible for cloning when the extraterrestrials arrive. And if linear time is indeed an illusion, I can look forward to a better rebirth, according to a member of Hare Krishna who suggested that I am a devotee of Swami Prahupada "in my heart."

Oddly enough, these assurances make me feel more secure on airplanes when I travel to conferences. . . .

THE SOCIOLOGIST AS UNDERCOVER AGENT

Three months after the Solar Temple perpetrated their shocking mass suicide/homicide ritual "transit" to Sirius, I found myself in an office being grilled by two policemen from the Securité Quebec concerning my belated and rather tentative research efforts into this controversial and criminal order. They wanted me to hand over a list of the Templars or ex-Templars I had met or interviewed. (It was impossible to tell the difference since none of them would admit to a current affiliation.) I refused, saying that to reveal the names of one's informants contravened ethics in the social sciences. "Excuse me, Madame," said one official, "What is that?" It was difficult to explain. Finally the "good cop" in the tweed suit joked, "Be very careful, Madame. But, if you find yourself on Sirius, send us a postcard."

THE SOCIOLOGIST AS SOFT DEPROGRAMMER

I have noticed that the visit of a researcher is sometimes welcomed by NRM adherents as an opportunity for hedonism, a chance to gain access to luxuries and indulgences not normally available within the strict regimen of a commune or the work space of even the more secularized religious institutions. This particular ethical problem has never been identified or discussed in anticult circles, because they view cultists as obedient robots incapable of rebelling. In my experience, the brainwashed are quite capable of sneakiness, of pursuing their own individualistic whims or vices.

The kind of situation I am talking about has occurred quite often, where the people assigned to host me and facilitate my research *very* often suggest we go outside to a local bar or restaurant and order a drink or a meal. Somehow, many NRMs seemed to have gained the impression that most sociologists are borderline alcoholics. After one round of beers (paid for by the cult budget) they have suggested we order another round. The first time this happened I unthinkingly and selfishly said "No thanks," and then saw the anxious, disappointed looks on their faces. I realized this was perhaps their *only* opportunity to indulge in alcoholic beverages for the next few years, so I said, "OK, maybe I will," and paid for the second round. When I left half a glass, I noticed one of them swilled it down quickly as we got up to leave.

Since I privately feel many of the new religions I study are too strict and overly Spartan, I am inclined to collude with my interviewees and encourage their secret rebellions—which places me in a morally dubious position, since I genuinely respect their religious principles and realize the rules are based on sound economics or communal ideals of humility and equality—or necessary measures to avoid assimilation. It puts sociologists like me rather in the position of being a "soft deprogrammer"—by encouraging members to disobey leaders, break out of their conditioning, and place their own selfish desires before the group goals—perhaps the first tentative steps towards eventually leaving?

On one occasion I had arranged to spend a few days living with a rather puritanical, biblically based commune in order to interview members and study communal patterns. Two members in their forties, who had recently been given the exciting task of dealing with the public, picked me up in a car to drive me to the commune four hours away in the countryside. On the way they suggested we stop off at a beautiful hotel by a lake to get some refreshment and so that I could admire the prospect of the mountains. I agreed, still feeling jet-lagged. Upon our arrival at the hotel front desk it became clear they had booked rooms—one for the two women, and the other for the man. Then they turned to me and said, "Susan, you must be really tired with all your teaching and travelling, we thought it would be great for you if we all stayed here for three days. You could interview us, and catch up with your writing projects. We'll double up and give you the private room so you can work in peace." It became clear that their real agenda was to indulge a secret passion they had been harboring for years. It turned out their love affair had started years ago, but had been squelched by the leaders, and they had been encouraged to marry more suitable partners. I was not unsympathetic to their romance, and I could appreciate their need for a little holiday away from the crowded commune.

In this situation we find the sociologist-as-chaperone. The two would no doubt later report to their leaders: "Dr. Palmer *insisted* on stopping at a hotel for three days en route," and they probably had been instructed to indulge a decadent sociologist. I had no problem personally with facilitating their affair, except that I really *did* want to conduct as many interviews as possible and realized if the situation became public this would not be good for my rep: I would very much look like a jet-setting, kept scholar using research trips to enjoy luxurious holidays. So I had to play the priggish spoilsport and say no, although I sat by the lake and reviewed my notes while they went to the room to "rest from the drive." Thus sociologists can have a corrupting effect upon the morals of members.

THE REAL ETHICAL QUESTION: WHO GETS HURT BY WHOM?

. . . Scholars and researchers play an important role as educators in the global process of the proliferating new religious pluralism. Often they are the only go-betweens, the ones who have traversed that no man's land between the "cult" and "normal society." In this situation it is tempting to fancy oneself as a "freedom fighter" or a *deus ex machina* who advises cult leaders on how to get out of trouble.

I find myself torn between the need to educate and the desire to entertain. By highlighting spiritual weirdnesses I grab my students' attention and please journalists, but I undermine the groups' struggle for respect. It is only too easy to forget that cult members are human beings too, and that many have found happiness, learned social graces, received spiritual gifts participating in less than respectable religions.

Recently I invited a Knight of the Golden Lotus to speak to my class, after giving the students a rather unfeeling satirical sketch of the late leader's eccentricities. Our speaker appeared in the knights' orange and yellow garments, with mirrors fastened on his headband. His companion wore amulets of swans, rainbows, and mandalas pinned to her ample bosom. I stifled a smirk, and was feeling particularly frazzled—the VCR wasn't working and the audiovisual man refused to help, and he launched into a tirade on the college cutbacks that robbed him of his assistant. My daughter had refused to brush her hair before leaving for school, and my students were now behaving badly, lurching in late and babbling at the back. My Knight of the Golden Lotus stepped forward: "Please be quiet! We have come to present to you our religion and would appreciate respect." The students immediately calmed down and he launched into a fascinating lecture.

Afterwards, walking down the hall beside him, I reflected that, in spite of his leader's execrable taste in architecture, here was an admirable human being. His swift social responses had shown considerable insight and intelligence. I suspected that on this particular day his mental health was superior to my own. In fact, he'd put me in a good mood—perhaps an altered state?

LEARNING HOW TO NAVIGATE THE CULT WARS

All the evidence at hand points to a future filled with a dizzying abundance of ever-proliferating new religions. This phenomenon begs to be studied and offers stimulating hands-on research opportunities for young scholars. And yet, inexperienced and ambitious aspiring academics are likely to be deterred by a kind of miasma hovering around the field, a miasma arising from rumors and stereotypes as well as occasional errors and poor judgment on the part of NRM researchers. Will the young field researcher who wishes to write about the vampire subculture and its rituals hesitate to embark on this project lest she later find herself branded as a morbid blood-drinker once she becomes a famous sociologist? Young scholars may feel reluctant to embark on the study of NRMs like the Church Universal and Triumphant, the Unification Church and The Family, groups that in the past have been known to exhibit "philomandarin" tendencies—to eagerly court, and even pay, scholars to study them. These groups continue to mature, mutate, and institutionalize charisma in fascinating ways... but by associating with these groups, are young researchers compromising their most precious commodity: objectivity? Or, even more important, are they compromising their reputations as objective social scientists?

Paradoxically, there is pressure in the academy to steer clear of cults, but the news media exerts considerable pressure on scholars to comment on, and hence to study, the more controversial, outrageous, or dangerous groups— and these are precisely the areas of unpredictable pitfalls. What NRM scholar does not feel trepidation upon hearing the following cautionary, but true tales? (1) A Japanese professor who wrote an encyclopedia entry on Aum Shinrikyo, and whose graduate student was recruited into the movement, was fired by the university—the rationale being, if he knew his stuff he should have been able to recognize danger signals and warn the proper authorities; and (2) an Oregon high-school teacher was fired after inviting two sannyasis from Rajneeshpuram to talk to his class.[1]

Like Dorothy on the yellow brick road, young researchers will occasionally lose their barking "Totos" of objectivity. They will rely on their Cowardly Lions (academic caution) and rusty Tin Woodsmen (quantitative methods) as they wander off into the yet undreamt-of spiritual landscapes of the future. Perhaps in a few years it will be considered quite as respectable to receive research funding from NRMs as it is from the Vatican. Perhaps "religious minority" will have the same earnest ring to it as "sexual minority" or "women of color." The best advice I can offer to my students who aspire to spiritual espionage is this: Be open about what you're doing, don't apologize for mistakes, grow a rhinoceros-hide, but cultivate an empathetic ear for spiritual confessions.

NOTE

1. From *The Oregonian*, a special issue on Rajneeshpuram, August 1985.

REFERENCES

Barker, Eileen. 1996. "The Scientific Study of Religion? You Must be Joking!" In *Cults in Context*, edited by Lorne L. Dawson, 5–27. Toronto: Canadian Scholars Press.

Baum, L. Frank. 1910. *The Emerald City of Oz*. Chicago: Reilly & Lee.

Erikson, Kai T. 1967. "A Comment on Disguised Observation in Sociology." *Social Problems* 14 (14): 367–73.

Palmer, Susan J. 1994. *Moon Sisters, Krishna Mothers, Rajneesh Lovers: Women's Roles in New Religions*. Syracuse, N.Y.: Syracuse University Press, 105–36.

Palmer, Susan J. 1995. "Women in the Raelian Movement." In *The Gods Have Landed: New Religions from Other Worlds*, edited by James R. Lewis. New York: SUNY.

Singer, Margaret Thaler, with Janja Lalich. 1995. *Cults in Our Midst: The Hidden Menace in Our Everyday Lives*. San Francisco: Jossey-Bass.

SUICIDE BOMBERS

The "Just War" Debate, Islamic Style

JOHN KELSAY

*For many scholars, an understanding of deviance should focus on the meaning
of the deviant act to the actor. For the symbolic interactionist, such meanings
are acquired in the process of social interaction, and these meanings are often
negotiated in the process. Though the following article was not formally written in the interactionist tradition, it allows us to see how the meanings of "suicide" and "martyrdom" are being negotiated in the Islamic community. The
outcomes of this negotiation, of course, can have substantial impact on the
manifestation of deviance and in crafting the appropriate response to such
deviance.*

Tucked away in an account of the Jewish resistance to Antiochus Epiphanes
is the story of a hero's sacrifice. The Book of Maccabees describes the prebattle
scene. Jewish forces are encamped at Bethzechariah with the enemy directly
opposite them, fully armed and ready to fight. As the Jewish soldiers watch,
their counterparts prepare elephants—the heavy artillery of ancient warfare.
Wooden towers are fastened onto elephants, with each tower bearing four
armed men who will fight from this raised position. The army is a fearsome
spectacle: "The sun shone on the shields of gold and brass, the hills were
ablaze with them and gleamed like flaming torches. . . . All who heard the
noise made by their multitude, by the marching of the multitude and the
clanking of their arms, trembled, for the army was very large and strong."
Fighting ensues, and then a member of the Jewish resistance makes
a move:

> Eleazar, called Avaran, saw that one of the animals was equipped with royal
> armor. It was taller than all the others, and he supposed that the king was on it.
> So he gave his life to save his people and to win for himself an everlasting name.
> He courageously ran into the midst of the phalanx to reach it; he killed men right
> and left, and they parted before him on both sides. He got under the elephant,
> stabbed it from beneath, and killed it; . . . it fell to the ground upon him and he
> died. (1 Macc, 6:43–46)

Eleazar's action offers one of the enduring images of war. In giving his life
for a cause, he also provides a context for discussing the suicide bombings
that are now a feature of the conflict between Palestinians and Israelis. If we
are to understand why Palestinians engage in such acts, we must begin with

their categories. For many Palestinians, the bombers are not "suicides" but like Eleazar, "martyrs." And their actions are "martyrdom operations."

In this context, the important issues have less to do with the social-psychological dynamics of suicide and more to do with the concerns of military ethics. Martyrdom operations are tactics by which Palestinians attempt to engage an enemy militarily. As such, they must be evaluated in terms of the criteria of the just war tradition, or in Muslim terms, of the Shari'a provisions governing armed conflict.

On March 27, 2001, a Palestinian detonated explosives next to a bus in the French Hill sector of Jerusalem, killing himself and injuring 30 Israelis. The next day, another Palestinian did the same in Neve Yamin, killing himself and two Israeli teenagers. These incidents occurred in connection with the al-Aqsa intifada, which began in the fall of 2000. But they fit a pattern that began after the 1993 signing of the Oslo Accords and has become ever more familiar. In these, as in most such attacks, responsibility was claimed by Hamas, which calls itself the specifically Islamic party within the larger Palestinian movement.

A month later, the highest-ranking official of the Saudi religious establishment questioned the legitimacy of such attacks. Fighting must be governed by the Shari'a, said Shaykh Abd al-Aziz bin Abdallah al-Shaykh, and he warned that the deaths of those who kill themselves "in the heart of the enemy's ranks" are "merely" suicides, and thus contravene God's command.

By appealing to the Shari'a, the Saudi scholar invoked well-established practices by which Muslims debate the rights and wrongs of particular acts. The term stands for the ideal way of living. Scholars like the shaykh are responsible for interpreting the Qur'an, the example of the Prophet, and precedents from prior generations in order to establish analogies between these sources and the questions of contemporary Muslims. The shaykh considered the practice of suicide bombings without precedent in Islam, and thus illegitimate.

Responding to this argument, Yusuf al-Qaradhawi, a prominent leader of the Muslim Brotherhood, emphasized the importance of intention and argued that the "mentality of those who carry out [martyrdom operations] has nothing to do with the mentality of one who commits suicide." Suicide involves taking one's life for selfish reasons; those who die in the course of suicide attacks aimed at Israeli targets are anything but selfish, he argued. They sacrifice their lives for the sake of others. As Shaykh Qaradhawi put it, to speak of these acts as "suicide attacks" is misleading because they are really "heroic acts of martyrdom [that] have nothing to do with suicide." Instead of sinful contraventions, they are "the supreme form of struggle in the path of God."

Up to this point, Qaradhawi spoke for the majority of Muslim scholars. But the Shaykh al-Azhar responded by noting that "the suicide operations are classified as self-defense and are a kind of martyrdom, so long as the intention behind them is to kill the enemy's soldiers, and not women or children." The intention of a martyr, in other words, is understood in relation to the target that he (or more recently, she) attacks. Here, the highest authority in Egyptian Islam had in mind the saying of Muhammad: "When you fight, do not cheat or commit treachery. Do not kill or mutilate women, children or old men." To put it another way: a just warrior never directly and intentionally targets civilians. In this matter, the Shari'a parallels the just war tradition and its concern for discrimination or noncombatant immunity.

How then do devout Muslims justify martyrdom operations? Civilians have died or been injured in attacks on buses, in restaurants and grocery stores, at discotheques and even during a Passover seder. Despite this apparent contravention of the Shari'a, the consensus of most of those participating in the discussion was summarized by Qaradhawi: "Israeli society is militaristic in nature. Both men and women serve in the army and can be drafted at any moment." In other words, there are no civilians in Israel.

What about children or elderly people? Qaradhawi says, "If a child or an elderly person is killed in this type of operation, he or she is not killed on purpose, but by mistake, and as a result of military necessity. Necessity makes the forbidden things permitted." In other words, if the bomber does not intend or plan for children or elderly people to be the target of attack, the operation does not violate Shari'a norms. All Israeli men and women who are eligible by age to serve in the military are legitimate targets for direct attack, whether they are currently on active duty, members of reserve forces on vacation, or not yet drafted.

As to children or elderly people killed as collateral damage, the martyr is excused from culpability. Those who participate in these attacks are fulfilling an obligation to defend the territory and values of Islam. The superior military capacity of the enemy justifies the unusual tactics. As two groups of scholars from al-Azhar put it: "When the Muslims are attacked in their homes and their land is robbed, the struggle in the path of God turns into an individual duty. In this case, martyrdom operations become a primary obligation and Islam's highest form of struggle."

Do extreme conditions justify indiscriminate tactics? This is a question not only for Muslims in Palestine; those who carried out the attacks on the World Trade Center and the Pentagon gave similar justifications for their actions. Ayman al-Zawahiri, an Egyptian known as "bin Laden's physician," argues that martyrdom operations should be the preferred tactic of a worldwide struggle for Muslim rights, since they inflict the most damage at the least cost to the Muslim community. Zawahiri and others consider distinctions between civilian and military targets irrelevant. Like Qaradhawi, they speak of an armed struggle imposed upon Muslims by anti-Muslim forces that have invaded historic Islamic territory.

Those forces deprive Muslims of basic rights; they threaten the very existence of the Islamic community, or at least its ability to carry out its historic mission of commanding good and forbidding evil. They are a threat to humanity, since God appointed the Islamic *umma* as an arbiter of the differences that lead the diverse nations into a state of perpetual war. Muslims are thus in an emergency situation in which armed struggle is a duty for each and every Muslim. And all of the enemy's people are guilty of oppression, for those who do not fight nevertheless support and benefit from the injustice of their political and military leaders.

Qaradhawi and representatives of al-Azhar unanimously condemned the attacks of September 11 and the al-Qaeda network's indiscriminate tactics. For example, in speaking of the 1998 attacks against U.S. embassies in Kenya and Tanzania, the Shaykh al-Azhar said: "Any explosion that leads to the death of innocent women and children is a criminal act, carried out only by people who are base cowards and traitors. A rational person with only a small portion of respect and virtue refrains from such operations." No fine points here about the "intention" or "mentality" of the one carrying out such attacks.

Yet the Shaykh al-Azhar supports Palestinian martyrdom operations. Is the Palestinian case different because it is "homeland defense"? Do those who justify martyrdom operations in Palestine simply disagree with bin Laden, al-Zawahiri and others regarding the scope of the legitimate struggle? Some advocates of Palestinian martyrdom operations draw a line between operations inside Israel's pre-1967 borders and operations in the rest of Palestine/Israel.

Apparently only a clear incursion of enemy forces into Muslim territory justifies extreme measures. Otherwise, the extraordinary measures involved in martyrdom operations are either not justified, or those carrying out such operations must exercise greater care in distinguishing between civilian and military targets.

For some Palestinians, these distinctions do not justify indiscriminate tactics. On June 19, a group of 55 Muslims and Christians issued a communiqué calling for an end to military operations aimed at citizens in Israel. Arguing on pragmatic grounds, the group noted that "these operations achieve no progress towards the realization of our plan calling for freedom and independence." Instead, they deepen hatred and "provide excuses" for the Sharon government to continue its aggressive policies. Sari Nusseibeh, president of Al Quds University and PLO representative in Jerusalem, later explained that the communiqué was aimed at indiscriminate military operations, those attacks that fail to distinguish between civilian and military targets. Such attacks are counterproductive, and should be stopped.

Judging from the response of Hamas and others, this argument was unconvincing. On June 30, 150 people signed a communiqué opposing Nusseibeh and his colleagues:

> What is required today from the Arab Palestinian people of all factions is to resist the occupation and remove from our land *by all ways and all means*, primarily armed struggle *with all weapons that can be found*, in response to the Zionist military

machine armed with American weapons and its overt bias against our people, our cause and all the causes of the Arab world (emphasis added).

In response to suicide bombings, many commentators focus on the despair fostered by political and economic hopelessness. It is hopelessness, they say, that leads people to suicide. Other commentators connect the motivation for bombings with promises of rewards, either heavenly (enjoying the pleasures of Paradise) or earthly (monetary rewards to families of martyrs). Still others worry about the countries and organizations that exploit young and desperate men and women. These concerns are a valid part of any inquiry into the phenomenon.

But if we take Palestinian, and especially Muslim accounts seriously, we are not talking about suicide bombings but about operations in which someone carries out an attack and sacrifices his or her life for a larger cause. Such martyrdom operations awaken feelings like those that accompany readings of the story of Eleazar, or of Muslim martyrs like Anas ibn Nadr, whose sacrifice during the battle of Uhud in 625 led his companions to exclaim to Muhammad: "O messenger of God, I could not fight as he fought." The annals of Islam are full of Eleazars who have given their lives to save their people and to win for themselves an everlasting name.

Like the acts of martyrs in these ancient stories, the suicide bombings take place in military contexts, involve military tactics, and should be evaluated accordingly. In Muslim discussion, the critical issue is the distinction between civilian and military targets. Despite disagreement among Muslim leaders, Shari'a precedents do not support a contravention of the rule "never directly and intentionally target civilians." Nor do they support the judgment that "there are no civilians in Israel." No society is so militarized as to have no distinction between civilian and military targets. Nor does an appeal to "intention" or "mental reservation" work. Targeting a bus that picks up and drops off passengers along a route designated for public transportation is a violation of Shari'a rules. The idea of an emergency in which each and every Muslim has a duty to fight makes sense in terms of Shari'a reasoning. But doing away with the need to distinguish between targets does not.

Many Palestinians will ask, "What about our civilians, killed or wounded by Israelis? Are the lives of all civilians of equal worth?" The answer must be yes. If the challenge for Muslims is to find ways to seek justice while honoring the distinctions between civilian and military targets, the challenge for Israel (and for the U.S. and its allies as they seek to limit the capacity of terrorists to inflict harm) is to honor the notion of proportionate means.

From the standpoint of both the just war tradition and the canons of Shari'a, the conduct of war must be governed by two concerns: discrimination between civilian and military targets, and proportionality in means. Both present new challenges as the conditions and technology of warfare change. Both must be honored if those who carry out military activity are to stand in the legacy of Eleazar.

PART 8

Mental Illness

ON BEING SANE IN INSANE PLACES

DAVID L. ROSENHAN

Sociologists are frequently critical of psychiatry, arguing that it has clouded the study of deviance with pseudoscientific nomenclature and biomedical explanations that have not risen to empirical verification. Through "medicalizing" deviance, critics argue, psychiatry has become little more than an institution of social control, much like the police and the courts—but more insidious than the police and the courts because psychiatry is not recognized for its control function.

In this classic article, Rosenhan calls into question the scientific validity and reliability of psychiatric diagnoses. Since this article was written in the 1970s, psychiatry has moved to improve the reliability of diagnoses; and, yet, still today, when a criminal defendant enters an insanity plea, there is almost certain to be an expert claiming he or she is sane and another claiming that he or she is insane.

If sanity and insanity exist, how shall we know them?

The question is neither capricious nor itself insane. However much we may be personally convinced that we can tell the normal from the abnormal, the evidence is simply not compelling. It is commonplace, for example, to read about murder trials wherein eminent psychiatrists for the defense are contradicted by equally eminent psychiatrists for the prosecution on the matter of the defendant's sanity. More generally, there are a great deal of conflicting data on the reliability, utility, and meaning of such terms as "sanity," "insanity," "mental illness," and "schizophrenia." Finally, as early as 1934, Benedict suggested that normality and abnormality are not universal.[1] What is viewed as normal in one culture may be seen as quite aberrant in another. Thus, notions of normality and abnormality may not be quite as accurate as people believe they are.

To raise questions regarding normality and abnormality is in no way to question the fact that some behaviors are deviant or odd. Murder is deviant. So, too, are hallucinations. Nor does raising such questions deny the existence of the personal anguish that is often associated with "mental illness." Anxiety and depression exist. Psychological suffering exists. But normality and abnormality, sanity and insanity, and the diagnoses that flow from them may be less substantive than many believe them to be.

At its heart, the question of whether the sane can be distinguished from the insane (and whether degrees of insanity can be distinguished from each other) is a simple matter: Do the salient characteristics that lead to diagnoses reside in the patients themselves or in the environments and, contexts in which observers find them? . . . [T]he belief has been strong that patients present symptoms, that those symptoms can be categorized, and, implicitly, that the sane are distinguishable from the insane. More recently, however, this belief has been questioned. . . . [T]he view has grown that psychological categorization of mental illness is useless at best and downright harmful, misleading, and pejorative at worst. Psychiatric diagnoses, in this view, are in the minds of the observers and are not valid summaries of characteristics displayed by the observed.[2, 3]

Gains can be made in deciding which of these is more nearly accurate by getting normal people (that is, people who do not have, and have never suffered, symptoms of serious psychiatric disorders) admitted to psychiatric hospitals and then determining whether they were discovered to be sane and, if so, how. If the sanity of such pseudopatients were always detected, there would be prima facie evidence that a sane individual can be distinguished from the insane context in which he is found. Normality (and presumably abnormality) is distinct enough that it can be recognized wherever it occurs, for it is carried within the person. If, on the other hand, the sanity of the pseudopatients were never discovered, serious difficulties would arise for those who support traditional modes of psychiatric diagnosis. Given that the hospital staff was not incompetent, that the pseudopatient had been behaving as sanely as he had been outside of the hospital, and that it had never been previously suggested that he belonged in a psychiatric hospital, such an unlikely outcome would support the view that psychiatric diagnosis betrays little about the patient but much about the environment in which an observer finds him.

This article describes such an experiment. Eight sane people gained secret admission to twelve different hospitals. Their diagnostic experiences constitute the data of the first part of this article; the remainder is devoted to a description of their experiences in psychiatric institutions. . . .

PSEUDOPATIENTS AND THEIR SETTINGS

The eight pseudopatients were a varied group. One was a psychology graduate student in his twenties. The remaining seven were older and "established." Among them were three psychologists, a pediatrician, a psychiatrist, a painter, and a housewife. Three pseudopatients were women, five were men. All of them employed pseudonyms, lest their alleged diagnoses embarrass them later. Those who were in mental health professions alleged another occupation in order to avoid the special attentions that might be accorded by staff, as a matter of courtesy or caution, to ailing colleagues. With the exception of myself (I was the first pseudopatient and my presence was known to the hospital administrator and chief psychologist and, so far as I can tell, to them alone), the presence of pseudopatients and the nature of the research program were not known to the hospital staffs.

The settings were similarly varied. In order to generalize the findings, admission into a variety of hospitals was sought. The twelve hospitals in the sample were located in five different states on the East and West coasts. Some were old and shabby, some were quite new. Some were research-oriented, others not. Some had good staff-patient ratios, others were quite under-staffed. Only one was a strictly private hospital. All of the others were sup-ported by state or federal funds, or in one instance, by university funds.

After calling the hospital for an appointment, the pseudopatient arrived at the admissions office complaining that he had been hearing voices. Asked what the voices said, he replied that they were often unclear, but as far as he could tell they said "empty," "hollow," and "thud." The voices were unfamiliar and were of the same sex as the pseudopatient. The choice of these symptoms was occasioned by their apparent similarity to existential symptoms. Such symptoms are alleged to arise from painful concerns about the perceived meaninglessness of one's life. It is as if the hallucinating person were saying, "My life is empty and hollow." The choice of these symptoms was also determined by the *absence* of a single report of existential psychoses in the literature.

Beyond alleging the symptoms and falsifying name, vocation, and employment, no further alterations of person, history, or circumstances were made. The significant events of the pseudopatient's life history were pre-sented as they had actually occurred. Relationships with parents and siblings, with spouse and children, with people at work and in school, consistent with the aforementioned exceptions, were described as they were or had been. Frustrations and upsets were described along with joys and satisfactions. These facts are important to remember. If anything, they strongly biased the subsequent results in favor of detecting sanity, since none of their histories or current behaviors were seriously pathological in any way.

Immediately upon admission to the psychiatric ward, the pseudopatient ceased simulating *any* symptoms of abnormality. In some cases, there was a brief period of mild nervousness and anxiety, since none of the pseudopa-tients really believed that they would be admitted so easily. Indeed, their shared fear was that they would be immediately exposed as frauds and greatly embarrassed. Moreover, many of them had never visited a psychiatric ward; even those who had, nevertheless had some genuine fears about what might happen to them. Their nervousness, then, was quite appropriate to the novelty of the hospital setting, and it abated rapidly.

Apart from that short-lived nervousness, the pseudopatient behaved on the ward as he "normally" behaved. The pseudopatient spoke to patients and staff as he might ordinarily. Because there is uncommonly little to do on a psychiatric ward, he attempted to engage others in conversation. When asked by staff how he was feeling, he indicated that he was fine, that he no longer experienced symptoms. He responded to instructions from attendants, to calls for medication (which was not swallowed), and to dining-hall instructions. Beyond such activities as were available to him on the admissions ward, he spent his time writing down his observations about the ward, its patients, and the staff. Initially these notes were written "secretly," but as it soon became clear that no one much cared, they were subsequently written on standard tablets of paper in such public places as the dayroom. No secret was made of these activities.

The pseudopatient, very much as a true psychiatric patient, entered a hospital with no foreknowledge of when he would be discharged. Each was told that he would have to get out by his own devices, essentially by convincing the staff that he was sane. The psychological stresses associated with hospitalization were considerable, and all but one of the pseudopatients desired to be discharged almost immediately after being admitted. They were, therefore, motivated not only to behave sanely, but to be paragons of cooperation. That their behavior was in no way disruptive is confirmed by nursing reports, which have been obtained on most of the patients. These reports uniformly indicate that the patients were "friendly," "cooperative," and "exhibited no abnormal indications."

THE NORMAL ARE NOT DETECTABLY SANE

Despite their public "show" of sanity, the pseudopatients were never detected. Admitted, except in one case, with a diagnosis of schizophrenia, each was discharged with a diagnosis of schizophrenia "in remission." The label "in remission" should in no way be dismissed as a formality, for at no time during any hospitalization had any question been raised about any pseudopatient's simulation. Nor are there any indications in the hospital records that the pseudopatient's status was suspect. Rather, the evidence is strong that, once labeled schizophrenic, the pseudopatient was stuck with that label. If the pseudopatient was to be discharged, he must naturally be "in remission"; but he was not sane, nor, in the institution's view, had he ever been sane.

The uniform failure to recognize sanity cannot be attributed to the quality of the hospitals, for, although there were considerable variations among them, several are considered excellent. Nor can it be alleged that there was simply not enough time to observe the pseudopatients. Length of hospitalization ranged from seven to fifty-two days, with an average of nineteen days. The pseudopatients were not, in fact, carefully observed, but this failure clearly speaks more to traditions within psychiatric hospitals than to lack of opportunity.

Finally, it cannot be said that the failure to recognize the pseudopatients' sanity was due to the fact that they were not behaving sanely. While there was clearly some tension present in all of them, their daily visitors could detect no serious behavioral consequences—nor, indeed, could other patients. It was quite common for the patients to "detect" the pseudopatients' sanity. During the first three hospitalizations, when accurate counts were kept, 35 of a total of 118 patients on the admissions ward voiced their suspicions, some vigorously. "You're not crazy. You're a journalist, or a professor [referring to the continual note-taking]. You're checking up on the hospital." While most of the patients were reassured by the pseudopatient's insistence that he had been sick before he came in but was fine now, some continued to believe that the pseudopatient was sane throughout his hospitalization. The fact that the patients often recognized normality when staff did not raises important questions.

Failure to detect sanity during the course of hospitalization may be due to the fact that physicians operate with a strong bias toward what statisticians call the type 2 error. This is to say that physicians are more inclined to call a healthy person sick (a false positive, type 2) than a sick person healthy (a false negative, type 1). The reasons for this are not hard to find: It is clearly more dangerous to misdiagnose illness than health. Better to err on the side of caution, to suspect illness even among the healthy.

But what holds for medicine does not hold equally well for psychiatry. Medical illnesses, while unfortunate, are not commonly pejorative. Psychiatric diagnoses, on the contrary, carry with them personal, legal, and social stigmas. It was therefore important to see whether the tendency toward diagnosing the sane insane could be reversed. The following experiment was arranged at a research and teaching hospital whose staff had heard these findings but doubted that such an error could occur in their hospital. The staff was informed that at some time during the following three months, one or more pseudopatients would attempt to be admitted into the psychiatric hospital. Each staff member was asked to rate each patient who presented himself at admissions or on the ward according to the likelihood that the patient was a pseudopatient. A 10-point scale was used, with a 1 and 2 reflecting high confidence that the patient was a pseudopatient.

Judgments were obtained on 193 patients who were admitted for psychiatric treatment. All staff who had had sustained contact with or primary responsibility for the patient—attendants, nurses, psychiatrists, physicians, and psychologists—were asked to make judgments. Forty-one patients were alleged, with high confidence, to be pseudopatients by at least one member of the staff. Twenty-three were considered suspect by at least one psychiatrist. Nineteen were suspected by one psychiatrist *and* one other staff member. Actually, no genuine pseudopatient (at least from my group) presented himself during this period.

The experiment is instructive. It indicates that the tendency to designate sane people as insane can be reversed when the stakes (in this case, prestige and diagnostic acumen) are high. But what can be said of the nineteen people who were suspected of being "sane" by one psychiatrist and another staff member? Were these people truly "sane," or was it rather the case that in the course of avoiding the type 2 error the staff tended to make more errors of the first sort—calling the crazy "sane"? There is no way of knowing. But one thing is certain: Any diagnostic process that lends itself so readily to massive errors of this sort cannot be a very reliable one.

THE STICKINESS OF PSYCHODIAGNOSTIC LABELS

Beyond the tendency to call the healthy sick—a tendency that accounts better for diagnostic behavior on admission than it does for such behavior after a lengthy period of exposure—the data speak to the massive role of labeling in psychiatric assessment. Having once been labeled schizophrenic, there is nothing the pseudopatient can do to overcome the tag. The tag profoundly colors others' perceptions of him and his behavior.

From one viewpoint, these data are hardly surprising, for it has long been known that elements are given meaning by the context in which they occur. . . . Once a person is designated abnormal, all of his other behaviors and characteristics are colored by that label. Indeed, that label is so powerful that many of the pseudopatients' normal behaviors were overlooked entirely or profoundly misinterpreted. Some examples may clarify this issue. . . .

All pseudopatients took extensive notes publicly. Under ordinary circumstances, such behavior would have raised questions in the minds of observers, as, in fact, it did among patients. Indeed, it seemed so certain that the notes would elicit suspicion that elaborate precautions were taken to remove them from the ward each day. But the precautions proved needless. The closest any staff member came to questioning these notes occurred when one pseudopatient asked his physician what kind of medication he was receiving and began to write down the response. "You needn't write it," he was told gently. "If you have trouble remembering, just ask me again."

If no questions were asked of the pseudopatients, how was their writing interpreted? Nursing records for three patients indicate that the writing was seen as an aspect of their pathological behavior. "Patient engages in writing behavior" was the daily nursing comment on one of the pseudopatients who was never questioned about his writing. Given that the patient is in the hospital, he must be psychologically disturbed. And given that he is disturbed, continuous writing must be a behavioral manifestation of that disturbance, perhaps a subset of the compulsive behaviors that are sometimes correlated with schizophrenia.

One tacit characteristic of psychiatric diagnosis is that it locates the sources of aberration within the individual and only rarely within the complex of stimuli that surrounds him. Consequently, behaviors that are stimulated by the environment are commonly misattributed to the patient's disorder. For example, one kindly nurse found a pseudopatient pacing the long hospital corridors. "Nervous, Mr. X?" she asked. "No, bored," he said.

The notes kept by pseudopatients are full of patient behaviors that were misinterpreted by well-intentioned staff. Often enough, a patient would go "berserk" because he had, wittingly or unwittingly, been mistreated by, say, an attendant. A nurse coming upon the scene would rarely inquire even cursorily into the environmental stimuli of the patient's behavior. Rather, she assumed that his upset derived from his pathology, not from his present interactions with other staff members. Occasionally, the staff might assume that the patient's family (especially when they had recently visited) or other patients had stimulated the outburst. But never were the staff found to assume that one of themselves or the structure of the hospital had anything to do with a patient's behavior. One psychiatrist pointed to a group of patients who were sitting outside the cafeteria entrance half an hour before lunchtime. To a group of young residents he indicated that such behavior was characteristic of the oral-acquisitive nature of the syndrome. It seemed not to occur to him that there were very few things to anticipate in the psychiatric hospital besides eating.

A psychiatric label has a life and an influence of its own. Once the impression has been formed that the patient is schizophrenic, the expectation is that he will continue to be schizophrenic. When a sufficient amount of time has passed, during which the patient has done nothing bizarre, he is considered to be in remission and available for discharge. But the label endures beyond discharge, with the unconfirmed expectation that he will behave as a schizophrenic again. Such labels, conferred by mental health professionals, are as influential on the patient as they are on his relatives and friends, and it should not surprise anyone that the diagnosis acts on all of them as a self-fulfilling prophecy. Eventually, the patient himself accepts the diagnosis, with all of its surplus meanings and expectations, and behaves accordingly.

The inferences to be made from these matters are quite simple. . . . [T]here is enormous overlap in the symptoms presented by patients who have been variously diagnosed, and so there is enormous overlap in the behaviors of the sane and the insane. The sane are not "sane" all of the time. We lose our tempers "for no good reason." We are occasionally depressed or anxious, again for no good reason. And we may find it difficult to get along with one or another person—again for no reason that we can specify. Similarly, the insane are not always insane. Indeed, it was the impression of the pseudopatients while living with them that they were sane for long periods of time— that the bizarre behaviors upon which their diagnoses were allegedly predicated constituted only a small fraction of their total behavior. If it makes no sense to label ourselves permanently depressed on the basis of an occasional depression, then it takes better evidence than is presently available to label all patients insane or schizophrenic on the basis of bizarre behaviors or cognitions. It seems more useful, . . . to limit our discussions to *behaviors*, the stimuli that provoke them, and their correlates.

It is not known why powerful impressions of personality traits, such as "crazy" or "insane," arise. Conceivably, when the origins of and stimuli that give rise to a behavior are remote or unknown, or when the behavior strikes us as immutable, trait labels regarding the *behavior* arise. When, on the other hand, the origins and stimuli are known and available, discourse is limited to the behavior itself. Thus, I may hallucinate because I am sleeping, or I may hallucinate because I have ingested a peculiar drug. These are termed sleep-induced hallucinations, or dreams, and drug-induced hallucinations, respectively. But when the stimuli to my hallucinations are unknown, that is called craziness, or schizophrenia—as if that inference were somehow as illuminating as the others. . . .

THE CONSEQUENCES OF LABELING AND DEPERSONALIZATION

Whenever the ratio of what is known to what needs to be known approaches zero, we tend to invent "knowledge" and assume that we understand more than we actually do. We seem unable to acknowledge that we simply don't know. The needs for diagnosis and remediation of behavioral and emotional problems are enormous. But rather than acknowledge that we are just embarking on understanding, we continue to label patients "schizophrenic," "manic-depressive," and "insane," as if in those words we had captured the essence of understanding. The facts of the matter are that we have known for a long time that diagnoses are often not useful or reliable, but we have nevertheless continued to use them. We now know that we cannot distinguish insanity from sanity. It is depressing to consider how that information will be used.

Not merely depressing, but frightening. How many people, one wonders, are sane but not recognized as such in our psychiatric institutions? How many have been needlessly stripped of their privileges of citizenship, from the right to vote and drive to that of handling their own accounts? How many have feigned insanity in order to avoid the criminal consequences of their behavior, and, conversely, how many would rather stand trial than live interminably in a psychiatric hospital—but are wrongly thought to be mentally ill? How many have been stigmatized by well-intentioned, but nevertheless erroneous, diagnoses? On the last point, recall again that a "type 2 error" in psychiatric diagnosis does not have the same consequences it does in medical diagnosis. A diagnosis of cancer that has been found to be in error is cause for celebration. But psychiatric diagnoses are rarely found to be in error. The label sticks, a mark of inadequacy forever.

NOTES

1. R. Benedict. *J. Gen. Psychol.* 10, 59 (1934).

2. See in this regard H. Becker, *Outsiders: Studies in the Sociology of Deviance* (New York: Free Press, 1963).

3. E. Goffman. *Asylums* (Garden City, NY: Doubleday, 1961).

SCHIZOPHRENIA IN THE THIRD WORLD

RICHARD WARNER

Paradoxically, while the United States is presumed to have among the most advanced medical treatments in the world, schizophrenia patients in many Third World countries often have better prognoses than those in the United States. That is, schizophrenia is generally considered incurable in the United States, whereas frequently patients in the Third World who exhibit the symptoms of the "disease" frequently get over it. As you will see in the following article, many of the factors that are strongly correlated with schizophrenia are social and environmental factors, thus calling into question the role of biological and medical factors alleged by Western psychiatrists.

Sixteen billion dollars was spent on the treatment of schizophrenia in the United States in 1990[1]—about 0.3 per cent of the gross domestic product. This figure excludes social security benefits paid to people with schizophrenia and other indirect costs. Such a substantial investment should surely have yielded Americans significantly better rates of recovery than in less affluent parts of the world. By contrast, psychiatric care is very low on the list of priorities in developing countries. Despite this fact, the evidence points overwhelmingly to much better outcome from schizophrenia in the Third World. It is worth looking at this evidence in some detail.

BRIEF PSYCHOSES IN THE THIRD WORLD

There are numerous reports that psychoses have a briefer duration in the Third World, and virtually none to indicate that such illnesses have a worse outcome anywhere outside the Western world. Transitory delusional states (*bouffées delirantes*) in Senegal, for example, with such schizophrenia-like features as "derealization, hallucinations, and ideas of reference dominated by themes of persecution and megalomania"[2] occasionally develop the classic, chronic course of schizophrenia, but generally recover spontaneously within a short period of time. Acute paranoid reactions with a favorable course and outcome are common in the Grande Kabylie of northern Algeria[3] and throughout East Africa.[4] Acute psychotic episodes with high rates of spontaneous remission are frequent in Nigeria,[5] and brief schizophrenia-like psychoses have been reported to account for four-fifths of the admissions to one psychiatric hospital in Uganda.[6] Indistinguishable from schizophrenia, acute "fear and guilt psychoses" in Ghana manifest hallucinations, inappropriate emotional reactions, grotesque delusions and bizarre behavior. Under treatment at local healing shrines, such illnesses are generally cured within a week or so, although they may occasionally progress to chronic schizophrenia.[7] Doris Mayer, a psychiatrist, also found typical schizophrenic states to be more readily reversible in the Tallensi of northern Ghana.[8] Many more examples could be given of the prevalence of such brief psychoses in Singapore, Papua and other developing countries.[9] "Acute, short lasting psychoses," according to Dr H. B. M. Murphy, a Canadian psychiatrist with much research experience in cross-cultural psychiatry, "form a major part of all recognized mental disorders . . . " in the Third World.[10]

NOT REALLY SCHIZOPHRENIA

But are they schizophrenia? Some psychiatrists would argue that these acute psychoses are indeed schizophrenia in view of the typical schizophrenic features such as hallucinations, delusions, bizarre behavior and emotional disturbances. They would also point to the minority of cases, initially indistinguishable, which develop the chronic schizophrenic picture. Others would deny that any brief psychosis can be schizophrenia precisely because schizophrenia, by definition, is a long-lasting illness. According to the American Psychiatric Association's Diagnostic and Statistical Manual (DSM-IV),[11] a psychosis must last six months to be labeled schizophrenia. This is a terminological issue that must not be allowed to obscure the point of logic. If schizophrenia has a more benign course in the developing world (and there is considerable evidence to show that this is the case), then we might well find many schizophrenia-like episodes in these societies that are of a shorter duration than six months. To argue that these are not schizophrenia is to prejudge the issue.

Could these be cases of organic psychosis? Certainly, some could be. There is a high prevalence in Third World countries of trypanosomiasis, pellagra and related parasitic, nutritional and infectious disorders that may develop into psychotic states. Malaria, in particular, is often associated with acute psychotic episodes.[12] It is unlikely, however, that all brief episodes in the Third World are organic in origin. In conducting their social psychiatric survey of four aboriginal tribes in Taiwan, two psychiatrists, Hsien Rin and Tsung-Yi Lin, were particularly concerned about the diagnosis of organic and functional psychoses. They carefully separated schizophrenia from malarial psychosis, drug-induced psychosis and unclassifiable cases. Although skeptical at the outset of the study, after cross-checking their information and cross-validating their diagnoses they were forced to conclude that psychoses in general, and schizophrenia in particular, had a particularly benign course among these Formosan farmers and hunters. Of ten confirmed cases of schizophrenia only two had been active for more than two years and five had been ill for less than a year.[13]

. . . Schizophrenia in the Third World has a course and prognosis quite unlike the condition as we recognize it in the West. The progressive deterioration that Kraepelin considered central to his definition of the disease is a rare event in non-industrial societies, except perhaps under the dehumanizing restrictions of a traditional asylum. The majority of people with schizophrenia in the Third World achieve a favorable outcome. The more urbanized and industrialized the setting, the more malignant becomes the illness. Why should this be so?

WORK

It [has been argued] that the dwindling cure rates for insanity during the growth of industrialism in Britain and America, and the low recovery rates in schizophrenia during the Great Depression, were possibly related to labor-force dynamics. . . . The picture that has now been drawn of schizophrenia in the Third World gives more support to the notion that the work role may be an important factor shaping the course of schizophrenia.

In non-industrial societies that are not based upon a wage economy, the term "unemployment" is meaningless. Even where colonial wage systems have been developed, they frequently preserve the subsistence base of tribal or peasant communities, drawing workers for temporary labor only.[14] In these circumstances, underemployment and landlessness may become common but unemployment is rare. Unemployment, however, may reach high levels in the urbanized and industrial areas of the Third World.

The return of a person suffering from psychosis to a productive role in a non-industrial setting is not contingent upon his or her actively seeking a job, impressing an employer with his or her worth or functioning at a consistently adequate level. In a non-wage, subsistence economy, people with mental illness may perform any of those available tasks that match their level of functioning at a given time. Whatever constructive contributions they can make are likely to be valued by the community and their level of disability will not be considered absolute. Dr. Adios Lambs, a psychiatrist well known for developing a village-based treatment and rehabilitation program in Nigeria, reports that social attitudes in Nigerian rural communities permit the majority of those with mental disorders to find an appropriate level of functioning and thus to avoid disability and deterioration.[15] In India, research workers for the World Health Organization's [WHO] follow-up study of schizophrenia encountered difficulty in interviewing their cases as the ex-patients were so busy—the men in the fields and the women in domestic work.[16] In rural Sichuan, China, more than three-quarters of people with schizophrenia who had never been treated were working; even people with significant psychotic symptoms were doing housework or farm work.[17] The more complete use of labor in pre-industrial societies may encourage high rates of recovery from psychosis.

But what of the nature of the work itself? John Wing, a British social psychiatrist who undertook a great deal of research on schizophrenia, identified two critical environmental factors that lead to optimal outcome from the illness. The first of these, which we will return to later, is freedom from emotional over-involvement—smothering or criticism—from others in the household. His second criterion, which is relevant here, is that there should be stable expectations precisely geared to the level of performance that the individual can actually achieve.[18] Industrial society gives relatively little leeway for adapting a job to the abilities of the worker. High productivity requirements and competitive performance ratings may be particularly unsuitable for a person recovering from schizophrenia. In a peasant culture he or she is more likely to find an appropriate role among such tasks of subsistence farming as livestock management, food- and fuel-gathering or child-minding. . . .

In each setting there is wide individual variation. In pre-revolutionary Russia, for example, peasant farmers in Volokolamsk worked between 79 days a year in the least industrious households and 216 in the most industrious.[19] This compares with an expectation of around 230 to 240 working days a year for employees in modern industrial society. Work demands in many cultures are particularly low for young, unmarried adults[20] (who may be at higher risk for developing schizophrenia), but whatever the usual pattern, workload expectations are more readily adjusted to meet the capacities of the marginally functional individual in a village setting than in the industrial labor market. There can be little doubt that it is simpler for a person with schizophrenia to return to a productive role in a non-industrial community than in the industrial world. The merits of tribal and peasant labor systems are apparent. As in the West during a period of labor shortage, it is easier for family and community members to reintegrate the sick person into the society, and the sufferer is better able to retain his or her self-esteem. The result may well be not only better social functioning of the sick person but also more complete remission of the symptoms of the illness.

OCCUPATION AND OUTCOME

[The] WHO Pilot Study data more clearly document an association between occupation and outcome. Farmers were more likely than patients of any other occupation to experience the most benign pattern of illness—full remission with no relapses—and the unemployed were least likely to experience such a mild course to the psychosis. In urbanized Cali and Taipei patients from high-status professional and managerial occupations were found to achieve good overall outcome, while this was not the case in the largely rural catchment area around Agra, India.[21] This pattern confirms the impression that schizophrenia may be more benign in the successful upper classes in the industrialized setting, but more malignant among the better educated in India who are known to suffer rates of unemployment several times greater than the poorly educated and illiterate.[22] The data from Nigeria do not fit as neatly. Even though many patients in the sample appear to have come from rural districts, Nigerians with schizophrenia in managerial jobs experienced good overall outcome.[23] This could be explained by a strong local demand for educated labor at that time or, again, the high mobility of the migrant labor force may confuse the picture; patients who were unable to continue in managerial positions could return to a less demanding role in their farming community.

Migrant-labor practices allow people with schizophrenia in the Third World to change occupation and residence after developing psychotic symptoms. Level of education, however, is less easily changed. It is therefore interesting to note that a *high* level of education is one of the few strong and consistent indicators of *poor* outcome in the Third World,[24] thus standing in contrast to Western patterns of recovery. This point, then, may be one of the most useful pieces of evidence in the WHO study, pointing to a link between good outcome for schizophrenia in the Third World and the maintenance of traditional occupational roles. . . .

A PSYCHOTIC EPISODE IN GUATEMALA

Maria, a young Indian woman living in a village on Lake Atitlan in Guatemala, alienates her close relatives and the people of the community by her irresponsible behavior before finally suffering a full-blown psychotic episode. She hallucinates, believing that spirits are surrounding her to take her to the realm of the dead, and she walks about the house arguing with ghosts. A local shaman perceives that she is *loca* (crazy) and diagnoses her as suffering the effect of supernatural forces unleashed by the improper behavior of certain relatives. He prescribes a healing ritual that calls for the active participation of most of her extended family. Her condition requires her to move back to her father's house, where she recovers within a week. Benjamin Paul, the anthropologist who describes Maria's case, points out several features of interest. Maria is never blamed for her psychotic behavior or stigmatized by her illness, because her hallucinations of ghosts are credible supernatural events and she is innocently suffering the magical consequences of the wrongdoing of others. The communal healing activities lead to a dramatic reversal of Maria's course of alienation from family and community. In the West, a psychotic episode is likely to lead to increased alienation. In the case of Maria, conflict resolution and social reintegration are central to her recovery and result from the folk diagnosis and treatment of her symptoms.[25]

THE FOLK DIAGNOSIS OF PSYCHOSIS

Throughout the non-industrial world, the features of psychosis are likely to be given a supernatural explanation. The Shona of Southern Rhodesia, for example, believe visual and auditory hallucinations to be real and sent by spirits.[26] In Dakar, Senegal:

> one can have hallucinations without being thought to be sick. A magical explanation is usually resorted to and native specialists are consulted. There is no rejection or alienation by society. The patient remains integrated within his group. As a result, the level of anxiety is low.[27]

The psychiatrist who gives this report claims that 90 per cent of the acute psychoses in Dakar are cured because the patient's delusions and hallucinations have an obvious culturally relevant content, and he or she is not rejected by the group.

Similarly, in the slums of San Juan, Puerto Rico:

> If an individual reports hallucinations, it clearly indicates to the believer in spiritualism that he is being visited by spirits who manifest themselves visually and audibly. If he has delusions . . . his thoughts are being distorted by interfering bad spirits, or through development of his psychic faculties spirits have informed him of the true enemies in his environment. Incoherent ramblings, and cryptic verbalizations indicate that he is undergoing a test, an experiment engineered by the spirits. If he wanders aimlessly through the neighborhood, he is being pursued by ambulatory spirits who are tormenting him unmercifully.[28]

In many cases where a supernatural explanation for psychotic features is used, the label "crazy" or "insane" may never be applied. I once remarked to a Sioux mental health worker from the Pine Ridge Reservation in South Dakota that most Americans who heard voices would be diagnosed as suffering from psychosis. Her response was simple. "That's terrible."

STIGMA

Psychiatrists working in the Third World have repeatedly noted the low level of stigma that attaches to mental disorder. Among the Formosan tribesmen studied by Rio and Lin, mental illness is free of stigma.[29] Sinhalese families freely refer to their psychotic family members as *pissu* (crazy) and show no shame about it. Tuberculosis in Sri Lanka is more stigmatizing than mental illness.[30] The authors of the WHO follow-up study suggest that one of the factors contributing to the good outcome for people with schizophrenia in Cali, Colombia, is the "high level of tolerance of relatives and friends for symptoms of mental disorder"—a factor that can help the "readjustment to family life and work after discharge."[31]

The possibility that the stigma attached to an illness may influence its course is illustrated by research on Navajos who suffer from epilepsy conducted by anthropologist Jerrold Levy in cooperation with the Indian Health Service. Sibling incest is regarded as the cause of generalized seizures, or Moth Sickness, in Navajo society, and those who suffer from the condition are highly stigmatized for supposed transgressions of a major taboo. It is interesting to learn that these individuals are often found to lead chaotic lives characterized by alcoholism, promiscuity, incest, rape, violence and early death. Levy and his co-workers attribute the career of the Navajo epileptic to the disdain and lack of social support that he or she is offered by the community.[32] To what extent, we may wonder, can features of schizophrenia in the West be attributed to similar treatment?

HIGH STATUS IN PSYCHOSIS

It seems strange in retrospect that tuberculosis should have been such a romantic and genteel illness to eighteenth- and nineteenth-century society that people of fashion chose to copy the consumptive appearance.[33] Equally curious, the features of psychosis in the Third World can, at times, lead to considerable elevation in social status. In non-industrial cultures throughout the world, the hallucinations and altered states of consciousness produced by psychosis, fasting, sleep deprivation, social isolation and contemplation, and hallucinogenic drug use are often a prerequisite for gaining shamanic power.[34] The psychotic features are interpreted as an initiatory experience. For example, whereas poor Puerto Ricans who go to a psychiatric clinic or insane asylum are likely to be highly stigmatized as *locos* (madmen), people who suffer from schizophrenia who consult a spiritualist may rise in status. Sociologists Lloyd Rogler and August Hollingshead report: "The spiritualist may announce to the sick person, his family, and friends that the afflicted person is endowed with *facultades* (psychic faculties), a matter of prestige at this level of the social structure. . . ."[35]

The study indicates that Puerto Ricans with schizophrenia who consult spiritualists may not only lose their symptoms, they may also achieve the status of mediums themselves. So successful is the social reintegration of the male Puerto Ricans with schizophrenia that, after some readjustment of family roles, their wives found them *more* acceptable as husbands than did the wives of normal men. . . .

GROUP PARTICIPATION

The process of curing in pre-industrial societies, it is clear, is very much a communal phenomenon tending not only to reintegrate the deviant individual into the group but also to reaffirm the solidarity of the community. Thus, the N'jayei secret society of the Mende tribe in Sierra Leone, which aims to treat mental illness by applying sanctions to those who are presumed to have committed a breach of social rules, provides members with a mechanism for social reintegration and, simultaneously, reinforces the integrity and standards of the culture.[36] Such a dual process of unification of the group and integration of the individual is seen to result from the great public healing ceremonies of the Zuni medicine societies[37] or from the intense communal involvement and dramatic grandeur of a Navajo healing ceremony. The Navajo patient, relatives and other participants alike take medicine and submit to ritual procedures in a symbolic recognition that illness is a problem for the community as a whole.[38]

Nancy Waxler, in her research on people suffering from psychosis in Sri Lanka, was impressed with the way in which the intense community involvement in treating mental illness prevents the patient from developing secondary symptoms from alienation and stigma and results in the sick person being reintegrated into society. She writes:

> Mental illness is basically a problem of and for the family, not the sick person. Thus we find among the Sinhalese that almost all treatment of mental illness involves groups meeting with groups. When a mad person is believed to have been possessed by a demon the whole family, their relatives and neighbors, sometimes the whole village, join together to plan, carry out and pay for the appropriate exorcism ceremony. The sick person is usually the central focus, but often only as the vehicle for the demon, and during some parts of these ceremonies the patient is largely ignored.[39]

The importance of this process of social reintegration is confirmed by data from the two WHO outcome studies. In both the developed and developing worlds, social isolation was found to be one of the strongest predictors of poor outcome in schizophrenia.[40] Several other researchers have found this factor to be important in the genesis and outcome of schizophrenia.[41]

THE FAMILY

One of John Wing's criteria for good outcome in schizophrenia mentioned earlier in the chapter was freedom for the patient from excessive emotional demands or criticism within the family. His recommendation is backed up by a good deal of social psychiatric research from the Medical Research Council in London. . . . The family environment for people with schizophrenia in the Third World is different from the West. In India, spouses, parents or siblings are willing to provide for a relative, however disabled.[42] The multiple caregivers in an Indian extended family will handle most of the problems presented by a family member with schizophrenia without seeking outside assistance—self-neglect and dirtiness seem to be of the greatest concern.[43]

At the end of the twentieth century, however, with urbanization, increased female employment and the break-up of the extended family, the level of tolerance was declining.[44] Increased acceptance, nevertheless, can bring better outcomes. In Qatar, on the Persian Gulf, people with schizophrenia in extended families have been reported to show better outcome at follow-up than those who return to nuclear family households.[45] The extended family structure, which is more common in the Third World, allows a diffusion of emotional over-involvement and interdependence among family members.

The emphasis on community involvement in the treatment of mental illness in non-industrial societies similarly tends to reduce family tensions. Responsibility is shared broadly and the patient often escapes blame and criticism, allowing the family to be more supportive. According to one study, for example, relatives of people with schizophrenia in Chandigarh, north India, are much less likely to be demanding or critical of their psychotic family member than are the relatives of people with schizophrenia in the industrial world. In London, nearly a half of patients with schizophrenia have such emotionally stressful relatives; in Rochester, New York, the proportion is similar; but in north India, fewer than a fifth of subjects with schizophrenia were found to have critical and demanding relatives . . . .[46] [T]his difference might be a consequence of the higher achievement expectations placed on Westerners suffering from psychosis or of the emotional isolation so common for families of people with schizophrenia in the West but so much rarer in the developing world.

In the Third World, it appears, the person with a psychotic disorder is more likely to retain his or her self-esteem, a feeling of value to the community and a sense of belonging. These are things that . . . sixteen billion dollars does not buy the person with schizophrenia in the United States or elsewhere in the Western world.

NOTES

1. Norquist, G. S., Regier, D. A. and Rupp, A., "Estimates of the cost of treating people with schizophrenia: Contributions of data from epidemiological survey," in M. Moscarelli, A. Rupp. And N. Sartorius (eds), *Handbook of Mental Health Economics and Health Policy: Volume I: Schizophrenia*, Chichester: John Wiley and Sons, 1996, pp. 96–101.1

2. Collomb, H., "Bouffées délirantes en psychiatrie Africaine," *Transcultural Psychiatric Research*, 3: 29–34, 1966, p. 29.

3. Schwartz, R., "Beschreibung einer ambulanten psychiatrischen Patienten-population in der Grossen-Kabylie (Nordalgerien): Epidemiologische und Klinische Aspekte," *Social Psychiatry* (West Germany), 12: 207–18, 1977.

4. Smartt, C. G. F., "Mental maladjustment in the East African," *Journal of Mental Science*, 102: 441–66, 1956.

5. Opler, M. K., "The social and cultural nature of mental illness and its treatment," in S. Lesse, (ed.), *An Evaluation of the Results of the Psychotherapies*, Springfield, Illinois: C.C. Thomas, 1968, pp. 280–91.

6. Tewfik, G. I., "Psychoses in Africa," in *Mental Disorders and Mental Health in Africa South of the Sahara*, CCTA/CSA-WFMH-WHO meeting of specialists on mental health, Bukavu, London: 1958.

7. Field, M. J., *Search for Security, An Ethno-Psychiatric Study of Rural Ghana*, Chicago: Northwestern University Press, 1962.

8. Fortes, M. and Mayer, D. Y., "Psychosis and social change among the Tallensi of northern Ghana," in S. H. Foulkes and G. S. Prince (eds) *Psychiatry in a Changing Society*, London: Tavistock, 1969, pp. 33–73.

9. Berne, E., "Some oriental mental hospitals," *American Journal of Psychiatry*, 106:376–83, 1949; Seligman, C. G., "Temperament, conflict and psychosis in a stone-age population," *British Journal of Medical Psychology*, 9:187–202, 1929; Jilek, W. G. and Jilek-Aall, L., "Transient psychoses in Africans," *Psychiatrics Clinica* (Basel), 3: 337–64, 1970.

10. Murphy, H. B. M., "Cultural factors in the genesis of schizophrenia," in D. Rosenthal and S. S. Kety (eds), *The Transmission of Schizophrenia*, Oxford: Pergamon, 1968, p. 138.

11. American Psychiatric Association, *Diagnostic and Statistical Manual of Mental Disorders (DSM–III)*, Washington, DC: 1968.

12. Wintrob, R. M., "Malaria and the acute psychotic episode," *Journal of Nervous and Mental Disease*, 156: 306–17, 1973.

13. Rin, H. and Lin, T., "Mental illness among Formosan aborigines as compared with the Chinese in Taiwan," *Journal of Mental Science*, 108: 134–46, 1962.

14. Harris, M., *Culture, Man and Nature. An Introduction to General Anthropology*, New York: Thomas Y. Crowell, 1971, p. 480.

15. Lambo, T., "The importance of cultural factors in psychiatric treatment," in I. Al-Issa and W. Dennis (eds), *Cross-Cultural Studies of Behavior*, New York: Holt, Rinehart & Winston, 1970, pp. 548–52.

16. World Health Organization, *Schizophrenia: An International Follow-Up Study*, Chichester, England: Wiley, 1979, p. 104.

17. Ran, M., Xiang, M., Huang, M. and Shan, Y. "Natural course of schizophrenia," *British Journal of Psychiatry*, 178, 2001.

18.Wing, J. K., "The social context of schizophrenia," *American Journal of Psychiatry*, 135: 1333–9, 1978.

19. Chayanov, A. V., *The Theory of Peasant Economy*, Homewood, Illinois: Richard D. Irwin, 1966, p. 77, cited in Sahlins, *Stone Age Economics*, p. 89.

20. Richards, A. I., *Land, Labor and Diet*, p. 402; Douglas, M., "Lele economy as compared with the Bushong," in G. Dalton and P. Bohannen, *Markets in Africa*, Evanston, Illinois: Northwestern University Press, 1962, p. 231, cited in Sahlins, *Stone Age Economics*, pp. 52–4.

21.World Health Organization, *Schizophrenia: An International Follow Study*, Chichester, England: Wiley, 1979, pp. 271, 283.

22. Squire, *Employment Policy in Developing Countries*, p. 71.

23. World Health Organization, *Schizophrenia*, p. 283.

24. Ibid., pp. 287–8.

25. Paul, B. D., "Mental disorder and self-regulating processes in culture: A Guatemalan illustration," in R. Hunt (ed.), *Personalities and Cultures: Readings in Psychological Anthropology*, Garden City, New York: Natural History Press, 1967.

26. Gelfand, M., "Psychiatric disorders as recognized by the Shona," in A. Kiev (ed.), *Magic, Faith and Healing*, New York: Free Press, 1964, pp. 156–73.

27. Collomb, "Bouffées délirantes en psychiatrie Africaine," p. 30.

28. Rogler, L. H. and Hollingshead, A. B., *Trapped: Families and Schizophrenia*, New York: Wiley, 1965, p. 254.

29. Rin and Lin, "Mental illness among Formosan aborigines."

30. Waxler, N. E., "Is mental illness cured in traditional societies? A theoretical analysis," *Culture, Medicine and Psychiatry*, 1: 233–53, 1977, p. 242.

31. World Health Organization, *Schizophrenia*, p. 105.

32. Levy, J. E., Neutra, R. and Parker, D., "Life careers of Navajo epileptics and convulsive hysterics," *Social Science and Medicine*, 13: 53–66, 1979.

33. Sontag, S., *Illness as Metaphor*, New York: Vintage Books, 1979.

34. Eliade, M., *Shamanism: Archaic Techniques of Ecstasy*, Princeton: Princeton University Press/Bollingen Paperback, 1972; Black Elk, *The Sacred Pipe*, Baltimore: Penguin, 1971.

35. Rogler and Hollingshead, *Trapped. Families and Schizophrenia*, New York: Wiley, 1965, p. 254.

36. Dawson, J., "Urbanization and mental health in a West African community," in Kiev, *Magic, Faith and Healing*, pp. 305–42.

37. Benedict, R., *Patterns of Culture*, Boston: Houghton-Mifflin, 1934, p. 72.

38. Kaplan, B. and Johnson, D., "The social meaning of Navajo psychopathology and psychotherapy," in Kiev, *Magic, Faith and Healing*, pp. 203–29; Leighton, A. H. and Leighton, D. C., "Elements of psychotherapy in Navaho religion," *Psychiatry*, 4: 515–23, 1941.

39. Waxler, "Is mental illness cured in traditional societies?," p. 241.

40. World Health Organization, *Schizophrenia*, p. 288; Jablensky et al., "Schizophrenia: Manifestations, incidence and course in different cultures. A World Health Organization ten-country study," *Psychological Medicine*, monograph supplement 20, 1991. Table 4.17.

41. Hare, E. H., "Mental illness and social conditions in Bristol," *Journal of Mental Science*, 102:349–57, 1956; Stein, L., "Social class' gradient in schizophrenia," British Journal of Preventive and Social Medicine, 11:181–95, 1957; Cooper, B., "Social class and prognosis in schizophrenia: Part I," British Journal of Preventive and Social Medicine, 15:17–30, 1961; Jaco, E. G., "The social isolation hypothesis and schizophrenia," American Sociological Review, 19: 567–77, 1954.

42. Thara, R. and Rajkumar, S. "Gender differences in schizophrenia: Results of a follow-up study in India," Schizophrenia Research, 7: 65–70, 1992.

43. Srinivasan, T. N., Rajkumar, S., and Padmavathi, R. "Initiating care for untreated schizophrenic patients and results of a one year follow-up," International Journal of Social Psychiatry, 47: 73–80, 2001.

44. Thara, "Gender differences in schizophrenia."

45. El-Islam, M. F., "A better outlook for schizophrenics living in extended families," British Journal of Psychiatry, 135: 343–7, 1979.

46. Wig, N. N., Menon, D. K. and Bedi, H., "Coping with schizophrenic patients in developing countries: A study of expressed emotions in the relatives" presented at the Seventh World Congress of Psychiatry, Vienna, July 11–16, 1983; Leff, Psychiatry Around the Globe, p. 157.

PART 9

Epilogue

A Freedom-Deviance Trade-Off?

LESSONS IN ORDER

DAVID H. BAYLEY

To end this volume full circle, we can return to Durkheim's assertion that crime and deviance are the price we pay for a free society. Many societies have less crime than we have in the United States, and a myriad of factors account for the differences. The following article concerns the extraordinarily low rates of street crime in Japan, relative to the United States. Bayley attributes the difference to the relatively extreme emphasis the Japanese place on conformity to the group. By contrast, the United States places a relatively extreme value on individualism. If the crime rates differ because of these cultural differences, then, on the one hand, crime and deviance may indeed be the price we pay for freedom and individualism in the United States. On the other hand, since, as we have seen, deviance is what the audience says it is, societies placing more emphasis on conformity are apt to define more activities as deviant.

The gangster office was located in a modern two-story detached structure in an open space at the end of a passageway between two tall brick buildings. On the first floor was a large office containing desks and filing cabinets, along with an alcove furnished with leatherette couches and easy chairs providing a view through glass panels of a well-tended Japanese-style garden. The name of the gangster organization was etched onto a large, lacquered cross section of tree trunk displayed prominently just inside the door. The boss was a tough-looking man of forty-five, dressed in dark slacks and a maroon turtleneck under a buttoned cardigan. As the two patrol officers and I sat drinking green tea prepared by one of the casually dressed male underlings, the boss explained that this was a headquarters supervising forty or fifty branch offices. The two patrol officers took their hats off and enjoyed a relaxed smoke while prompting the boss with questions that they thought would interest me. After fifteen minutes, we were bowed out the door, past conical piles of salt arranged for good luck on the doorstep.

Police estimate that there are at least 80,000 *yakuza* in Japan—that is, full-fledged members of 1,500 organized criminal groups, loosely federated into several larger competing syndicates.[1] They commit 6 percent of all Penal Code crimes—3 percent of murders, 16 percent of robberies, 15 percent of rapes—and are instrumental in drug and gun smuggling.[2] Frequently fighting among themselves for turf and position, they commit most of the crimes involving firearms, as well as most of the offenses against the gun laws. Their illegal activities include gambling, prostitution, selling protection, strike-breaking, blackmail, and loan-sharking, although increasingly they are investing their illegal proceeds in legitimate businesses, especially in the entertainment industry. Uniformed patrol officers routinely visit their offices to show the flag, and also to note the names of gang members displayed on wall-mounted rosters and the schedule of monthly events written on large chalkboards, as in any Japanese office.

The visibility of organized criminal gangs and their close surveillance by the police does not mean that Japan's reputation for being the safest country among the developed democracies is false. Japan's rate of serious crime is indeed less than one-third of the American, and there is no reason to doubt the figures.[3] But it certainly raises questions about how this orderliness has been achieved and what the role of the police is in it. To understand what is going on in Japan, I shall compare factors that are commonly expected to affect crime and its control in order to see if they can account for the remarkable difference in orderliness between Japan and the United States. I shall begin by examining criminalogenic conditions.

REASONS FOR PUBLIC ORDER

In searching for an explanation of Japan's dramatically lower crime rates, several factors can immediately be set aside. Japan is fully as modern as the United States, transformed equally during the last century by processes of urbanization, industrialization, and technological development. Japan is not a Third World backwater. Especially confounding is the fact that its population congestion, sometimes suspected of being associated with social disorganization and high crime, is much greater than that of the United States. To appreciate what it would be like if the United States were as densely populated as Japan, imagine California if half the U.S. population moved there. If they did, can one believe that our crime rate would fall?

Japan is also not politically repressive; its people are not subjected to the iron hand of government regimentation. It is as democratic as the United States, with the rights of speech, expression, association, and electoral competition protected by law and an independent judiciary. This has not always been the case. Democracy is less than fifty years old in Japan, dating from the Allied Occupation in 1945. For centuries government had exercised very tight control. While it seems doubtful that many Japanese are inhibited by fear of governmental abuses of power, one might argue that the habits of subservience to authority learned in earlier times remain a part of Japan's political culture and might inhibit expressive behavior. The sole serious contemporary exception to its fine human rights record is the practice of extended pre-charge detention.[4] Because it is used so seldomly and the cultural promptings of confession are so powerful, I doubt that this practice has any important effect on either crime—or clearance—rates.

Turning to economic conditions, informative differences between Japan and the United States begin to emerge. Although per capita wealth is about the same, the distribution of income is significantly more egalitarian in Japan than in the United States. That is, rich people earn a larger proportion of the country's income in the United States than they do in Japan.[5] Furthermore, unemployment is generally much lower in Japan than in the United States by a factor of two or three.[6] And a much smaller proportion of the working population is involved in strikes in Japan.[7] Although there is poverty in Japan and homelessness, there are few slums—that is, areas of chronic poverty, unemployment, family pathology, and high crime.[8] There are probably only two in all of Japan that qualify—the Airin area of Osaka, home to 20,000 day laborers, and the Sanya section of Tokyo, which has 7,000.[9] These areas are notorious throughout Japan.

More important, Japan does not have ghettoes, meaning areas inhabited by chronically impoverished people who are members of groups that are subjected to discrimination by the general population. Only about one-half of 1 percent of the population is ethnically not Japanese, mostly Koreans and Chinese.[10] By contrast, about 13 percent of the American population is African-American and 8 percent is Hispanic.[11] As Japanese often point out, Japan probably has the largest homogeneous population of any country in the world. This is not to suggest that crime is mostly interracial or interethnic. It is not. Rather, Japan lacks the kind of racial and cultural diversity that so frequently reinforces economic inequality to produce successive generations of the misery, hopelessness, rage, and family disintegration that are so strongly associated with crime.

Americans expect the operations of the criminal justice system to inhibit crime. Comparing its operation in Japan and in the United States, however, the few differences would seem to work to give Japan higher rather than lower crime rates. The two systems are very similar in form, which is hardly surprising, since the Japanese system is the product of American reform after World War II, overlaying earlier borrowings from Germany and France. The Japanese actually invest less of their gross national product in police, courts, and corrections (0.88 percent) than does the United States (1.26 percent).[12] Japan spends a smaller proportion of government revenues on criminal justice (2.5 percent) than does the United States (3.2 percent).[13] Japan does spend proportionately more of its gross national product on police—0.76 percent versus 0.50 percent—but per capita expenditures on police are higher in the United States.[14] Altogether, criminal justice investments would hardly seem to account for Japan's lower crime rates.

Contrary to what Americans would expect in a country with low crime rates, sentences for similar crimes are invariably more lenient in Japan than in the United States, which is reflected in the fact that five times as many Americans as Japanese, proportionate to population, are in prison. . . .[15] If the Japanese criminal justice system is having an impact on crime, it is not, therefore, through the greater rigor of its punishments. It may, however, be doing so through its sureness. A suspect is charged and officially dealt with in some manner in more than one-third of all crimes reported to the Japanese police. In the United States, the comparable figure is a meager 5 percent.

Crime is much more risky in Japan than in the United States. The sureness of punishment in Japan, even if it is mild, may have a more deterrent effect than the more severe but uncertain punishments in the United States.

There is only one difference in legal context that might help to account for the disparity in crime rates. Japan has the toughest laws on the ownership of firearms, especially handguns, of any democratic country in the world. Registration is required for all firearms, knives, and swords.[16] No handguns are permitted in private hands, even registered, with the exception of people who participate in international shooting competitions. . . .[17] Even they cannot take their guns home, but must deposit them at a police station or with registered administrators of shooting ranges. Shotguns and small-caliber rifles are permitted for hunting. . . . Permits for owning weapons are issued by prefectural public safety commissions.[18] No one knows how many handguns are privately held in the United States, although estimates run into the hundreds of millions. Surveys have shown that 23 percent of American homes have handguns.[19]

As a result, the use of firearms in Japanese crime is negligible. . . . The uncertainty, wariness, and honest fear that American police officers feel in making street contacts and responding to summonses for assistance are totally unfamiliar to the Japanese police. Less than twenty officers are killed feloniously each year, hardly ever by firearms. In the United States eighty-four officers on average were killed each year during the last decade, three-quarters of them by handguns.[20]

The National Rifle Association, the major source of opposition to efforts to restrict gun ownership in the United States, developed a slogan that many believe makes the case convincingly against legislation restricting gun ownership. "When guns are outlawed, only outlaws will have guns." This is exactly what has occurred in Japan. And the Japanese think this is a very good thing.[21]

A final factor that is often considered influential in explaining crime, especially violent crime, is popular culture. Japan's is hardly less violent than that of the United States. Its history is certainly as blood-soaked. For centuries justice was meted out on the basis of class; until a little over a hundred years ago a samurai had the right to cut down with a sword any peasant who insulted him. Executions for crime were quick and brutal. There was and still is a cult of the sword in Japan similar to the cult of the gun in the United States. Martial values and regimen, which Americans tend to deprecate, have been extolled in Japan for generations. Political assassination has been far more common in Japanese history than in American. Since 1945 eight political leaders have been killed or injured in attacks.[22] Several assassination plans are discovered in their early stages each year. Both countries fought civil wars at approximately the same time. Although the bloodletting was less extensive in Japan, the parochial loyalties overcome were probably as intense. Furthermore, two generations ago Japan launched a fanatical imperial war whose excesses are still remembered throughout Asia as well as in the United States.

Contemporary popular culture, too, is replete with violence. Theater, films, television, and the ubiquitous "manga"—adult comic books—are saturated with violence, much of it with strong erotic overtones that feature women as victims.[23] Violence on television, on which many American ills are blamed, appears to be as prevalent in Japan as in the United States.[24] Samurai dramas are a staple of television, as Westerns used to be and police detective shows now are in the United States. The sword-wielding warrior, especially if he has turned outlaw, fascinates the Japanese. However, there may be some important differences in the portrayal of violence in both countries. Violence in Japan is more ritualized, more easily recognized as theater, distanced more from the settings of contemporary life. Furthermore, violence is usually portrayed tragically; people who use it die, often with their problems unresolved.[25]

Looking generally then at the circumstances within which Japanese and Americans live, there are some differences that would explain the lower crime rates in Japan. On the one hand, income distribution is more equitable in Japan, unemployment is less, and poverty is less concentrated in particular localities, especially neighborhoods defined by race or ethnicity. Japan also regulates gun ownership much more stringently than does the United States. On the other hand, its popular culture is as violent as that of the United States', and its criminal justice system, while more efficient, is less rigorous in its punishments. Criminal prosecution is hampered by civil rights, very much as in the United States except for the extended pre-charge detention period.

It is impossible to determine scientifically, given limitations on data in both countries, whether these differences in social circumstances can account entirely for Japan's enviable crime record. At the same time, it is clear that there are other processes at work in Japan that help to produce its remarkable orderliness. These are processes of social interaction, part of general culture, that bear directly on the behavior of the Japanese. Crime, more generally the impulse to deviance, is inhibited by mechanisms that are peculiar to Japan in their strength and extensiveness. Although these mechanisms can be found in American society too, they are much weaker and more attenuated. Control of deviant behavior in Japan, I shall argue, is obtained through a unique combination of propriety, presumption, and pride.

First: Propriety

Japanese are bound by an infinite number of rules about what is proper. To an American, Japan is supremely upright. There is nothing casual or relaxed about it. In order to avoid giving offense, modes of speech shift as one addresses a man or a woman, a child or an adult, an older or a younger sibling, an elderly person, one's peer, a first-time acquaintance or a long-time friend, a workmate or an outsider, and so forth. Informal dress codes are strict, and people dress exactly so as to conform to what is expected on particular occasions as well as in particular roles. All schoolchildren wear the uniform distinctive of the school they attend, identical down to purses, backpacks, width of trousers, and length of skirts. Businessmen and government bureaucrats invariably wear dark suits, dark ties, white shirts, and black shoes. Construction workers can be recognized by knickers, soft two-toed boots, and woolen belly-warmers. Female street sweepers wear long scarves; truck and taxi drivers often wear white gloves. Revealingly, a customer in a Western-style dress shop will be asked, "What size are you?" in a kimono store, "How old are you?"[26] People in Japan are what they look like, which means they must conform in order to be what they want to be.

Decorum is all-encompassing: not sitting on desks and surfaces people use for work; not putting shod feet on chairs, so that mothers carefully take off the tiny tennis shoes of their children when they pull them onto subway seats; encasing wet umbrellas in disposable plastic sacks when entering department stores; tying a *ukata* (bathrobe) one way for a man, another for a woman; and not looking directly into the eyes of another person in public. Japanese calculate the depth as well as the number of bows so that proper deference is shown. Department stores have mechanical calibrators that help personnel learn the appropriate bowing angle for different sorts of people.[27] Late one morning in a popular Tokyo restaurant I heard chanting from the kitchen. Peering surreptitiously through an open door, I saw the manager rehearsing the staff in saying, "What can I do for you?" "How can I help you?" and "Thank you, come back," in the proper bright and cheery way.

Japanese are surrounded by rules in all they do, from the serious to the trivial. In relation to Americans, they are compulsively watchful about decorum. Etiquette, civility, morality, and law blend together. Japanese learn early that someone is paying attention to everything they do, and that departures from propriety will be met with visible expressions of disapproval. A sense of constraining order is always present in Japanese life. A person is never offstage.

The pervading sense of propriety produces startling demonstrations of orderliness. An English businessman was so astonished at the absence of litter that he personally inspected 1,200 yards of subway corridors in the Yurakicho-Ginza subway station during an evening rush hour to count discarded trash. Although this complex is ten times larger than London's Piccadilly Circus Underground station, he found only nineteen cigarette ends, twenty-eight matchsticks, eleven candy wrappers, and four pieces of paper.[28] Japanese pedestrians rarely jaywalk, dutifully waiting for the crossing-lights to turn green even if there is no car in sight and it is late at night.

The instinctive obedience to shared rules of order is wonderfully captured in a story about a burglar who was caught fleeing an apartment in the daytime. It is important to understand that Japanese remove their shoes on entering a private home, especially if its floor is the traditional raised floor made of thick woven-straw (tatami). The burglar had crossed such a room to ransack a bureau, but was apprehended by the police because, when he heard them, he had stopped to put his shoes back on.[29]

Japanese orderliness in large matters, such as crime, seems to be related to orderliness in small things. If this is true, then the lack of regimentation that Americans value in personal life may affect the amount of criminal disorder in public life. Would Americans, one wonders, be willing to obtain a greater measure of safety if they were required to tie their bathrobes in a prescribed way?[30]

Second: Presumption

Japanese are enmeshed in closely knit groups that inhibit behavior through informal social controls. Japanese are not raised to stand alone, develop their individual potential, or "do their own thing." They are taught to fit into groups and to subordinate themselves to the purposes of those groups. The most important and enduring groups are family, school, and workplace. Becoming an organic part of them—belonging—is the source of the deepest emotional satisfaction Japanese feel. Thus, fitting in becomes the ultimate discipline in Japan. Japanese are encapsulated in small groups of well-known people who have the presumptive right to tell them how to behave.

Accepting the obligations of belonging is not like being directed to conform, though that is the result. Japanese tolerate the presumptions of membership because in exchange they are nurtured, supported, and cared for. This may take the form of lifetime employment, or the covering up of errors, or assistance in carrying out tasks, or simply an understanding of personal problems. Americans are more calculating about the costs and benefits of membership. Groups are instruments of individual purpose, rather than being ends in themselves. Americans are therefore less bound by the obligations of membership in any particular group, whether it be family, marriage, job, sports team, or social club. Because Japanese depend so entirely on a much smaller number of affiliations, they lose the ability to discriminate between the claims of the individual and those of the group, the obligations of the personal as opposed to those of the public.

The difference between Japanese and Americans is not in valuing the favorable regard of others or in the need to conform; it lies in the range of significant external references. Americans are "outer directed," to use David Reisman's famous phrase, in a generalized way; Japanese are "outer directed" in a focused way.[31] Studies have in fact shown that among strangers Americans conform more quickly than Japanese.[32] Japanese do not accept the presumptions of any group, but only of a small number of groups. The universal desire for fellowship and community provides enormous leverage in Japan because it is not counterbalanced by the obligations of other affiliations.

The presumptive control that immediate social groups can exercise can be seen in the importance placed on unspoken communication in Japan. People who properly belong do not have to be told; they understand instinctively what the wishes of the group are. For example, a husband in a properly attuned marriage does not need to apologize to his wife if he spills hot tea-water on her hand, because she understands without being told that he did not intend to hurt her and also that he is sorry. The most cutting remark a man can make about his wife is that she has to be told what he needs.[33] Businessmen complain that they do not like to be sent abroad for long periods because they lose instinctive knowledge of their group. When they return they feel like strangers, having to be told what everyone else understands. As the Japanese say, the expectation in most of life is that when you talk "others can finish the sentence." It is not an acceptable excuse in Japan to say "I wasn't told."[34]

Japanese learn the value of belonging early in life. In schools children advance automatically, as a group, helping one another as they go. Individual achievements are de-emphasized in favor of group accomplishments. Children learn not to embarrass schoolmates by showing them to be wrong. Instead, they correct others by saying "I want to help Yakuda-kun" or "I agree with Kato-san but I also think this way."[35] Individual test scores are not known among classmates. Separation according to ability occurs impersonally, usually as the result of formal examinations allowing students to move from one level of schooling to another. Young children compete athletically by classes, not as individuals. Students also perform together many of the custodial chores at schools, like sweeping floors, washing dishes after lunch, picking up trash, putting away equipment, and rearranging chairs. Teachers and students explain constantly to laggards what is expected, reiterating that unless something or other is done the class will be disappointed, the student will be letting down the side, or everyone will be ashamed if the student does not try. Emotional blackmail, Americans would call this, and would resent it.

Even before schooling, Japanese children learn that fitting in brings warmth and love. Observers of early child-raising practices have noted that Japanese mothers carry their children with them everywhere, both inside and outside the house. Children sleep with their parents until the age of four or five. American mothers put down happy children, encouraging them to play by themselves. American children are left with baby-sitters, a practice still uncommon in Japan. They learn early to attract attention by crying and demanding; Japanese mothers anticipate the needs of their children so they do not have to cry or demand.[36]

When Japanese preschool children misbehave, parents threaten them with being locked out of the home. They tearfully bang on the front doors, pleading to be allowed back in. In the United States parents threaten badly behaving children with exactly the reverse-being kept in. The children are "grounded." The effect is that American children are taught that it is punishment to be locked up with one's family; Japanese children are taught that punishment is being excluded from one's family.[37] Small wonder, then, that Japanese schools and work groups have leverage over individual behavior later in life—and that adult affiliations in the United States have less.

The power of informal social control is what the Japanese criminal justice system relies on when it accepts apologies for minor infractions, does not insist on arresting suspects, allows people to be free without bail pending trial, and suspends prosecution or the execution of sentences. The vitality of group supervision is what allows police, prosecutors, and judges to act on the philosophy that they "hate the crime but not the criminal." The Japanese criminal justice system is founded not on deterrence but rather on "reintegrative shaming."[38] The purpose of the system is to shame individuals into accepting the obligations of their social setting and to shame groups into accepting responsibility for the errant member. Individuation makes sense in Japan, as it often does in the United States as well, when people are situated in specific, binding social networks.

Learning to accept the presumptions of groups does not mean that groups are without conflict and disagreement. Japanese often feel frustrated and inhibited. Unlike Americans, however, they are more willing to manage the conflict, deflecting or repressing it.[39] They make an explicit distinction linguistically between what is apparent and what is real in social situations. *Tatemae* refers to the appearance that must be maintained; *honne* is the inside story, what is truly felt. Americans too understand the tension between gut-feeling and propriety, but are more likely to be led by the former. Conversely, they value sincerity, being uncomfortable with hollow conformity. Japanese stifle nonconformity for the sake of maintaining the *tatemae* of group harmony, even though they know it is a pretense.

Social order in an individualistic society like the United States requires the discipline of conscience; social order in a communitarian society like Japan requires the discipline of presumption. Both societies learn to accommodate some of the other perspective. Japanese society does not wholly trample individual identity; American society does not forfeit entirely the capacity for cooperative endeavor. But the balance is different. As two observers of both countries have said, "One may even venture to suggest that while Americans learn to live with an illusion of complete self-reliance, self-sufficiency and autonomy, many Japanese tend to live with an illusion of total harmony, mutual understanding and consensus among them."[40]

Third: Pride

Discipline is maintained in Japan because people take enormous pride in performing well the roles demanded of them. Distinctive occupational dress is one indication of the prideful identification people have with their work. Japanese society is hierarchical in terms of authority, but it is egalitarian in its evaluation of the worth of work. What is important is the dedication brought to the job, not its status. Interestingly, anyone who teaches in Japan, from university professors to instructors in cutting up raw fish, are called *sensei*.

One reason Japanese women have accepted differentiated sex roles more readily than American women may be that the emotional rewards are greater. Being a wife and mother is regarded as a demanding and responsible job in Japan. It is not denigrated as being "just housework."[41]

The essential ingredient in achieving success at anything is *seishin*, literally "spirit." But the word has strong overtones of effort, discipline, self-control, and even suffering. Inner fulfillment comes from developing the *seishin* necessary to accept demanding obligations willingly, whether artistic and craft skills, work routines, athletic feats, or social responsibilities. Japanese respect the *seishin* shown by the daughter-in-law who uncomplainingly performs her duties in the house of an overbearing mother-in-law for the sake of the family, or the student who practices tea-ceremony for years in order to achieve a higher ranking, or the baseball player who trains despite personal injury without asking for time off.[42] In arts, crafts, and social relations, Japanese learn by rote, by endlessly copying approved behavior. High achievement is obtained by fanatical application, not by gifted innovation. Great effort earns great respect. Indeed, Japanese tend to excuse marginal performance as long as exemplary *seishin* was shown. By being perfectionist in effort, Japanese protect themselves against censure. Americans, on the other hand, are more ends-oriented, excusing slipshod preparation if the results are good.

Pride given to work helps Japanese accept conformity. As Edwin O. Reischauer, former ambassador to Japan, has said, "social conformity to the Japanese is no sign of weakness but rather the proud, tempered product of inner strength."[43] A symbol of this is the bonsai tree, a unique expression of aesthetic taste with which Japanese identify. Bonsai is a dwarf tree that has been restricted by binding and pruning so that it grows into strange, artificial shapes. A bonsai tree achieves beauty by being constricted, some might say deformed. Japanese orderliness is achieved in the same way.

In conclusion, propriety, presumption, and pride can be analytically and anecdotally separated, but they are part of a single dynamic. The enwrapping web of propriety is held in place by the myriad presumptive corrections of primary social groups. Careful attention to the forms of human interaction allows tightly knit groups to hold together despite the vagaries of circumstance and personality. Pride allows for the internalization of the discipline necessary for subordination to small groups. Presumption becomes bearable when society rewards those who accept it.

Americans can understand, perhaps even empathize with, this dynamic. But they reverse the values. Propriety in the United States is limited, individuals being free to live their lives bound only by the commodious limits of the law. Behavior is bound more exclusively by law, or a very general morality, because the texture of American society is too loosely knit to rely on the presumptive enforcement of small groups. Norms of decorum and civility are not shared across the spectrum of American life. American pride is rooted in individual accomplishment, not in the acceptance of the disciplines of primary social groups. Americans kick against the restrictions of propriety, having been taught to question conventions of dress, language, taste, and morality.

If crime is caused to an important extent by customary patterns of social interaction, then Japan and the United States may both be getting what they have contrived.

NOTES

1. *Yakuza* is a slang word for gangster. More politely, gangsters are known as *boryokudan*.

2. M. Tamura, "Yakuza and Stimulants: Drug Problems in Japan" (Paper for the International Conference on Crime, Drugs, and Social Control, Hong Kong, December 14–16, 1988), p. 3; S. Miyazawa, "Learning Lessons from Japanese Experience: Challenge for Japanese Criminologists" (Paper prepared for the U.S./Japan Bilateral Session, Tokyo, 1988), Appendix 25. See also the *White Paper on Police*, 1987.

3. See chapter 1. *Forces of Order*, Bayley, 1991.

4. See chapter 7, the issue of "substitute prisons." *Forces of Order*, David H. Bayley, Berkely: University of California Press, 1991.

5. Income inequality as measured by the gini-coefficient was 0.278 in Japan, 0.366 in the United States. *Japan Times*, 24 February 1989, p. 24, from data provided by the European Economic Community and the Japanese Economic Planning Agency. Values for the gini-coefficient run from 0 to 1, with higher values indicating greater inequality. Elliott Currie, *Confronting Crime: An American Challenge* (New York: Pantheon, 1985) 1, p. 161, says that Japan's equality of income was exceeded among OECD countries only by Holland, Sweden, and Norway.

6. In 1987, for example, unemployment rates were 2.8 percent in Japan and 6.2 percent in the United States; in 1989, 2.5 percent in Japan, 5.5 percent in the United States. *Japan Times*, 24 February 1989.

7. In 1987, 256,000 person-days were lost to strikes in Japan, 4,481,000 in the U.S. Ibid.

8. H. Wagatsuma, "Social Control of Juvenile Delinquency in Arakawa Ward of Tokyo" (Paper prepared for the Social Science Research Council Workshop on the Japanese City, April 1976), pp. 34–39.

9. Figures supplied by the respective police forces.

10. See chapter 5, *Forces of Order*, Bayley, 1991.

11. *Statistical Abstract of the United States*, 1989, pp. 14,16.

12. Japan spent Y2, 900 billion in 1988 on police, prosecution, courts, and corrections; the United States, $53.5 billion in 1986. Information from the Ministry of justice and National Police Agency, 1989, and the *Sourcebook of Criminal Justice Statistics*, 1988, p. 2. The GNP of Japan was Y330,116 billion in 1987; of the United States, $4, 235 billion in 1986. Japan, 1989, p. 14.

13. Same sources as n. 12.

14. See chapter 8, *Forces of Order*, Bayley, 1991.

15. See chapter 7, *Forces of Order*, Bayley.

16. This includes rivet guns, rope-discharging guns, and signal guns for athletic games. "Law Controlling Possession, Etc., of Fire-arms and Swords," Article 3(1), clause 8 (Law No. 6, March 1958). Swords and knives over six inches long or with blades that automatically extend by mechanical action are prohibited except under permit.

17. Article 4.

18. Article 4.

19. Ministry of Justice, 1989, *Sourcebook of Criminal Justice Statistics*, 1988, pp. 231–232.

20. Federal Bureau of Investigation, *Uniform Crime Reports: Law Enforcement Officers Killed and Assaulted 1988* (Washington, D.C.: U.S. Department of Justice, 1989).

21. The place of firearms in Japan is even more interesting because they were once fairly widely used and manufactured in Japan. Japan is disarmed today as a result of deliberate government policy. This experience, and the reasons for the government decision, is described in a short illustrated book by Noel Perrin, *Giving Up the Gun: Japan's Reversion to the Sword* (Boston: Godine, 1979).

22. National Police Agency, 1989.

23. Ian Baruma, *Behind the Mask* (New York: Pantheon, 1984), Chapter 10.

24. Albert Axelbank, *Black Star over Japan* (London: Allen and Unwin, 1972), and George Comstock, Syracuse University, speech, May 12, 1982.

25. Baruma and Comstock.

26. W. Caudill and H. Weinstein, "Maternal Care and Infant Behavior in Japan and America," in *Japanese Culture and Behavior*, T. S. and W Lebra, eds. (Honolulu: University of Hawaii Press, 1974), pp. 225–76.

27. Peter Hazelhurst, formerly Tokyo correspondent for the *Sunday Times* and the *Straits Times*.

28. Peter Hazelhurst.

29. Robert Trumbull, formerly Tokyo correspondent for the *New York Times*. I once saw a squad of plainclothes detectives break into a yakuza apartment on a drug-bust and stop inside the front door to remove their shoes before undertaking their search.

30. James Q. Wilson and George L. Kelling have argued that police should concentrate on maintaining decorum on the streets in order to discourage more serious criminal behavior. "Broken Windows," *Atlantic Monthly* (March 1982), pp. 29–38. Experimental evidence for a connection between visible signs of disorder and criminal actions was found by Professor Philip Zimbardo, Stanford University, in 1969.

31. David Reisman, *The Lonely Crowd* (Garden City, N.Y.: Doubleday, 1953).

32. H. Wagatsuma and Arthur Rosett, "Cultural Attitudes toward Contract Law: Japan and the U.S. Compared" (Draft article, 1982), p. 22.

33. Robert J. Smith, *Japanese Society: Tradition, Self, and the Social Order* (Cambridge: Cambridge University Press, 1983), pp. 57–58.

34. In *Hidden Differences: Doing Business with the Japanese* (New York: Anchor Press/Doubleday, 1987), Part I, Edward T. and Mildred R. Hall describe Japan as a "high context" society, meaning that people need a great deal of information about the people they work with in order to work together successfully. Americans, on the other hand, need much less, preferring to limit the dimensions of interaction with the people they work with. The same distinction is made by Howard Gardner, *Frames of Mind* (New York: Basic Books, 1985), in distinguishing "particle" societies, where autonomous individuals interact, from "field" societies, where individuals are subordinated to groups.

35. Takie S. Lebra, *Japanese Women: Constraint and Fulfillment* (Honolulu: University of Hawaii Press, 1984), chap. 5.

36. See Caudill and Weinstein (n. 26 above).

37. *Mura hachibu* is the term for being excluded. It was a very serious punishment in villages. This is similar to the practice in the British labor movement of sending colleagues "to Coventry," not talking to them, when they defied group norms.

38. John Braithwaite, *Crime, Shame, and Reintegration* (Cambridge: Cambridge University Press, 1989).

39. Takie S. Lebra, "Nonconfrontational Strategies for Management of Interpersonal Conflicts," in Ellis S. Krauss et al., *Conflict in Japan* (Honolulu: University of Hawaii Press, 1984), chap. 3.

40. Wagatsuma and Rosett, "Cultural Attitudes."

41. Suzanne H. Vogel, "Professional Housewife: The Career of Urban Middle Class Japanese Women," *Japan Interpreter* 12, no. 1 (Winter 1978): 16–43.

42. Robert Whiting, *You Gotta Have Wa* (New York: Macmillan, 1989), p.317.

43. *The Japanese Today* (Cambridge: Harvard University Press, 1988), p. 166.